DATE DUE			
Apr 21 78			

POWER AND EQUITY

POWER AND EQUITY

An Introduction to Social Stratification

William McCord
City College of New York, City University of New York

Arline McCord
Hunter College, City University of New York

Praeger Publishers
New York

Published in the United States of America in 1977
by Praeger Publishers.
200 Park Avenue, New York, N. Y. 10017

Library of Congress Cataloging in Publication Data

McCord, William Maxwell, 1930-
    Power and equity.
    Includes index.
    1. Social classes—History. 2. Equality. 3. Power
(Social sciences) 4. Elite (Social sciences) 5. Caste.
I. McCord, Arline F., joint author. II. Title.
HT607.M3   301.44'09   75-36205
ISBN 0-275-22750-2

Printed in the United States of America

789 074 987654321

To
William Maxwell McCord
and
Elinor Mary McCord

PREFACE

"How does your father earn money?" I said to the little girl who sat next to me on a school bus in Arizona. "Stocks and bonds?" I added, helpfully.

The girl wore no shoes. Her dress was in rags. Her face, if I had had the knowledge to recognize it, was emaciated from malnutrition.

"Welfare," she said.

My incredibly naive question emerged from the stunted mentality of a spoiled upper-class child. My ancestors included distinguished politicians and writers; my father had once headed a powerful New York bank, and his father had presided over a large railroad. Servants ran our house; prime ribs of beef materialized on our table even during the worst days of war-time rationing; family names regularly appeared in Who's Who; *and "everyone" assumed that we would be listed in* The Blue Book, *attend the Junior Assembly, go to an Ivy League college, swim at the country club, and enter the Junior League or the "Old Pueblo Club." Most importantly, money, money, money smoothed the way of our pampered lives.*

The little girl on the bus, "Red" she was nicknamed, lived on charity (there were no food stamps in the 1940s), suffered from a club foot, which her father could not afford to have treated, and existed in a rat-infested, tarred shanty.

vii

She went on to become first in our high-school class. I limped in 550 out of 1,000, having turned down my parents' offer to send me to a private school.

Since that time of innocence, I have learned that not all people live off "stocks and bonds." I have experienced the prisons, ghettoes, and dilapidated schools of the American system. I have learned that wealth, not merit, buys the good things of life: abundant food, a good education, political influence, proper medical care, and even a dignified burial.

Is this equitable? Should we allocate power in the fashion we do? Should I, a lump-headed football player in high school, receive more privileges than "Red," the crippled poor girl who accompanied me on the school bus? Can we alleviate the unfairness of American life? These are the fundamental subjects of this book.

Throughout this work we will be concerned with power: the differential ability of people to command the obedience of others, to influence them, or to secure a high proportion of the resources of their society. This differentiation in power has been an enduring element in human history.

In Part I, we are particularly concerned with five basic types of inequality in power: (1) slavery, as exemplified in ancient Rome and in America; (2) the caste system, as practiced in Hindu and some Moslem states until it was officially attacked by colonial powers and by the legal prohibitions of newly independent nations; (3) serfdom, as witnessed in such societies as those of medieval Europe and nineteenth-century Russia, in which people were differentiated by their ownership of land and by military prowess; (4) class distinctions in industrialized nations whereby people are differentiated primarily by the degree to which they own the means of production and the wealth that flows from such dominance; and (5) bureaucratic inequality, a new form of social stratification that has emerged as characteristic of such diverse postindustrial nations as the United States, England, and the Soviet Union. We are concerned with the reasons why each of these systems emerged as well as the reasons for their continuance, erosion, or disappearance.

It is also important to consider the philosophical positions of various thinkers who have questioned whether or not inequality is inevitable. On the one hand, there are those who believe that social inequality is an inevitable part of the human condition and necessary for the survival of civilization. In these ranks, one should count such distinguished figures as Plato, Aristotle, Gaetano Mosca, Vilfredo Pareto, José Ortega y Gasset, and Sigmund Freud. On the other hand, some intellectuals—such as Pierre Proudhon, Peter Kropotkin, Karl Marx, Martin Buber, and John Galbraith—have argued that inequality could be abolished if statesmen paid more attention to the public interest or, more radically, if they engaged in establishing socialist states, communes, or kibbutzim.

In an attempt to provide some evidence for the examination of these issues, we turn in Part II to an examination of the actual impact of inequality and differentials of power in America. Here, we are concerned with a variety of studies that illustrate the specific effect of social inequality on opportunities for higher education, death in war, infant mortality, mental disorder, crime, values, and life styles. In addition, we must pay close attention to racism and sexism, their intimate relation with the class system, and their impact upon Americans.

We are also concerned with various strategies to end inequality since, in recent decades, there have been many attempts to reduce some of the inequalities in American society. The particular measures we examine include the "War on Poverty"; the provision of new legal protections for the poor; extensions of public education and medical care; and attempts to "mobilize" the poor into political action.

In Part III, the philosophical arguments that surround the problems of power and equity in any society are presented. Most Americans believe that equality of opportunity in the pursuit of happiness is a desirable objective. Yet, some intellectuals have attacked this goal as unattainable or, if reachable, as undesirable.

We will examine the lines of argument of the following: the elitists, who believe that inequality is just and necessary for the preservation of a good society; the liberals, who wish to protect individual freedom and provide equality of opportunity; the libertarians, who regard liberty as their foremost goal and are willing to tolerate inequalities as long as people are "entitled" to their privileges; and the egalitarians, who wish to see all people share alike in the goods and resources of this world.

Our own biases affect this enterprise. It should be known, for example, that we believe that every human being is entitled to life, liberty, and the property he or she earns. Further, each person should be guaranteed a basic annual income, receive health care, have some form of shelter, and clothing. Each should receive an education that fits his or her fullest potential. We believe that every person should be offered full equality of opportunity to achieve goods beyond this level.

There are, of course, means to eliminate the more blatant and arbitrary inequalities that remain in modern society. Yet, we recognize that inequity and inequalities in wealth, status, and power are inevitable aspects of human life.

W. M.
A. M.

CONTENTS

INTRODUCTION: POWER AND EQUITY

Wherever people have lived together, one of their primary concerns has been the relative distribution of resources. Power and privilege have always been accorded some people in every group. Even the most cursory reading of history or contemporary affairs shows the pervasiveness of inequality:

1. In primitive societies, men generally own women as pieces of property who have no rights and who, in some societies such as ancient India, are obliged to kill themselves upon the death of their husband.[1]

2. In some simple societies where food is scarce, strong children grab food from the mouths of those who are weakened by age or infirmity.[2]

3. In caste-ridden nations, orthodox believers in supernatural predestination drink a mixture of cow's urine and dung to "purify" themselves if they have been "defiled" by the sight of an untouchable.[3]

4. In ancient Rome, patricians could kill slaves without punishment,[4] and centuries later, in the American South, whites whipped slaves for playing drums at night.[5]

5. In nineteenth-century Russia, serfs who appealed to government officials because of maltreatment were banished and forced to walk 3,000 miles to Siberia.[6]

Industrialization modified many of these forms of inequality. In some cases, modernization has resulted in the abolition of a particular type of inequality, such as slavery. This does not mean, however, that the modern world has eradicated inequality, for humankind appears infinitely ingenious in creating new forms of human subjugation.

In the contemporary United States, for example, the top 20 percent of the nation's families receive 41 percent of all personal income while the bottom 20 percent receive less than 5 percent.[7] While wealthy Americans enjoy a privileged style of life and leisure, the poor suffer such indignities as the following:

1. In 1965, poor children in Mississippi received less than 32 cents a day for food.[8]

2. In the 1960's many children in Washington, D.C., attended school without food.[9]

3. At the same time, the food allowance for welfare recipients in the nation's capital amounted to 17.5 cents per person per meal.[10]

4. For lack of medical care, twice as many black as white infants died in the 1960s. If a black male survived, he could expect to die seven years earlier than his white counterpart.[11]

5. In 1967, because of educational discrimination, 80 percent of intelligent males and 86 percent of intelligent females who came from the lower class in Wisconsin did not graduate from college.[12]

6. American women spent enough money on cosmetics to double all the national budgets of black Africa.[13]

7. In 1976, the richest 10 percent of the American population still received fifteen times the income that the poorest 10 percent gets.[14]

These are only a few of the results of various types of *social stratification,* a system of human organization in which one group enjoys more power, privilege, wealth, or material goods than another. In one way or another, all contemporary societies exhibit this inequality. Within the borders of a nation such as the United States, particular groups—lower-class blacks, Puerto Ricans, or Chicanos—lose in the race for material bounties, housing, education, and even life itself. Internationally, a favored handful of nations in North America, Western Europe, and Asia enjoy the benefits of industrialization while much of the rest of the world starves.

In this book we address some of the fundamental issues raised by social stratification throughout the world. We are concerned with three general problems.

1. *What is the nature and source of inequality in human affairs?* Why does a society develop a particular form for distributing power—say, slavery, serfdom, or bureaucracy? What accounts for the demise of a special type of inequality? These are essentially historical and empirical questions that can be answered by the resources of social science.

2. *Is inequality inevitable?* Some social thinkers, including defenders of slavery such as Aristotle and John Calhoun, political conservatives like José Ortega y Gasset and T. S. Eliot, and social scientists from Herbert Spencer to Edgar Z. Friedenberg, believe that social ordering and ranking is (or should be) an inevitable part of the social fabric. Other social philosophers, from Jean Jacques Rousseau to John Rawls, Condorcet to Marx, Babeuf to Kropotkin, have argued that inequalities of power and privilege are artificial, unneeded, unjust appendages of our civilization. To correct the stratification systems of their time, slaves revolted in Rome, Frenchmen launched a revolution, Zionists created kibbutzim, and socialists throughout the world have sought to establish classless societies. Are they pursuing a chimera or is it possible that a society without discrimination, without ranks, and without inequalities in power might be created? This issue is at the heart of the many political and social debates of our time.

Closely related to the question of the inevitability of stratification is that of equity; that is, if the hierarchical ordering of people is inevitable, then a third problem must be confronted.

3. *What would be an equitable social order?* Throughout history people have portrayed social orders different from their own that would come closer to their concept of justice. The content of these visions has differed drastically: Comte, Saint-Simon, and Fourier, who wrote during the beginning stages of industrialization, depicted scientifically managed communities run by a technocratic elite;[15] Babeuf and Proudhon fought for an egalitarian society where classes and the power of the state no longer prevailed;[16] Marx and Engels believed that the inevitable drift of history would create a society in which each person was his or her own master and each would receive material rewards according to his or her needs;[17] Spencer and Nietzsche wished for a society that recognized biological differences and allowed the superior person to pursue his or her interests untrammeled by the petty desires of the masses.[18]

History has swept some of these depictions of equity into obscurity. Other conceptions of power and equity—most notably those of Marx, Mao, Hitler, and Mussolini—have, for good or ill, changed the course of humankind's development.[19] Despite the wishes of those who rule a particular status quo, the demand for equity cannot be ignored. Although an outsider may view a particular society as unfair, the majority of its citizens must believe in it for the sake of internal cohesion. Intricate religious, political, economic, and philosophical justifications have been elaborated to preserve a particular brand of inequality.

The question of equity remains open, however, and even in present-day America, a land that proclaims the ideal of equal opportunity, there remains much debate. Ayn Rand proclaims the sacredness of wealth;[20] Robert Nozick argues that each person is "entitled" to whatever wealth he or she may receive;[21] and B. F. Skinner longs for a perfect society of people conditioned by "supervisors."[22] In contrast, Michael Harrington issues pleas for socialism;[23] Herbert Gans wishes to create more equality among people;[24] and John Rawls foresees no conditions that justify any form of inequality except for the general benefit of all.[25] Obviously, the issue of how power and privilege should be justly settled in the modern world is far from being resolved.

Before confronting the multifaceted issues involved in this debate, let us establish a few basic definitions of the concepts important to our discussion.

Basic Concepts of Social Stratification

An individual's position in the stratification system potently affects almost every aspect of his or her life: dress, eating habits, education, physical health, outlook on life, as well as the very ability to live. By *stratification system* we mean the hierarchical ordering of people in a society differentiated according to their power, privilege or status. A collectivity of people who occupy similar positions in the hierarchical order constitutes a *stratum*. Most American sociologists have been interested primarily in one form of social stratification: the social-class system that dominates modern societies. By *social classes* we mean groups of people identified on the basis of their relationship to the economic market who have differential access to wealth, power, and certain styles of life.

Although debated by some social scientists,[26] we believe that every society creates some form of social stratification. There are two prerequisites for the appearance of a stratification system: (1) differentiation of the population along some dimension with a degree of permanence and (2) a system of rewards attached to the specific tasks performed by the different individuals or groups. However, the exact nature of the stratification system to be found in a society depends upon the state of its technological development and its prevailing cultural ideology.

Varieties of Social Stratification

Distinct varieties of social stratification have developed in each of three technologically different types of human society.

SIMPLE SOCIETIES

Simple societies are those in which hunting and gathering techniques are used for survival. In these societies, three types of social stratification prevail.

1. *Equalitarianism,* a minimal hierarchical organization, exists only in a handful of small societies where food and other resources are distributed among the members of the group on the basis of their desires and needs. Among the Tasaday of the Philippines[27] and the Andaman Islanders,[28] two examples of this type of stratification, group members share food and tend not to compete with one another. Such societies enjoy an abundance of resources. With only a vestige of a social-class system as we know it, such people do, however, accord honor and prestige to one another on the basis of skills such as hunting, utility as arbiters in familial disputes, or generosity in distributing food.[29]

2. *Anarchy** occurs when neither government nor law inhibits the use of brute strength, a situation that exists in those simple societies where food is extraordinarily rare. Members of the Ik tribe of Uganda[30] do not help each other; on the contrary, they steal food whenever possible, abandon children if they prove cumbersome, and kill the aged and infirm. The Ik's social stratification is based simply on the supremacy of the physically strong, and finding food is the imperative of their lives.

3. *Patriarchy,* where the father is ruler of the family, predominates in many simple societies where food is scarce and the skill of the male hunter is valued. Among the Kalahari Bushmen of Africa,[31] for example, harsh desert conditions have created a society in which the strongest males rule and in which all men dominate women. The men receive honor as hunters and are quick to eliminate those who are too weak to follow their nomadic wanderings.

---

*This term should, of course, not be confused with *anarchism,* the political theory that all systems of government and law are harmful and prevent individuals from reaching their fullest development.

AGRARIAN SOCIETIES

Agrarian societies, where people live primarily on what they produce from their gardening and cultivation of the land, are associated with three other types of social stratification.

1. *Slavery,* a situation in which one person is the legal property of another, has existed in every agrarian society. In settled agricultural communities or large plantations, slaves became an asset in production rather than simply more mouths to feed. Economic surpluses produced in agrarian nations have commonly allowed for military expeditions during which captives were taken who were made slaves.[32]

2. The *caste* system, particularly as practiced in India, is based on the assumption that each person is preordained a place and occupation in society at birth. Contact between persons of the different strata is "impure," and intermarriage between castes is forbidden. Even the most trivial acts of life—such as sipping water or eating—are governed by particular rules for each caste.[33] The Indian caste system derives its authority from the Hindu belief in *karma,* the opinion that each person's soul follows a prescribed destiny governed by that individual's actions in a presumed previous life.

3. *Estate* systems, best symbolized by feudal European society, have appeared in some agrarian regions.[34] In such a system, people are assigned to their strata according to their birth, military strength, or land holdings. Each stratum has specific legal rights in relation to the others, as well as various privileges. For example, the lords of medieval Europe provided military protection to their serfs in return for a portion of the serfs' produce. Estate systems have blossomed during periods of social turmoil, such as the disintegration of the Roman Empire, where security could be assured only by allying oneself with the most powerful local lord, who could protect one within his fortress.

Each of these different forms of social stratification allows for some degree of *social mobility,* a situation in which individuals or groups rise above or fall from the stratum to which they have been assigned by birth. Even in India, subcastes (although not individuals) may move upward in the caste system by achieving increased wealth and education and by changing their rituals to conform with those of the higher caste.[35] In feudal Europe, urban merchants achieved the status of lord by financing military expeditions.[36]

In areas of the globe where industrialism has superseded agrarian forms of production, the distinctions between master and slave, hunter and the weak, noble and serf, have given way to new types of social stratification.

INDUSTRIAL SOCIETIES

In those societies where machine energy has replaced human and animal energy as the primary source of economic production, an entirely new set of *social classes* in the modern sense of that term has been created. With the advent of industrialism, in seventeenth-century Europe, two important social classes appeared: the *bourgeoisie,* merchants and industrialists who owned the means of production, and the *proletariat,* former peasants who had become workers in factories. A variety of theories emerged concerning the role of these social classes.

Karl Marx and Friedrich Engels in their historic *Communist Manifesto* argued that the interests of the bourgeoisie and the proletariat were fundamentally opposed, and that contradictions within the capitalist form of economic development would result in a classless society; that is, a society in which everyone contributed according to his ability and received rewards according to his needs. Marxism postulated a growth in *class consciousness,* a recognition of one's location in the class structure by persons who share similar economic positions. Marx and Engels viewed history as an outgrowth of *class conflict,* an opposition between those who owned the means of production and those who labored for the owners, which would end only with the establishment of a communist society.[37]

Max Weber, the great German sociologist, on the other hand, viewed class differences in modern society as based on considerations that extended beyond the economic realm.[38] In Weber's opinion, three criteria were used to differentiate people in modern society: *class* (power, based on one's relationship to the means of production); *status* differences, based on esteem given to individuals because of their membership in an hereditary aristocracy or their possession of special skills or knowledge; and *party* power, derived from one's dominance over a political, legal, or administrative system.

Recent writers such as Talcott Parsons, Kingsley Davis, and Wilbert Moore have argued that inequality is inherent in any society and that the particular rewards a society gives to its members are the result of their "functional" utility.[39] Critically important social positions must be filled with properly talented people who are, in turn, rewarded with more money, prestige, or power. Critics of this theory argue that it merely glorifies the existing class system, and that little evidence can be provided which clearly demonstrates that the members of the upper stratum in modern societies actually *deserve* more wealth, power, or prestige because of their contributions to the welfare of the whole society.[40]

Today's sociologists have also debated the political consequences of the new system of social stratification ushered in by industrialism. Gerhard Lenski maintains that "the appearance of mature industrial societies marks the first significant reversal in the age old evolutionary trend toward ever increasing inequality."[41] Lenski views the development of industrialized nations as a prelude to political democracy. Other writers—most notably Floyd Hunter and C. Wright Mills—have contended that industrial societies have produced a new type of *power elite,* an intertwined group of business executives, political leaders, and military administrators who control the destiny of modern nations.[42]

Whatever their political persuasion, few sociologists deny that a distinctly stratified class system exists in the United States and in other industrialized nations, the impact of which on every facet of life has been fully documented.

The Impact of the Class System

Whether people are consciously aware of their societal placement or not, their *objective* location in the stratification system has many important implications for their lives. Objective location of individuals has been studied by social scientists through analyses of indicators such as income, education, occupation, power (that is, the ability to influence the alternatives open to others) or esteem (that is, the prestige accorded to an individual).

Americans, for example, have traditionally believed that education can overcome the handicap of a lower-class position in society. In contrast to this prevailing belief, most studies indicate that one's social-class position rather than one's intelligence has a powerful effect upon educational attainment. A study by William Sewell and Vimal Shah recorded that males of high intelligence have three times the chance of graduating from college if they came from the upper classes than if they came from the lower classes, as measured by their fathers' occupations.[43]

Clearly, social class correlates strongly with the possession of political power in modern-day America. Donald R. Mathews and William Domhoff have shown that only 4 percent of politically powerful individuals in the nation were raised in a lower-class environment, whereas most high government officials (such as cabinet officers) come from the highest classes.[44]

Social class also correlates with the mental and physical health of America's population. Severe mental disorders such as schizophrenia have been found to be most prevalent in the lowest social classes.[45] The same pattern holds for physical health, mortality rates being higher among the lower than the upper classes. During the Vietnam War twice as many men from the lower, compared to the upper, classes were killed,[46] since infantrymen come overwhelmingly from the lower class. In deaths from any type of disease, the lower class in America exceeds the upper class in ratios ranging from 2:1 to 1.3:1.[47]

As industrial economies have matured, and as the creation of new positions has allowed many individuals to become upwardly mobile, a variety of new social classes have emerged.[48] Upwardly mobile persons include party functionaries in socialist nations, as well as industrial managers, professionals (particularly lawyers) and clerical and sales people in industrial societies in general. These groups derive their power and income primarily from their control over or participation in *bureaucracies,* formalized hierarchical organizations of people with specialized tasks directed toward specific goals. In fact, new *service classes,* or people devoted to providing "help" to others rather than producing food or industrial products, have displaced both agricultural workers and industrial workers as the major social classes in the United States today.[49]

The emergence of new groups of workers has led many social commentators to argue that the industrially advanced nations of Western Europe, the United States, Russia, and Japan are entering a new stage of social stratification; that is, a postindustrial as opposed to a simple agricultural or merely industrialized society.

Social Stratification in Postindustrial Societies

In postindustrial societies the majority of the labor force is engaged in the provision of services: technical and professional workers increase in number, and scientific knowledge becomes crucially important in the direction of economic, political, and social affairs.[50]

New systems of social stratification not necessarily based upon the possession of wealth are created. Some social scientists have argued, for example, that a *managerial class* (a group of administrators of large economic organizations) has emerged that possesses power independent of those who technically own the means of production.[51] Communist nations, dedicated to the ideal of equalitarianism, have produced bureaucratic administrators who, in effect, dominate the society.[52] *Technocrats* —specialized technicians, scientists, and professionals—have also proliferated at an amazing rate in postindustrial societies. In addition, the ranks of the lower *white-collar* class, such as salespeople and clericals, and other nonmanual occupations have drastically expanded.[53]

The changes in the social stratification systems of postindustrial societies have prompted some writers to envision a new society. Michael Young, for example, has written a fable on the rise of *meritocracy,* a type of utopian society in which everyone receives a place in life according to his or her measured intelligence.[54] Ralf Dahrendorf believes that we are entering a *postcapitalist* era where ownership of property no longer is a prerequisite to membership in the upper classes; rather, those who exercise control in the political and economic realms now constitute a governing class.[55] Daniel Bell foresees a period in which those who have knowledge will increasingly gain power.[56] Utopians, such as Immanuel Wallerstein, Herbert Marcuse, Melford Spiro, and Paul Goodman, foresee different futures for postindustrial civilization ranging from the organization of society along "communal" lines, such as the Israeli kibbutzim, to the supremacy of "temporary," technocratic dictatorships.[57] These changes in postindustrial society have stirred intense debates about the philosophical implications of stratification.

Philosophical Aspects of Social Stratification

From Plato to Marx to current thinkers, social philosophers have considered the issue of social justice. Some seek a society based on *equality,* or the complete leveling of wealth, prestige, and rank; others have emphasized *equity,* or the distribution of rewards on the basis of the individual's contribution to society. Philosophers of social stratification may be roughly divided into three categories.

1. *Conservatives* generally wish to keep things as they are, viewing inequality as the natural condition of humankind. Aristotle considered social inequality as an inevitable condition of humankind and went so far as to defend slavery.[58] Conservatives assume that if each person receives a fair share from society, each should get exactly what he or she deserves in wealth, power, or prestige on the basis of his or her contribution.[59] Little consideration is given to providing resources to those who cannot contribute or to establishing the basis of a fair return.

A variety of conservatism labeled "libertarianism," or the political belief that everyone should have the greatest liberty possible, has recently been proposed by Robert Nozick. Nozick argues that there is no justification for believing that the state should seek greater equality among people. Redistribution of power or wealth is, in his opinion, a matter of private choice. Thus, the ideal state would have as its motto, "From each as they choose, to each as they are chosen."[60]

2. *Liberals* adhere to the political position that the state should assure abundance and liberty for all, although they agree with the conservatives that inequality is inevitable. Nonetheless, those who take the liberal stance argue for the restructuring of society so that the distribution of power and wealth within it corresponds with the talents and actual contributions of its members. This perspective focuses on *equity* rather than inequality. Equity involves consideration of the just rewards expected by a given population.

Writers such as Herbert Gans have argued not only for *equality of opportunity* (a fair chance for each person to fulfill his or her potential) but also for *equality of results.* By the latter term is meant some guarantee that gross inequalities in income, health, and status will be eliminated.[61] John Rawls has contended that each person must have an equal right to the most extensive liberty compatible with the liberty of others, and that social hierarchies should afford advantages, yet remain open to all.[62]

3. *Egalitarians,* those who oppose differences in wealth, power, or privilege, have condemned society as essentially unjust and have sought a complete leveling of the social order. Marxism represents the most influential school of thought among those who hold this opinion.

Clearly, the existence of inequality in human life presents serious problems. The belief that it is often inequitable and the hope of creating a just distribution of power have been prevailing concerns in intellectual circles of the world.

American sociologists became involved in this issue relatively late in the nation's history. Influenced perhaps by the prevailing nineteenth-century ideology of equality and by the openness of a frontier that allowed some people to escape from the burdens of inequality, American sociologists did not seriously confront the problems of inequality until the 1930s.* In the 1940s, they devoted themselves to meticulous studies of prestige in small communities. In the 1950s, some of them, most notably C. Wright Mills, examined the effects of concentrated class power in the United States.[63] In the 1960s, social scientists devoted much of their attention to solving the immediate problems of poverty,[64] and by the 1970s, the burgeoning interest in problems of power and equity resulted in an onslaught of both empirical studies and philosophical contemplations of equity. We now sketch briefly some of the major contemporary approaches to problems of stratification.

---

*Admittedly, a handful of early social thinkers, such as Edward Ross and Thorstein Veblen, were concerned with inequality and the "conspicuous consumption" of wealth in America; others, such as William Graham Sumner, absorbed Darwinian theories and glorified the "survival of the fittest."

Some Approaches to the Study of Social Stratification

In considering the various manifestations of stratification throughout history, scholars have employed a variety of approaches in attempting to understand how power and privilege are actually distributed. Within the ranks of American sociologists, five schools of thought have been dominant.*

1. *Marxism* has deliberately emphasized the role of economic power in determining social and political relationships. For Marx and Engels, social classes represented basic divisions between those who owned the means of production and those who did not.[65] This difference, in turn, defined the degree of personal freedom, political power, and general ideology of each class. Since class determines the conditions of one's life and the degree of one's freedom, and since it can never be escaped, the first question a Marxist asks in viewing any society is: Who holds economic power?

2. *Weberians* believe that the social structure of a community is far more than a reflection of the economy. For Weber, as we have noted, people may well derive power from their economic situation. Yet, their position in the society is also determined by two other factors: their "status" (that is, the position they hold because of family background, race, religion, and the like) and their "party" (that is, their power over the political state, administration, and law).[66] These various aspects of social life may not be congruent: for example, an economically poor individual might wield great power because of his or her inherited position as an aristocratic member of an officer's family. The Weberian approach has allowed an examination of various issues ranging from the nature of class consciousness to the independent role of religion in history. Thus, the basic question asked by a Weberian in viewing any society is: Who holds economic power, who has prestige, and who controls the state?

3. *Functionalists,* unlike Marxists, have contended that the specialization of labor entailed in social stratification may be a source of harmony.[67] They have also depicted stratification as an inevitable part of human life. Functionalists believe that specialization of labor and social stratification are necessary to maintain an ordered human life. Further, the majority of people in the society have to believe that the arrangement is just or legitimate. People receive different rewards for different posi-

---

*Each of these positions is more fully described in later sections of the book, particularly in Chapter 4. At this point, we would merely like to introduce the reader to these general orientations.

tions because the occupations are functionally more useful to the society.

Thus, for functionalists, the basic question in viewing social stratification is essentially: Who serves the most important function in the society?

4. *Status analysts,* such as W. Lloyd Warner, Robert S. Lynd, Helen Lynd, Floyd Hunter, Arthur Vidich, and Joseph Bensman, have examined various communities in America and concluded that the informal status of a particular group, not necessarily its economic situation or political office, gives it power over the affairs of a community. In Warner's classic studies of "Yankee City" and "Jonesville," for example, he found that one's reputation in the community was the prime determinant of whether one belonged to the "upper-upper" class.[68] In their anthropological study of a particular town ("Middletown"), the Lynds found that all the rulers came from a family of high economic status and political involvement but that other wealthy families had no political influence.[69] Arthur Vidich and Joseph Bensman, in their classic study of a town in upstate New York, found that a handful of diverse people ruled the community but that official political figures had no power.[70] In a study of a larger area, New Haven, Robert Dahl did not find a concentration of power in the hands of a small group; rather, he noted the existence of a number of equally influential "veto groups" that derived their power from a number of different sources.[71] All these studies implicitly emphasize what Joseph Bensman has called a "status community," that is, a group that shares the same technical and social skills, as well as similar values and loyalties, and that uses the community as a base for its style of life.[72]

5. *Conflict theorists* derive their inspiration from Marx but have seriously deviated from the original Marxist position.* Georg Simmel, for example, viewed conflict as inevitable in human society but did not subscribe to the belief that an end to property ownership would abolish conflict.[73] Most conflict theorists believe that social stratification is dysfunctional for society in that it limits opportunity and quashes individual freedom. Writers like Ralf Dahrendorf view economic classes as but one of many groups eternally involved in a struggle for power. Further Dahrendorf believes that there are an infinite number of power hierarchies in modern society, any one of which may generate conflict.[74] Writers in Eastern European countries, such as Milovan Djilas, see new conflicts emerging there because of the misuses of power by bureaucrats.[75]

Clearly, these various approaches to the study of social stratification differ in their premises, their objects of study, their results, and the con-

---

*Denis Wrong, for example, is often considered a conflict theorist and yet he believes the whole concept of class is outmoded since Americans have no class consciousness. Nevertheless, he believes that inequalities in power are still a major problem.[76]

clusions that flow from them. Although these approaches diverge in these regards, their end results may be complementary. The integration of these different approaches to the nature of power and privilege might best be illustrated by four concrete examples.

Examples of the Complementarity of Approaches to Social Stratification

Just as there is no complete theory of social stratification, there is no single approach that fully explains the situations and experiences of those enmeshed in a particular stratification system. Briefly, let us illustrate the necessity for an eclectic approach to stratification by describing four situations we have personally experienced: an American concentration camp in 1941; a California enclave of "Rentiers" in the 1950s; Northern Ireland in 1973; and Rhodesia in 1976.

An American Concentration Camp, 1941[77]

In December FBI agents swept through the homes of some Japanese-Americans on the West Coast. They arrested men who were labeled "suspicious" aliens.

Shortly thereafter all Japanese-Americans were asked to move voluntarily from the West Coast to locations east of the Rocky Mountains. Only a few moved voluntarily, whereupon orders for a compulsory evacuation were given. Within four months more than 100,000 men, women, and children, three-quarters of whom were American citizens, were "escorted" to temporary quarters—racetracks, fairgrounds, parks, and pavilions—and placed under army guard. They were then relocated and scattered in camps from California to Texas.

Triggered by the Japanese attack on Pearl Harbor, American agents imprisoned citizen and alien, aged and infant, rich and poor alike. There were no trials and no concern for rights except for those of young Japanese-American men who volunteered to fight on the European front or left for industrial or agricultural labor. Many Japanese-Americans remained in American concentration camps for four or more years. The last camp was closed in March 1946.

Within the camps, the inmates tried to maintain family life, an educational system, their religions, and their basic customs. Various social hierarchies developed within the camps—those who collaborated and those who did not, those who renounced citizenship and those who clung to it, those who chose to join the United States Army and those who longed to return to Japan. Significantly, Japanese-Americans in

Hawaii, a majority of the population, were not imprisoned by the army. Only a handful of Germans and Italians, also the official enemies of the United States, were put in jail. No Japanese-American was ever convicted of any act of espionage or sabotage; yet, they were imprisoned and held with barbed wire, tanks, and bayonets. Fellow (white) Americans took over their homes, furnishings, businesses, farms, and incomes.

How can one explain this "betrayal," this blatant display of majority power, this stripping from Americans not only of their possessions but also of their legal rights and their freedom? No single sociological approach suffices.

Marxists might analyze the causes of World War II, Japan's capitalistic expansion into Manchuria and eventually into Asia, and the economic attack upon the Japanese-American community as examples of capitalism's rapacity. The confiscation of Japanese-American property by whites on the West Coast would be just another demonstration of the inevitability of class conflict in capitalist societies. Weberians would possibly view the denigration of Japanese-Americans not primarily in economic terms but as an example of the exercise of "party" and "status" power. Since German-Americans were left unmolested, Weberians would be more interested in the greater prestige and political power that protected Germans in such cities as Milwaukee. Functionalists could point to the superior status of Japanese-Americans in Hawaii: they were not imprisoned because of their usefulness to those islands. Conflict theorists, while recognizing other causes, might well emphasize the nationalistic hysteria gripping America at that time. No single view offers a total explanation for the imprisonment of Japanese-Americans, but, taken together, the various rationales offer a portrait of the factors that entered into the situation.

A California Enclave of "Rentiers," 1950s

At the opposite extreme in social status from concentration camps, La Jolla, California, in the 1950s represented social prestige on the West Coast. A town of approximately 20,000 people located on beautiful beaches and foothills of the Pacific Ocean, La Jolla boasted the highest percentage of millionaires and retired admirals of any town of similar size in America.[78] Mansions lined the Muirlands above the town; each home maintained a staff of butlers and maids; and magnificent cars roamed the palm-lined streets as their drivers caught glimpses of bronzed, idle youths surf-boarding.

"Rentiers," those who received money from stocks, bonds, or munificent pensions, ruled La Jolla. Well-paid service classes of doctors, lawyers, stockbrokers, teachers, and merchants pandered to their needs. Maids, butlers, and gardeners either lived with the rentiers or occupied modest residences below the hills.

Money alone did not distinguish the rentiers from the lower classes. Typically, they attended St. James Episcopal Church, received their medical care at the expensive Scripps Clinic, sent their daughters to the exclusive Bishop's School, rode horses at Rancho Santa Fe, swam at the Beach and Tennis Club, sent their more talented sons to Stanford and the less talented ones to the University of Southern California. They bought their jewels at Cartier's and voted Republican. The women lifted their faces at Elizabeth Arden's. They detested Mexicans and tolerated Japanese in their gardens. They staunchly defended Senator Joseph McCarthy, Robert Taft, Chiang Kai-shek, the John Birch Society, Cadillacs, the stock market, M.G. roadsters, the University Club, the United States Navy and Marine Corps, and laissez-faire economic policies. They disliked Adlai Stevenson, taxation, Plymouths, city colleges, "egghead" intellectuals, "uppity" people, the Unitarian Church, *The New York Times,* Jews, communists, "pink fellow travelers," the gaucherie of Mays department store, China, and people who could not play golf, tennis, bridge, or canasta.

What accounts for this situation? Clearly, the rentier class had developed a set of institutions, preferences, prejudices, ideologies, customs, and religion that fit a social system they controlled.

In analyzing tbe peculiarities of this breed, the approach of the status analysts might be most appropriate since American sociologists have devoted much of their attention to problems of status in small communities. Undoubtedly, such a study would reveal who actually controlled political power in La Jolla, or why Jews were excluded from the country club, or what the lower ranks in La Jolla really thought of their employers. Yet, does a study of a single community shed much insight on the rest of the nation or the world? Marxists could inquire into the American economic system, which allows the existence of a rentier class; conflict theorists would be interested in the actual power of La Jollans on the national political scene; and functionalists would probably question why American society rewards such a group, since the rentiers' function, other than supporting classes that service them, is not immediately apparent.*

---

*This is, of course, one of the classic problems of functional analysis: some sociologists would say that since the rentiers existed, they *had* to serve some further overt or hidden function—perhaps as "status symbols," or as objects of contempt for lower classes, or as examples of society's rewards, and so on. Supposedly, the larger society somehow valued these "functions."

Northern Ireland, 1973

Many Ulster Protestants were like the La Jollan rentiers in that they saw themselves as landed English gentry. This group had long dominated the Northern Irish polity, economy, and society. Yet, late in the 1960s and into the 1970s, after generations of smouldering hatred, the elite of Ulster found its power threatened by violent uprisings by the (Catholic) Irish Republican Army and by "police powers" exercised by the central government in London. Observers attributed the murders, bombings, and shoot-outs that shook Belfast and Londonderry during these years to any number of factors: religious hatred, economic disputes, educational differences, political dissension, and even Irish romanticism.

No one who witnessed the internecine, interreligious devastation wrought by mail-bombs, hidden assassins, or the explosions of gelignite-loaded cars could doubt that by 1976 the social structure of Northern Ireland had fallen apart.[79]

In contemplating the disintegration of Ulster's social system, one could use any number of points of view. Obviously, religion marked the geographic lines of battle. The dominant Protestants believed they were defending themselves against "popery" and absorption into a theocratic system. The minority Catholics believed that continued Protestant ascendancy involved the destruction of their churches, subordination of their parochial schools, and political disaster. Thus, Weberians might take religious beliefs and subcultural development as a point of departure in analyzing the Irish conflict.

Marxists, in contrast, could well focus on the economic differences that split the two groups.[80] Condemned to a "proletarian" class, Catholics are excluded from most well-paying jobs and from the higher ranks of the civil service. Among young male Catholics, unemployment rose to 40 percent. Protestant-dominated unions kept Catholics from joining their ranks. Systematic discrimination has forced thousands of young Catholic men to seek jobs in England or the United States.

Conflict theorists might seek out other sources of the deadly dispute. In the educational realm, for example, Catholics were virtually excluded from Queen's University until 1945. Since that date, when scholarships were provided, Catholic enrollment has jumped to about 30 percent of the student body. Thus, a new class of intellectuals able to articulate their grievances was created. Similarly, in politics, Protestants managed to exclude Catholics from power. Until 1972, for example, no one could enter parliament unless he or she was a householder, a luxury few Catholics could afford. Even in 1976, Protestants refused to allow Catholics proportional representation in government.

Status analysts could well be concerned with the subtle differences between the different social strata in Northern Ireland. One could easily detect Catholic-Protestant differences by simply knowing the person's name, address, and the school he or she attended. Even hair color or the shape of a pram pushed by a mother indicated the person's social stratum.

Thus, as in the other examples, an analysis of the stratification system of Northern Ireland must necessarily include an understanding of status differences, political power, and economic leverage. In addition, however, in that disturbed province, no one could ignore the element of religious cleavages.

Rhodesia, 1976

Like the Protestants of Ireland, whites in Rhodesia held a supreme place of privilege. Rhodesia, a landlocked bastion of white power in the middle of black Africa, exploded into violence in 1976. Some 280,000 whites, mainly English and Portuguese emigrés, had traditionally ruled over 6 million blacks. Salisbury, the capital, was a modern city in the green rolling hills of the nation. Whites lived in lovely suburbs around the city or on sprawling plantations. Rich in cattle, chrome, and other resources, whites who had often come from lower-class English backgrounds, enjoyed lovely houses set on well-clipped lawns and backed by swimming pools. In 1964, England attempted to force its colony to accept black participation in the political process. The Rhodesian government, led by Ian Smith, steadfastly refused to allow majority rule and declared its independence. Although its exports were supposedly embargoed by the United Nations, Rhodesia flourished because nations such as the United States ignored the blockade. In 1976, because of the sudden collapse of Portuguese rule in neighboring black territories, Rhodesia was infiltrated by black guerrilla forces on several different fronts. Led by educated blacks who had been allowed to attend mission schools or the University of Rhodesia and abetted by urbanized blacks, the black independence movements seriously threatened the survival of the white supremacist regime.

The issue of race must be considered in any analysis of the social stratification system of Rhodesia. White Rhodesians argued that blacks had free access to schools, jobs, the army, and the university. Although white Rhodesians, like white South Africans, could legitimately claim that blacks had a higher standard of living than any place else in Africa, they steadfastly refused to allow blacks any genuine political power or higher offices in the economic structure until 1976.[81]

Marxists could view this situation as merely another example of capitalistic colonialism since the whites obviously benefited from their domination of blacks. However, to consider the Rhodesian conflagration as simply another example of proletarian exploitation would not do justice to this complex situation. Weberians would note that racial issues were paramount and that status differences between various black tribes prohibited them from forming a united front against the minority whites. Conflict theorists would be likely to consider the entire international arena and to contemplate the various interests Zambia, Tanzania, South Africa, and other nations had in either fomenting or calming the rebellion.

Thus, whether one considers the Rhodesian conflict, Ulster's explosion, the apparent calm of La Jolla, or the imprisonment of Japanese-Americans, issues of power and equity must be considered. Although these examples illustrate the potency of social stratification, no single sociological approach can exemplify the complexities of each situation. Therefore, in this book we are committed to an *eclectic* approach, a viewpoint that encompasses the political, economic, and social aspects of the phenomenon of human life. We believe that only this tactic can widen our understanding of why humankind has distributed power and privilege so unequally throughout history. By adopting such a catholic view of the problem, we also hope that the problem of social justice may be illuminated.

Now, let us look at the historical record.

Notes

1. F. Muller-Lynes, *The Evolution of Modern Marriage* (New York: Macmillan, 1930).
2. Elliot Skinner, ed., *Peoples and Cultures of Africa* (Garden City, N.Y.: Doubleday, 1973).
3. J. H. Hutton, *Caste in India* (Bombay: Oxford University Press, 1969).
4. S. Dill, *Roman Society in the Last Century of the Western Empire* (Oxford: Clarendon, 1898).
5. John Hope Franklin, *From Slavery to Freedom* (New York: Knopf, 1963).
6. Jerome Blum, *Lord and Peasant in Russia from the Ninth to the Nineteenth Century* (Princeton, N.J.: Princeton University Press, 1964).
7. Paul Blumberg, ed., *The Impact of Social Class* (New York: Crowell, 1972).
8. Philip M. Stern and George de Vincent, *The Shame of a Nation,* (New York: Obolensky, 1965), p. 1.
9. Ibid.
10. Ibid., p. 2.
11. Aaron Antonovsky, "Social Class, Life Expectancy, and Overall Mortality," *Millbank Memorial Fund Quarterly* 45 (April 1967).
12. William Sewell and Vernal Shah, "Socioeconomic Status, Intelligence, and the Attainment of Higher Education," *The Sociology of Education* 40 (Winter 1967).

13. William McCord, *The Springtime of Freedom* (New York: Oxford University Press, 1965).
14. Organization of Economic Cooperation and Development, Paris, 1976.
15. J. B. Bury, *The Idea of Progress* (New York: Dover, 1932).
16. George Woodcock, *Anarchism* (New York: World, 1962).
17. Karl Marx and Friedrich Engels, *Manifest des Kommunistishen Partei*, J. E. Burhard Printer, 1848.
18. F. Nietzsche, *Thus Spake Zarathustra* (London: Everyman, 1946).
19. George Paloczi-Horvath, *Mao Tse-tung* (Garden City, N.Y.: Doubleday, 1963); Richard Collier, *Duce!* (New York: Viking, 1971); and Joachim C. Fest, *Hitler* (New York: Harcourt Brace Jovanovich, 1973).
20. Ayn Rand, *The Virtue of Selfishness* (New York: Signet, 1964).
21. Robert Nozick, *Anarchy, State, and Utopia* (New York: Basic Books, 1975).
22. B. F. Skinner, *Beyond Freedom and Dignity* (New York: Knopf, 1971).
23. Michael Harrington, *Socialism* (New York: Bantam, 1973).
24. Herbert Gans, *More Equality* (New York: Vintage, 1974).
25. John Rawls, *A Theory of Justice* (Cambridge: Harvard University Press, 1974).
26. See Jon Van Til for an opposing point of view in Arthur B. Shostack, Jon Van Til, and Sally Bould Van Til, *Privilege in America* (Englewood Cliffs, N.J.: Prentice-Hall, 1973).
27. Rebecca Marcus, *Survivors of the Stone Age* (New York: Hastings House, 1975).
28. A. R. Radcliffe-Brown, *The Andaman Islanders* (Glencoe, Ill.: Free Press, 1948).
29. Gerhard Lenski, *Power and Privilege* (New York: McGraw-Hill, 1966).
30. Skinner, *Peoples and Culture of Africa*.
31. Elizabeth M. Thomas, *The Harmless People* (New York: Knopf, 1959).
32. See M. J. Finley, *Slavery in Classical Antiquity* (Cambridge: W. Heffer and Sons, 1960).
33. Hutton, *Caste in India*.
34. Marc Bloch, *La Société Féodale* (London: Routledge and Kegan Paul, 1961).
35. Hutton, *Caste in India*.
36. Bloch, *La Société Féodale*.
37. Marx and Engels, *Manifest des Kommunistishen Partei*.
38. H. H. Gerth and C. W. Mills, eds. and trans., *From Max Weber: Essays in Sociology* (New York: Oxford University Press, 1946).
39. Talcott Parsons, "A Revised Analytical Approach to the Theory of Social Stratification," in R. Bendix and S. M. Lipset, eds., *Class, Status, and Power* (Glencoe, Ill.: Free Press, 1953).
40. Melvin Tumin, "Some Principles of Stratification," *American Sociological Review* 18 (August 1963).
41. Lenski, *Power and Privilege*, p. 308.
42. C. Wright Mills, *The Power Elite* (New York: Oxford University Press, 1967).
43. Sewell and Shah, "Socioeconomic Status."
44. Donald R. Mathews, *The Social Class Background of United States Senators* (Chapel Hill: University of North Carolina Press, 1960); and William Domhoff, *Who Rules America?* (Englewood Cliffs, N.J.: Prentice-Hall, 1967).
45. August Hollingshead and Frederich C. Redlich, *Social Class and Mental Illness* (New York: Wiley, 1958).
46. Maurice Zeitlin, "A Note on Death in Vietnam," in Maurice Zeitlin, ed., *American Society, Inc.* (Chicago: Markham, 1970).
47. Aaron Antonovsky, "Social Class, Life Expectancy, and Overall Mortality."
48. Seymour Lipset and Reinhard Bendix, *Social Mobility in Industrial Society* (Berkely and Los Angeles: University of California Press, 1959).
49. Alain Touraine, *La Societe Post-Industrielle* (Paris: Denoel, 1969).

50. Daniel Bell, *The Coming of Post-Industrial Society* (New York: Basic Books, 1973).
51. James Burnham, *The Managerial Revolution* (Bloomington: Indiana University Press, 1960).
52. Milovan Djilas, *The New Class* (New York: Praeger, 1957).
53. Bell, *Coming of Post-Industrial Society.*
54. Michael Young, *The Rise of Meritocracy* (London: Penguin, 1958).
55. Ralf Dahrendorf, *Class and Class Conflict in Industrial Society* (Stanford, Calif.: Stanford University Press, 1959).
56. Bell, *Coming of Post-Industrial Society.*
57. See T. R. Bottomore, *Sociology as Social Criticism* (New York: Pantheon, 1974), for cogent criticism of some of the more unrealistic neo-Marxist positions as well as of the functionalist branch of sociology.
58. See Aristotle, *Politics,* trans. Benjamin Jowett (New York: Modern Library, 1943).
59. See Stanislau Ossowski, *Class Structure in the Social Consciousness,* trans. Sheila Patterson (New York: Free Press, 1963), for an interesting discussion of this position from a Marxist point of view.
60. Nozick, *Anarchy, State, and Utopia.*
61. Gans, *More Equality.*
62. Rawls, *A Theory of Justice.*
63. Mills, *The Power Elite.*
64. Shostack et al., *Privilege in America.*
65. *Karl Marx: Selected Writings in Sociology and Social Philosophy* (New York: McGraw-Hill, 1964).
66. Gerth and Mills, *From Max Weber.*
67. Parsons, "A Revised Analytical Approach."
68. W. Lloyd Warner and Paul S. Lunt, *The Social Life of a Modern Community* (New Haven, Conn.: Yale University Press, 1941).
69. Robert S. Lynd and Helen M. Lynd, *Middletown* (New York: Harcourt, Brace, 1929).
70. Arthur Vidich and Joseph Bensman, *Small Town in Mass Society* (Garden City, N.Y.: Doubleday, 1958).
71. Robert A. Dahl, *Who Governs?* (New Haven, Conn.: Yale University Press, 1961).
72. Joseph Bensman, "Status Communities in an Urban Society: The Musical Community," in Holger R. Stub, ed., *Status Communities in Modern Society* (Hinsdale, Ill.: Dryden Press, 1972), pp. 92-107.
73. Georg Simmel, *Conflict and the Web of Group Affiliations,* tr. Kurt H. Wolff (Glencoe, Ill.: Free Press, 1956).
74. Ralf Dahrendorf, *Class and Class Conflict in Industrial Society.*
75. Djilas, *The New Class.*
76. See Dennis Wrong, "Social Inequality Without Social Stratification," *Canadian Review of Sociology and Anthropology* 1 (1964).
77. Brewton Berry, *Race and Ethnic Relations* (Boston: Houghton Mifflin, 1951), p. 200.
78. No analysis of the social structure of La Jolla, California, exists. The *La Jolla Blue Book,* however, offers some hints about the nature of that small society. Residents could identify each other's social status by address and by listed occupation.
79. Liam de Paor, *Divided Ulster* (London, Penguin, 1970); Sunday Times Insight Team, *Ulster* (London: Penguin, 1972); and Andrew Boyd, *Holy War in Belfast* (London: Anvil, 1971).
80. See, for example, Bernadette Devlin, *The Price of My Soul* (London: André Deutsch, 1972).
81. Clive Kileff, ed., *Urban Man in Southern Africa* (Rhodesia: Salisbury, 1975).

PART I

Varieties of Inequality

A useful framework for categorizing the historical differences in social inequality has been provided by Celia Heller.[1] She has suggested that the major differences between systems of stratification can be viewed in terms of at least four types of issues.

1. Normatively, is the system of stratification open or closed? (That is, can people from the lower stratum theoretically enter the higher stratum?)
2. Normatively, is it based on ascription or achievement? (That is, is a person assigned to a position in society simply because of his or her parents, or may that person change position by personal efforts?)
3. Is access to changes in status formalized or prohibited by such institutions as law? (That is, could a slave achieve a freeman's status during the period of the Roman Empire?)*
4. What is the actual, as opposed to the theoretical, source of inequality? (That is, are religious justifications of inequality really a cloak for differences in wealth?)+

*Heller becomes a bit vague at this point since it is unclear how her categorizations differentiate between, on the one hand, the ascription-achievement axis and, on the other hand, "the degree and types of institutionalization."

+Similarly, if the law, the wealthy, the church, and the military all agree on certain types of inequality, how is one to judge which is the "true" rationale?

1

Agrarian Society

Dimensions of Stratification	Simple Society	Agrarian Society			Industrial Society	Postindustrial Society
		Slavery	Caste System	Estate System		
Normative openness	Achieved	Ascribed	Ascribed	Achieved ascribed	Achieved	Achieved
Normative source	Physical prowess in production of food	Law	Religious	Military prowess	Entrepreneurship	Knowledge and expertise
Normative justification	Custom	Law	Religion "virtue"	Military protection	Economic productivity	Economic, cultural, and bureaucratic productivity
Amount of mobility	Open	Closed, except for some selected individuals	Closed, except for subcastes	Closed, except for rare individuals and groups	Relatively open	Relatively open
Actual source of obtaining control	Production of food	Heredity and military prowess	"Control" by priests and heredity	Heredity military prowess	Wealth	Control over bureaucracy
Impact	Sharing of food, male dominance	Legal subjugation of entire groups	Economic, political, and social as well as religious distinctions	Supremacy of lord over serf	Economic class system	Bureaucratic and economic class system

Although Heller's categorical distinction may be useful as a framework for comparing the stratification systems of different societies, it certainly does not exhaust the many questions that can be posed about the systems that people have established to assure their supremacy over other people. As our examination of simple, slave, caste, and estate societies illustrates, one may also ask questions such as:

1. What is the impact of different forms of inequality upon humankind?
2. What are the roles of religion, wealth, and military power as the sources of social inequality?
3. What are the actual possibilities for mobility in the system?

Thus, drawing together the issues raised by Heller and a few others, the four types of societies that we examine in this part are viewed in terms of the dimensions in the accompanying table.

In some detail, then, let us proceed to an examination of the origins, form, and results of social stratification in different societies. The simple societies, those characterized by the most primitive of technologies, have often been regarded and even idolized as the most egalitarian.

Note

1. Celia S. Heller, *Structured Social Inequality* (New York: Macmillan, 1969).

1
SIMPLE SOCIETIES

The Beginnings of Inequality

In 1754 Jean Jacques Rousseau presented his picture of man in an "original state of nature." The invention of the idea of private property, in Rousseau's opinion, removed man from a condition of untrammeled liberty and equality. This led to inequalities that in turn corrupted man's nature. In his pure state, according to Rousseau, man wandered in the forests, "without industry, without speech, without home, without war, without ties, without any need of his fellows, without any desire to hurt them, perhaps without recognizing any of them, individually . . . but sufficing to himself alone."[1] Rousseau did not, of course, have much experience outside of the sophisticated enclave of Geneva, and he had never actually visited a primitive society.

In spite of their gross idealization and simplicity, Rousseau's views concerning "primitive" man proved immensely popular and influential. Karl Marx, for one, accepted the opinion that man at the very beginning of society lived in a state of "primitive communism" where each person shared his goods equally with others.

Although our knowledge of simple, nonagricultural societies has been increased in recent years, some modern scholars continue to cling to the belief that the "natural" or "original" state of man was one of basic equality. For example, Jon Van Til contends "that there are situations in which human beings live in virtual equality."[2] He cites primitive societies such as the Bushmen of South Africa's Kalahari Desert, the Pygmies of the African Congo, and the Indians of Tierra del Fuego as instances where social inequality is virtually unknown and where food, the most important of commodities, is shared equally. These surviving examples of the presumably original state of man have prompted scholars such as Van Til to question the inevitability of inequality. He suggests that every inquiry concerning modern class-conscious societies should begin with the question: "Why is it that a very natural way of organizing society has given way in our own time to a much more inegalitarian social form—with all the attendant costs that tax us so?"[3]

Unfortunately, contemporary anthropology cannot provide us with a completely unambiguous picture of human beings in the earliest stages of their development. In order to reconstruct the unwritten past, we must accept the assumption that the surviving remnants of Stone Age people (those untouched by knowledge of bronze, iron, or agricultural techniques) truly resemble our most distant ancestors. Even accepting this premise, when we review contemporary evidence concerning those simple societies that have somehow survived in modern times (the Bushmen, the Pygmies, the Tasaday of the Philippines, the Jivaro of Brazil, the Ik of Uganda) a picture of idyllic equality does not emerge. Some of these groups live in relative harmony; others hate everyone around them and do not hesitate to steal from anyone, including their mothers. Some groups place the aged at the top of the social hierarchy, while some despise them. Some give special privileges to warriors or shamans, while other groups ignore such social distinctions. A consideration of the varied mosaic of "simple" societies allows for few unqualified generalizations:

If a "simple" society exists in an area where food is abundant, social distinctions are usually kept at a minimum.

Adult men—at the expense of women, children, and sometimes the aged—generally are dominant since they are most adept at food gathering.

Social honor in such societies is usually accorded to people who (1) possess wisdom, which is at times attributed to the old; (2) have access to the supernatural; or (3) possess special skills, such as ability in hunting.

The Technology of Simple Societies

A *simple society* is defined as a human group that lives primarily by hunting and gathering food. The society manufactures tools from stone, bone, or wood but is unable to forge them from iron. With their primitive instruments, members of a simple society can gather wild plants, fruits, and seeds, and they can perhaps hunt and kill certain animals. Some have learned to use fire, to herd animals, and to plant seeds. A primitive technology sustains those simple societies that existed three million years ago and survive in rudimentary form today, but it seldom produces an economic surplus that is not immediately eaten.

Clothing, if worn, is made from palm leaves or other accessible materials. Medicine, except for the magical spells cast by shamans, is unknown. Religion may exist, but it is confined to beliefs in vague great spirits (for instance, the forest represents such a spirit to the Pygmies of the Congo).

The culture of these simple societies is not necessarily primitve. They do have, for example, comprehensive, highly imaginative, and complicated kinship systems that dictate who may marry whom. Clearly, however, without an advanced agricultural technology or a resulting economic surplus, simple societies seldom develop an elaborated system of art, theology, politics, literature, or philosophy. The social interaction between members of such societies may be described as cruel or kind, hierarchical or egalitarian, ruthless or worshipful toward the aged, playful or mean toward children.

In handling differences of skill and presumed wisdom among people, then, simple societies have created vastly different systems of inequality. Because of variations in geographic situation and social experience, we examine each of the simple societies in terms of its own development and culture. At one extreme, one may find examples of relatively equalitarian, harmonious societies that lack most of the distinctions of power and privilege characteristic of modern life. At the other extreme, brute strength creates distinctly unequal societies.

"Equalitarian" Societies:
The Tasaday and the Andaman Islanders

The Tasaday are a tiny tribe of people who live in a secluded area of the Philippines. They have no contact with other people except for an occasional exchange of women. They might be seen as the contemporary followers of Rousseau's ideal. As Rebecca Marcus states:

> The Tasaday have no chief or leader, and they need none. They share their food, just as they share their few tools. They compete with no one, for they live in peace and harmony with each other. They are gentle, non-aggressive people, with no words in their language for anger, war, weapons, or hostility.[4]

The Tasaday's basic social unit is the family, which consists of father, mother, children, and perhaps a widowed father or mother. Each family is self-sufficient, collecting its own firewood and food. Beyond this level there is apparently no greater social organization. Any disputes among family members are handled by the father. Older children care for the young in a tender, playful manner.

The Tasaday have not created any art forms, and they lack a sophisticated religion (although they believe that a huge, dangerous bird lives in some supernatural realm). They can create fire but have no cooking techniques. Their prime ethical injunction forbids incest, which is conceived of as intermarriage within the ranks of those who speak the Tasaday language. Thus they must seek mates from tribes in the surrounding forest. They are hardly a prolific people. Investigators who first came to their realm in 1971 found only twenty-seven people who identified themselves as Tasaday.[5] Living in caves and sheltered by dense underbrush, they have almost totally escaped contact with the outside world.

The Tasaday, like all "equalitarian" simple societies, enjoy one great benefit: an abundance of food. They neither grow food nor store it since they can dig up wild yams, gather bananas, berries, crabs, frogs, and small fish. They have not invented fishing tackle because the fish are so abundant in their region that they catch them with their hands. Whether contact with the Philippine government and with American television crews (complete with helicopters, tape recorders, and cameras) will change the life of this feckless people remains an open question.

The Onges of the Andaman Islands closely resemble the Tasaday in their spirit of egalitarianism and have often been cited as examples of the basically equalitarian nature of humanity. The Andaman Islanders, who were first described by A. R. Radcliffe-Brown in 1922, provide a classic example of "primitive communism."[6] They own land jointly, share their abundant food, exchange presents of private property, and accord honor to those who are most generous.

Like the Tasadays, the approximately seven hundred Onges of Little Andaman Island enjoy beneficent weather, a large food supply, and plenty of fresh water drawn from streams. They have not developed the arts except for necklaces and other body decorations. Their religion consists of the belief that there is a supreme being who resembles a crocodile. Because the island is located in an isolated zone of the Indian Ocean, they have escaped most contact with other peoples, although the Indian government has recently established health clinics there.

In terms of social organization, the Onges of the Andamans have chosen to live in villages consisting of eight to twelve families, all of whom live in one huge hut. Private property (such as nautilus-shell drinking cups) is kept in woven baskets. Men limit themselves to one wife and often "lend" their children to childless couples.

To handle the minor disputes that may emerge in the communal hut, the islanders elect a leader who serves as an arbiter though he has no unique powers. All important decisions about the group are made democratically. Stealing, a rare but serious crime, is punished by banishment, which usually eventuates in death.

Although the Andamanese do not suffer from major inequalities in power and privilege, they do accord honor and prestige to their people in a differential manner. Usually, "the benefits and honors enjoyed by the few represent a return for services rendered to the many under conditions free from any form of social coercion or man-made shortage."[7] The group, for example, extols the virtues of the skilled hunter who divides his food with others. "By this spontaneous and uncoerced exchange, those who are generously endowed by nature with talent and energy are stimulated to produce more, and those who are not have greater assurance of obtaining the necessities of life."[8]

In the Andaman Islands the benevolence of nature assures that no one will be absolutely deprived of food or face death because of famine. Thus social distinctions have been kept to a minimum since even the weakest members of the group may gather enough food in an hour to feed a family. In contrast to the Tasaday and the Andamanese, the people of simple societies who live under harsher conditions have developed systems of inequality based for the most part on physical strength.

Anarchic Societies: One against All (the Ik)

The Ik of Uganda, some two thousand strong, once enjoyed the same abundant food as other Stone Age tribes. Their land teemed with baboons, leopards, hyenas, antelope, and ostriches. In 1939 the British colonial government of Uganda forbade the killing of these animals, which were designated as "endangered species." The Ik refused to obey these laws and continued their customary patterns of hunting. Even as their prey disappeared, however, the Ik retained their Stone Age implements, declined to adopt agricultural techniques, and increasingly faced a shortage of food. The critical change in their environmental situation led to a new social organization, one that contrasts sharply with the utopian vision of the life style and innate equalitarianism of "simple" societies.[9]

Among the contemporary Ik, "nobody helps anyone else. Each person thinks only of himself, his ever-present hunger, and ways to satisfy it."[10] Social distinctions in this tribe are based solely on strength. The person who can seize food for himself survives and owes no obligation to the weaker members of the group. The Ik do not fit in with the utopian pictures of the happiness and equalitarianism of the simpler peoples as described by Rousseau; rather, they exist in a state of nature such as Thomas Hobbes hypothesized, where "the life of man is solitary, poor, nasty, brutish, and short."

As one observer has characterized a daily experience among the Ik:

A weak old woman has dragged herself into the woods near the village and found a handful of berries. She puts them into her mouth, and before she can swallow them, two boys of six who had followed her stealthily attack her. One holds her arms while the other pries open her mouth, puts his fingers in, and scoops out the berries. He and his friend share the meager food.[11]

The Ik live in small villages composed of the huts of individual families. The compound can be entered only through hatches, which force a visitor to run a gauntlet of spears. The Ik have very little social life and families do not even eat together. Because of distrust, husband and wife go off separately each morning to find food, gulp it down, and rarely if ever bring it back to the hut. The Ik have no marriage ceremonies, no celebrations at the birth of a child, and no mourning for the dead. The dead are hidden and buried in a secluded place since, if one publicly announces a death, he might be required to give a funeral feast for the entire village.[12]

Children are despised and forbidden to enter the family hut. They are forced to join bands when they are three or four. Temporarily, they cooperate in hunting, but when one member of the band proves superior to the others, he leaves them to go out on his own. The youngest children in the bands are humiliated and tortured until they are big enough to take out their hostility on even smaller children. The games of the children, both male and female, consist in hunting exercises and attacks upon others. As Rebecca Marcus has observed, "Early in childhood, an Ik learns the selfish and cruel behavior that stays with him for the rest of his life. When he leaves his senior band he makes no other friends. By this time, he has also learned to laugh, not in fun, but at someone else's misfortune."[13]

The only sources of humor for the Ik are the old and weak. A great laugh goes up, for example, when a blind or crippled man tries to find food; the stronger people kick him out of the way and find enormous fun in mocking his plight.

The Ik maintain a vague religious belief in a god that created them and continues to live on a mountain. They do not worship this god, however, for they believe that he has abandoned them. They have no ethical beliefs. Their knowledge of medicine is limited to herbs used by shamans.

Ik social organization consists simply of the supremacy of the physically strong. Finding food is the imperative of their lives. If someone is weak or old, a stronger person kicks him out of the compound and leaves him to die. Neither water nor food is furnished to the weak. It is not even quite clear to the Ik why they should breast-feed infants and, as soon as they can, Ik mothers force their children away from them. Based on studies of deprived children in other cultures, the Ik as an entire group have developed a psychopathic personality devoid of love or conscience.[14]

Patriarchal Societies:
The Kalahari Bushmen

Despite the fact that other simple societies such as the Jivaro of Brazil,[15] the Pygmies of Africa,[16] and the peoples of Papua[17] have been idealized, they cannot be considered equalitarian societies. Although hardly as brutal as the Ik, these peoples have constructed societies in which strong, younger males dominate others. The Bushmen of the Kalahari Desert represent one example of this mode of life. It is a style characteristic of those groups that have neither the good fortune to live in an area of material abundance nor the bad fortune to exist in an environment that cannot sustain them.

The Bushmen of South Africa live in a barren, inhospitable desert where they have been driven by Bantu and Caucasian invaders.[18] There are approximately forty thousand Bushmen of the Kalahari Desert who roam the land in search of game. Each group (generally composed of fifteen to forty people) has its own home base near a waterhole. When rain is abundant, however, the band ranges across the desert within a radius of seventy miles.

The nomadic Bushmen follow a strict division of labor. Women are in charge of filling ostrich eggs with water, caring for the children, building shelter, and carrying children. The men and older boys hunt and take charge of making fires out of stone flints. The men kill hartebeests, wilde-beests, antelope, and giraffes. They use a variety of weapons, including poisoned arrows, clubs that resemble boomerangs, and spears. The game they bring back to the encampment serves purposes other than as food; the skins are turned into sandals, strings for bows, sacks, or clothes. While hunting, the men attempt to suck water from the ground with straws made of reeds. One basic rule of the bands is never to steal the water or food of another man.

The environment of the Bushmen is harsh and totally without the lush variety of foods that provide other groups such as those of the Andaman Islands with ample diets. It is, however, less cruel than the conditions of severe shortage under which the Ik live. Through their skill the Bushmen have been able to track down quarry for over five hundred years. They share their food among all members of the band and smoke meat that is not immediately used.

Although food sharing is a common practice among the Bushmen, the society cannot be considered equalitarian. As the most respected provi-ders, young adult men stand at the top of the social hierarchy. The band accepts the authority of a headman, who inherits this position of chief from his father. His primary function is to lead the group from one camp-ground to another. The headman receives no special portions of food, but the band is organized around him. Usually, the chief has several wives. His group is made up of the wives, their children, and perhaps other relatives and those of his wives. Everyone in the band must bear some relationship to the chief.

Men dominate not only the women of the band but also those who are too weak to keep up their nomadic wanderings. A sick person or an older, weak person is often separated from the group when the band is engaged in its search for food. They are left behind in special shelters built for them by the stronger members of the group, given a small amount of food and water, and—after some weeping and mourning—abandoned to face their inevitable death.

This pattern of male dominance appears to be characteristic of these simple peoples who have neither been blessed with an abundance of food nor condemned to a life of near starvation.

"Civilized" People in a Simple Society: The Uruguayan Cannibals

People who have been raised in technologically advanced societies may find that under extreme and rare circumstances, they are plunged back to dependence on Stone Age technology. In the ravages of war or famine, for example, some have stepped back three million years to an earlier technology. How do they react? Usually, they develop a system of stratification in which the physically strongest hold power and in which the "civilized" customs of class, caste, religion, and other social distinctions are dispensed with.

A dramatic illustration of a return to the simple state of life occurred in 1972. An Uruguayan air force plane destined for Chile crashed in the high Andes Mountains. The plane carried, among others, a team of young rugby players. The people who survived the crash soon exhausted their meager supplies of food, and it became apparent that their only means of survival was to devour the frozen corpses of their comrades who had been killed in the crash. The Uruguayans justified their cannibalism by regarding the consumption of the corpses as similar to the symbolism of the Catholic Mass.

At first, the flesh was divided equally. When it became evident that rescue parties that had been sent out would not reach them, a team of the strongest mountain climbers among the survivors was chosen to undertake an arduous trek to Chile. Since the survival of the entire group depended upon the success of this expedition, the four men were awarded extra portions of flesh, were allowed to rest, and were not required to do any "housekeeping" duties around the survivors' camp.

As Piers Paul Read, who wrote about this expedition in *Alive*, indicated, these men emerged as the "elite" among the cannibalistic survivors.

> Once the four expeditionaries had been chosen, they became a warrior class whose special obligations entitled them to special privileges. They were allowed anything which might improve their condition in body or mind. They ate more meat than the others and chose which pieces they preferred. They slept where, how, and for as long as they liked. They were no longer expected to share the everyday work of cutting meat and cleaning the plane.[19]

Although the expeditionaries formed a privileged class, and all the others literally prayed each night for them, their power was curtailed by two factors that emerged. First, three cousins who had been on the airplane formed a type of "judiciary" that decided disputes between the survivors and limited the power of the four chosen expeditionaries. Second, the expeditionaries allowed some bending of the rules so that those who worked at cutting up the corpses received more nourishment than the injured (or those who faked injury):

> There arose outside the rules an unofficial system of pilfering. This was why the task of cutting up the larger pieces (of bodies) was so

popular; every now and then a sliver could be popped into one's mouth.
. . . One piece in the mouth for every ten cut up for the others was more
or less normal. . . .
   This system, like a good constitution, was fair in theory and flexible
enough to allow for the weakness of human nature, but the burden fell
on those who either could not or would not work.[20]

Eventually, after great suffering, the expeditionaries marched across
the mountains and the group was saved. In such terrible conditions of
privation, it is hardly surprising that a system of social stratification developed among highly religious, "civilized" people that was not too remote from that of certain Stone Age tribes.

Advances in technology have doomed the way of life of most simple
societies. Although one may admire the simplicity of the Tasaday and the
Andaman Islanders, their happiness depends upon an abundance of food
that only a few simple societies enjoy. Yet, ironically, an advance in
agricultural techniques usually entails the decline of simple societies and
the demise of their particular social organizations.

Decline of Simple Societies

Approximately ten thousand years ago, most simple societies scattered
throughout the world created agricultural technologies that allowed them
to cultivate necessary food. With the invention of the hoe, terracing,
irrigation, fertilization, and rudimentary metal tools came totally new
forms of stratification. Among the major social changes produced by the
revolution in agriculture, Gerhard Lenski has noted six that seem of
particular importance.[21]

1. The production of nonessential goods increased as an economic
   surplus developed.
2. People devoted more of their time and energies to ceremonial activities, particularly religion.
3. Warfare (and the warrior), although not totally absent in simple societies, grew in importance.
4. Social roles, particularly in the political and economic realm, became increasingly specialized.
5. Secret societies and social clubs for men emerged apart from the
   family and kin group.
6. Inequality—based on political power, knowledge of the supernatural, wealth, skill in oratory, or military prowess—increased.

As Lenski observed, in agricultural societies, in comparison to hunting and gathering ones, "inequalities in power and privilege are nearly always more pronounced. . . . Not only are the inequalities greater, they are more institutionalized, a development made possible by the increase in 'leisure' and the greater opportunities for specialization."[22]

Thus the technological evolution of agrarian societies produced an increase in warfare and inequality—two social institutions that have been vigorously condemned throughout history. Yet, simultaneously, the arts, religion, and economic complexity also increased. This historical development raised a basic issue that continues to haunt modern social thinkers: is inequality a necessary handmaiden of economic advance and the cultivation of "higher" cultures?

In even the simplest of horticultural societies as well as advanced agrarian ones, a particularly severe form of social inequality—slavery— made its appearance. It is this form of inequality, one of the most durable institutions in human history and found in some of the greatest civilizations of the world, to which we next give our attention.

Notes

1. Jean Jacques Rousseau, "Discourse on the Origin of Inequality," 1754.
2. Jon Van Til, "Social Inequality: How Did We Get Here Anyway?" in Arthur B. Shostak, Jon Van Til, and Sally Bould Van Til, *Privilege in America* (Englewood Cliffs, N.J.: Prentice-Hall, 1973), p. 1.
3. Ibid.
4. Rebecca B. Marcus, *Survivors of the Stone Age* (New York: Hastings House, 1975), p. 16.
5. "Cave People of the Philippines," *The New York Times*, October 8, 1972.
6. A. R. Radcliffe-Brown, *The Andaman Islanders* (Glencoe, Ill.: Free Press, 1948).
7. Gerhard Lenski, *Power and Privilege* (New York: McGraw-Hill, 1966), p. 200.
8. Ibid., p. 106.
9. Elliot P. Skinner, ed., *Peoples and Cultures of Africa* (Garden City, N.Y.: Doubleday, 1973).
10. Marcus, *Survivors of the Stone Age*, p. 23.
11. Ibid., p. 24.
12. Simon Ottenberg and Phoebe Ottenberg, *Cultures and Societies of Africa* (New York: Random House, 1960).
13. Marcus, *Survivors of the Stone Age*, p. 31.
14. William McCord and Joan McCord, *The Psychopath* (Princeton, N.J.: Van Nostrand, 1965).
15. J. Michael, *The Jivaro* (Garden City, N.Y.: Doubleday, 1973).
16. Colin Turnbull, *The Forest People* New York: Simon & Schuster, 1968).
17. James Sinclair, *The Highlanders* (Brisbane, Aust.: Jackagranda Press, 1971).
18. Elizabeth M. Thomas, *The Harmless People* (New York: Knopf, 1959).
19. Piers Paul Read, *Alive* (New York: Avon, 1974), p. 122.
20. Ibid., p. 125.
21. Lenski, *Power and Privilege*.
22. Ibid., p. 131.

2

AGRARIAN SOCIETIES: SLAVERY, CASTE, AND ESTATES

Slavery

All known agrarian societies have at one time or another produced a system of slavery. In settled agricultural communities, slaves became an asset in production, whereas in nomadic, simple societies, captives were considered other mouths to feed. Furthermore, the increased militarism characteristic of agrarian societies allowed conquerors to take prisoners who could serve as slaves. Throughout recorded history, in fact, slavery has been an integral part of most societies. Philosophers such as Aristotle, statesmen such as Seneca, and religious prophets such as Jesus accepted slavery as a natural part of society. It has only been in the last one thousand years that slavery has been questioned as an economically profitable system, and only in the last four hundred years has its equity been seriously challenged.

Slavery has disappeared under the following conditions: (1) when it was replaced by an equally severe system of stratification, such as castes prescribed by religious oracles; (2) when it collapsed because of economic or military disasters suffered by the central governing power; or (3) when it became irrelevant and unprofitable because of industrialization. Humane people in modern times have cried out against slavery, but their voices were heard only when economic conditions propitiously decreed that the old system was dead.

Slavery, as opposed to other systems of social stratification, exhibits two unique features: (1) the slave is regarded as property, as the possession of another person; and (2) the slave's position is justified by the law, another creation of agrarian societies. In a few societies, the slave's position has been regarded as hereditary; in some societies the slave had no escape from ascribed status; in some societies slavery became identified with racial or national prejudices. The central fact about slavery in all societies, according to the best historian of ancient Greece, is that slavery is a system where "a man is in the eyes of the law and of public opinion and with respect to all other parties a possession of another man"[1]

Slavery did not exist in simpler societies but arose only with the growth of more advanced horticultural techniques. When land was cultivated, there tended to be an "increasing utilization of wives as an income-producing form of property. This and the raising of small livestock such as pigs provide certain resources which can be used throughout the whole of a man's life."[2] Simultaneously, man developed the institution of slavery, for it provides an easy way of transmitting power and privilege from one generation to another. For the first time in human history, Gerhard Lenski has observed, men regarded other men as a form of property.[3]

In most agrarian societies, slaves were gathered during punitive expeditions against other societies. The captives' sons, in turn, remained in slavery, and the ranks of this group grew. As slavery became an indispensable part of agrarian economies, various theorists offered normative justifications for the system. Some, like Aristotle, believed "that some men are by nature free, and others slaves, and that for these latter slavery is both expedient and right."[4] In other societies, such as Mameluke Egypt, China during the T'ang dynasty, and the American South, slavery was regarded as the natural condition of inferior, docile, conquered peoples. On the other hand, others did not attempt to claim that slaves were by nature inferior. Florentinus, the Roman jurist, for example, declared that "Slavery as an institution of the *jus gentium* whereby some are subject to the *dominum* of another is contrary to nature."[5] Generally, in ancient Rome and Greece, philosophers viewed slavery as a disgraceful but necessary accompaniment to their economy and civilization.[6] At times, religion has been invoked to justify the "natural inferiority" of slaves, as American Southerners did in their interpretation of Christianity.[7]

In the conditions of warfare which prevailed in ancient Greece and Rome, as M. J. Finley has expressed it, "the condition of servitude was one which no man, woman, or child regardless of status or wealth, could be sure to escape in case of war or some other unpredictable and uncontrollable emergency."[8]

In spite of differences in justifications, remarkably similar systems of slavery developed in ancient China, Greece, Rome, eighteenth-century Latin America, and nineteenth-century North America. These systems were all based upon the legal ownership of one human being by another, and all regarded the slave as property. Variations on this theme occurred because of regional differences. In Rome, Greece, and Latin America, for example, the slave was considered a human being (perhaps endowed with a soul) and was therefore at times treated with more paternalism than in the American South.[9] In other areas, such as the American South, the slave was regarded at best as an inferior being and at worst as subhuman.

In some highly significant ways, the American South had a unique form of slavery. As Celia Heller has pointed out, "The tie between race and slavery accounts for all major differences between American and ancient slavery."[10] Most important, this link between race and slavery encouraged white Southerners to think of slaves as intrinsically inferior. When manumission occurred voluntarily, the freedman was still subjected to legal restrictions. For example, he was prohibited in most parts of the United States from intermarriage with whites.

The institution of slavery can perhaps best be illustrated by examining it as it existed in ancient Rome and in the American South, where its defenders put up the last battle in its defense.

Roman Society

THE ORIGINS OF SLAVERY

In 800 B.C. Rome was a relatively minor city that, in myth and probably in fact, had very few slaves. The *classicus* (the original noble class) were often farmers who lived a simple form of life. However, they contributed one hundred members to the Senate, which ruled the Republic and furnished it with generals, consuls, lawyers, and philosophers.[11] The *equites* (or rich merchants) constituted a second economic class and stood below the patricians in power. The *populus,* artisans and tradesmen, made up a third class and were generally free men. They, however, may have allied themselves with patrons.

During this early part of Roman history, slaves constituted only a small proportion of the population. They were usually captives taken during wars and were generally considered to be valuable members of a household. They served as nurses, teachers, managers of household monies, writers, or craftsmen. Since these original slaves had been captured in a military defeat, enslavement was regarded as a merciful exchange for death. The slave was not treated as inherently inferior and could, with relative ease, buy freedom through payments to the master. Commonly, a slave could earn enough in Rome to secure his manumission within seven years.[12]

By 200 B.C. the economic and military conditions in Rome had changed drastically. First, Rome had vastly extended her boundaries by conquering fertile areas of southern Italy, Spain, and northern Africa. In the process the Republic acquired unprecedented numbers of slaves. Second, Rome had developed a system of large farms in conquered lands that made the use of slaves an economically profitable operation. These *latifundia* were awarded to merchants or artisans as spoils of Rome's various wars, and served to spread the Empire. Third, the *latifundia,* utilizing cheap slave labor, produced goods that could be sold for less than those of free farmers. Gradually, the originally free peasants gave up the competition, migrated to the city, and lived off the free corn and other forms of the "dole" distributed by officials. All these factors worked to increase the economic importance of slaves in the Roman Empire, as their free competitors disappeared from the farms.

By 145 B.C. "Roman society, once a community of free farmers, now rested more and more upon external plunder and internal slavery."[13] In Rome itself, slaves carried out the work of servants, tradesmen, bankers, and factory labor. Mistrusted by their owners, slaves were not generally considered as loyal and were not subject to the military draft.[14] Thus their servitude became even more profitable to large landholders or urban patricians who required able-bodied men. The huge influx of captured slaves severed the intimate relations between master and slave that had existed in early Rome. Consequently, slave revolts plagued the Roman Empire. In 196 B.C. the slaves of Etruria revolted. In 185 B.C. 7,000 slaves rebelled in Apulia; in 139 B.C. 70,000 rebel slaves took over Sicily.[15] These sporadic revolts were crushed speedily and brutally by efficient Roman legions. Leaders of slave revolts were crucified, drowned, or, more mercifully, beheaded. The strongest were dispatched to Rome to fight as gladiators against each other or animals in the "circuses" of the Empire.

The greatest revolt against slavery erupted from the ranks of the gladiators. In 73 B.C. 200 gladiators fought their way out of Capua and occupied a slope of Vesuvius. They were led by Spartacus, whom Plutarch considered "a man not only of high spirit and bravery but also in understanding and gentleness superior to his condition."[16] Spartacus rallied 70,000 slaves and successfully fought off punitive expeditions sent out to recapture the revolutionaries. Since Roman slaves at that time composed about one-half of the population of Italy, Spartacus had little difficulty in rallying 120,000 men. As they marched toward the Alps, he promised the recruits that the land or farms that the men had originally owned would be returned. Roman armies eventually forced Spartacus to turn his troops back toward Rome.

By 72 B.C. the patricians gathered their forces and fought against their former slaves with a vengeance born of the fear that their entire way of life might disappear. Harassed by Roman legions, Spartacus fled south, avoiding a direct invasion of Rome. He found, however, that he could no longer control the ex-slaves under his command. Thousands of them formed marauding bands and ravaged the countryside. Alarmed by the impudence of the rebels, Rome sent huge armies to pursue Spartacus. In 71 B.C. the Roman legions surrounded the ex-slaves and decimated their ranks. The legionnaires crucified 6,000 captives and exhibited their bodies along the Appian Way from Capua to Rome. Decomposed corpses were left hanging on the crosses for months as a deterrent to potential revolts.

Slave revolts nevertheless continued throughout the Roman Empire because of the brutality of the system. None were successful.

STYLES OF LIFE AND SLAVERY

By the first century after the birth of Christ, slaves, who had witnessed the futility of earlier efforts, seldom revolted against their condition. In addition, for a minority, freedom was still possible. As the Roman Empire expanded, urban slaves could make a fortune in the service of their masters. Also, they could still be freed, and their sons could even achieve the status of senator, or in one case (Pertinax) that of emperor. Since slaves, primarily of Greek or Syrian origin, held important positions as financiers, managers of mines and waterways, a person of the lowliest birth could hope to accumulate a great deal of wealth.[17]

Slaves performed every imaginable function in the empire. Aside from their indispensable services on the great farms, they constituted about 80 percent of the people in retail, clerical, or artisan trades in the empire's major cities. As "household" slaves, they served as musicians, librarians, and physicians as well as personal servants. But despite their varied activities, slaves were still considered as property and treated as such. According to Seneca, they could be beaten or even killed at the whim of the master; slaves were the objects of pointless cruelty and the butt of many jokes.[18] Slave markets in Rome offered legless, armless men, dwarfs, and hermaphrodites for the amusement of potential buyers. Prices for human beings ranged from about $1 for farm slaves up to $105,000 for an especially gifted philosopher.[19]

Some household slaves during the first century A.D. were treated almost as members of the noble's family. On certain feast days, some masters would even serve the slaves at dinner; other masters freed their slaves and married them; slave nurses cared for nobles' children with great affection; and some slaves died in battle for their masters. Seneca, the epitome of the humane man in this age of slavery, chose to take all of his meals at the same table with his servants.[20] Some slaves were admitted to the *collegia,* a type of trade union that bargained for the rights of urban workers.

The fact that slaves could be of any race or region, the belief in brotherhood espoused by Roman philosophers, and the relatively high price of slaves all served to moderate the brutality of masters toward their subjects. The advent of Christianity in Rome may have offered some solace to the slaves. Proponents of the faith promised eventual liberation in heaven. The supremacy of Christianity did not, however, basically change the slave's life style. The Gospels describe Jesus as a person who called upon slaves to protect the property of their master, who praised slaves who increased the wealth of their conquerors, and who supposedly said, "blessed is the slave whom his master, returning, finds performing his charge."[21] Thus the coming of Christianity did not in itself promote the freedom of slaves but, like most ancient beliefs in agrarian societies, justified slavery as a necessary part of this mortal life.

Although rationalized by religion and enforced by military power, the Roman slave system allowed ample opportunity for individuals to escape their servitude.

SOCIAL MOBILITY IN THE SLAVE SYSTEM

Emancipation could be bought by a resourceful slave who had a valued skill. Having earned enough money (approximately seven times his original purchase price), the slave could buy his freedom and enter any economic or political pursuit he wished. It was also possible for old or sickly slaves to be freed because their masters could then place them on the state "dole" and feed them from public monies. The advent of the dole hastened the abolition of slavery. Once freed, slaves could, theoretically at least, achieve any economic or political goals they wished.

By the beginning of the Christian era, freedmen began to outnumber native Romans. Fearful that the growth in freedmen might change the ethnic character of Rome and destroy the military prowess of her army, Augustus, in 2 B.C., imposed strict limits on the number of slaves who could be freed by their masters. No one was allowed to free more than one hundred slaves.[22]

The influence of the ex-slaves is perhaps best portrayed in the life of Epictetus. Epictetus was born a slave in A.D. 50 but became the confidant of emperors and the most prominent philosopher in this period in Roman history. As the son of a slave, Epictetus received no formal education. In addition, he was a lame, weak person who required constant medical attention. After a series of moves, he became the slave of Epaphroditus, who was himself a freedman. His master was apparently thoughtful and kindly. Epictetus was allowed to study with the leading philosophers of Rome and, upon recognizing his talent, Epaphroditus freed him.

Epictetus migrated from city to city, gathering a following behind him. He argued, as did the other founders of Roman stoicism, that man must accept whatever fate befalls him. All men were brothers, he believed, under a fatherly but enigmatic God. Whatever God ordained—humiliation, slavery, or death—man must accept with equanimity.[23]

In the name of brotherhood, Epictetus condemned slavery and advised men to treat each other with kindness. He advocated an end to capital punishment and asked that man return evil with good.[24] Many of the great nobles, particularly Marcus Aurelius, tried to follow his advice. Nonetheless, slavery flourished in Rome until about A.D. 300.

THE DECLINE OF SLAVERY

In the third century after Christ's birth, political anarchy and economic disaster overwhelmed the Roman Empire. As agricultural stability and the central state dissolved under the attacks of "barbarian" German tribes, the institution of slavery slowly eroded.

No one can specify the exact reasons for the decline of Rome: the rise of Christianity, the military power of the German tribes, the dole system, dependence upon listless slaves, a weakening of original beliefs in Roman nobility, are all factors that have been suggested. Rome's decline, however, can be definitively traced to A.D. 193, when Pertinax—the grandson of an ex-slave—briefly held the position of emperor. Pertinax was a respected man who had ruled Rome as a prefect; he replenished the treasury, encouraged the arts, and attempted to enforce discipline upon the army. Rebelling against the instituting of disciplines, the Praetorian Guard formed an alliance with the freedmen who had become the urban merchants of Rome. Ironically, Pertinax fell to the swords of his own bodyguards and his fellow freedmen.

A period of economic and political chaos followed the death of Pertinax. Ominously, German armies drew closer to Rome from the north while Balkan and Greek troops (allied with Germans) pillaged the south. Rome continued as a relatively stable center, but the empire disintegrated.

By the third century A.D., the Roman Empire had declined to the point where slavery was no longer a profitable institution. Among the many reasons for the demise of slavery in Rome, several factors can be noted:

1. *Latifundia* could no longer function. The ravages of enemy bands made settled, large-scale agriculture (and hence, slavery) a difficult enterprise to maintain.[25]
2. The military decline of the empire made slaves expensive pieces of property since they could no longer be replaced as easily as in past centuries. The *Pax Romana,* which originally supplied an abundance of slaves, could no longer replenish them.[26]
3. Landowners often found it more profitable in this circumstance to emancipate their slaves and treat them as *coloni*—that is, individuals who cultivated the land of the owner in return for payments of rent. These newly freed men, out from under the control of their former owners, survived for many centuries as tenants and virtual "serfs."
4. As the power of the central state eroded, each locality—with self-sufficient trades, a barter system (instead of the imperial coinage), and small-scale agricultural operations—gained in power. These local enterprises could satisfy the needs of each community and, in turn, served to weaken the power of most absentee landlords, who owned the largest numbers of slaves. Severed from their masters, these ex-slaves often unilaterally declared their independence.

Slavery declined, therefore, as an empire based upon universal ambitions distintegrated into local, isolated fortresses; as intense urbanization gave way to the rise of sheltered, protected villages; as the force of cosmopolitan legions fell prey to the attacks of roving bands of "barbarians." Slavery in ancient Rome was the product of imperial ambitions, the spread of huge farms, and a growth in urbanization. As "barbarism" advanced, Roman armies collapsed, nobles fled to the safety of enclosed villas, giant farms fell infertile. Concomitantly, slavery became increasingly unprofitable.

Wherever huge agrarian societies flourished under the protection of military power, slavery continued to exist. Such was the case of the American South until Northern weapons silenced this last bastion of slavery in Western civilization.

The American South

ORIGINS OF SLAVERY

Like ancient Rome, the American South developed a full-scale slave system based on huge plantations. Virginia, one of the first slave-holding states, provides a typical example of the system's evolution. Englishmen first arrived in 1607 and struggled to earn a living. They soon bename aware that they could sell crops of tobacco in London. The production of tobacco, however, was most profitable when conducted on a "labor-intensive" basis. Thus in 1619 the whites began to import black slaves to farm their growing plantations and, by 1650, slave-supported tobacco plantations became the richest enterprise in the American economy. By 1700 the powerful plantation owners commanded the labor of thousands of slaves.[27]

By 1800, due to technological innovations, the planting of cotton on huge plantations also proved profitable and spread throughout the American South. Cotton plantations, like those raising tobacco, also became dependent upon large sources of human labor. Although large-scale slaveholders accounted for no more than 25 percent of the Southern whites, they considered themselves an American aristocracy. The invention of the cotton gin made the growing of cotton even more profitable, and those who owned as few as five slaves stoutly advocated the system of slavery. The spread of huge cotton-growing areas caused an increase in the price for slaves as well as rewards to those who bred or traded slaves. Prices for slaves boomed. In 1852 a prime field hand was worth as much as $1,500.[28]

During the eighteenth century, Europe found that slave labor was no longer profitable. European nations, particularly England, continued as the prime slave traders, exporting most of their captives to North America, where large-scale plantations utilizing human labor were still practical and economical.[29] Captured off the west coast of Africa (often in collaboration with hostile African chiefs), slaves were brought into the Americas at an average rate of at least 10,000 per year from 1550 to 1750.[30] Only a tiny fraction of those who started the journey reached American shores: the majority died en route; some sabotaged their ships, revolted, or even took control of the slave traders themselves.[31] Nevertheless, slave traders usually made a 100 percent profit on their merchandise and were encouraged by the money to be made in the American South. The growth in the number of slaves led white American planters to pressure the government to enact a series of laws that put black slaves irrevocably under their control.

JUSTIFICATIONS FOR SLAVERY

The slavery system in the American South expanded rapidly. By 1860 more than 50 percent of the population of Virginia, South Carolina, Georgia, Alabama, Mississippi, and Louisiana were slaves. With the expansion of the system of slavery, a variety of apologists for it emerged. Writers such as George Fitzhugh, a Virginia slaveholder, claimed that the Bible proved the innate inferiority of blacks. Fitzhugh argued that white rule over blacks was progressive and benevolent. It provided a greater degree of security, more food, and more medical attention for the slaves than they had ever received in Africa. In comparison to the factory workers of the North, Fitzhugh continued, slaves were far better off in health, nutrition, and morals.[32]

The most influential proponents of slavery seldom bothered to invoke idealism concerning its status. John C. Calhoun, for example, contended that the historical processes of all civilizations justified slavery. Calhoun looked at ancient Rome or Athens and maintained that the labor provided by slaves alone freed others to create the philosophies, architecture, and the forms of government that characterized these great civilizations. Like Marx, Calhoun believed that the leaders of every civilized society had lived off the labor of others. Northern merchants who paid their laborers meager wages were not, in his opinion, different from slaveholders. Unlike Marx, however, Calhoun could not see an end to this situation. This Southern senator honestly admitted that slavery was a form of exploitation necessary for the development of elites. His beliefs were encapsulated in an 1837 speech before the Senate in which he said:

I hold that in the present state of civilization, where two races of different origins, and distinguished by color and other physical differences, as well as intellectual, are brought together, the relation now existing in the slave. iolding states between the two is, instead of an evil, a good—a positive good . . . . I hold, then, that there never has yet existed a wealthy and civilized society in which one portion of the community did not, in point of fact, live on the labor of the other. Broad and general as is this assertion, it is fully borne out by history.[33]

Slavery was, therefore, justified by some sophisticated Southern spokesmen on the grounds that the system existed in one form or another throughout the civilized world. This assertion was not different from, say, Aristotle's defense of Athenian slavery or Seneca's views of Roman slavery.

American Southerners added a final justification: blacks, they contended, were intrinsically inferior to whites and deserved subordinate status. As Arnold Sio makes clear, the racial factor in American slavery was the crucial element that differentiated it from the Roman variety.[34] For slaves, this difference had monumental effects. Manumission, for example, was extraordinarily difficult for Southern blacks to achieve, although in Rome it was not uncommon. Even the few freedmen who lived in the American South were still regarded as innately inferior.[35]

Thus, Biblical, "realistic," and racial arguments served to salve the conscience of whites who held slaves as their possessions. Regardless of their justifications, whites, particularly plantation owners, derived enormous economic benefits from their slaves and this, in itself, was enough justification for most slave owners.[36]

SLAVERY AND REPRESSION

As in ancient Rome, Southern slaveholders lived in constant fear that their slaves might revolt. Aside from declaring slaves to be nothing more than property, the slave owners passed into law a series of "black codes" that further ensured the subjugation of slaves. Slaves could not possess guns; they could not leave a plantation without the owner's permission; they could not assemble without the presence of a white man. In Mississippi a slave could not even beat a drum. Theoretically, the "black codes" ensured that contacts between black people would be kept at a minimum, and that slaves could never conduct themselves as free people. Patrols of whites roamed the Southern states searching for infractions of the codes.[37]

Slaves did in fact violate the proscriptions of their masters. Usually, they were punished by whipping. In some states, regular courts made up of white slaveholders tried slaves for "crimes." These trials were reserved only for cases such as conspiracy to rebel. Since slave owners wished to protect their investments, they hesitated to hand over their property to a court that might order an execution.

In spite of the black codes, frequent whippings, and occasional executions, slaves intermittently revolted against the system. These rebellions never occurred on the scale of that led by Spartacus, but when they occurred, Southerners responded with savage repression. Nat Turner's rebellion in 1831 was typical of these relatively minor attempts by slaves to achieve their freedom.[38] Frightened even by these infrequent uprisings, the whites strengthened the black codes and whipped to death slaves who were implicated in "conspiracies." White "citizens literally stayed awake nights waiting for the negroes to make another break."[39] Although some present-day scholars have attempted to portray revolts such as Nat Turner's as massive revolutions,[40] blacks in the South remained relatively "quiet," nonviolent, and complacent compared to Roman slaves.[41]

This outward "complacency," as Stanley Elkins has recorded, could not be attributed to the slaves' acceptance of the system. Rather, the black slaves—torn irrevocably from their original cultures, devoid of hope that they could someday return to their homes, and placed in complete subjugation—commonly reacted by assuming outwardly "Sambo" behavior: in general, they were stoic, seemingly cheerful, passive except for incidental pilfering and sabotage, and not particularly prone to active revolt.[42] Elkins has argued that the Southern slaves very much resembled concentration camp victims.[43] Consequently, active, large-scale revolts in the South were relatively infrequent. Under their outward behavior, however, slaves were in a constant state of agony and fury as their oral accounts and diaries clearly indicate.[44] Despite idyllic accounts of slave life found in the propaganda of the time or in modern novels such as *Gone with the Wind,* the lot of the American slave was hardly a happy one.

STYLES OF LIFE AND SLAVERY

By 1830 the majority of black slaves (approximately 2,800,000) lived on plantations. Most of these (about 1,800,000) worked on cotton farms where each slave was expected to cultivate roughly three acres. A relatively small number of slaves (400,000) had been moved by their owners to urban areas where they served as artisans and servants. During harvest seasons, they were rented out to surrounding plantations.[45]

On the plantations, a few slaves worked in the large mansions as relatively privileged "house" servants, but most labored only in the fields. On smaller farms, the white owner worked side by side with his slave. As John Hope Franklin has observed, the life of neither the slave nor the owner on a small plantation was a happy one:

> Even for the planter, life was not always pleasant, and there was little in the way of recreation and other diversions to foster a zest for living on the plantation. . . . Life was so barren generally that it can hardly be described as "the good life" even under the most favorable circumstances; and the plantation with its inherent isolation and consequent social and cultural self-sufficiency frequently bordering on stagnancy tended to perpetuate the barrenness.[46]

Slaves lived in small, rude houses. Their work was supervised by poor whites who were not successful on their own farms. On the larger plantations, these whites were responsible for punishing and disciplining the slaves. As overseers, they applied the whip mercilessly to slaves who had little motivation to work.[47]

Slaves in urban areas commonly became carpenters or other types of artisans but, unlike Roman slaves, they did not develop into a large middle class of well-paid freedmen. The black codes ensured that even the most industrious worker could not secure freedom. Furthermore, urban white artisans objected strongly to competition from the slaves and refused to teach them many of the necessary skills.

The social activities of slaves were quite limited and centered primarily on their churches. Missionary influences came from the North and, in response, blacks were allowed to set up a number of independent churches. As long as the ministers promised redemption in heaven, whites permitted black churches to function independently, but when the sentiment for abolition grew, the whites decided to outlaw black churches as possible sources of rebellion. Between 1830 and 1835 most Southern states stripped black ministers of their credentials and replaced them in their posts with white men.

The basic family system of the slaves was consciously destroyed by slave traders.[48] Family units left intact could aid in provoking rebellions. Slave owners had little compunction about trading the men, women, or children of a family separately. Nonetheless, under ordinary circumstances, slave owners cooperated in the establishment of slave families on their own plantation.[49] The children bred of such unions became property and, naturally, the owners were most interested in garnering further profit from their human possessions.

In a recent controversial examination of American slavery, Robert W. Fogel and Stanley L. Engermen have illuminated the life style of slaves.[50] These authors stress that slave owners, motivated by economic self-interest, were eager to protect the health of their slaves (as they were of their cattle) and that they watched carefully over the mating of their slaves for fear of debasing their stock. Further, Fogel and Engermen report that even as the Civil War approached, slave owners were optimistic about the economic viability of the system. According to their analysis, there appeared to be no inherent economic reason for the downfall of slavery since agriculture with slave labor was economically more profitable than farming carried out by free men. Indeed, they maintain that slaves' productivity was 35 percent higher on the plantations than similar agrarian systems of family farming in the North. Thus, unlike the Roman system of slavery, the American system did not decline because of its own "inner dynamics." Rather it required a war and external attack to destroy it.

The Decline of American Slavery:
The Civil War

The Civil War, which erupted in 1861, was fought on strictly sectional grounds. Southerners, frustrated in their attempts to extend slavery to Western states, believed that their rights had been abrogated. Northerners, prompted perhaps by a desire to expand their industrial activities, fought primarily to secure the Union. Although abolitionists and Northern "radicals" had long argued for the end of slavery, the immediate cause of the war was the South's refusal to obey the majority opinion laid down by the North. Abraham Lincoln expressed Northern indifference to slavery when he wrote Horace Greeley in 1862:

> My paramount object in this struggle is to save the Union, and it is not either to save or to destroy slavery. If I could save the Union without freeing any slave, I would do it.[51]

As an incidental part of his strategy to save the Union, Lincoln issued the Emancipation Proclamation on September 22, 1862. By this act, a gesture to unite Northerners against the South, and to ensure that England would not aid the South, he legally freed the slaves. Freedom came as a hollow gesture, however, since Lincoln and subsequent Northern governments failed to provide economic, military, or political guarantees for the freedom of the South's ex-slaves.

By 1862 slavery had ended as an official policy of Western societies, although it has continued in various forms in a few agrarian societies, notably Saudi Arabia and the Sudan, until recent times. Throughout the world, the demise of slavery may be considered a tribute to the technological power of industrialized, urbanized nations that no longer need the energy and labor provided by slaves.

Another form of stratification, other than slavery, has also been characteristic of agrarian societies and has proved more durable. The caste system differs from slavery in that human beings are not considered as masters or property, but rather as souls whose position in life has been predetermined by their past actions in another life. The caste system, particularly as practiced in India, has a religious justification that has proven more durable than the arguments used to justify slavery.

Caste Systems

"In order to protect this universe," Hindu priests announced in 200 B.C., "He, the most resplendent one, assigned separate occupations to those who sprang from his mouth, arms, thighs, and feet."[52] Thus Manu, the great lawgiver of India, divinely ordained inequalities among people. In contrast to the Judeo-Christian tradition, which viewed worldly inequalities as unjust or, at best, tolerable, Hindu religious thinkers have treated inequality as a divinely sanctioned, unavoidable, and just fact of life. Despite contemporary movements to abolish some aspects of the caste system (such as the Indian government's attempt to protect "untouchables"), this ancient system of inequality has been extraordinarily durable.

Those who believe in the caste system assert that each person is assigned a place in society at birth, that contact between different ranks is "impure," that intermarriage between castes is forbidden, and that every social act is governed by caste rules. In India, the prime and perhaps sole example of the caste system, the Hindu religion has sanctioned the systematic practice of caste inequality in almost every sphere of human interaction. It is assumed that supernatural forces have placed each person in the exact social position that he or she deserves. If an individual led a good life in an assumed prior existence, then the person has a high social position in this life; if one acted immorally in one's previous existence, then one falls to a servile rank in one's present incarnation. Theoretically, one may not complain about inequality since heaven has ordained one's life in an equitable manner.

The word "caste" derives from the Portuguese *casta* and was first used in 1563 when Garcia de Orta observed in India that "no one changes from his father's trade and all those of the same *casta* of shoe-makers are the same."[53] *Caste* today signifies a collection of people who bear a common name for their group, claim descent from a common ancestor, follow the same hereditary calling, forbid intermarriage with members of another caste, and observe extremely strict rules concerning contact with other castes, particularly when consuming water or food. Thus, *Brahmans*, members of the highest caste, may marry only a fellow Brahman and, more specifically, one who comes from their particular subcaste; they may serve water to members of a lower caste but they may not accept it; they must cleanse themselves ritually if the shadow of an "untouchable" falls upon them; and, before British invasions, they could kill members of the lower castes with impunity.

In the caste system's obscure beginnings some thousands of years before Christ, unnamed Hindu priests declared that humankind had been divided into four basic castes (or *varna):*

The *Brahmans* were priests and teachers who stood at the top of the hierarchy.
The *Kshatriyas* took second place as warriors and political leaders.
The *Vaisyas* performed agricultural and mercantile functions.
The *Sudras* were servants, menials, and peasants who supported the other three castes.

The belief in *karma,* the idea that the human soul follows a prescribed destiny in this life, rendered the unequal distribution of social functions palatable. It was part of the divine order of the universe and human passage through it. According to Vedic hymns, the castes emerged respectively from the various organs of *Purusha,* the God or life-giving element in all animate beings.

With the passage of time, the four original castes have been subdivided into at least three thousand categories encompassing many different occupations. Each subcaste has its own rules, privileges, and taboos.[54]

For devout Hindus, the caste system governs almost all aspects of life. If one violates the rules of one's caste, that person may be punished or ostracized by the caste *panchayat* (council). Before British rule, an individual could be killed by order of the council. If one refused to do penance for one's violation, that individual became an "out-caste" in this life and was condemned to a lower caste in the next life. For believers, caste permeates their very existence. Although conditions and beliefs in modern India have altered slightly, the observations of S. J. Wilson in 1877 still have relevance in the twentieth century. The caste system, he noted:

. . . gives its directions for recognition, acceptance consecration, and sacramental dedication, and vice versa, of a human being on his appearance in the world. It has for infancy, pupilage, and manhood, its ordained methods of sucking, sipping, drinking, eating, and voiding; of washing, rinsing, anointing, and smearing; of clothing, dressing, and ornamenting; of sitting, rising, and reclining; and of meditating, singing, working, playing, and fighting. It has its laws for social and religious rights, privileges, and occupations; for instructing, training, and educating; for obligation, duty, and practice; for divine recognition, duty, and ceremony; for errors, sins and transgressions; for intercommunion, avoidance, and excommunication; for defilement, absolution, and purification; for finesse, chastisements, imprisonments, mutilations, banishments and capital executions. It unfolds the ways of commiting what is called sin, accumulating sin, and of putting away sin; and of acquiring merit, dispensing merit, and losing merit. It treats of inheritance, conveyance, possession, and dispossession; and of bargains, gain, loss and ruin. It deals with death, burial, and burning; and with commemoration, assistance, and innury after death. It interferes, in short, with all the relations and events of life, and with what precedes and follows life.[55]

This all-encompassing system, deeply ingrained in the religious life of a subcontinent, has withstood generations of invaders; it has influenced other religious faiths, such as Islam, to take up its practices; it has provided the social cement to a deeply divided nation and offered divine consolation to those who have been condemned to the lowest positions in society. As Charles Drekmeier has observed,

In India the concept of karma, the belief that character is stamped by the deeds of the earlier lives of the soul, could only discourage hopes for social melioration. For the orthodox there was nothing accidental about birth into a particular class. There was no logical basis for social protest. Here was as convincing an answer to Job as has been devised.[56]

Even in contemporary India, where Western ideals of liberalism, equalitarianism, and socialism have affected the elite, the caste system continues to affect the everyday lives of 600 million people.

CASTE AND STYLES OF LIFE

Some of the rigid inequalities of the ancient caste system have been softened in modern India because of the combined influence of Western rule, egalitarian political beliefs, and the humanitarianism of such leaders as Gandhi. In ancient times, for example, a Brahman who killed a Sudra felt no more compunction than if he had killed a dog; the penance was the same.[57] In contrast, a Brahman who drank water from a well used by outcastes was so defiled that he had to live on cow's urine for a certain period of time until the impurities had been removed from his system.[58]

These practices no longer flourish in India. Indeed, the government has proscribed persecution of untouchables, established quotas for them in universities, and afforded them de jure political rights that they never possessed before. Nonetheless, the practice of caste continues in India's innumerable villages, which remain the backbone of this essentially agrarian nation.

Our own experience in the villages of India testifies to the tenacity of the caste system.[59] In the north of India, no one dares to drink from the wells touched by lower castes, and breaking the marriage taboo is unthinkable to an average villager. The lowest castes eat grain deposited in cow dung for lack of any other food; upper castes give them neither money nor food for they believe that it is the natural situation of these lower castes. In southern India, where caste hatreds run deep, the "light-skinned" Aryan (the presumed ancestor of Brahmans) is blamed for all crimes by the lower castes; walled fortresses prevent women of an upper caste from leaving their village; strict Hindus still drink the *panchgavya*— a mixture of cow's milk, butter, curds, urine, and dung—as a way of purifying the body of defilement.

Although the caste system is outwardly rigid, its adaptation to modern technology reflects a degree of flexibility. Castes of metal workers change their name to adopt to the ways of a steel plant. As names of an entire caste change, their position in life may go a little higher, but they retain the customs of those who work metal with their hands. Similarly, the introduction of automobiles led A. Enthoven to comment, "Modern India, having created a caste of chauffeurs from the menials who tend motor-cars, is almost ripe for a Rolls Royce caste rejecting food or marriage with the Fords."[60]

Intermarriage is a hazardous course to undertake for even the most modern of Indians. As one Kshatriya man who was also a university professor commented about his friend,

> She is a pupil of mine. . . . We should like to get married, but my girl friend is a *brahman*: her parents would never allow her to choose a husband from the warrior caste. Nor would it help me to have a wife from a higher caste than my own. My own caste would expel me. . . . Our relations and our friends would no longer know us. . . . No suitor would regard the hand of her sister as desirable any longer.[61]

Justice for the different castes differed as dramatically as marriage patterns. Ancient Indian law, for example, decreed that a Brahman could not be executed for any crime whatsoever. A Sudra who mentioned the name of an upper caste, however, should have a huge, red-hot iron nail thrust into his mouth.[62] In remote districts some untouchables continue the practice of shrieking and howling when they see a Brahman, so that the Brahman may be warned not to approach them and risk impurity.[63]

Touching a portrait of a member of another caste or the skin of a leather worker, seeing a grave digger, marrying the wrong person, charging bank interest at the same rate for a Brahman as for lower castes— these and many other transgressions still preoccupy contemporary Indians and, for the orthodox, require purification.

Thus ritualism permeates life in India, particularly in the rural regions, and, as Max Weber pointed out, constitutes an essential element of the caste system.[64]

Although members of the lower castes acquiesce in the system, they do not ordinarily accept their particular position as individuals within the caste hierarchy.[65] When unobserved by members of the upper castes, they complain of economic, political, and even sexual exploitation by the higher castes.[66] In their everyday life, members of the lower castes react to their situation by adopting one of several psychological responses.

PSYCHOLOGICAL RESPONSES OF THE LOWER CASTES

Members of the lower castes have several possible reactions to their despised and deprived position in life:

1. *Passive resignation.* Although they accept ritual practices, some members of the lower castes try to "play the fool" and act as if they were irresponsible, simple-minded, and "shiftless."[67] This response, similar to that of slaves in many societies, helps them to avoid contact or trouble with the higher castes.

2. *Sullen resignation.* Members of the lower castes may follow the rules and obey the orders of the upper castes but express their resentment in minor acts of sabotage, irresponsibility, or passive resistance.[68] Again, as in the slave system, the resentment felt by this group seldom results in a total rejection of the system.

3. *Rationalization by denial.* Members of a lower caste may claim that they are in their subordinate position merely because of their lack of economic power or numerical inferiority.

4. *Rationalization by a "mistake."* Members of a lower caste may acknowledge that their family belonged to a low caste but argue that the caste was given a subordinate status by some type of mistake. They may, for example, contend that they should be Brahmans because of their father's lineage but that, in their particular region, caste is unjustly traced through the mother.

5. *Rationalization by an "accident."* Members of a lower caste may argue that they "really" belonged in the ranks of the Brahmans but had lost their status because of some accident in their previous lives. Thus astrologers may tell an individual that he was a highly meritorious individual in his last incarnation but that he had been tricked by jealous servants into inadvertently polluting himself.[69] Heaven had punished him but not because of an evil act that he had voluntarily committed.

As Berreman has summarized the Indian caste situation, no one who is in a deprived status says,

> I am of low status and so are my family members and my caste-fellows, and justly so, because of our misdeeds in previous lives. To do so would lead to a psychologically untenable position. . . . Rationalizations indicate something less than enthusiastic acceptance of caste position and, meanwhile, they perhaps alleviate or divert resentment. . . . That people remain in an inferior position, therefore, does not mean that they do so willingly, or that they believe it is justified.[70]

In whatever way they rationalize their position, very few individuals can escape the embrace of caste. Even Gandhi's son (who belonged to the merchant caste of Vaisya) was condemned and became the subject of national scandal when he married the daughter of a Brahman. Whereas efforts by individuals are often fruitless, joint action by members of entire castes to improve their lot in life can sometimes succeed in moving them up a notch or two in the caste system.

SOCIAL MOBILITY IN THE CASTE SYSTEM

The doctrine of *karma* gives remarkable stability to the caste system. To question one's status in life or to attempt to change one's lot as an individual is regarded as literally impossible. The *Bhagavad Gita,* India's rough equivalent to the Bible or the Koran, commands each person to follow his *dharma* (his duty as prescribed by the rules of his caste) and thus to reach perfection. The greatest sin is to violate a caste rule. As J. H. Hutton has observed:

> It is quite clear that the caste system has been effectively utilized by the Brahman priesthood to maintain the existing form of Hindu society with the Brahmans as a privileged class, and that caste has been taken advantage of generally by the higher castes to keep the inferior and exterior castes in their respective stations, if not to reduce them to the lowest status possible.[71]

The rigidity of the system, however, does not preclude the possibility that an entire subcaste, rather than an individual, may experience social mobility. Over a period of years, members of a particular subcaste may gain economic power or a majority of their members may attend modern educational institutions. Once this has occurred, caste members' self-esteem tends to rise. Gradually, by adopting some of the customs of an upper caste, such as the number of days prescribed for mourning, and adding a new prefix to the name of their subcaste, the upwardly mobile group may also achieve recognition from others that they have indeed gained in importance. In this fashion, members of the Sudra caste have gained admittance to the Vaisya group, and subgroups of Vaisyas have moved into the Kshatriyas. Although some scholars believe that it was once possible to be admitted to the Brahman caste, in recent times this appears to come only at birth.[72]

ANALOGOUS CASTE SYSTEMS

Premodern Japan, Burma, and Sri Lanka all exhibited vestiges of a caste system in that certain occupations were hereditary, others were considered impure, and contact between different groups often required purification rites.[73] Each of these societies had been affected by Buddhism, which, in turn, was "Hinduized" in India. Similarly, a vestigial caste system exists in Pakistan, a Moslem society that melded with Hinduism in the centuries preceding the partition of the Indian subcontinent.

Other societies that have had no historical contact with Hinduism have independently created caste systems that closely resemble but are not identical to India's. The Theodosian Code of the Western Roman Empire of the fith century A.D., for example, compelled every man to follow his father's occupation or that of the family into which he married. People could not marry outside of their guild. These injunctions were created during a period of social turmoil and served to ensure some form of stability in a crumbling Roman Empire.[74] The Roman caste system, however, did not prescribe a rigid series of taboos and lacked the strong religious sanction imposed by Hinduism.

Ancient Egypt may well have possessed a caste system similar to India's. Herodotus records the existence of seven "clans" in Egypt that were hereditary in nature. Some of these, such as swineherds, were regarded as impure, and people who had contact with them had to bathe. Priests, who were the highest class, could not eat certain foods. The system was not, however, as extensive as India's since intermarriage was allowed.

Parts of Africa also exhibit signs of a rudimentary caste system. The Masai look down upon two classes, a completely tabooed group of blacksmiths and a despised group of hunters. Masai do not permit intermarriage with these groups, and the blacksmith's products must be purified with grease before they can be used. Certain magical elements are involved in the system (for instance, the use of the word for blacksmith "causes" lions to attack at night), but the Masai lack the full religious jutifications for their customs that the Indians have developed, and the caste system does not extend throughout all occupations.

Some American scholars—most notably, John Dollard—have contended that white American discrimination against blacks constitutes a caste system.[75] Clearly, American blacks have long suffered from occupational and residential discrimination; intermarriage with whites was forbidden by laws in certain states; and in parts of the South, the provision of separate drinking fountains and bathrooms implied that contact between the two "races" would be impure. Like lower-caste Indians, American blacks have a darker skin color than their masters and have traditionally occupied subservient positions.

The correspondences among systems of inequality should not, however, blind us to their differences. Although American slavery and discrimination were at times strongly supported by religion, they were equally strongly attacked by religious abolitionists. The Christian religion did not provide the same unquestioned, divinely ordained, anciently accepted, and pervasive justification for slavery and discrimination as Hinduism did for the caste system.

Moreover, the concept of "impurity," which is so central to India's caste system, was never as paramount a belief among the American whites who subordinated blacks. Whites mated with blacks without the certainty that they had damaged their immortal souls; white children were suckled by black women; and individual blacks escaped the rank servility of their condition without waiting for the general emancipation of their group or rebirth with a white skin.

Other differences distinguish the systems of inequality in India and the United States. In India, Brahmans perform the lowly task of serving water in a railroad station to lower castes, but it would have been unthinkable in the American South for a white "gentleman" to act as a servant to blacks in a similar situation. Conversely, blacks have often served as valets or maids to American whites, preparing and touching their clothes and food, but in India, the higher castes would not conceive of a Chandal cook serving a Brahman master.

No system of inequality, then, is identical to that found in India. In those areas where similar systems have arisen, vestigial caste systems have developed but have tended to lack the full support of religion or the panoply of prescriptions and proscriptions that accompany the Indian caste system. The historical origins of the various castelike systems do, however, shed some light on the genesis of India's unique social organization. All the known caste or pseudo-caste systems arose in times of social and politcal turmoil in agrarian (rather than industrial) societies; were imposed by a conquering group upon a defeated population; were fully or partially sanctioned by the priests of the time; and normally involved a color or supposed "racial" difference between the upper "caste" and the subordinate groups. These similarities offer some clues as to the often debated origins of the caste system in India.

ORIGINS OF THE INDIAN CASTE SYSTEM

The origins of the caste system are shrouded in the mists of unrecorded history. The caste system of India cannot be viewed as merely the imposition of power by a wealthy Brahman caste. It apparently existed before priests had consolidated their position in society and before the Brahman class had been declared hereditary.[76] The caste system was not imposed by invaders in ancient India since many of its elements, including the idea of impurity, preceded the first known invasions.[77] It was not a necessary, inevitable by-product of an agrarian society since slavery, serfdom, and other forms of inequality sprang up in this economic environment whereas the caste system did not.[78] With the historical knowledge now possessed by scholars it can be said that the caste system originated in a concatenation of events—the ascendance of a priestly class after a period of turmoil, the invasion of "Aryan" outsiders, the correlation between skin color and social taboos—which took place uniquely in India at a point in time that cannot be precisely identified.

Most historians and sociologists agree that a period of intense social conflict devastated India between 1500 and 600 B.C., resulting in a codification of laws and customs depicted by the Vedic hymns, which date from approximately the sixth century B.C. Charles Drekmeier has noted that "in the seventh and sixth centuries B.C. social changes threatened the traditional allotment of functions, and it became imperative that the system be provided with a definitive rationale."[79] The conflict apparently stemmed from a long battle between the ruling nobility and the priests (or Brahmans).[80] The Kshatriyas apparently added their military prowess to the "divine" commands of the priests. By the end of the Vedic period, the priests and their allies triumphed. They accorded themselves the two highest ranks in Indian society but did not yet subdivide the lower ranks into specific groups.[81] Although priests in every agrarian society have been among the first recipients of the economic surplus produced by innovations such as the plow, India represents a rare case where the priestly class managed to impose their demands upon other economically and politically powerful groups in the society.

The establishment of the caste system was undoubtedly aided by the Aryan invasions of India, which began approximately in 1750 B.C. and had been fully consolidated by the sixth century B.C. The Aryans, who probably came originally from lands north and east of the Caspian Sea, poured through the Afghan gorges and overwhelmed the original Indus culture. They were of a lighter skin than the original Dravidian inhabitants. The Aryans absorbed the preexisting elements of the caste system and extended it to the conquered masses by creating further divisions. Most of the original Indians were consigned to the Sudra caste. The three higher castes, the "twice-born," could be reborn by ceremonial initiation into the Aryan tribes.[82] The twice-born castes were specifically forbidden contact with any occupations or groups that dealt with decay or disease, a religiously sanctioned rule that may have, incidentally, prolonged the Aryan life span.

The color or "race" of the original Indians may well have influenced the development of the caste system as it was transformed by the Aryans. *Varna,* the Indian word for caste, also means color. The Aryan invaders apparently associated black with evil and lighter colors (their own) with the forces of goodness. Because of little geographical mobility (extensive travel involved risks of impurities), most ethnic groups remained in their original habitations, and modern caste names often stem from geographical locations. It is not surprising, then, that caste distinctions today often go hand in hand with skin color.

Color prejudice, the results of conquest, and the supremacy of a priestly class—allied with many other Indian elements such as ancient ideas of totemism, taboo, pollution, purification, beliefs in reincarnation, and the (possibly) pre-Aryan theory that occupations should be hereditary —joined together to create the uniquely Indian caste system. The fact that this system has lasted for several thousand years testifies not only to the durability of its religious justification but also to its socially stabilizing functions.

STABILITY OF THE CASTE SYSTEM

As we have noted, the Indian caste system imposes a number of strictures upon every area of life and is reinforced by a series of sanctions that range from the political and legal to the supernatural. In an otherwise unreliable, impoverished society, the caste system offers obvious religious, political, and economic advantages to the Indian upper castes. In addition, the lowest castes may hope for reincarnation in a better life and can rationalize their present sufferings.

Even the most deprived members of the *Sudra* caste can look down upon such defiling groups as the *Chamars* (who make leather products), the *Dhobis* (who wash dirty, impure clothes), and the *Doms* (who deal with corpses). The vast majority of Indian society can take pleasure in comparing themselves with the lower castes and out-castes; by following their duty, they pave the way for future happiness. Certain curious elements in the caste system actually allow some castes to despise subgroups of Brahmans. The *Mahabrahmans,* for example, officiate at the cremation of the dead. Although they are Brahmans, they are regarded by everyone else as polluted. The varied, diverse pleasures of snobbery that allow almost anyone to regard himself as better than someone else help to ensure the caste system's stability.

In addition to its severe religious sanctions, the system's stability is also aided by secular punishments. Caste panchayats enforce the rules by issuing penalties to people who have eaten polluted food, married a widow from a different caste, insulted a Brahman, or "killed" a cow by neglect. The governing council of the caste may impose a variety of penalties. The most extreme would be total ostracism from the caste.

Reinforced by both religious and secular sanctions, then, it is not surprising that the caste system has survived for so many centuries. Most observers agree that a total abolition of the caste system would be highly improbable. Berreman, for example, has reviewed much of the evidence concerning the caste system in Indian villages. He has concluded:

> In the multicaste system of India, abolition of the system evidently seems impossible from the point of view of any particular caste. . . . Abolition would destroy the caste as a group which is superior to at least some other groups, and, while it would give caste members an opportunity to mingle as equals with their superiors, it would also force them to mingle as equals with their inferiors.[83]

Although no observer of the Indian scene would be rash enough to predict the disappearance of the caste system, currents of change have developed within the last century.

CHANGES IN THE CASTE SYSTEM

As we have already remarked, the caste system can be subtly altered as subcastes change "the rules of the game" and gradually move upward in the hierarchy. Urbanization, industrialization, the introduction of new technology, and increased education can accelerate this tendency.

On the highest political levels in India, many leaders privately or publicly deplore the caste system. Some view it as a distinct hindrance to economic development, since the caste system restricts geographic mobility and, at times, hinders the acceptance of economically beneficial innovations. Merely a change in tools used or seeds planted may be stubbornly resisted by particular castes since it fundamentally changes the nature of their hereditary occupation. However beneficial a particular economic change may be, believers in the caste system may adamantly and successfully oppose material progress.[84]

Politically, Indian leaders led by Gandhi have been strongly opposed to aspects of the caste system on humanitarian grounds. They have particularly attacked discriminations against the untouchables, who numbered some 60 million people in 1970.[85] Officially, the Indian parliament has laid down severe penalties for anyone who hinders the untouchable castes in their use of temples, wells, or public places of any kind. The central and state governments reserve one post of eight for untouchables.[86] All higher schools also maintain a quota of placements for the untouchables. Untouchables may receive a government subsidy for building a new home.[87]

These measures have led Hindus of a higher caste to complain that "injustice has been replaced by privilege . . . the *harijans* [untouchables] are hardly worthy of their privileged position. Centuries of contempt have made them genuinely contemptible."[88] Moreover, the base economic lot of the untouchables, or of any of the lower castes, has not been fundamentally altered because India's economic development has barely kept step with its population growth. In general, the psychological attitudes of the masses have not altered.[89] As the Indianologist J. H. Hutton has commented, although

> . . . the intelligentsia of India today seem to have made up their minds that the caste system should be got rid of . . . they fail to comprehend the difficulties, and perhaps the dangers, of such an undertaking —one indeed which would, if carried out at a stroke, wreck the edifice of Hindu society and destroy a growth of some three thousand years or more.[90]

Despite vigorous political and legal attempts to change the caste system, it appears that this particular form of human inequality will continue to prove resistant to such changes.

Estate Systems

In addition to the caste system, slavery, and primitive variations of inequality, preindustrial societies produced still another form of social stratification—a ranking of humankind by their "estate" (the possession of land and military prowess). This form of social organization historically followed other types of social differentiation. Slavery during the Roman Empire, for example, gradually gave way to a pseudo-caste system and, because of intense economic pressures, to serfdom. In ancient

Egypt, slavery preceded a caste system very much like India's, which, in turn, evolved into a society of "estates." Despite Egypt's 1952 revolution, carried out in the name of "socialism," the estate system still characterizes the rural sections of this predominantly agrarian nation.

By asserting a certain "progression" in history that has been ignored by other scholars, we are not, of course, implying that the system of estates is a higher or better form of stratification, but merely that it has usually evolved from a prior epoch of slavery or of a pseudo-caste system. Clearly, there is no inevitable development from one stage to another. Some societies, like those in most of tropical Africa, have moved from slavery to a colonial status, to incipient industrialization. Other societies, after abandoning slavery, have, like India, remained caste-ridden with only the vestiges of untenured serfdom.

By the *estate system* we mean a system of social organization that (1) assigns men to a higher or lower strata according to birth, military strength, and possession of land; (2) specifies the legal rights of each group in relation to other groups; (3) ordains that the higher strata officially grant certain privileges (for instance, protection in warfare) to the lower groups; and (4) allows the lower strata to claim this protection in return for various property rights, particularly their own labor and the produce of their lands, which they give to the upper strata.

The system of estates differed from the caste system in certain respects. It tended to lack religious sanctions; it enabled individuals to change their position in life through various military or economic achievements; and it did not proclaim the usual taboos and impurities associated with caste. The system of estates also differed from the system of slavery in certain ways. It was based upon "contractual" justifications; it gained authority through mutual exchange rather than brute conquest; it offered greater opportunities than some forms of slavery for a person to rise in the hierarchy; and it presumably offered rights in exchange for obligations.

The specific nature of the system of estates may best be understood by a review of the history of feudalism in medieval Europe between approximately A.D. 600 and 1200 and in Russia until the middle of the nineteenth century. Although these periods differ in their customs and justifications for serfdom, they offer the best illustrations of pure feudal or estate systems.

The Estate System of Feudal Europe

SOCIETY BETWEEN 600 AND 1200

With the collapse of the Roman Empire, Italy, Gaul, parts of Germany, and Spain lost the imperial center that held them together, and the cities of this period underwent a pronounced decline. Nobles retreated to their country manors, drawing with them the peasants, artisans, and soldiers necessary to control their domains. Each castle became a fortress, defended by the inhabitants who huddled in shacks near the walls.

As we have noted, a long history of war in the Roman Empire and its eventual collapse at the hands of "barbarian" Germans destroyed the system of commerce, made roads impassable, and forced the great estates to become self-sufficient in food and artifacts. Repeated invasions of Western Europe by the Saracen, the Norse, and the Magyar between the eighth and tenth centuries A.D. served to further erode the power of the central state and the kings who had ruled it. For their own protection, the various kings parceled out huge chunks of land in return for the vassalage and sworn loyalty of military people or monasteries.

Former Roman slaves, who had for the most part become freedmen during this period of social turmoil, sought protection from the more powerful local lords. In return for the lord's care, they swore that their labor, land, and, for limited periods of time, their military abilities would be at his disposal. In medieval Europe the system of estates arose in a period of political and social disintegration and constant military threats, and the consequent need of men to subject themselves economically to stronger lords in return for the lords' military protection.

As Marc Bloch, a historian of feudal society, has observed:

> Feudalism coincided with a profound weakening of the State . . . an outcome of the violent dissolution of older societies. . . . In an age of disorder, the place of the adventurer was too important, the memory of men too short, the regularity of social classifications too uncertain to admit of the strict formation of regular castes.[91]

Slavery, as a form of social stratification, declined because the lord needed the loyalty, hard work, and military prowess of his subordinates almost as much as they needed his protection.

The growth of the estate system not only entailed the demise of slavery and the supremacy of the strongest armed men, "it also involved a far-reaching restriction of social intercourse, a circulation of money too sluggish to admit of a salaried officialdom, and a mentality attached to things tangible and local."[92] As T. R. Bottomore has noted, the resulting estate system closely approximated Karl Marx's general conception of society, for it represented the clear supremacy of a warrior class that possessed military power and, usually, control over the land.[93]

GRADATIONS IN SOCIAL STATUS

The Lords: At the top of the pyramid stood the lord (or *dominus, seigneur, Herr*), who possessed horses, armor, weapons, and the allegiance of enough vassals to command control over a particular territory. Theoretically, he was ruled by a king, but the distinctions between the two ranks were minimal. As a price for buying the loyalty of the lords, most kings during this period had given away so much of their land that they were little more than "first among equals" in the noble ranks.

By the ninth century A.D. the lords had developed various mechanisms to protect their privileged status. In theory, no one could become a knight unless he had inherited that rank from his father. In addition, feudal law protected the privileges of the knights, although it made little mention of their previous obligations. The lords developed a distinctive ethic, based on loyalty, courtly love, and bravery, which exalted them as "chivalrous"—men above the common herd.

The nobles served a distinct function in their society. They were committed body and soul to their role as warriors. In a time when brigandage was rife and knights felt free to launch their private wars as a way of securing loot, the common folk had a direct and immediate need for a military protector. The interminable wars of the medieval period were disastrous for the common people since the lords ravaged their lands.[94] In most battles, the knights did not fight to kill since it was much more profitable to take a lord as prisoner and sell him back for ransom. Moreover, true battles to the death would have damaged the fragile system of knighthood. Because each lord wanted to protect his own life and that of the system, they seldom fought to the death. At Tinchebrai (1106), where England conquered all of Normandy, not a single lord was slain. At the decisive battle of Brémule (1119), only 3 of the 900 knights who fought lost their lives.[95]

In return for their "valor" and presumed protection of their serfs, the lords led relatively good lives—albeit marked by illiteracy, constant fear of outlaw attacks, and disease—in their besieged castles. Their closest, most trusted supporters came from the ranks of *serjeants.*

The Serjeants: The lords, who frequently absented themselves from their manors in order to conduct war, had need of a trusted class of subordinates to serve as stewards of their estates. Drawn originally from the ranks of peasants, these serjeants directed the duties of the castle's household servants, saw to the cultivation of the estate's lands, and levied taxes. They ranged in rank from bailiffs, who were the lord's chief servants, down to messengers and domestic servants.

The lords reimbursed their serjeants either by providing for their maintenance in the castle or, more frequently, by granting them control over "fiefs," or rural tenements. Not unexpectedly, the higher-ranking serjeants gradually accumulated their own lands, stores of wealth, mills, and, eventually, weaponry, castles, and serfs.[96]

The Clergy: Priests, bishops, and abbots ranked at every social level in the estate system. Some were immensely wealthy lords who, like Alcuin of Tours, claimed as many as twenty thousand serfs under their control. Other priests lived the meager life of a peasant. And some monks followed the path of asceticism. The clergy constituted a legal class as it possessed its own law and, in terms of secular law, was allowed certain privileges. Yet, the diversity of its economic status led Marc Bloch to observe, "It was in no sense a social class; within its ranks coexisted human types differing widely in mode of life, power and prestige."[97]

The Church served the lords by providing religious ceremonies to elevate men to knighthood;[98] it participated in the system of serfdom by offering religious as well as military protection to the lower orders. At times, the Church tried to stop the recurring wars that ravaged Europe by proclaiming interludes of the "peace of God"; at times, it encouraged military adventures such as the Crusades.

Serfs: The greatest number of people under the estate system were serfs. Drawn from the ranks of formerly free men or of slaves, the serfs tilled the land and produced the food and other goods supporting the higher estates. Typically, the lord gave the serf a lifetime tenure on a piece of land in return for rent, which was paid in products, labor, or money. In return for the lord's protection, the serf was bound by taxes and rents: he owed his lord a part of his produce (usually a tenth), unpaid labor in constructing roads or castles, fees for grinding his corn at the lord's mill, payments for fighting or hunting, a tax on goods sold in the market, a fine if his son went on for an education, and a forfeiture of all his land if he did not produce a son. This list of obligations could be greatly extended. In addition, the serf could be tossed off his land if the owner became displeased with him and, at death, the land passed to his sons only if the lord gave his permission. Clearly, serfs led lives of bondage. Yet, it has been noted that

. . . the peasants, till the thirteenth century, looked up to him [the lord] with admiration, often with affection; if the lord became a childless widower they sent deputations to him to urge remarriage, lest the estate be left without a regular heir, and be despoiled in a war of succession. Like most economic and political systems in history, feudalism was what it had to be to meet the necessities of place and time and the nature of man.[99]

Slaves: Although slaves were few in number compared to the time of the Roman Empire, slavery did persist, particularly in western Germany, northern Italy, and southern France. Increasingly, however, their ranks were diminished as serfdom became the predominant mode of economic bondage. Eventually, only people captured from pagan groups (Moslems and Slavs) received religious sanction (from such moralists as Pope Gregory I and St. Thomas Aquinas) as slaves.

Urban Merchants: Toward the end of the feudal period a new group emerged—the urban merchants. Their economic power and relative independence upset the system of estates and paved the way for a different type of class system. The merchants gained their living from commerce, essentially by buying goods at a certain price and reselling them at a higher price. This practice was condemned as sinful by the Church and was regarded with disdain by the lords. At the beginning of the feudal period, the merchants carried arms and attempted to defend themselves, as did the knights. Along with their mercantile activities in the remaining cities of the era, they also plowed lands for food and often led the life of a peasant. But as their wealth increased (and as wars decreased), they gained a certain degree of stability in their position as merchants.

Their power was essentially enhanced by the establishment of *communes*. Merchants, who had been relatively helpless as individuals at the mercy of marauding bands and armies, joined together to pledge their mutual support against outside attacks on their cities. To secure guarantees of their security, they often pledged their entire commune to the military service of a particular lord. Unlike the usual exchanges between lord and serf, however, the commune gave its loyalty as an equal in power to the lord. Often unknowingly, the lord contributed to the growth of a group of urban patriarchs who paid richly in taxes. Yet, this new form of communal power gradually challenged that of individual nobles. Thus, "the increasing power of the burgesses [urban merchants] tended to undermine one of the most characteristic features of feudalism—the subdivision of authority.[100] In addition, the rise of the urban merchants paved the way for the birth of capitalism.

ORIGINS OF THE ESTATE SYSTEM

From the sixth to the twelfth century the estate system flourished for a variety of reasons. Successive invasions focused power in more and more decentralized political units. The ravages of war decreased populations, reduced the viability of many cities as economic and political units, and most important, rendered the European population totally dependent upon local "warlords." The circulation of currency dropped, necessitating the payment of troops in land rather than cash, eliminating salaried classes. Often the powerful classes could not impose taxes unless they could be paid in produce and labor, which would then be locally and immediately consumed. Peasants could not hope to survive the constant brigandage of the period without the protection of a militarily powerful lord. In consequence, serfdom was a relatively low price to pay for survival.

By the twelfth century the customs of feudal Europe had been codified into law and the privileges of the elite had become almost completely hereditary in nature. During this period, too, the urban merchants began to rise in power. As Celia Heller has commented:

> The warriors recognized them [urban merchants] as foreign to their own mentality and therefore as constituting a special threat, because their numbers would endanger the noble way of life. On the other hand, they were farsighted enough not to exclude from their ranks the "new forces."[101]

In response to the challenge of urban merchants, the lords developed an intricate system of laws and sanctions that protected them but that did not entirely forbid the entrance of new people into the nobility. The laws of the twelfth century specified that no one could be knighted who was not the descendant of a knight in the male line. Although these laws were generally adhered to, exceptions were sometimes made.

SOCIAL MOBILITY

By the twelfth century, despite legal restrictions, the new class of urban merchants had accumulated enough wealth to make it impossible for the lords to exclude them from the highest ranks of the estates. In recruiting armies, for example, the lords often turned to the urban merchants for money to buy armor, weapons, and horses. In 1302, for instance, Flemish princes ennobled a group of rich merchants who produced necessary military equipment for them. Kings also exercised the right of raising commoners to the rank of knighthood. Various "letters of nobility" were issued either for acts of exceptional gallantry or because the lords needed the services and monies the urban merchants were capable of providing them. "These 'letters of nobility' not only permitted a new knight to be created . . . they in effect brought into being each time a whole new line of knights."[102]

In theory, lords could fall in the social scale if they ever cultivated land, carried hay or manure, or engaged in commerce, but in fact, those who descended from the ranks of nobility were few, if any. The rise of the urban merchants, however, was steady and marked the decline of the system of estates.

DECLINE OF THE ESTATE SYSTEM

After the thirteenth century feudal estates declined gradually as power was increasingly centralized again. Nation-states, based on common language, began to emerge. There are several reasons for this transformation: (1) the growing influence of princes and kings, who no longer faced the incessant invasions of "barbarians"; (2) expansion in the ranks of urban merchants, who desired peace (after money, that is); (3) the stabilization of cities, whose "communes" had linked themselves with lords; (4) the recirculation of money, which allowed different forms of taxation; (5) the re-establishment of a class of salaried officials. With relative peace in Europe came an upsurge in population, cultivation of more arable land, the direct payment of servants and troops (rather than providing them with hereditary allocations of land), and, relatively speaking, a cessation of private wars in face of the overwhelming superiority of the new states' financial resources.

Feudal Europe: Analogous Systems

Although the rise and fall of the estate system in Europe has been regarded by some as a unique event in history, other periods have exhibited extremely similar traits: the legal subservience of vassals to lords; ties of obedience and protection based not on slavery but on the hereditary supremacy of a class of nobles (or warriors); and a fragmentation of political authority down to the level where each person owed obeisance to a local lord. Perhaps the best-known, most extensive system of estates, and one that survived into the nineteenth century, was the system of serfdom in Russia.

The Russian System

LORD AND SERF

Although the estate system had begun to deteriorate in Western Europe in the twelfth century, it bloomed in Russia during the fifteenth century. Between the sixteenth century and final emancipation of 1861, formerly free Russian peasants were engulfed in a full system of serfdom.

As in medieval Europe, lords in Russia provided military protection and economic organization for the peasants in return for their labors. Unlike those of medieval Europe, however, Russian peasants looked up to an absolute tsar who theoretically acted as their protector against both outside invasions and the whims of their own lords.[103]

During the height of Russian serfdom in 1824, all people except the nobility and clergy had to pay a "soul tax." To be entered on the tax rolls, and to ensure that they would pay their obligations, men had to register as serfs, soldiers, or state peasants (serfs of the tsar).

Serfs owed two basic types of duties to their lords. *Barschcina* forced the peasant to pay the lord an average of three days of labor per week for his use of the land; *obrok*, a milder form of serfdom, required the peasant to pay the lord in cash or produce for use of the land. During the height of serfdom, all land legally belonged either to the lords or to the state, although many peasants maintained the belief that they owned the land while their lives belonged to the lord.[104]

Until the beginning of the nineteenth century, serfs, like slaves, could be sold to the highest bidder. Normally, the lords would sell a piece of land together with the necessary number of serfs attached to it. Although technically free men, serfs were treated as little more than pieces of property.

The lords had virtually complete legal power over their serfs. They enforced the laws and imposed penalties. Mild punishments for disobedient serfs involved forty blows with a rod or fifteen with a cudgel. Serfs who had mutilated themselves to avoid serving in the army could be ordered by their masters to run the gauntlet of 500 soldiers using whips. Lords were recompensed with a "recruit allowance" for every man drafted into the army. More severe penalties allowed the lord to imprison his serf for up to three months. The ultimate punishment was banishment to Siberia.[105]

Exile in Siberia forced the peasant to walk to the outermost reaches of Russia. At times, his wife and family were allowed to go with him. The state paid the lord for his loss of a workingman. Once in Siberia, the exile became a "state peasant" with his own piece of land. Approximately 75 percent of exiled serfs, however, died while trying to complete the journey.[106]

Serfs who wished to marry had to receive the permission of their lord. If they married a woman outside of the lord's estates, they were liable to severe penalties. Serfs held property—horses, furniture, pots and pans—only at the whim of the lord, for ultimately all property on the land belonged to him. A generous lord would allow a serf to take his property with him after he had sold him.

In spite of some protective ordinances, serfs had no real legal recourse against their masters. In 1767 Catherine II even forbade serfs to present petitions of complaint about their lord. No credence was placed in the word of a serf unless he said that his master was treasonous, planned to kill the tsar, or had juggled his roll of serfs to avoid paying taxes to the central government. The mere act of appealing to a state official could result in banishment to Siberia. Unorganized and without leadership, the serfs had no recourse except for sporadic, abortive revolts, and these flared up throughout Russian history.[107]

ORIGINS OF SERFDOM

Between the eighth and eleventh centuries a type of serfdom made its first appearance in Russia. Here, as in Western Europe, warriors took control of the land, participated in minor wars, and lived off the booty they could steal. Again as in Western Europe, the peasants were the primary victims of this depredation.

Major and minor lords set themselves up as custodians of estates. As part of their conquest, they took over lands that had formerly been held in common by free peasants. By the eleventh century, the peasants, oppressed by the threat of famine, had little choice but to rent out their labor and their remaining landholdings to the lords. This was the beginning of Russian serfdom.

In the thirteenth century Mongols invaded central Russia. The result was economic stagnation, a population decline, the break-up of large landed estates, and the disintegration of both military and administrative centers of power. The Mongols allowed the original rulers to keep their personal lands, but the resulting decline of trade and commerce forced the Russian lords to seek labor from the peasant ranks. As population fell, the Russian lords made a variety of concessions to formerly free Russian peasants. In return for men who would till the land and pay their rents, the lords gave up huge sections of their territory as a way of attracting settlers. The peasants virtually owned the land except for meeting constant obligations to the nobles. Other peasant communities, fearing the incursion of Mongols or the attacks of local Russian lords, voluntarily became the subjects of the most powerful lords and monasteries. Until this point in history, peasants retained the right of free movement: if they wished to leave the land, they could not legally be prevented from doing so.

By the end of the fifteenth century, however, both political and economic conditions eroded almost all peasant rights. The grand dukes of Moscow, the greatest power opposing the deteriorating Mongol hegemony, gradually extended their influence over much of European Russia. In a series of continuing battles, the grand dukes granted land and peasants to the lesser nobility as a way of ensuring their allegiance. Unlike the peasants in medieval Europe, those in Russia had no say in the matter and apparently made no pledges of loyalty other than to guarantee their labor and some of the produce of their lands.

STABILITY OF THE ESTATE SYSTEM

Between the sixteenth and nineteenth centuries the Russian system of serfdom gained stability from two forces: economic and political. Economic depressions during the sixteenth century made it increasingly difficult for serfs to leave their lands in search of other jobs. The depopulation of Russia that accompanied the crises made it all the more important for lords to ensure that they had a secure labor supply on their lands. Consequently, through a gradual series of legal moves from the fifteenth to the seventeenth century, the lords gained the power to tie the serfs to the land. From about the 1580s on, no serf could leave this land against his lord's will.[108]

Simultaneously, the new state created by the grand dukes of Moscow solidified the system of serfdom. The central government found the institution useful as a way of collecting taxes. Since free movement of peasants might have allowed them to escape their fiscal and military obligations, the central state increased and legalized the power of the local lords over their serfs. In return, the lords themselves had to serve the state for a large part of their lives in a military or administrative fashion. As Jerome Blum has noted:

In the unique Service State that the Muscovite rulers created, each of their subjects, from the greatest to the least, was assigned a role that was determined by the interests of the state. The lord was bound to state service, and the peasant was bound to the lord, in order to provide him with the means to perform his service to the state.[109]

The state required the services of the lower nobility and in return granted increasing power to the nobility over the lives, movement, and economic organization of peasants, which it required. In return for the political and economic tranquility of the upper classes, the fiscal security of the central state, and the elimination of labor difficulties, each social group gave up some share of its power. Caught in inexorable economic and political pressures, the peasantry relinquished whatever freedom it had once possessed.

SOCIAL MOBILITY IN THE ESTATE SYSTEM

Although minor and major nobles scrambled for power during this period, there were no major opportunities for either individuals or groups to change their social position in a dramatic fashion. Occasionally, a noble would lose his land to state confiscation or a rare peasant would escape to an urban center where he established a new identity, but for the most part, the Russian estate system remained remarkably stable. It has been reported that in 1724 approximately 55 percent of the male population were serfs; by 1796 this had fallen to 49 percent; in 1811 it rose to 58 percent; and by 1858 (on the eve of emancipation) it fell to 44.5 percent.[110] These statistical fluctuations probably reflect the general inaccuracy of the census rather than real changes within Russian society.

The only two actual outlets for serfs were to flee to Siberia, where they became state peasants, or to be drafted into the army. Serfs who were drafted were freed from their bondage, but the conditions of military life severely discouraged people from choosing this alternative. Still, through forced ravages of the countryside, the central government managed to increase the size of its army from about 200,000 in the eighteenth century to over a million in the 1850s.

In sharp contrast to medieval Europe, in Russia a powerful urban-merchant class never arose; thus the Russian masses were denied this source of social mobility and countervailing power. Urban areas grew during the sixteenth and seventeenth centuries, but with few exceptions, urban areas fulfilled agricultural trading functions. Most important, the central government denied urban people the right to move about freely. Peasants who came to the cities remained bound to their lords. Even if they became traders and resided in cities for a long period of time, they had to continue to pay their obligations to their lords. Interregional trade remained in the hands of special types of lords and of agents of the tsar. Under these conditions a distinctive urban bourgeoisie with wealth and power of its own could not develop. This lack of an urban bourgeoisie with the poltical and economic influence to challenge the estate system fundamentally altered the course of Russian history. As Jerome Blum has argued:

The divergence between East and West in the nature of the relationship between lord and peasant turned out to be the decisive watershed in the history of freedom in the modern world. . . . A tradition of compulsion and servility, and acquiescence in the right of a few men to hold millions of their fellows in bondage, became the heritage of the peoples of Eastern Europe. The West moved forward into an era where the idea of freedom to live as one wished, and the conviction that individual liberty was a natural and inalienable right, could take root and flourish.[111]

THE DECLINE OF THE ESTATE SYSTEM

In 1861, by decree of the tsar, serfdom was abolished in Russia, but despite the 500-page declaration of intent, most still remained in virtual bondage. An important qualification of emancipation was that the serfs had to indemnify the lords for the loss of their services. In an agrarian society, where forms of income other than land were extremely scarce, it was most difficult to satisfy this obligation. Despite its restrictions, the emancipation of 1861 represented a major change in Russian life. It sparked vigorous opposition from the nobility and hostility from serfs who believed they had a right to the land above all else. Subsequent uprisings by peasants, as well as the revolutions of 1905 and of 1917, partially emanated from this reform.

Several reasons have been proposed for the 1861 emancipation: changes in the Russian economy may have made the estate system unwise; Western European ideas of liberalism had affected many in the educated classes; the Crimean War signaled major dangers in the society; and smouldering opposition within the ranks of the serfs may have convinced the tsar that continuance of the system endangered the survival of the state. Each of these explanations has some degree of merit in explaining the decline of serfdom.

Russian intellectuals, many of them drawn from the noble class, imbibed the ideas of the French Revolution and of nineteenth-century liberalism. For them, holding people as chattel violated all notions of human rights that they had received from the lessons of Western civilization. Few would claim that sheer humanitarian impulses prompted them to advocate freeing of the serfs, yet it cannot be denied that many in the educated classes abhorred a system that they had come to regard as unjust.

The failure of Russia to win the Crimean War taught the upper classes in general and the tsar in particular that Russia was dangerously enfeebled by a serfdom that owed only grudging loyalty to the existing society.

As a result of the Crimean War, continuing peasant uprisings, and intellectual agitation, Tsar Nicholas became convinced that serfdom imperiled the survival of the state. In a state such as Russia, the tsar's opinion was of paramount importance. Thus, to ensure political tranquility the tsar decreed partial emancipation, even over the protests of the nobility.

As in medieval Europe, in Russia the estate system gradually deteriorated because of changes in the economic realm, the growth of cities, the emergence of a class opposed to the system, and political decisions by the rulers of the central state who viewed this system as offering few tangible returns. Remnants of the estate system still exist in parts of Latin America, Asia, and Africa, albeit in highly modified forms. As in feudal Europe or nineteenth-century Russia, however, one may reasonably anticipate that due to processes of economic development a new system of social inequality will eventually replace the estate system.

Conclusions: Inequality in Simple and Agrarian Societies

A consideration of such different societies as the Andaman Islanders and the Ik of Uganda, the Roman Empire and the American South, India before and after the introduction of Western ideas, medieval Europe and nineteenth-century Russia, can prompt few generalizations about the nature of social inequality. Human beings have devised numerous, ingenious, devious ways to extract an economic surplus from their fellows and to declare them inferior. It does seem clear, however, that two related elements have greatly affected the nature, origins, and forms of social inequality in preindustrial society.

First, the *nature of technology* available to a particular society has a dramatic effect. In societies such as that of the Tasaday, where food is abundant, relative egalitarianism emerges. In societies where food is in short supply, such as that of the Ik, severe differences in rank based upon physical strength appear to take precedence. In societies where large-scale agriculture demands a supply of manual labor, slavery and the caste system are attractive options. Disintegration of a society—because of military invasion, the rise of new classes such as urban merchants, or the decline of large farms—has normally entailed the end of slavery or of serfdom. *Thus the nature and effects of the technology largely determine the form of inequality that will prevail in a simple or agrarian society.*

Second, *ideology* or *religion* will affect the particular form of inequality in an agrarian society. Surely the caste system would not have arisen in India and allowed priests to triumph over warriors if the peoples of India had not previously accepted ideas of reincarnation, impurity, and taboos. Nor would American slavery or Russian serfdom have collapsed under their own weight simply because of technological changes. These systems declined—at least in part—because they had been affected by Enlightenment beliefs in humanitarianism. *Thus the ideology or religion that pervades a particular society plays a highly significant role in shaping inequality.*

Our examination of simple and agrarian societies has indicated that two crucial factors affect the nature of inequality. The nature of technology in a given region determines the possibilities open to a particular people: they may choose any form of stratification from relative equalitarianism to the lord-serf relation, dominance of the hunter or a slave-master relationship, anarchy or a caste system. In addition to the nature of their technology, the ideological framework of a people leads them to choose, for example, an estate system versus a caste system.

There is, in fact, a genuine choice. Both medieval Europe and ancient India experienced periods of political and social turmoil, economic disintegration, and foreign invasions. Indians, because of their religious heritage, chose to re-establish stability by instituting a caste system. Europeans replaced slavery with an estate system. Both societies experienced the same objective social and economic circumstances, but because of their cultural heritages they took different paths.

Consequently, having reviewed the rise, nature, and fall of several types of inequality, it is possible to venture several generalizations:

1. *The nature of inequality in a particular simple or agrarian society is affected primarily by the form of technology that it adopts.* In simple societies the relative abundance of food affects whether or not the society is relatively egalitarian, anarchic, or male-dominated. Once an economic surplus has been achieved, three forms of inequality take precedence over the types created in simple societies: slavery, the caste system, or the estate system. "Civilized" people who are forced to return to Stone Age technology normally adopt a stratification system based on strength.*

---

*The Israeli kibbutzim have generally been cited as a type of "simple" or agrarian society that has harbored civilized people, utilized modern techniques of production, and yet produced a fairly egalitarian social order. It does not, on the whole, represent an exception to the general rule.

2. *The form of inequality in agrarian societies has generally been molded by the religious and political ideology that prevailed at the time as well as by the technological status of the society.* Religion, for example, made decisive changes in India's caste system. Europe's estate system arose in a situation where an empire had disintegrated and "free men" believed that they could make contracts with each other that would be of mutual benefit. Slavery waned and waxed according to a variety of legal codes.

3. *The decline of systems of inequality—whether expressed in terms of male dominance, slavery, the caste system, or the estate system—appears to be governed by technological and military considerations.* If an agrarian society collapsed and it was impossible for a central power to maintain its military control, as occurred in ancient India, Rome, and the American South, the slavery system went out of existence. In some situations— Russia, for instance—serfdom replaced slavery; in others, such as medieval Europe, urban merchants gained ascendance over feudal lords. Thus, as technology changed and produced new social groups, new forms of social stratification emerged.

In all the societies we have examined in this chapter, the slow advance of industrialization and the consequent development of urban bourgeois and proletarian classes have spelled the end of the more "primitive" forms of inequality. Slavery in the American South collapsed in the 1860s when urbanized, industrialized forces put an end to the practice; serfdom finally ceased in Russia under similar pressures; and the caste system, although still viable in a largely rural society such as India, shows some signs of relaxation as the political forces unleashed by modernization continue to advance.

Clearly, however, the decline of simpler, agrarian forms of inequality did not entail the death of stratification systems. In Chapter 3 we will concern ourselves with new forms of inequality—the class and bureaucratic systems—which emerged as parts of the world passed from an agrarian to an industrial and then to a postindustrial stage of existence.

Notes

1. M. J. Finley, *Slavery in Classical Antiquity* (Cambridge, England: Heffer, 1960), p. 145.

2. Gerhard Lenski, *Power and Privilege* (New York: McGraw-Hill, 1966), p. 182.

3. Ibid.

4. Aristotle, *Politics*, trans. Benjamin Jowett (New York: Modern Library, 1943), p. 60.

5. Quoted in Finley, *Slavery in Classical Antiquity*, p. 153.
6. David Brian Davis, *The Problem of Slavery in Western Culture* (Ithaca, N.Y.: Cornell University Press, 1966).
7. Eugene D. Genovese, *The Political Economy of Slavery* (New York: Pantheon, 1965).
8. Finley, *Slavery in Classical Antiquity*, p. 145.
9. Davis, *Problem of Slavery in Western Culture.*
10. Celia S. Heller, *Structured Social Inequality* (New York: Macmillan, 1969), p. 55.
11. E. Gibbon, *Decline and Fall of the Roman Empire* (London: Everyman Library, 1900).
12. Will Durant, *Caesar and Christ* (New York: Simon & Schuster, 1944), pp. 11–112.
13. Ibid., p. 11.
14. Livy, *Epitome of Book XC.*
15. Ibid.
16. Aupelius, *Apology.*
17. W. S. Davis, *Influence of Wealth in Imperial Rome* (New York: Columbia University Press, 1913).
18. Seneca, *Epitulae Morales*, Loeb Library.
19. Ibid.
20. Ibid.
21. Matthew XXIV: 46 and Luke XVII: 7–10.
22. Augustus, *Lex Fufia Caninia.*
23. Epictetus, *Discourses*, III, 3.
24. Ibid.
25. Davis, *Problem of Slavery in Western Culture.*
26. L. West, "Economic Collapse of the Roman Empire," *Classical Journal* (1932): 106.
27. See Charles M. Andrews, *The Colonial Period of American History*, 4 vols. (*New Haven, Conn.: Yale University Press*), 1934-38.
28. W. E. Dodd, *The Cotton Kingdom* (New Haven, Conn.: Yale University Press, 1919).
29. See John Hope Franklin, *From Slavery to Freedom* (New York: Knopf, 1963).
30. Ibid., p. 49.
31. Ibid.
32. Max Savelle, *American Civilization* (New York: Dryden Press, 1957).
33. John C. Calhoun, Speech to the Senate, quoted in ibid., p. 348.
34. Arnold A. Sio, "Interpretations of Slavery," *Comparative Studies in Society and History* 7 (April 1965): 289–308.
35. Ibid.
36. Genovese, *Political Economy of Slavery.*
37. See Franklin, *From Slavery to Freedom.*
38. See Herbert Aptheker, *American Negro Slave Revolts* (New York: International Universities Press, 1943).
39. Franklin, *From Freedom to Slavery*, p. 211.
40. Aptheker, *American Negro Slave Revolts.*
41. See Stanley Elkins, *Slavery* (Chicago: University of Chicago Press, 1959).
42. Ibid.
43. Ibid.
44. Roy Simon Bryce LaPorte, "Review Symposium of Time on the Cross," *Contemporary Sociology*, Vol. 10 (August 1975).
45. See Franklin, *From Slavery to Freedom*, p. 189.
46. Ibid., p. 197.
47. Ibid., p. 191.
48. Ibid., p. 201.
49. Robert W. Fogel and Stanley L. Engerman, *Time on the Cross* (Boston: Little, Brown, 1974).

50. Ibid.
51. Abraham Lincoln, quoted in Savelle, *American Civilization,* p. 381.
52. *The Laws of Manu,* trans. G. Buhler, in *Sacred Books of the East,* ed. Max Muller (Oxford: Clarendon Press, 1886).
53. See H. Yle and A. C. Burnell, *Hobson-Johnson* (London: Crooke, 1886).
54. See J. H. Hutton, *Caste in India* (Bombay: Oxford University Press, 1969).
55. S. J. Wilson, *Indian Caste History of the Suppression of Infanticide in Western India,* 1877, cited in ibid., p. 113.
56. Charles Drekmeier, *Kingship and Community in Early India* (Stanford, Calif.: Stanford University Press, 1962), p. 70.
57. Ibid., p. 87.
58. Ibid., p. 88.
59. See William McCord, *The Springtime of Freedom* (New York: Oxford University Press, 1965).
60. A. Enthoven, "Review of Origins and Growth of Caste in India," *Journal of the Royal Asiatic Society* 1 (January 1932): 84.
61. Cited in Peter Schmid, *India: Mirage and Reality* (London: George Harrow, 1961), p. 154.
62. Sir Percival Griffiths, *Modern India* (London: Ernst Benn, 1957), p. 31.
63. Ibid.
64. Max Weber, *The Religion of India* (Glencoe, Ill.: Free Press, 1958), pp. 39–45.
65. Gerald D. Berreman, "Caste in India and the United States," *American Journal of Sociology* 66 (September 1960).
66. Ibid.
67. Ibid.
68. Pauline M. Mahar, "Changing Caste Ideology in a North Indian Village," *Journal of Social Issues* 14 (1958).
69. Berreman, "Caste in India and the United States."
70. Ibid.
71. Hutton, *Caste in India,* p. 125.
72. Ibid., p. 122.
73. Ibid., Chapter IX.
74. S. Dill, *Roman Society in the Last Century of the Western Empire* (Oxford: Clarendon, 1898).
75. John Dollard, *Caste and Class in a Southern Town* (New Haven, Conn.: Yale University Press, 1937).
76. See Drekmeier, *Kingship and Community in Early India,* p. 80.
77. Ibid., p. 77.
78. See Lenski, *Power and Privilege.*
79. Drekmeier, *Kingship and Community in Early India,* p. 70.
80. Ibid.
81. Ibid.
82. Ibid., p. 29.
83. Berreman, "Caste in India and the United States."
84. See Kussum Nair, *Blossoms in the Dust* (London: Duckworth, 1961).
85. *The Times,* New Dehli, May 22, 1971.
86. Hutton, *Caste in India,* p. ix.
87. Schmid, *India.*
88. Ibid., p. 158.
89. Hutton, *Caste in India,* p. xi.
90. Ibid., p. x.
91. Marc Bloch, *Feudal Society,* vol. 2 (Chicago: University of Chicago Press, Phoenix Books, 1964), p. 11.

92. Ibid., p. 443.
93. T. R. Bottomore, *Elites and Society* (New York: Basic Books, 1964).
94. P. Builhermoz, *Essai sur Les Origins de la Noblesse en France au Moyen-Age* (Paris: 1902).
95. Will Durant, *The Age of Faith* (New York: Simon & Schuster, 1950), p. 571.
96. K. H. Roth von Schrekenstein, *Die Ritterwurde und der Ritterstand* (Berlin: Feiburg im Briesgau, 1886).
97. Bloch, *Feudal Society*, p. 345.
98. Michel Andrieu, *Les Origines Roman du Haut Moyen Age* (Louvain: 1931).
99. Durant, *The Age of Faith*, p. 556.
100. Bloch, *Feudal Society*, p. 354.
101. Heller, *Structured Social Inequality*, p. 58.
102. Bloch, *Feudal Society*, p. 323.
103. A. Gershenkron, "An Economic History of Russia," *Journal of Economic History* 12 (1952).
104. I. Polosin, "Le Servage Russe et Son Origine," *Revue Internationale de Sociologie* 36 (1928).
105. Jerome Blum, *Lord and Peasant in Russia from the Ninth to the Nineteenth Century* (Princeton, N.J.: Princeton University Press, 1964).
106. Ibid., p. 430.
107. M. Szeftel, "La Condition Juidique des Desclassés dans La Russie Ancienne," *Archives de Histoire du Droit Oriental* 2 (1938).
108. Ibid.
109. Blum, *Lord and Peasant*, pp. 605–606.
110. Ibid.
111. Ibid., p. 611.

3
INDUSTRIAL SOCIETIES

"The history of all hitherto existing society," Karl Marx observed in the *Communist Manifesto,* "is the history of class struggles."[1] Although Marx's observation has validity, as we have seen from the case histories presented in Chapter 2, it cannot be accepted as a completely accurate description of all societies. Historically, inequalities have been based not only on class but also on distinctions of status and power, and this is true in the modern world as well. The stratification systems of agrarian, nonindustrial societies are qualitatively different from that of industrial nations. Class, status, and power tend to be inextricably fused in traditional, nonindustrial societies, whereas the stratification systems of modern industrial nations are characterized by a relative separation of these three dimensions.[2]

In 1848, when Marx and Engels wrote the *Communist Manifesto,* technological advances and social changes entailed in the political centralization, industrialization, and urbanization of Europe had produced a true class system based on the ownership of the means of production. Hence these scholars focused on class as the pivotal point in their theory of social change. To continue our analysis of power, inequality, and the stratification system, we must examine two key phenomena more closely —industrialization and urbanization.

The Nature of Industrial Society

Industrial society as it has progressed from Marx's time to our own has two basic characteristics. First, machines became substitutes for tools, and inanimate sources of energy replaced animate sources. In recent times, only a minority of people in advanced industrial nations have been engaged in the production of goods for their own consumption or for sale in the marketplace.

Second, the basis for differentiation among social groups has changed. Groups of managers, military administrators, clerical and sales staffs, lawyers and industrial workers have grown and eclipsed the differentiation of people based on birth, brute strength, physical power, or supernatural considerations. Most industrial societies are now characterized by a true *class* system in which income, control over the means of production, education, political power, and social status are highly, but not necessarily, related.

The Rise of Industrial Society

Industrial societies arose as early as the fifteenth century in Europe, the eighteenth century in the United States, and the nineteenth century in Japan and Russia. A variety of technological and social changes occurred in these areas. Social scientists continue to debate the importance of technological and social structural factors in the emergence of industrialization.

On the technological level, by the middle of the twentieth century, all the advanced industrial societies had experienced these major changes in productive activity:[3]

1. The major sources of energy became machines rather than human or animal labor or other "natural" sources of power such as wind or water. People rapidly learned how to harness energy, smelt metals, and provide heat and light. In the United States in 1850, for example, human or animal labor supplied 65 percent of the energy used in production. By 1955 this figure had dropped to only 1.6 percent.[4]

2. The consumption of the earth's resources by industrial nations rose sharply as people found more and more ways to utilize these resources. Gerhard Lenski has estimated that the per capita consumption of iron ore, for example, increased by a hundredfold from 1800 to 1950.[5] Similar statistics would reflect the industrial nations' increased consumption of stone, sand, phosphates, gypsum, sulphur, copper, and zinc.[6]

This extraordinary rate of consumption has had two unexpected but potentially devastating results. First, the world has become increasingly divided between nations that produce raw materials and industrial nations, which disproportionately consume them.[7] Second, many experts believe that the rate of consumption cannot possibly be maintained and that even the additional heat generated by industrial production may well destroy this planet.[8]

3. Per capita income rose dramatically as industrialization progressed. Gerhard Lenski estimated in 1966 that "the per capita income of the United States today is already at least twenty times that of the typical agrarian society of the past."[9] By 1976 the energy used by the United States alone was equivalent to all the energy consumed by developing nations.[10]

4. These technological advances have also entailed increasing specialization in work as well as the growth of huge enterprises that can produce goods at relatively low prices.

5. Advances in food production and medical technology have resulted in a burgeoning of the world's population. The population of Great Britain approximately tripled between 1800 and 1960; France doubled its population, and Russia increased its population fivefold during the same period.[11] Developing nations because of the same factors have more recently followed this trend.

These great technological alterations were accompanied by (or sometimes preceded by) equally momentous social changes.

Social Bases of Industrial Society

During the earliest periods of industrial development in Europe, America, Japan, and Russia, two new social classes developed that had not previously occupied important positions in the estate systems. First, a group of bourgeoisie emerged. These were primarily urban merchants who had accumulated capital and were willing to risk it in industrial enterprises. At times, their ranks were joined by former lords who had also set aside an economic surplus.[12] These entrepreneurs provided the funds for—and some scholars such as Joseph Schumpeter would say the "spirit" behind—industrial development.[13]

Second, a group of industrial, urbanized workers grew in importance. They ran the machines in the new industrial societies. These people were often drawn from the ranks of peasants who had been dispossessed from land and forced into industrial activity in order to survive.[14]

Other social changes occurred that some observers believe were fundamental to industrialization:

1. Politically, power was held by increasing numbers of groups, rather than simply by the lords, slave owners, or Brahmans of a particular society. The state extended its powers over many segments of human life as industrialized nations increasingly concentrated upon the uses of industrial and military might.[15] There is a vast divergence of opinion as to whether these political changes accompanied, preceded, or followed industrialization.[16]

2. Educationally, the scope of knowledge vastly expanded and, simultaneously, more people became literate and able to understand technological developments. Public education became the norm of industrialized nations, and the number and scope of educational institutions grew at an accelerated rate. Some observers, such as Daniel Bell, regard this "knowledge explosion" as a crucial element in industrial societies as well as the precursor of a new "post-industrial society."[17]

3. Religiously, people increasingly abandoned their beliefs in a personal God and adopted impersonal religious beliefs.[18] In industrialized societies, religion stressed a secular orientation and lost its emphasis upon myths, superstition, and miracles.[19] In most industrialized nations, the affiliation between church and state was weakened or disappeared.[20]

4. As industrialization matured, more people were freed for the "service" sector of the economy. Thus a service" class—managers, administrators, clerical and sales people—appeared. This class supported the large-scale bureaucracies, which dominate the later stages of industrialization.[21] This new class grew for a variety of reasons. The family firm, the traditional form of economic organization, could no longer handle all the complex problems that advancing industrialization entailed.[22] Technological advances, symbolized by automation, made industrial workers increasingly redundant; yet an industrial economy required people who earned wages from some sector of the economy and could purchase the goods that the economy produced.[23] The increase in knowledge required the development of more and more specialists and educational institutions to retain and relay it to succeeding generations of workers.[24] Increasing specialization and growth in the size of business, military, educational, and political enterprises brought about the growth of specialists who understood, above all, the workings of the particular bureaucracy within which they were involved.

As industrialism advanced, a variety of theories of social inequality were suggested to account for the development and nature of the new class system. Perhaps the most important theories were put forward by Karl Marx, Max Weber, and, in more recent times, the functional theorists and Gerhard Lenski. Let us consider each of these positions.

Theories of Social Stratification in Industrial Society

MARX

Karl Marx and Friedrich Engels proposed the most comprehensive explanation of the changing nature of social inequality in a society that was becoming increasingly wealthy. Marxism attempted to explain why poverty persisted in nations undergoing industrialization. It offered a "scientific" explanation of the class system through use of historical data. In so doing, it drew directly upon a Judeo-Christian tradition, which condemned the exploitation of one person by another, the degradation of the human spirit, and the alienation of a person from his or her labor.

Marxism proffered both an explanation and a cure for the severe economic crises that long plagued industrial societies. Marx contended that there was a fundamental contradiction between the realities of industrial production and the ideology of the bourgeoisie. Industrial production, Marx said, required close coordination, planning, and rationalization of economic processes. However, the ideology offered by the bourgeoisie, while emphasizing a lack of planning, also maintained the sacredness of private property and individualism.[25] In Marx's opinion this contradiction, inherent in capitalistic industrial society, ultimately doomed the system.

Marx believed that the *bourgeoisie,* or the class composed of those who owned the means of production, and the *proletariat,* composed of workers, made up the entire class system of industrial societies. These two groups stood in direct opposition to each other. Certain sub groups, such as the *lumpenbourgeoisie* (lower-middle-class merchants and bureaucrats), remained in an ambiguous position.

In his most important statement, *Das Kapital,* Marx dissected nineteenth-century capitalist society and predicted its downfall. Essentially, he argued that all industrial capitalists competed with each other in the marketplace. The most efficient form of competition is to expand production so that all goods are produced at the lowest possible price. As competition ensues in a capitalist society, Marx argued, the demand for laborers rises and so do their wages. As wages increase, the profit made by a capitalist decreases since his or her profit derives solely from *surplus value* (that is, the extra amount of money derived from not paying workers the full value of their labor). As profits decrease, typical capitalists introduce labor-saving machinery to reduce the cost of hiring more workers. As workers are dismissed from a factory, their surplus value is lost and a particular capitalist firm enters a period of depression, if not bankruptcy.

This theory of capitalism predicted the eventual demise of the system. Inevitably, as depressions got more and more severe, the expropriated, alienated groups in society would unite. Class consciousness would increase and, eventually, the workers of the world would unite and overthrow the bourgeoisie. A socialist and finally a communist society would follow.

Marx's prediction of a cataclysmic class struggle has not proved accurate. In fact, Marxist-oriented governments have come to power only in relatively backward, agrarian societies. Some Marxists, such as Paul Baran,[26] Paul Sweezy, and Adam Schaff, attribute this trend to imperialism and argue that advanced industrial nations have used the surplus value derived from developing nations as a way of restraining class antagonisms in their own nations.

Although Marx's prediction of an ultimate class struggle has not come true, his legacy cannot be ignored. He was undoubtedly the most influential social thinker in the nineteenth century to argue that the modes of production of a society determined its social relationships. He was the first to point out that, as modes of production change, conflict would arise among the new and the old groups. Although he did not deny the influence of ideas in historical development, he also argued that the ideological "superstructure" of a society—its government, philosophy, religion, and so on—was, in fact, a by-product of its system of social stratification.

It was this last point in Marx's theory of social stratification which brought him into conflict with Max Weber.

WEBER

Max Weber contended that the class system produced by industrialism had to be examined not only in terms of property relationships but also in regard to dimensions such as power and status. Weber, a social theorist who first came to prominence in the early twentieth century and now exerts an important influence over contemporary sociology, maintained that all positions in a social hierarchy were fundamentally based upon differences in power. But unlike Marx, Weber emphasized that power flows from a variety of sources and is not limited simply to the economic realm. By power, Weber meant, "the chance of a man or of a number of men to realize their own will in a communal action even against the resistance of others who are participating in the action."[27]

In Weber's view, there were three types of power that, in turn, generated three types of differences within modern society: power based on economic control ("class" power), power based on social distinctions ("status"), and power based on dominance over the political or legal system (one's "party").

Class power derived from one's position in the economy and, more specifically, from the possession of goods and the opportunity for income. Weber acknowledged the tremendous importance of class distinctions in determining, for example, political activity. Yet, he argued that a second type of power, one's social status, could be equally important. Status might be inherited or ascribed to people who were, for example, members of the aristocracy. Such people might defend their status interests, such as the possession of a prestigious piece of land, at the cost of entrepreneurs, who pursued only class interests and who wished to turn the land into a subdevelopment.

In addition, a third type of power difference related to control over the political administration of a society. A political judgment such as the expansion of the frontiers of an empire might well conflict with the economic interests of a particular class.

On one level, Weber's contribution was his description of a class system composed of economic as well as other, at times conflicting, interests. In addition, he argued that different class or status groups might find themselves in conflict although they were in the same objective economic position.

Weber must also be credited with the observation that a bureaucratic structure dominated industrial societies.[28] He argued that the rise of huge factory systems, large armies, and complex groups in many areas of life demanded the growth of bureaucracy as an efficient mode of organization.

The validity of Weber's observation is supported by the fact that modern society continues to be bureaucratic. With few exceptions, the massive, formalized, hierarchical structure pervades the lives of people in industrial societies and provides the setting for inequalities based on criteria different from those of years past. The bureaucratic mode of assigning positions is based presumably on the possession of special skills or expertise. To highly simplify the case: the shift in the basis of establishing social inequalities appears to have been from ascribed to achieved characteristics.

A delineation of the characteristics of bureaucracy as an "ideal type" has been furnished by Max Weber. The basic conditions of the Weberian model include:

1. The regular activities required for the purpose of the organization are distributed in a fixed way as official duties.

2. Offices are organized along the principle of hierarchy; that is, each lower office is under the control and supervision of a higher one.

3. Operations of the organization are governed by a consistent system of abstract rules that are applied to particular cases.

4. The ideal official within a bureaucracy conducts his or her office in a formalistic, impersonal manner.

5. One's position in a bureaucracy is based strictly on technical qualifications and one is protected from arbitrary dismissal from this job.[29]

Deviation from the ideal type has been assumed to be accompanied by a decrease in efficiency.[30] However, the advantages that accrue from the efficacy of bureaucratic organization present a problem for anyone concerned with the problem of the balance between individual freedom and social control. In order to meet the collective requirement for efficient organization, individual initiative and creativity are curtailed. Weber himself was reportedly concerned with the implications of bureaucracy for the quality of human life.[31] Although he apparently applauded the efficacy of such organizations, he deplored a situation in which people with broad, intellectual interests and skills might be stifled by restrictive specialization, standardization, and hierarchical control.

Prognostications for bureaucracy range from catastrophic consequences to more positive effects; they have been issued by persons such as Bruno Rizzi, C. Wright Mills, and William H. Whyte, Jr.[32] Progress toward a resolution of the apparent conflict between the oppressive social control of bureaucracy and individual freedom has been made slowly in the series of empirical investigations by such sociologists as Robert K. Merton,[33] Alvin Gouldner,[34] Philip Selznick,[35] Peter Blau,[36] and Michael Crozier.[37] Although most of these scholars remained in the tradition of Weber's analysis of bureaucracy, they have suggested a different tack to the problem of control and freedom.

Merton, for example, concluded on the basis of an analysis of the bureaucratic "personality" that the requirement of standardized behavior necessary for internal efficiency commonly resulted in an ineffectual organization in terms of the bureaucracy's goals. In addition, Selznick's examination of the TVA, Gouldner's study of a manufacturing plant, and Blau's report on social workers and a federal agency extended the Weberian model through analyses of relationships within the bureaucratic structure that affected the functioning and development of organizations. Most of these researchers concluded their studies by emphasizing the routine and oppressive aspects of bureaucracy. For the most part they tended to ignore the interplay of human factors with the requirement for rationality.

Michael Crozier, on the other hand, while agreeing with the social scientists who concluded that bureaucratic structure provides an obstacle to change and social development, explicitly considers internal variations and the evolution of bureaucratic characteristics such as modes of control from a cross-cultural as well as from a historical perspective. In regard to the evolution of bureaucracies, he noted:

Only two centuries ago, conformity within an organization was obtained through very harsh and direct means with a great deal of open
coercion. . . . Modern organizations, in contrast to their predecessors
use a much more liberal set of pressures. . . The modern organization
can tolerate more deviance, restrict its requirements to a more specialized field, and demand only temporary commitments. For all these reasons, it can and does rely more on indirect and intellectual means to
obtain conformity: communication structure and work flow, the technical setting of jobs, economic incentives, and also, perhaps, rational
calculus of a higher sort.[38]

Further, Crozier reported, in spite of the proliferation of rules that
abound in an organization, unanticipated events do occur. Power, he
contends, accrues to those in the bureaucratic structure who can gain
control of the "areas of uncertainty."[39] The portrait of modern bureaucratic structure as oppressive thus appears to be grossly oversimplified
and perhaps even inaccurate. A question germane to the discussion of the
stratification system in modern society is that of the implication of the
processes and alteration of bureaucratic control. A consideration of this
problem is presented in Chapter 4 as part of our examination of postindustrial society.

FUNCTIONALISM

Another discussion of the bases of stratification that has been extremely influential during the mid-twentieth century is found in the writing of those identified as functionalists. This school of thought represented in the writings of Talcott Parsons, Kingsley Davis, and Wilbert
Moore has been called "functionalism." The functionalists have generally argued that inequality is inherent in any society and that the particular
rewards that a society gives to its members are justified by their functional utility as determined by the values of a particular society.

Talcott Parsons, long regarded as the most important spokesman of
functionalism, has argued that social stratification is "a generalized aspect of the structure of all social systems" that arises because the various
elements "are subject to the process of evaluation, as desirable or undesirable, as useful or useless, as gratifying or noxious."[40] The evaluative
process, he has argued, is based on standards or common value patterns
shared by members of society and provides a mechanism of integration
necessary for a society's survival.

Parsons has noted, however, that the actual hierarchical structure of inequality found in all societies is not perfectly matched to the "ideal" ranking order prescribed by the society's values. In regard to this discrepancy, he has written: "It is convenient to conceptualize this element of discrepancy between the normatively defined 'ideal' ranking order and the actual state of affairs, in terms of the relation between value terms and 'power.' "[41] Rather than choosing to explicate the implications of power, Parsons focused on the common value pattern. In his view, this focus provides "the stable points of reference for a technical theoretical analysis of the empirical influence of the other components of the system process."[42]

Adherents of the functionalist school have generally agreed with the Parsonian position. In the most significant article of this genre, Kingsley Davis and Wilbert Moore[43] concluded that the universal presence of stratification was explicable in terms of the requirements faced by all societies in placing and motivating people to perform the duties important to that society. The determinants of rank include differential functional importance of a position to society and the scarcity of personnel to fill all positions.

In one of the early critiques of the Davis and Moore position, Melvin Tumin identified the following propositions, which summarize the logic of the functionalist argument:

1. Certain positions in any society are more functionally important than others and require special skills for their performance.

2. Only a limited number of people in any society have the talents that can be trained into the skills appropriate to these positions.

3. The conversion of talents into skills involves a training period during which sacrifices of one kind or another are made by those undergoing the training.

4. In order to induce the talented persons to undergo these sacrifices and acquire the training, their future positions must carry an inducement value.

5. Scarce and desired goods consist of rights and perquisites attached to or built into the positions and can be classified into things that contribute to sustenance and comfort, humor and diversion, self-respect and ego expansion.

6. This differential access to the basic rewards of the society has as a consequence the differentiation of the prestige and esteem that various strata acquire.

7. Therefore, social inequality among different strata in terms of the amounts of prestige and esteem that they receive is both positively functional and inevitable in any society.[44]

In line with this summary, Tumin presented a point-by-point critique that in essence questioned the inevitability and positive functionality of institutionalized social inequality.

A seemingly endless debate has ensued on the validity, logical adequacy, and testability of the functionalist argument.[45] Revision of the initial Davis-Moore formulation has been suggested by many social scientists.[46] Richard Simpson, for example, would substitute the economic concept of "supply and demand" for the term "functional necessity."[47] Some of the attempts to extend the Davis-Moore theory of stratification have been linked to empirical tests of propositions suggested by the theory.[48] One of the most recent empirical reports in this vein was conducted by Burke D. Grandjean and Frank D. Bean. Based on a national sample of 1,569 male family heads in Italy, Grandjean and Bean concluded that "while Italians believe that rewards are *in general* allocated in proportion to one's social usefulness, their *own* rewards bear little relationship to the importance of their *own* occupation, as they perceive this importance."[49] This conclusion, Melvin Tumin noted some years ago, suggests the possibility of "feelings of distributive injustice."[50]

Conflict Theory and Structural Functionalism

A few contemporary theorists have attempted to bridge the gap between *conflict theorists* (that is, those who focus on power relationships and conflicts) and functionalism. Rather than asking which position is correct, social scientists such as Stanislau Ossowski,[51] Piere van den Berghe,[52] and Gerhard Lenski[53] have worked toward a synthesis of the two theories. They acknowledge both as partial but complementary views of social reality.

More recently, Theodore Kemper[54] developed an argument for quantitative indicators that permit empirical tests of the applicability of the two formulations. Kemper noted four problems that must be answered in order to assess the relative contributions of the two types of theory:

1. To what extent is there an evaluative consensus that there should be differing concrete rewards, such as income, for different positions in society?

2. Even if there is societal agreement on the rank order of positions according to the differential reward that ought to be accorded to them, the question of the statistical properties of the ranks themselves must be analyzed. If there is a relatively high variance around many rank positions, for example, "this would mean that there is actually low evaluative

consensus on the reward appropriate for these positions, and a fundamental part of the functional theory of stratification is thereby put into question."[55]

3. What is the agreement between the *ideal* rank order of the evaluative consensus on deserved rewards with the rank order of *actual* rewards for the same position?

4. As a test of the contrasting emphases of the functionalist and Marxist theories on the importance of power in the determination of stratification, Kemper suggests an examination of the relationship between "the shape and the variance of the distribution of ranks according to the evaluative consensus and the shape and the variance of the actual or real distribution of ranks."[56]

A most comprehensive attempt at synthesis is provided in the work of Gerhard Lenski.[57] Building from basic assumptions about the nature of people and society, Lenski developed a series of hypotheses, which he tested with materials drawn from anthropology, history, and sociology. In summary, Lenski argued that the growth of industrial societies produced a decline in inequality. He pointed out that industrialism has usually entailed a growth in political democracy and a decrease in income differences between classes. Moreover, even though the wealthiest people in the United States earn several thousand times the average income and the highest officials in the Soviet Union receive a hundred times the average wage, Lenski contends that despite these broad income differences, industrial nations show a major decline in income inequality when compared to agrarian nations.

A number of trends in industrial societies are cited as important. First, as technology becomes more complex, it is increasingly difficult for a small elite to understand the functioning of economic, military, or bureaucratic systems. Consequently they must rely upon a greater number of experts who are, in turn, rewarded for their expertise with money, power, and privilege.

Second, the rapidity of growth in the industrial sector allows the elite to share the economic surplus because that will reward specialists and eventually maximize profits for the ruling class.

Third, in an expanding industrial economy, elites are more willing to pursue other goals, such as cultural, educational, or status-conferring rewards, rather than simply economic advantage. Therefore, they spread the economic surplus to other sectors of the society.

Further, the extension of literacy and expertise increasingly involves the masses in political participation. In consequence, new groups enter into political competition with the elite.

Lenski views the development of political democracy in industrialized nations as an indication of the clear decline of the political power of agrarian elites. He acknowledges that an egalitarian political ideal has not been realized in contemporary societies. Nonetheless, he believes that it is difficult to prove that the power of a "ruling class" has actually increased in modern times. There are, of course, other writers, most notably Floyd Hunter and C. Wright Mills, who have argued that industrial societies have produced a new type of "power elite." The new elite in their opinion differs in nature but not in the extent of privilege characteristic of old agrarian elites.[58]

Lenski was among the first social scientists to focus on the complexities in the distribution of power and privilege in modern society. He did so by noting that many individuals were inconsistent in the levels of positions they held in society.[59] An individual, for example, may have obtained a college degree but, because of race or sex discrimination, be relegated to a relatively low-paying job. Such an individual is described as occupying an *inconsistent status position*. Of course, the tendency for different types of strata to reach a common level, after a time, has been recognized. In other words, for example, politically powerful people usually attain wealth and high status. There is little doubt, however, that substantial numbers of people in industrial society occupy inconsistent strata.

The concept of status inconsistency refers to a nonvertical dimension of the stratification system. It also implies attitudinal and behavioral correlates not directly associated with a specific location in the stratification hierarchy. The central thrust of Lenski's original empirical study demonstrated a relationship of status inconsistency with specific political attitudes.

A range of studies have been undertaken to examine the correlates and consequences of inconsistent status. One researcher, for example, concluded that the social position of those who occupied inconsistent strata was resolved in terms of the higher status dimension, and that expectations regarding deference from others conformed with this resolution.[60] Research by Lenski[61] and by Himmelfard and Senn,[62] however, suggests the frustration of these expectations. These researchers have concluded that those who interact with status-inconsistent individuals tend to attribute lower status to the individual than that person has attributed to himself or herself.

The findings of the various researchers who have undertaken an examination of the effects of status inconsistency have not always provided clear answers as to its effect. For example, following the lead by Lenski, a number of researchers have studied political attitudes and the preferences for political change by those occupying inconsistent status positions. Whereas the research by Lenski[63] and Erving Goffman[64] supported the proposition that these individuals preferred political change, data gathered by William Kenkel,[65] Gerard Brandmeyer,[66] Kevin Kelly and

William Chamblis[67] did not. A few researchers have found that the relationship noted by Lenski and Goffman held only for specific types of inconsistencies such as that between race and income or between religion and occupation.[68]

The differences in the findings of researchers concerned with the effects of status implication have been explained by Elton Jackson and Richard Curtis[69] in terms of the different methods employed. They have noted that many of the earlier findings should probably be discarded because "such methods as simple frequency counts or four cell 'fold-over' technique are not generally regarded as inadequate or unreliable."[70] Further, they suggest that the mixed results may also be attributed to the large number of dependent variables studied: "There is certainly no reason to expect that mobility or inconsistency should affect every aspect of human attitudes and behavior; so some researchers may have obtained results, while others did not because they focused on the correct dependent variable."[71]

Aside from the methodological problems and the choice of dependent variables that may affect the results of empirical studies, Jackson and Curtis also suggest that alternative hypotheses may be implied by the many negative findings reported in the literature. For example, the social context of the group or individual experiencing the effects of mobility and inconsistent status may be important in ascertaining the degree of desire for social change or of personal stress. In the words of Jackson and Curtis: "Mobility or inconsistency effects perhaps only occur in a rigid stable class structure. In the United States, rates of mobility and inconsistency are so high as to make them the modal experience."[72] Under these conditions, then, individuals would be assisted in resolving the stress of status inconsistency. Of course this hypothesis remains in the realm of speculation until the focus of research in this area has been broadened.

In addition, researchers interested in the effects of status consistency might also consider the more immediate social context and history of the groups or individuals who are the focus of examination. Most people, after all, base their attitudes on their perception of the immediate rather than the broad social environment.[73] This factor, as a case in point, has been used to explain why black children continue to maintain a high degree of self-esteem in spite of the racism institutionalized in American society.[74] There would appear to be much research left to be done.

Industrialization has entailed not only the growth of new social classes and bureaucracy but also the burgeoning of cities. Since the effects of urbanization per se have often been confused with the results of industrialism, we now discuss the impact of urbanization as a related but not inevitable consequence of industrialization and its effect upon the stratification system.

Urbanization

The growth of modern urban areas was based on two "revolutions": the industrial revolution, which made possible the urban domination of the modern world, and the agricultural revolution, which made urban growth possible.

As has already been noted, the agricultural revolution enabled a family to produce a surplus of food in excess of that it could use itself. Because of the surplus, not everyone had to be a food producer, and many people were able to move away from the farm and to create social systems independent of kinship ties. Specialists such as craftsmen, tradesmen, administrators, record keepers, and service personnel emerged as full-time workers early in the development of preindustrial cities. They exchanged their services for the excess food produced by farmers.

Noel P. Gist and Sylvia Fava[75] have estimated that the first cities appeared approximately five or six thousand years ago. They have observed that "the 6,000 years of man's urban existence represent only slightly more than one percent of his total existence on earth and ten percent of his existence as physically modern man."[76] Preindustrial cities were typically characterized by a relatively small population. Cities of 100,000 persons or more were rare. It has only been since the industrial revolution in Europe and the United States that the concentration of large masses of people has occurred. With the introduction of technological advances such as steam and, more recently, electrical power, it became more economical to concentrate manufacturing in large factories rather than maintaining cottage industries.

The centralization of large numbers of factory workers, in turn, encouraged even more people to flock to the city. Workers were needed not only to manufacture goods but also to transport and distribute them. The migrants were filled with the promise of economic rewards, freedom from the surveillance of the family, and the novelty of urban life. Since the mechanization of farming paralleled the growth of the factory system, ever increasing numbers of rural dwellers were relieved of the necessity to produce agricultural products.

The rapid shift in population after industrialization is apparent. In 1870, shortly after the onset of the industrial revolution in the United States, more than half the labor force was employed in agriculture. One century later less than 5 percent of the population was engaged in agricultural occupations.[77]

Approaches to studies of the city have generally followed their historical development. For instance, the spatial aspect of cities in the United States and other industrial nations has been conceptualized by scholars to include larger and larger proportions of the outlying areas. Gist and Fava[78] report that two new concepts were introduced by the Bureau of the Census in the 1950s: the Urbanized Area and the Standard Metropolitan Statistical Area (SMSA). Both measure the extent of the influence of particular contiguous areas.

According to the Bureau of the Census definition, an Urbanized Area consists of "a city (or 'twin cities') of at least 50,000 persons (central city) and its surrounding closely settled territory."[79] Outside of the Urbanized Area, places with 2,500 inhabitants were classified as urban. An SMSA boundary, on the other hand, has as its starting point a county containing a city of at least 50,000 inhabitants and surrounding counties. To qualify as part of an SMSA, the county must serve as a place of work or home for workers and maintain regular social and economic ties with the central-city county.

In 1970 the metropolitan population of the United States was 68.6 percent of the total population. Of course, the growth of urban areas is not restricted to the United States. Gist and Fava report, "The most rapid growth (among the world's large cities) is occurring in developing countries."[80] The urbanizing trend of the world's population, in fact, has led to the introduction of the concept of overurbanization. In nonstatistical terms, countries are described as "overurbanized" "if the economic system is not expanding rapidly enough to provide employment and income for the employable urban inhabitants, whether locally born or immigrants, and if urban institutions are unable to provide adequate housing, education, sanitation, medical care and other basic needs."[81]

The growth of urban areas along with that of industrialization is an accepted fact. However, urbanization has had effects on social class, power, and status that are independent of the effects of industrialization.

The Effects of Urbanization on Social Structure

Many different approaches have been employed in attempts to conceptualize the social nature and the dynamics of urban areas. Early discussions of urbanism focused on the development of typologies differentiating urban from rural communities. Based on the earlier distinction of differences in modes of social organization noted by Emile Durkheim (mechanical versus organic), Ferdinand Tönnies (*Gemeinschaft* versus

Gesellschaft), and Henry Maine (status versus contract), Robert Redfield characterized folk societies as "small, isolated, nonliterate and homogeneous with a strong sense of group solidarity. . . . Behavior is traditional, spontaneous, uncritical and personal . . . the familial group is the unit of action, the sacred prevails over the secular; the economy is one of status rather than of the market."[82] Redfield did not attempt to characterize urban societies. Rather, he assumed that the characteristics of urban societies were the opposite of those of folk societies.

Typologies such as the folk-urban continuum, though providing some insight and stimulating much discussion, remain a crude analytic tool. Whether cities or societies are the unit of analysis remains unclear, and the effects of urban areas on environment cannot be examined. Moreover, the use of this approach precludes separating the effects of industrialism from those of urbanization.

The most instructive attempt to discern the differential effects on the social structure of urbanization and industrialization has been provided by Gideon Sjoberg.[83] In his historical and cross-cultural examination of preindustrial cities, he concluded that major differences between the industrial and preindustrial cities, aside from their economic structure, were to be found in the organization of the political structure and the stratification system.

Preindustrial cities, noted Sjoberg, were dominated by a small, privileged upper class, which made up perhaps 5 to 10 percent of the population.[84] The number of ruling families in the elite, though small,[85] occupied most of the leading positions in governmental bureaucracies as well as in the religious and educational organizations that dominated both cities and society. They were able to do so, commented Sjoberg, because of the "sizeable progeny of many of the elite."[86]

Sjoberg contended that the stratification structure of preindustrial society was essentially bifurcated and consisted of the elite and the lower class. In addition, "outcasts" who were isolated from the upper and the lower classes of "respectable" people were found in most preindustrial cities.

The elite of preindustrial societies were found to control instruments of authority and power, which enabled them to defend themselves against any attack from within or from the elite from another society. They were also able to obtain "luxury" items, giving them a life style that set them dramatically apart from the members of the lower class.

The lower class in preindustrial societies, according to Sjoberg, was made up of members of the lower echelons of the religious and governmental structures, soldiers, merchants, artisans, and a large number of unskilled laborers. He noted that there was some internal gradation of status in both the elite and the lower-class group. The lower-class groups in various regions of a nation differed from each other because of a lack of communication between them over very great distances.

The two classes, according to Sjoberg, maintained highly contrasting life styles. Only the elite possessed the means to buy richly furnished homes, jewelry, and elaborate clothing and to patronize the arts. Further, upper-class persons were not only identified by birth into a "proper" kinship group, they were also educated and therefore able to engage in mental, rather than physical, work. For example, Sjoberg noted: "The educated elite utilize lexical and grammatical forms that the abysmally poor and illiterate rarely have the opportunity to hear, much less acquire."[87] Differences between the upper and the lower classes were also manifested in personal attributes such as manners, dress, and speech. Such status indicators served not only to identify persons of elite status but also helped to perpetuate their position.

Two general characteristics would appear to differentiate the stratification system found in preindustrial cities from that of its counterpart in industrial societies: the pervasiveness of the class structure and the rigidity of classes. The pervasiveness of class in preindustrial cities results from the interlocking nature (because of intermarriage) of families and the monopoly of privileges held by the elite. The elite in industrialized societies has not maintained as much of a monopoly of privileges, such as in education, nor can it easily resort to the bases of legitimation used by those in preindustrial society; that is, the appeal to absolutes and tradition.[88] Rather, the justification for the power of one body of persons over another in an industrial or postindustrial society has been based on presumed expertise as well as an appeal to the governed.[89]

Research by Alex Inkeles[90], concerned with the relative impact of industrialization and urbanization on the attitudes of urban people, helps us to understand some of the reasons for the change in bases of legitimating the power of one group over another. Inkeles argued that the move into the modern era has required that individuals:

1. Be informed, participating citizens.

2. Have a marked sense of personal efficacy.

3. Be highly independent and autonomous in their relations with traditional sources of influence.

4. Be ready for new experiences and ideas; that is, be relatively open-minded and cognitively flexible.[91]

Such individuals could not accept absolutes or tradition as a basis for legitimating privilege and power.

Based on data obtained in Argentina, Chile, East Pakistan, India, Israel, and Nigeria on the levels of modernity of specific populations, Inkeles concluded that education, an urban phenomenon, has proved to be the single most powerful force in creating the attitude of modernity.[92] Formal schools, suggests Inkeles, use rational organizations centered on individual comprehension and logic while teaching a time perspective, subject matter, and other values and attitudes important in orienting an individual to the natural and social environment.[93]

However, any generalization concerning the effect of education (as one facet of urbanization) on the attitudes of industrial workers must be qualified. As Inkeles himself noted:

> Factory experience had a much greater impact on men of rural background and of little education than it did on men of urban origin who had more education. Indeed, in explaining the modernity scores of the less educated men of rural origin, we found that their occupational experience could be of equal, or even greater importance than was the amount of schooling they had received.[94]

Change in the mode of differentiating and stratifying populations from ascribed to achieved characteristics accounts in part for the change in the degree of rigidity in the stratification systems from preindustrial to industrial societies. The relative lack of rigidity in the class structure of industrial society is also based on the rapidity of technological change, which constantly creates new categories of workers. In addition, the mass production of goods has helped to hide gross differences in the quality of clothing and other material goods, which in preindustrial society helped to set the elite apart.

Industrial Cities

The study of industrial cities has served as the focus of many modern social scientists. Among various scholars, Louis Wirth has been a paramount guide to the nature of industrial cities and their stratification systems. Wirth, in his classic article "Urbanism as a Way of Life,"[95] described cities in terms of occupational specialization, secularization, and segmental, transitory social relationships. Such characteristics, he argued, resulted in impersonality and anonymity.

Building on the work of men such as Wirth, and supporting the view that industrial cities dominate society, Eshref Bell and Wendell Shevsky formulated their theory of "social areas."[96] Unlike the typological approach, which focuses on the contrast between rural and urban areas, or Wirth's approach, which focuses on internal aspects of the city, Bell and Shevsky contended that the organization of industrial societies, although converging in cities, has vastly expanded beyond easily definable limits. They view the city as a dominating force extending throughout the society.[97] Urbanism, from this point of view, is not restricted to a specific localized area—namely, the city.

The almost universal consensus about the people identified as belonging to a particular stratum in a preindustrial city and even in a modern small town[98] is no longer possible in a large industrial city. There are a number of reasons for this. First, social relations in industrial cities are commonly segmented and transitory. Second, technological changes have altered occupational groupings so that status is blurred. Third, there are a number of voluntary associations that confer status on their membership. Fourth, the heterogeneity of the population in cities, particularly American cities, complicates the understanding of life styles and symbols that might otherwise be employed as indicators of social status.

As Wirth noted in 1938, the density of population in urban areas commonly resulted in many transitory social contacts.[99] Individuals and families may, of course, develop intense relationships with others in their neighborhood or place of work, but the average urbanite is confronted with many people each day, perhaps even on a regular basis, with whom contact is minimal. In addition, friendships at work or school may not be carried through to other spheres of life, thus limiting the amount of knowledge about people, which is readily available in a small town.

A sense of anonymity is created under urban conditions, and the identification of others on the basis of criteria other than superficial ones such as dress, manners, or occupation is difficult. However, because mass-produced clothing is available to almost everyone and knowledge about "socially acceptable" behavior can be learned from books or television, these superficial criteria are commonly inaccurate.

Occupation, together with source of income, has long been regarded as a key indicator of social class in American society. People generally regard the answer to the inquiry "What do you do?" to be sufficient to place a person in a particular social class. Yet occupation alone may not identify the social status of a particular person. There is much occupational differentiation in modern industrial society, and technological changes continually create new categories of workers. Both of these facts help to obscure information about the social status of an occupation. For example, Paul Hatt,[100] indicated that respondents in a nationwide occupational ranking were unable to make fine distinctions of status with a high degree of confidence when ranking occupations relatively distant from their own.

In addition to a lack of information, the ranking of new occupations may also be obscured by the aura of glamour that tends to surround work that is not fully understood. Just as astronauts are surrounded by a degree of mystery and prestige today, train engineers of yesteryear received social recognition beyond that which most Americans in the 1970s would be willing to attribute to them.

In addition to a diversity of occupations, modern industrial cities have a large number of voluntary associations such as the Parent-Teacher Association, the Council of Social Workers, and the League of Women Voters. These organizations are generally of two kinds: those geared toward achieving specific goals and those whose primary function is to afford satisfaction in the fellowship of people who share similar characteristics.

Among the most important goal-directed associations in modern industrial society are occupational and trade unions. These associations have not only upgraded working conditions, fringe benefits, and remuneration for their members, they have also acquired political power. In addition, they have provided a vehicle for increasing the status of their leadership.[101]

Similarly, many civil rights groups that came to the forefront in the 1960s focused the attention of the American public on the real and potential role they could have in effecting social change. Groups such as the Urban League, the National Association for the Advancement of Colored People (NAACP), SNCC, and CORE have forced legal changes that increase equity in housing, establishing credit, education, employment opportunity, and the voting franchise.

The goal-directed and social functions served by voluntary associations are not necessarily separate. Participants in organizations such as parents' associations, unions, and religious and civil rights groups successfully merge the two functions. At times, as in the instance of voluntary associations of the elite in cities, social contacts, contracts, and decisions may be made that have broad implications for the distribution of power as well as status in society.

The upper class in industrialized cities has also been organized into a series of "clubs" that combine social activities with business and politics.[102] Although supposedly devoted to such entertainments as squash or bridge, such clubs as New York's Union League, San Francisco's Bohemian, and St. Louis' University Club serve equally well as houses of commerce and political congresses.

Thus, since modern industrialized cities contain all classes of people, it becomes difficult to identify the truly powerful groups without an insider's knowledge of a particular city. For example, Richard Coleman and Bernice Neugarten,[103] in their study of Kansas City, identified seven social "classes" and thirteen substrata that included the:

Upper class: "capital society" (inheritors of large fortunes and descendants of prominent families); "noncapital society" (very successful professionals or executives)

Upper middle class

Lower middle class

Working class

Lower class: poor but reputable

Slum dwellers and disreputables

Assignment of families to the different classes was based on such diverse variables as character and reputation of the residential neighborhood, type of housing, income, occupation, membership and participation in social clubs, religious affiliation, and amount and type of schooling. However, Coleman and Neugarten emphasized their inability to make precise placement of individuals due to the status inconsistency of many of their respondents.

Each of the "classes" and substrata identified by Coleman and Neugarten was described in terms of different styles of life and association. These many distinctions in the social structure are cross-cut by a variety of ethnic and racial groups. Many of these groups, in varying degrees, have retained or developed a unique subculture.

Herbert Gans's analysis of the social relationships in the Italian working-class neighborhood in the West End of Boston before it was razed concluded that outside of their place of work, the social life of the community members tended to revolve around "peer groups" made up of compatible kin of similar age, economic level, and cultural interests.[104] Informally, these peer groups usually met in someone's home to discuss weddings or other celebrations, local anecdotes, neighborhood activities, and deviant behavior. They were not interested in politics or social developments that did directly affect their lives. Labor unions, churches, and a few social clubs, together with these peer groups, made up the social life of most of Gans's lower-class West Enders.

Elliot Liebow has provided an account of lower-class life in the District of Columbia. Social life for many of the black men in this district revolved around cliques that formed a "personal community" for the men involved. Friends formed within these cliques were "walking buddies," best friends or girls who spent much of their nonworking time together, "drinking, dancing, engaging in sex, playing the fool or the wise man, talking about nothing or everything."[105] The clique consisted of people who were turned to for help and counsel and, in turn, who expected to receive the same favors.

In the descriptions of both the Italian and black subcultures by Gans and Liebow, respectively, norms and behavior at variance with the majority of middle-class Americans were noted. For example, the notion of privacy, commonly cherished by middle-class Americans, is foreign to Gans's Italian population. Gans reports that these people live almost constantly in groups and feel much discomfort when left alone. And members of the streetcorner cliques described by Liebow have developed unconventional "family" lives as well as "deviant" attitudes toward work and morality.

The formation of subcultural differences in modern industrial cities derives in part from voluntary or enforced physical segregation based on differences in social class, religion, national origin, and race.[106] Black laborers, Jewish merchants, Italian vegetable and fruit sellers, and middle-class white professionals tend to cluster together in different areas of the city and to lead very different lives. Such differences often reinforce one another. Minimal contact between groups has implications for power and social status as well as for attitudinal and behavioral differences, which may perpetuate or create new differences.

Conclusions

The coming of industrial society brought with it the substitution of mechanical sources of energy for human labor. As industrialism spread throughout the world, the old stratification system of agrarian societies collapsed. New groups—most important, capitalists and workers—emerged as significant factors in social development.

A variety of social theorists have emphasized different facets of the transformation in human society. Marx focused on the issue of the prevalence of poverty in an economy of increasing abundance. Weber observed the growth of bureaucracy with both wonder and dismay. The functionalists attempted to understand the pervasiveness of social hierarchies. And other sociologists, such as Lenski, considered industrialization as the nemesis of inequality.

Although major cities existed throughout the agrarian age, industrialism promoted the growth of huge urban centers. These, in turn, spawned new occupations, interests, and mentalities. Interweaving racial, ethnic, class, and cultural concerns, the cities have created a variety of subcultures ranging from the quiet harmony of New York's Harvard Club library to the cacophony of street life in Washington's "Tally's Corner."

As cities, bureaucracies, and affluence have grown, a new era of social life and stratification has dawned: the postindustrial society. Some contemporary social scientists—Daniel Bell, Raymond Aron, Milovan Djilas, for example—have charted the course of this new way of life and its consequences for the distribution of power and privilege. We turn to this topic in our next chapter.

Notes

1. Karl Marx, *The Communist Manifesto,* in *Selected Works,* 2 vols. (New York: International Publishers).
2. Reinhard Bendix, "Inequality and Social Structure: A Comparison of Marx and Weber," *American Sociological Review* 39 (April 1974): 149–161.
3. See Gerhard Lenski, *Power and Privilege* (New York: McGraw-Hill, 1966), for the best summary of the common features of industrial society.
4. See Frederick Dewhurst et al., *America's Needs and Resources* (New York: Twentieth Century Fund, 1955).
5. Lenski, *Power and Privilege,* p. 299.
6. Dewhurst et al., *America's Needs and Resources.*
7. William McCord, *Springtime of Freedom* (New York: Oxford University Press, 1965).
8. Robert Heilbroner, *An Inquiry into the Human Prospect* (New York: Harper & Row, 1974).
9. Lenski, *Power and Privilege,* p. 300.
10. *The New York Times,* October 24, 1976, p. 31.
11. Lenski, *Power and Privilege,* p. 302.
12. See M. M. Bober, *Karl Marx's Interpretation of History* (Cambridge: Harvard University Press, 1948).
13. Joseph Schumpeter, *Imperialism and Social Classes* (New York: Meridian, 1955).
14. Philip Taft, *Economics and Problems of Labor* (Harrisburg, Pa.: Stackpole, 1942).
15. Morris Silver, "Toward a Consumption Theory of Political Democracy," in Robert D. Leiter and Gerald Saikin eds., *Economics of Public Choice* (New York: Cyrco Press, 1975).
16. See William McCord and Arline McCord, "Comments on 'Toward a Consumption Theory' " in Leiter and Saikin, *Economics of Public Choice.*
17. See Daniel Bell, *The Coming of Post-Industrial Society* (New York: Basic Books, 1973).
18. Lenski, *Power and Privilege,* p. 307.
19. Harvey Cox, *The Secular City* (New York: Macmillan, 1968).
20. Lenski, *Power and Privilege,* p. 307.
21. Bell, *Coming of Post-Industrial Society.*

22. David Granick, *The European Executive* (Garden City, N.Y.: Doubleday Anchor, 1964).
23. Bell, *Coming of Post-Industrial Society.*
24. Ibid.
25. Karl Marx, *Capital* (Chicago: Kerr, 1909).
26. See, for example, Paul Baran, *The Political Economy of Growth* (New York: Monthly Review Press, 1960).
27. H. H. Gerth and C. W. Mills, eds. and trans., *From Max Weber: Essays in Sociology* (New York: Oxford University Press, 1946), p. 180.
28. Ibid.
29. Peter M. Blau, *Bureaucracy in Modern Society* (New York: Random House, 1956), pp. 28–30.
30. Peter M. Blau and W. Richard Scott, *Formal Organization* (San Francisco: Chandler, 1962).
31. See J. P. Mayer, *Max Weber and German Politics* (London: Faber & Faber, 1943).
32. See Michael Crozier, *The Bureaucratic Phenomenon* (Chicago: University of Chicago Press, 1964), especially Chapter 7; and Alvin Gouldner, "Metaphysical Pathos and the Theory of Bureaucracy" in Amitai Etzioni, ed. *Complex Organizations* (New York: Holt, Rinehart, 1961).
33. Robert K. Merton, "Bureaucratic Structure and Personality," *Social Forces,* 18 (1940): 560–568.
34. Alvin Gouldner, *Patterns of Industrial Bureaucracy* (Glencoe, Ill.: Free Press, 1954).
35. Philip Selznic, *T.V.A. and the Grass Roots* (Berkeley: University of California Press, 1949).
36. Peter Blau, *The Dynamics of Bureaucracy* (Chicago: University of Chicago Press, 1955).
37. Crozier, *Bureaucratic Phenomenon.*
38. Ibid., pp. 184–185.
39. Ibid.
40. Talcott Parsons, "A Revised Analytic Approach to the Theory of Social Stratification," in *Essays in Sociological Theory,* rev. ed. (Glencoe, Ill.: Free Press, 1954), pp. 386–387.
41. Ibid., pp. 390–391.
42. Talcott Parsons, "A Revised Analytic Approach to the Theory of Social Stratification," in *Essays in Sociological Perspective,* p. 393.
43. Kingsley Davis and Wilbert Moore, "Some Principles of Stratification," *American Sociological Review* (April 1945): 242–249.
44. Melvin Tumin, "Some Principles of Stratification: A Critical Analysis," *American Sociological Review* 18 (August 1953): 389–394.
45. See G. A. Huaco, "The Functionalist Theory of Stratification: Two Decades of Controversy," *Inquiry* (Autumn 1966): 215–240.
46. See, for example, Burk D. Grandjean, "An Economic Analysis of the Davis-Moore Theory of Stratification," *Social Forces* 53 (June 1975): 543.
47. Richard Simpson, "A Modification of the Functional Theory of Social Stratification," *Social Forces* (December 1956): 133–138.
48. See, for example, M. Abrahamson, "Functionalism and the Functional Theory of Stratification: An Empirical Assessment," *American Journal of Sociology* 78 (March 1973): 1236–1246; Burke D. Grandjean and Frank D. Beau, "The Davis-Moore Theory and Perceptions of Stratification: Some Relevant Evidence," *Social Forces* 54 (September 1975): 166–179; A.L. Stinchcomb, "Some Empirical Consequences of the Davis-Moore Theory of Stratification," *American Sociological Review* 28 (October 1963): 387–394.

49. Grandjean and Beau, "Davis-Moore Theory."
50. Tumin, "Some Principles of Stratification."
51. Stanislau Ossowski, *Class Structure in Social Consciousness,* trans. Sheila Patterson (New York: Free Press, 1963).
52. Piere van den Berge, "Dialectic and Functionalism: Toward a Theoretical Synthesis," *American Sociological Review* 28 (1963): 695–705.
53. Lenski, *Power and Privilege.*
54. Theodore Kemper, "Marxist and Functionalist Theories in the Study of Stratification," *Social Forces* 54 (March 1976): 559.
55. Ibid., p. 575.
56. Ibid., p. 576.
57. Lenski, *Power and Privilege.*
58. Ibid., p. 325.
59. Gerhard Lenski, "Status Crystallization: A Non-Vertical Dimension of Social Status," *American Sociological Review* 19 (1954): 405–415.
60. J. Galtung, "Rank and Social Integration: A Multi-Dimensional Approach," in Joseph Berger, Morris Zelditch, Jr., and Bo Anderson, eds., *Sociological Theories in Progress* (Boston: Houghton Mifflin, 1966).
61. Lenski, "Status Crystallization."
62. S. Himmelfard and D. J. Senn, "Forming Impressions of Social Class: Two Tests of an Averaging Model," *Journal of Personality and Social Psychology* 12 (May 1969): 38–51.
63. Gerhard Lenski, "Social Participaton and Status Crystallization," *American Sociological Review* 21 (1956): 458–464.
64. Erving Goffman, "Status Consistency and Preference for Change in Power Distribution," *American Sociological Review* 22 (1957): 275–281.
65. William Kenkel, "The Relationship of Status Consistency and Political Economic Attitudes," *American Sociological Review* 21 (June 1956): 365–368.
66. Gerard Brandmeyer, "Status Consistency and Political Behavior: A Replication and Extension of Research," *Sociological Quarterly* 6 (July 1965): 241–256.
67. Kevin Kelly and William Chamblis, "Status Consistency and Political Attitudes," *American Sociological Review* 31 (June 1966): 375–382.
68. See, for example, Elton Jackson and Peter J. Burke, "Status and Symptoms of Stress: Additive and Interaction Effect," *American Sociological Review* 30 (August 1965): 556–564.
69. Elton Jackson and Richard Curtis, "Effects of Vertical Mobility and Status Inconsistency: A Body of Negative Evidence," *American Sociological Review* 37 (December 1972): 701–713.
70. Ibid., p. 710.
71. Ibid., p. 711.
72. Ibid., p. 712.
73. See, for example, Morris Rosenberg and Roberta G. Simmons, *Black and White Self Esteem: The Urban School Child* (Washington, D.C.: American Sociological Association, 1971).
74. Alvin F. Poussaint, "The Black Child's Image of the Future," in Alvin Toffler, ed., *Learning for Tomorrow* (New York: Random House, 1974), chap. 4.
75. Noel P. Gist and Sylvia Fava, *Urban Sociology,* 6th ed. (New York: Crowell, 1974).
76. Ibid., p. 4.
77. U.S. Bureau of the Census, *Statistical Abstracts 1975.*
78. Gist and Fava, *Urban Sociology,* p. 67.
79. Ibid.
80. Ibid., p. 122.
81. Ibid., p. 133.

82. Robert Redfield, "The Folk Society," *American Journal of Sociology* 52 (January 1947).
83. Gideon Sjoberg, *The Preindustrial City Past and Present* (New York: Free Press, 1960).
84. Ibid., p. 110.
85. Ibid.
86. Ibid., p. 221.
87. Ibid., p. 128.
88. Ibid., p. 225.
89. Ibid., p. 226.
90. Alex Inkeles, "A Model of Modern Man: Theoretical and Methodological Issues," in N. Hammond, ed., *Social Science and the New Societies: Problems in Cross Cultural Research and Theory Building* (Lansing: SSRB, Michigan State University, 1973).
91. Alex Inkeles, "Becoming Modern: Individual Change in Six Developing Countries," *Ethos* 3 (Summer 1975): 327.
92. Ibid., p. 332.
93. Ibid.
94. Ibid., p. 333.
95. Louis Wirth, "Urbanism as a Way of Life," *American Journal of Sociology* 44 (July 1938): 3–24.
96. Eshref Bell and Wendell Shevsky, *Social Area Analysis* (Stanford, Calif.: Stanford University Press, 1955).
97. Ibid.
98. See, for example, Leonard Reisman, *Class in American Society* (Glencoe, Ill.: Free Press, 1959).
99. Wirth, "Urbanism as a Way of Life."
100. Paul Hatt, *Occupation and Social Status* (New York: Free Press, 1961).
101. See, for example, Seymour Lipset, Martin Trow, and James S. Coleman, *Union Democracy* (Glencoe, Ill.: Free Press, 1956).
102. See, for example, E. Digby Baltzell, *The Protestant Establishment* (New York: Vintage, 1966).
103. Richard Coleman and Bernice Neugarten, *Social Status in the City* (San Francisco: Jossey-Bassey-Bass, 1971).
104. Herbert Gans, *The Urban Villagers* (New York: Free Press, 1962).
105. Elliot Liebow, *Tally's Corner* (Boston: Little, Brown, 1967), p. 10.
106. See, for example, Brewton Berry, *Race and Ethnic Relations* (Boston: Houghton Mifflin, 1958), chap. 10.

4

POSTINDUSTRIAL
SOCIETIES

The Nature of Postindustrial Society

Daniel Bell, the most influential analyst of postindustrial societies, has cogently argued that the major industrial nations of the world—preeminently, the United States—have entered a new era of social development.[1] Bell has suggested that five characteristics differentiate postindustrial from industrial nations.

First, the majority of the labor force in postindustrial societies engage in the provision of services rather than the actual production of agricultural or manufactured goods. In 1973, for example, 61.0 percent of America's labor force provided services ranging from education to office work; 35.4 percent were blue-collar workers; and only 3.8 percent were involved in agriculture.[2] Other advanced nations show remarkably similar patterns: service occupations occupy 49.8 percent of the labor force in the Netherlands, 49.7 percent in Britain, and 48.8 percent in Sweden.[3]

Second, the biggest change in America's occupational structure, Bell contends, is an astounding leap in the number of technical and professional workers. These occupations, which usually require an advanced education, have been growing at twice the average rate of other occupations.[4] In his opinion, scientists, professionals, and technicians have assumed paramount importance in the government, in the management of the economy, and in the development of technological advances. Bell argues that in a limited sense, the "technocrats" have become a new ruling class displacing landowners and businesspeople.[5] They achieve their power because of technical skill and political organization. In a postindustrialized society, education (rather than inheritance or patronage) becomes the main mode of access to the upper classes.

Third, Bell argues that theoretical knowledge has become the primary source of technological innovation and policy formation.[6] For example, technological advances in postindustrial society have made many traditional military theories obsolete. Developments in the synthetic production of nitrogen, as one illustration, allowed Germany to continue World War I far beyond the calculations of the Allied staff. And advances in atomic physics before and during World War II radically changed older conceptions of the balance of power. Similarly, Bell argues, the creation of post-Keynesian economics, aided by sophisticated computers, has transformed governmental policy in handling the economy. Thus governments, businesses, and all large organizations have become dependent upon the development of scientific, theoretical knowledge.

Fourth, postindustrial societies increasingly require the conscious planning of technological advances and a calculation of their "social costs" as well as their material effects.

Fifth, both in science and in human affairs a new intellectual technology has arisen. The development of systems theory, decision theory, game theory, and their supplementary techniques has entailed a major change: they allow scientists to consider the combined impact of numerous variables upon a particular phenomenon. On the level of military technology, this new approach has led "to the installation of technocrats in the Defense Department, the creation of Program Planning Budget Systems responsible in large measure for the realignment of strategic and tactical programs."[7] Bell makes this observation concerning the social level:

> The goal of the new intellectual technology is neither more nor less [than] to realize a social alchemist's dream: the dream of "ordering" the mass society. In this society today, millions of persons daily make billions of decisions about what to buy, how many children to have, whom to vote for, what job to take . . . . any single choice may be as impredictable as the quantum atom responding erratically to the measuring instrument, yet the aggregate patterns could be charted as neatly as the geometer triangulates the height and the horizon. . . . So the decision theorists seek their own *tableau entier*—the compass of rationality, "best" solution to the choices perplexing men.[8]

All these developments have produced major changes in the social structure of postindustrial societies: the rise of bureaucracy and a new set of people who attach themselves to bureaucratic systems.

Bureaucracy and the Rise of a New Elite

As a consequence of the change from an industrial to a "service" society, the decline of family-managed businesses and small farms, and the emergence of huge organizations with gigantic budgets (such as the Pentagon, the City University of New York, and General Motors), a new group of "bureaucrats" has emerged. The new elite commands immense power and privilege; others act as mere functionaries of a bureaucracy. They share in common, however, the fact that they derive their income and status from a combination of expertise, role in the bureaucracy, and "inside knowledge" of how to manipulate the system. Several of these bureaucratic classes have received particular attention.

In 1941 James Burnham first brought attention to the growth of a *managerial class*.[9] Burnham argued that the managers of large enterprises both in capitalist nations and in the Soviet Union were taking over economic and political power. In capitalist nations, he noted, administrative control over an enterprise had succeeded actual ownership as the most potent tool for wielding power. Stockholders had become mere appendages of a business. Boards of directors were, more often than not, "rubber stamps" who acknowledged decisions already made by the highest managers and their technocratic subordinates.

As C. Wright Mills noted, however, Burnham ignored the fact that the managerial elite readily merged "into the more or less unified statum of the corporate rich."[10] Similarly, Gerhard Lenski presented evidence that indicates "that those who become members of the managerial elite in private industry are almost certain to be, or become, members of the property elite as well."[11]

Nevertheless, the tie between ownership of property and direct control over business enterprises has been directly weakened. Presidents of great corporations in America are more often nameless individuals who have risen in the bureaucratic hierarchy rather than the entrepreneurs and founders of these large enterprises. Talcott Parsons in his critique of C. Wright Mills noted this change. He wrote that "control has passed by— by no means freely but for the most part—to professional executives, who have not reached their positions through the exercise of property rights but through some sort of process of appointment and promotion."[12]

The growth of large bureaucracies in almost all spheres of life—military, the civil service, education, and trade unions—has resulted in a phenomenal growth of the managerial class. An air force genral, a president of a state university, or the head of the Teamsters' Union has great power and privilege as well as a substantial if not enormous income. Such individuals have the capacity to decide the fate of thousands of people

below them in the hierarchy. They may have connections with traditionally wealthy upper-class people and may in fact consolidate their position
through increasing their own holdings. Their primary influence, however,
derives from the fact that they are able to control highly complex, specialized organizations.

The relative mobility of many of this newly emerged elite is facilitated
by their ability to transfer skills in heading gigantic bureaucracies from
one area to another. A general, for example, may use his background to
assume a role of leadership in a large corporation or a prestigious college
or even to serve as president of the nation. Those who occupy positions
only slightly removed from this apex of an organization's hierarchy, such
as most professionals, technicians, or other specialists, have less of a
chance to transfer their skills. This is due to the nature of their work and
the prolonged preparation necessary before beginning it.

Clearly, there has been a change in the bases of power in postindustrial
society. The implications of this change, however, are subject to a wide
range of speculation and cannot be understood without some knowledge
of other changes that have occurred in the social structure of modern
societies. At the most elementary level at least two dimensions of change
in the overall stratification system should be noted: its shape and span.

The *shape* of the stratification system is most simply depicted in terms
of some sort of triangular form. It may be truncated at the top (for
instance, where a few monopolize power, prestige, and resources), or it
may be set on a relatively small base indicating that the lower groups are
less numerous than the groups immediately above it. The *span* of the
stratification system refers to the distance between those at the top and
those at the bottom of the social structure. The distance can reflect any
sort of differences such as income, power, or prestige.

Span and shape of the social structure can be altered independently.
The shape of the stratification system may be altered because of changes
in industrial technology and the development of increased numbers of
"middle-class" occupations, yet the span may be unaffected by these
changes. For the most part, in postindustrial societies around the world,
the shape and not the span of the stratification system has been affected
by technological advances. Not only have the managerial ranks expanded;
so, too, have the numbers of technocrats and clerical and sales personnel.

THE TECHNOCRAT

With advances in knowledge, increases in specialization, and the demand for reliable knowledge in every sphere from population forecasting
to medical services, the ranks of the technocrats have steadily expanded.

By the term "technocrats," we mean individuals who have specialized knowledge in a particular field. The individuals have usually undergone a long apprenticeship, resulting in a certification of presumed expertise.

Many technocrats, such as physicians, have a great deal of influence over people. Such influence varies with the degree of expertise that the professional "monopolizes," but it is usually limited to a relatively confined area.

The stability of power in any society presumes a legitimating rationale that attributes proficiency to particular individuals or groups. Persons in each society learn norms and values that grant others (or specific positions) the right to dictate to them. Societies that revere the aged and allow them to influence its policies assume that accumulated life experiences are tantamount to wisdom. And in societies in which power is based on sexual differentiation, the assumption is that one or the other sex (usually men) is mentally superior in determining desirable or rational plans of action. But in postindustrial society, with its emphasis on rationality, legitimation is based on the position obtained by the individual. And this position (such as doctor, judge, or chemist) is presumed to be occupied by those individuals who have appropriate knowledge.[13] The criteria of expertise in this instance are determined by specific certifying agencies such as institutions of higher education or professional organizations.[14]

The ever increasing amounts of information presumed necessary to acquire expertise on matters from the most complex (for instance, world economy) to the most common (for instance, personal health) may help to maintain the social distance between the average person and the "expert." This allows the latter to maintain relative control over the area of specified competence.

Regardless of the manner in which one measures the rate of occupational change, it is clear that the numbers of technocrats have increased greatly in a relatively short period of time. For example, the American Bureau of Labor Statistics estimated that between 1960 and 1975 the total number of professional and technical people doubled, growing at about twice the rate of the total labor force.

This is not unique to the United States. In communist nations, which are nominally dedicated to the equalization of classes, the emergence of increased numbers of technocrats and managers within the hierarchy of the Communist party has caused concern among various theoreticians. In Yugoslavia, Milovan Djilas[15] has warned that this trend can have an upsetting effect on the social structure; in Czechoslovakia, Radovan Richta[16] has discussed similar developments that he has found evidenced.

CLERICAL AND SALES STRATA

The spread of bureaucracy has also entailed the rise of a third group: clerical and sales people, commonly known as "the (lower) white-collar class." This group has replaced traditional industrial occupations at a very rapid rate.

In 1870, clerical workers were only 0.6 percent of the American labor force, but by 1962 they had increased to 15.2 percent.[17] Virtually all clerical personnel in the nineteenth century were males, but by the twentieth century, as women generally increased their participation in the labor force, the majority of clerical workers were women. While the numbers of white-collar workers increased absolutely and as a proportion of the labor force, and their sexual composition changed, their incomes relative to those of industrial workers declined.[18]

In very recent years, many of the functions of clerical workers have been taken over by machines, an occurrence similar to that which was seen in the factory. Floyd Mann and Lawrence Williams[19] describe the changes in the office as the transfer of functions, the centralization of control, and the greater interdependence of the various units. Some jobs were subdivided and others enlarged; first-line supervisors were eliminated; and communication was formalized in order to maximize efficiency, coordinate work efforts, and to promote the rapid transmission of information. These types of transformations in office structure parallel earlier, similar changes in production lines.

In addition, Mann and Williams reported that as the most routine office tasks were eliminated with the introduction of machines, the work pace became more subject to control; work shifts were introduced into some offices and promotional opportunities were reduced in others. Mann and Williams suggested that office workers, in contrast to factory workers, were less prepared for the changes that took place. They noted:

> The value orientations of the white collar worker in large utility, insurance company and government offices are apparently different from the unskilled worker in the plant. The stability of these organizations has been an important factor for these security minded employees; the instability of the change over probably finds them, by personality and experience, less ready to meet the demands for adjustment.[20]

Office workers, then, though subjected to changes familiar to many production workers, faced different types of problems. In addition, in the United States, white-collar workers have traditionally rejected unionization, which no doubt exacerbated the problem of the individual worker as he or she struggled to adjust to the uncertainties created by the technological change.[21]

As the size of the clerical staff has grown, the personal relationship that many clerical workers had with their employers or immediate supervisors has disappeared. Clerks occupy a much more anonymous status in the bureaucracy today than they did some years ago.

The total number of persons involved in the sales of products has also grown astoundingly. Consistent with the development of specialization in other employment spheres, people are now increasingly becoming "specialists" concerning the particular product that they peddle. Totally new sales occupations—insurance, real estate, computer "engineer" salesperson—have emerged in postindustrial society. In the last century the percentage of salespeople in the labor force has approximately tripled.[22]

The epoch of postindustrialism, then, has led to a great increase in bureaucrats: managers, technocrats, and white-collar workers. But the omnipotence of modern bureaucratic structures should not cause us to lose sight of its historic development.[23] The emergence of this organizational form can be traced to the necessity of conducting a multitude of tasks in the coordination and control of large numbers of people. T. F. Tout[24] observed that public servants whose special sphere was administration and finance could be found in the earliest days of the English state. Tout reports, however, that the earliest English administrators held positions similar to the domestic servants of the ruler's court and were considered mere members of the king's household. It was not too long before the king's desire to obtain as much from his subjects as possible made the financial administration the first branch of the bureaucracy to achieve a separate, more prestigious life of its own. Changes in all institutional structures of the society eventually led to the organization of ever increasing numbers of spheres of social life along bureaucratic lines.

Social analysts who have contemplated postindustrial society have viewed these developments both positively and negatively. On the one hand, rule by bureaucracy decreases the possibility of an arbitrary exercise of power by an individual ruler or by the physically strong. When adhering to principles of rationality and efficiency, the leaders of a particular enterprise cannot treat their subordinates with the same erratic whimsy as did feudal chieftains, kings, or entrepreneurs. Yet rule by bureaucracy can stifle creative spirit and serve as a bulwark against the forces of social change.

Because of the ambiguous results that bureaucracy generates, many contemporary sociologists have addressed themselves to dissecting its nature and relating it to the social stratification of postindustrial societies.

The Characteristics of Postindustrial Society

Bell foresees a period in which those who control knowledge and institutions such as higher education will increasingly gain power. Scientists and researchers will become the dominant figures in the society. Education will replace inheritance as a primary means of access to power.[25] Merit based on expertise will have almost completely displaced both nepotism and evaluation on the basis of ascribed characteristics.

Michael Young, the English sociologist, does not take such a sanguine view of postindustrial society.[26] In an analysis written in the form of a fable not too far removed from reality as we know it, Young has predicted the rise (and possible fall) of "meritocracy." Young describes a postindustrial society in the year 2033; it is a place where inequalities due to accidents of birth have been abolished. People rise to the higher positions in organizations because of their intelligence, measured by increasingly refined tests, and their effort. Once they have been admitted to the "meritocracy" at the top of the bureaucracy, they contribute their abilities to the welfare of society and are rewarded accordingly. Everyone with an IQ score over 125 finds a position in the elite. This elite group demands special educational privileges for its children and marries only people with equally high intelligence scores. Social groups such as trade unions, which represent the lower classes in society, progressively lose their more talented leaders. In time the "masses," led by a group of discontented intelligent women, revolt against the meritocracy and it is eventually destroyed.

Although Young's book is fiction, it raises some serious questions about whether equalized opportunity based on achieved rather than ascribed characteristics can have the virtuous results that some of its defenders believe. As Bell points out, "The post-industrial society, in its initial logic, is essentially a meritocracy, since differential status and differential income are based on technical skills and higher education."[27] How may the processes of differentiation and differential evaluation in such a system create their own opponents and conflicts? At least two sources of potential discontent can be identified in postindustrial society: education and conditions within the bureaucracy itself.

The educational system would seem, superficially at least, to be an unlikely source for creating feelings of inequity. After all, a good part of the ideological defense of a society is presumed to be rational and democratic in its basic organization and rests heavily on the shoulders of the schools.[28] It is asserted that public schools, particularly in the United States, equalize opportunity and allow those who are diligent and capable to obtain positions in the social structure commensurate with these characteristics.

However, Samuel Bowles has argued that schools, as they have emerged in the United States, serve to perpetuate rather than alleviate certain inequalities in the social structure.[29] He contends that the use of testing to track youngsters into "honors," average, or slow groups and of counseling to send children into academic or trade curricula within schools, as well as variation in educational experiences between schools, parallels the stratification of the work force found in large-scale bureaucracies.[30] Hence the majority of children of blue-collar workers receive an education different from that of children of professionals or wealthy families, which restricts their social mobility. Further, because of increased opportunities to pursue higher education since World War II, the expectation that one would receive a reward commensurate with the increased number of years spent in schools has been created. But during periods of severe economic recession, rewards in the form of desired occupations may not be available.[31] Under such conditions, public schools can contribute to the creation of groups that come into conflict with those who are more privileged. Simultaneously, many people may also reject the importance of schools, thus undermining the school's capacity to serve as a mechanism for legitimating the structure of power.

In addition, two characteristics of bureaucratic growth in postindustrial society may also contribute to the emergence of disenchanted people. First, although the expertise required of elite positions in bureaucratic organizations allows mobility via the transferability of administrative skills, the prolonged and highly specialized knowledge of technicians and many professionals prohibits their career movement outside of narrowly defined areas.

Second, the characteristics of bureaucratic organization commonly conflict with the values of the professional or with the daily tasks confronting staff engaged in providing services to people.[32] In the first instance the definition of professionalism includes having a range and depth of specialized knowledge and discretion as to the application of expertise to fit the needs of a particular situation. Prolonged socialization and periodic certification procedures are used as assurance that knowledge is adequate. Evaluation or social control of professionals is to be provided by colleagues since only they share the presumed expertise. Hierarchical control over the activities of professionals or a detailed a priori specification of work characteristics in bureaucratic settings conflicts with the nature of professionalism.

Professionalism itself has been undergoing changes in recent decades. Whereas the established professions were limited to doctors, lawyers, the clergy, and professors a few decades ago, Martin Oppenheimer has observed that "more recently, scientists, engineers, nurses, school teachers, social workers and others have swelled the ranks of what are defined as the professions.''[33] Many of these professionals are employed directly or indirectly by the public sector. Between 1940 and 1969, for example, the number of government employees (local, federal, and state) increased from 4.4 million to 12.7 million. In addition, many scientists and engineers, though employed by private industries, are dependent on government contracts.[34]

The employment of many professionals by large-scale bureaucratic organizations in recent years has led to much research and discussion.[35] However, alienation and the formation of discontented groups of professionals are not necessary facts of postindustrial society. The enormous scale of units where many professionals work requires much coordination and efficient recordkeeping. Dual structures have developed in such organizations as hospitals and universities. In these organizations large numbers of professionals work together with the bureaucratic administrative personnel to provide their services.

The nature of the relationship between the administrative and professional staff may vary. Although the work is not exhaustive of the possible types of relationships that occur, Robin Pardini[36] has described university administrations from four divergent perspectives:

1. The *angel above* perspective operates on the assumption that the welfare of the institution is best served by professional administrators who alone have a broad and long-run picture.

2. The *devil above* perspective views administrators as individuals who serve the interests of business people and politicians who control the university.

3. The *angel below* perspective views the administration as supportive of the expert faculty members.

4. The *devil below* perspective pictures administrators as police officers and bookkeepers who enforce policies, account for the expenditure of funds, and monitor the faculty.

Clearly, when any but the *angel below* perspective is followed, professional discretion and autonomy may be limited in any bureaucratic setting, resulting in the deterioration of job satisfaction.

Caution must be exercised in reaching oversimplified conclusions. Data reported by Gerald Moeller[37] in his investigation of teachers were initially collected with the expectation that teachers working in highly bureaucratized schools would be more likely to report an attitude of powerlessness in their ability to affect specific courses of action than those teachers in less bureaucratized settings. Contrary to this expectation, however, Moeller concluded on the basis of his data that faculties employed in *more* bureaucratized schools felt they had *more* power than those in less bureaucratized schools.

In reviewing his data, Moeller found that in less bureaucratic schools many people (for example, teachers, parents and the public) had access to those who set school policy. In these schools he found an air of uncertainty based on the unpredictability of decisions, and this in turn operated to abrogate a sense of power. Greater bureaucratization, on the other hand, allowed teachers to feel that they were being dealt with rationally and they therefore felt less alienated.

Nonetheless, in mammoth hierarchical systems such as General Motors, the City University of New York, or the federal government, procedures, lines of authority, communication channels, and areas of responsibility may be obscured, thus creating an air of uncertainty and a feeling of powerlessness. Further, since in these organizations, the staff of the various subunits (each bureaucratically organized) provides input into the decision processes of the larger administrative unit, the complexities of the enormous structures can serve to *decrease* rather than increase the perception of rationality and efficiency, resulting in more rather than less intense feelings of powerlessness on the part of the participants.

Disaffection with the conditions of bureaucratic existence can have many consequences ranging from withdrawal of the individual[38] to active organization as a mode of confronting the power of the bureaucracy. As we have already observed, there has been a traditional distaste for unionization among professional and white-collar workers. In the past, professionals for the most part chose to participate only in professional societies, and white-collar workers remained detached from any organization.

Recently some professional societies as well as individual lawyers, professors, school administrators, scientists, physicians, and other professionals have chosen to affiliate with unions.[39] In 1972, for example, professors in eight schools of the New Jersey state university system elected to join with the American Federation of Teachers (an AFL-CIO affiliate) rather than remain with the National Education Association, which is a professional society and not a union. Oppenheimer has noted that while the overall proportion of unionized labor declined about 1 percent (from 23.6 to 22.6 percent) between 1960 and 1970, the proportion of white-collar workers among all American unionists increased by 4 percent (from 12 to 16 percent) during the same period. Although this represents only a minority of the professional and white-collar population, it perhaps reflects some change in attitudes. Certainly the strikes of many professionals during the 1960s and 70s, including teachers, medical workers and lawyers, document a change in attitudes of these workers.

The alteration of the social structure consistent with the bureaucratic inequalities noted in the United States is not restricted to nations of similar economic and political systems. Analogous, if not identical, changes have been reported even in those nations with political and eco-

nomic systems designed to decrease the span between the managers and
the managed and the shape of the stratification system.

Milovan Djilas, formerly a high member of the Yugoslavian Communist party, has considered this issue in the context of socialist nations.[40]
He has argued that the bureaucrats of the communist nations, and technicians and scientists, constitute a new stratum that holds unprecedented
power. However, instead of obtaining power on the basis of control over
economic resources, as predicted by orthodox Marxists, the new class of
managers and bureaucrats has achieved its position through politics and
control over the administrative apparatus. They have not benefited from
direct inheritance or from other economic advantages enjoyed by the elite
in capitalist nations. They are, nonetheless, a privileged class with untrammeled power.

Djilas's analysis of stratification in socialist postindustrial countries
parallels that of James Burnham, who has described capitalist nations as
well as communist ones.[41] Although Burnham's description of this new
managerial class was often vague and some of his more specific political
predictions (for instance, that Germany would win World War II) were
flatly wrong, few can deny that postindustrial corporations, enterprises,
and governments have produced groups that experience a relatively high
degree of autonomy and enjoy economic privileges.

Alain Touraine has noted tendencies in France[42] similar to the ones
Bell has pointed out in the United States and Djilas has found in Yugoslavia. Touraine believes that the changes may have a positive rather than
negative impact on the society. He argues that advanced industrial nations are moving into a "programmed" age of large-scale political and
economic planning. He contends that the elite who control the "programs" of the postindustrial society may conflict with those at the bottom
of the social ladder who are manipulated and controlled. But he believes
in the possibility of merging the new technocratic elite with the more
"advanced" segment of the working class. Possibly, argues Touraine, a
new "participatory regime" will emerge allowing workers, technocrats,
and managers to cooperate in the running of postindustrial societies.

Other scholars, such as Ralf Dahrendorf, also recognize that society
has been altered by the ongoing industrial revolution.[43] He has noted that
ownership of property is no longer a prerequisite of "postcapitalist"
societies. Authority exercised administratively in the economic sphere
has assumed paramount importance. Consistent with such analysis, Norman Birnbaum has noted that the increased power on the part of management is a result of integration of knowledge with the command process.[44]
Unlike Touraine, however, Birnbaum does not foresee any advance in
political awareness on the part of the lower strata in postindustrial
societies.

Despite different outcomes posed by the many analysts of postindustrial society, there appears to be one recurrent theme: social power and advantage have shifted in the postindustrial era from a real-property-class base to differentiation based on achieved skills and mental abilities. The result of this change for the social stratification of particular nations can be seen only in the study of particular case histories. Let us look at two politically and economically diverse regions of the world: Eastern Europe and Scandinavia.

Social Stratification in Eastern Europe

By choice or force, Eastern European nations have adopted a system that theoretically espouses the goal of equality. Social classes, in the sense of groups that own the means of production, have been abolished. Yet a bureaucratic system of elites who have power and privileges extending far beyond that of the average citizen of these nations has emerged.

In Russia, for example, as Trotsky observed, "the means of production belong to the state. But the state, so to speak, 'belongs' to the bureaucracy. . . . It is in the full sense of the word the sole privileged and commanding *stratum* in Soviet Society."[45] Although Trotsky's original judgment in 1937 was undoubtedly ideological, a variety of recent empirical studies within the Soviet Union have confirmed the emergence of a new bureaucratic stratum in this supposedly classless society. A. M. Rumiantsev, a member of the Communist party, has reported data that indicate that the "intelligentsia" (that is, people who earn their living by "mental labor") comprised about one-fifth of all workers in Russia in 1965 and earned much more money than the average laborer.[46] These "mental" laborers (roughly the equivalent of managers, bureaucrats, and the white-collar class in America) have a strong tendency to grant similar positions and even their wealth to their descendants.[47] Further, members of the bureaucratic stratum send their children to special "prep schools."[48] As N. M. Blinov has observed, "class differences still have a strong influence upon social advancement of the individual and, therefore, the class structure as a social element plays a leading part in the formation of individual personality."[49]

In addition, traditional "interest groups" tied in with particular professions have continued to wield power within the Russian system. The military, for example, adhere to certain goals and maintain a set of values that set them apart from the common citizenry and often lead to conflicts with the ruling Communist party.[50] Russia's emergence as a superpower has necessarily entailed the growth of a sophisticated, well-trained officer corps that often asserts its prime interest of defending the Soviet Union *against* the wishes of political leaders. Specifically, the officer corps desires a high level of investment in heavy industry (which puts it into conflict with those who are oriented to the production of consumer goods) and a high level of investment in the military sector (thus depriving other units of the Soviet economy). It often depicts the activities of other nations as aggressive (undermining those in the political hierarchy who seek detente) and it seeks to maintain its authority and prestige in the formulation of strategic policies (so formulating them at times to conflict with other political interests). The military in Russia have apparently developed an ideology of their specialized function, high duties, and their selfless service to the nation that is not too different from that of the military professionals in other nations.[51]

In revering their own profession, many military officers implicitly deny the economic determinism of Marxism. They would appear to believe in a militaristic ideology best summarized by General Makeev, the editor-in-chief of *Red Star:*

> The concept of military honor has existed since time immemorial. . . bravery, selfless dedication, and military skill were revered. . . . The officer is at war for a lifetime. . . . How many inconveniences, how many trials! But the officer withstands all, overcomes all. He holds high his honor, the honor of the officer and citizen.[52]

In upholding the "immemorial" concept of "military honor," however, the officer corps may find itself at odds with Marxist ideals, which portray the eventual classless society as the final antidote to war.

Russian officers are not, of course, alone in defending their particular interests. Peasants, intellectuals, industrial managers and workers, and political bureaucrats also form distinct strata in conflict with each other.[53] The abolition of social classes in Russia, then, has not resulted in equality but in a transformation of the forms of social stratification.*

In Poland, a similar phenomenon has occurred. Before World War II, Poland was essentially an agrarian nation ruled by a landed aristocracy.[55] The devastation of the war resulted in the destruction of 22 percent of all Poles, the obliteration of the landed aristocracy, and a decimation of the "intelligentsia" (high civil service and "intellectual" workers). With the

---

*Even in China, the closest approximation to a modern equalitarian society, distinct and often bloody differences arise between peasants, industrial workers and managers (who apparently view their interests as similar), and the party bureaucracy. Those who "represent" the interests of these various groups within the party hierarchy sometimes find themselves in irreparable conflict.[54]

advent of a People's Republic after the war, Poland vastly increased its industrial production, rebuilt its cities, essentially abolished its old class system, and underwent rapid urbanization.[56]

One result of these changes, as in Russia, was to produce a great increase in managerial, clerical, and scientific workers, who, in the 1970s, make up about 18 percent of the working population.[57]

This new bureaucratic class possesses many advantages over the average worker in income, in the ability to secure comfortable housing, in the possession of cars and other amenities, and in the capacity to gain admission for its children into institutions of higher learning.[58] Although the Polish government imposed a quota of working-class or peasant students who must be admitted to institutions of higher education, there has been a steady *decline* since 1951 in the proportion of students who actually came from these backgrounds.[59] Most Polish sociologists recognize that the emergence of these "class" distinctions was a necessary, if undesirable, feature of their society, required in order to achieve even more rapid economic growth.[60]

Radovan Richta and other scholars in Czechoslovakia, in a unique deviation from sociological thinking in other Eastern European nations, have considered the consequences of the emergence of postindustrial societies in relation to the assumptions of Marxist theory. Although squarely within the Soviet sphere of influence, these Czech scholars have noted that the emergence of a postindustrial society (in their nation as well as in capitalist lands) requires a drastic revision in Marxist thought concerning social stratification.[61]

In effect, Richta recognizes the emergence of a new class that derives its power from technical knowledge, the emergence of "service" classes that eclipse the traditional working class in influence, and the possibility that the new conflicts will emerge between the managers and the managed. This analysis, if correct, undermines the traditional Marxist conception of classes with its preoccupation with the industrial proletariat as the vanguard of the future and its conception of a property-owning bourgeoisie as a ruling class in capitalist countries.

Whether they wish it or not, then, it appears that Eastern European theorists must deal with the emergence of new forms of social stratification, just as scholars of other advanced but capitalist nations must do.

Social Stratification in Scandinavia

Although the Scandinavian countries—Sweden, Denmark, Norway, Iceland, and Finland—have been ruled by "social democratic" political parties, they have remained essentially capitalist nations. Despite extensive social welfare programs, an average of 90 percent of the productive wealth of these nations is held by private interests. Like the United States and Eastern Europe, Scandinavia has entered the postindustrial period.

During the twentieth century, Scandinavian nations have experienced increasing urbanization and affluence and have established welfare states. Advanced programs of social welfare—child allowances for families, nationalized medicine, comfortable homes for the aged, and an extension of public education—have reduced the span of inequality between the landowning and bourgeois classes and the peasant and laborer classes. In 1800, for example, a supreme court judge in Norway received about sixty times the income of an unskilled worker.[62] In the late-twentieth century, he earns about six times the income of a worker.[63]

The reduction in the gap between incomes, however, has not automatically resulted in changes in social prestige or power between different groups. Occupation, particularly of the postindustrial category, strongly affects one's social standing. The Danish *Who Is Who,* for example, lists not only an individual's occupation, but the father's occupation and that of the father-in-law.[64]

Education, as in the United States, is increasingly important as a measure of social prestige. Although a somewhat higher proportion of all children pass the matriculation examination for entrance to a university than in the past, university students still come overwhelmingly from the ranks of those whose fathers hold high-status occupations. For example, 58 percent of the sons of professionals in Norway passed the crucial examination but only 3 percent of the children of forest or agricultural workers passed it.[65]

The most vital changes in Scandinavia's system of social stratification, according to Kaare Svlastoga and Gosta Carlsson, have been the decline in importance of the nobility and farmers, the disappearance of slaves, and the emergence of a well-educated, technocratic group with predominant importance.[66] As in other nations, white-collar postindustrial groups have gained in influence and power:

> Social power seems to be quite unevenly distributed in Scandinavia. . . . Such power will most of the time appear in the form of authority vested in an office. . . . With the increasing predominance of large-scale organizations (the expanding government, employers' unions, and employees' unions, larger productive units, etc.) it seems that the power gap between the top and the bottom may be widening.[67]

Since education is of increasing importance as a way of gaining power in large organizations, and since access to higher education is largely limited to the children of parents who already hold such positions, it would appear that Scandinavia may also be developing a privileged bureaucratic class with a strong tendency to exclude outsiders from their ranks. In this characteristic, the Scandinavian groups—despite a different political orientation—exhibit the same trends as do Eastern Europe, most of Western Europe, and the United States.

Conclusions

As we survey the span of human history—the extinction of male-dominated "simple" societies, the erosion yet continued durability of the caste system, the rise and fall of slavery, the emergence of new classes of bourgeoisie and proletarians, and, most recently, the appearance of new bureaucratic classes in industrial and postindustrial societies—five basic questions about social stratification must be faced:

1. Is inequality an inherent part of human society?
2. If it is, should we strive to produce a system of equality of opportunity where all will run the race for social distinction and power unhobbled by arbitrary shackles?
3. Should we seek a system of equality where no person will be deprived of health, welfare, or freedom, at least as far as this can be humanly achieved?
4. If we search for greater equality in power and privilege, what will be the consequences in other spheres of our society? Will economic productivity be affected? Will "culture"—art, literature, philosophy—be changed to fit the taste of the "average" person?
5. What, in philosophical terms, would be an ideally equitable (fair or just) distribution of power, privilege, status, and wealth in society?

These are both empirical and ethical problems. Some "elitists"—such as Aristotle, Mosca, Pareto, Ortega y Gasset, and Freud—have argued that the search for equality is fruitless, inequitable, and damaging to civilization. "Egalitarians" like Proudhon, Kropotkin, Marx, and Buber have contended that the creation of equalitarian societies is both practical and equitable.

Before we can consider the philosophical implications of these questions for the United States, we must examine the nature and impact of social stratification as it exists in contemporary America. Once having reviewed the nature of this class system, its effects on various aspects of life, its close links with racism and sexism, and various recent attempts to eliminate inequality, we will then be in a better position to evaluate the various philosophical judgments concerning equality and equity. Only through a fusion of empirical evidence and philosophical contemplation can we propose rational policies that may lead to the creation of a just society.

Notes

1. Daniel Bell, *The Coming of Post-Industrial Society* (New York: Basic Books, 1973).
2. Department of Commerce, Bureau of Labor Statistics, cited in *The New York Times*, Part 3, February 23, 1975, p. 1.
3. Organization for Economic Cooperation and Development, *Economic Report*, Paris, 1969.
4. Bell, *Coming of Post-Industrial Society*, p. 17.
5. Ibid., p. 358.
6. Ibid., p. 18
7. Ibid., p. 33.
8. Ibid.
9. James Burnham, *The Managerial Revolution* (Bloomington: Indiana University Press, 1960).
10. C. Wright Mills, *The Power Elite* (New York: Oxford University Press, 1956), p. 147.
11. Gerhard Lenski, *Power and Privilege* (New York: McGraw-Hill, 1966).
12. Talcott Parsons, *Structure and Process in Modern Society* (New York: Free Press, 1960), pp. 209–210.
13. See J. R. French and B. Raven, "The Bases of Social Power," in D. Cartwright, ed., *Studies in Social Power* (Ann Arbor: University of Michigan, Institute for Social Research, 1959).
14. See, for example, Burton Clark, *Educating the Expert Society* (San Francisco: Chandler, 1962).
15. Milovan Djilas, *The New Class* (New York: Praeger, 1957).
16. Czechoslovak Academy of Science, *Civilization at the Crossroads: Social and Human Implications of the Scientific and Technological Revolution*, 1967.
17. Lenski, *Power and Privilege*, p. 369.
18. Ibid., p. 371.
19. Floyd Mann and Lawrence Williams, "Organizational Impact of White Collar Automation," *Annual Proceedings*, Industrial Relations Research Association, 1958.
20. Ibid., p. 60.
21. Seymour Martin Lipset, "White Collar Workers and Professionals—Their Attitudes and Behavior Toward Unions," in William A. Faunce, ed., *Industrial Sociology* (New York: Appleton-Century-Crofts, 1967), pp. 525–548.
22. Lenski, *Power and Privilege*, p. 373.
23. H. H. Girth and C. W. Mills, eds., *Max Weber: Essays in Sociology* (New York: Oxford University Press, 1946), p. 204.
24. T. F. Tout, "The Emergence of a Bureaucracy," in R. Merton et al., eds., *Reader in Bureaucracy* (Glencoe, Ill.: Free Press, 1952), pp. 68–78.
25. Bell, *Coming of Post-industrial Society*, p. 359.
26. Michael Young, *The Rise of Meritocracy* (London: Penguin, 1958).
27. Bell, *Coming of Post-industrial Society*, p. 409.
28. See, for example, David W. Swift, *American Education: A Sociological View* (Boston: Houghton Mifflin, 1976), Chapter 1.
29. Samuel Bowles, "Unequal Education and the Reproduction of the Social Division of Labor," in Elizabeth Useem and Michael Useem, eds., *The Education Establishment* (Englewood Cliffs, N.J.: Prentice-Hall, 1974).
30. Ibid., p. 21.
31. See, for example, "Who Needs College?" *Newsweek*, April 26, 1976, pp. 60–69.

32. See, for example, Ronald G. Corwin, *Education in Crisis* (New York: Wiley, 1974), Chapter 2.
33. Martin Oppenheimer, "The Unionization of the Professional," *Social Policy* (January–February 1975): 34–40.
34. Ibid., p. 34.
35. See, for example, William Kornhauser, *Scientists in Industry: Conflict and Accommodation* (Berkeley: University of California Press, 1962); Simon Marcson, *The Scientist in American Industry* (New York: Harper & Row, 1960); Harold Wilensky, *Intellectuals in Labor Unions* (Glencoe, Ill.: Free Press, 1956).
36. Robin J. Pardini, "A Problem for Every Solution: Perspectives on the Study of University Administration," *Journal of the Society of Research Administrators* 4 (Summer 1972): 6–27.
37. Gerald Moeller, "Relationship Between Bureaucracy in School Systems and Teachers' Sense of Power," *School Review* (Summer 1964).
38. See, for example, Robert K. Merton, *Social Theory and Social Structure,* (Glencoe, Ill.: Free Press, 1957), chap. 8.
39. Oppenheimer, "Unionization of the Professional."
40. Djilas, *New Class.*
41. Burnham, *Managerial Revolution.*
42. Alain Touraine, *La Société Post-industrielle* (Paris: Denoel, 1969).
43. Ralf Dahrendorf, *Class and Class Conflict in Industrial Society* (Stanford, Calif.: Stanford University Press, 1959).
44. Norman Birnbaum, *The Crisis of Industrial Society* (New York: Oxford University Press, 1969).
45. Leon Trotsky, *The Revolution Betrayed* (1937), cited in Bell, *Coming of Post-Industrial Society.*
46. Ibid., p. 103.
47. See Tev Katz, *Hereditary Elements in Education and Social Structure in the U.S.S.R.,* University of Glasgow, Institute of Soviet and East European Studies, 1969.
48. Ibid.
49. Cited in ibid., p. 4.
50. See Roman Kokowicz, "Interest Groups in Soviet Politics: The Case of the Military," *Comparative Politics* 2 (April 1970).
51. Morris Janowitz, *The Professional Soldier* (New York: Free Press, 1960).
52. Quoted in *Izvestia*, February 12, 1963.
53. Leonard J. Cohen and Jane P. Shapiro, eds., *Communist Systems in Comparative Perspective* (New York: Doubleday Anchor, 1974).
54. Michel Oksenberg, "Occupational Groups in Chinese Society and the Cultural Revolution," *The Cultural Revolution: 1967 in Review,* Michigan Papers in Chinese, No. 2, Ann Arbor: University of Michigan, Center for Chinese Studies.
55. Michalina Vaughan, "Poland," in Margaret Soctford Archer and Salvador Giner, eds., *Contemporary Europe* (New York: St. Martin's, 1975).
56. Ibid.
57. Ibid., p. 325.
58. See, for example, William McCord, *The Springtime of Freedom* (New York: Oxford University Press, 1965).
59. J. Szczepanski, *Sociological Problems of Higher Education* (Warsaw: Academy of Arts and Sciences, 1963).
60. J. Lagneau, *Stratification et Egalitairisme,* doctoral thesis, Paris University, 1968.
61. Radovan Richta, *Civilization at the Crossroads* (Prague: Czechoslovak Academy of Science, 1967).

62. S. Steen, *Det Gamle Sanfunn* (Oslo: 1957).
63. Kaare Svlastoga and Gosta Carlsson, *Scandinavia in Contemporary Europe* in T.R. Bottomore, *op. cit.*
64. Ibid., p. 359.
65. O. Ramsøy, *Samfunnsbygning og Skolesokning* (Oslo: 1957).
66. K. Svlastoga and G. Carlsson, *Scandinavia in Contemporary Europe*, p. 364.
67. Ibid., p. 361.

PART II

Power and Equity in Contemporary America

All postindustrial, capitalist nations exhibit gross differences in income between the rich and the poor. Some countries—notably the Netherlands, Sweden, and Norway—have reduced this inequality and yet maintained vigorous economic growth over the last few decades. The United States, Spain, and France, in contrast, exhibit the most pronounced inequalities in wealth.

In 1976, the pattern of income distribution looked like this:

The poorest percent of households get:	
France	1.4 percent
Spain	1.5 percent
Australia	1.6 percent
United States	1.7 percent
Britain	2.4 percent
Norway	2.4 percent
Sweden	2.6 percent
Japan	2.7 percent
Germany	2.8 percent
Netherlands	3.2 percent

The richest percent of households get:	
Sweden	18.6 percent
Netherlands	21.8 percent
Norway	21.9 percent
Britain	23.9 percent
Canada	24.7 percent
Australia	25.2 percent
United States	26.1 percent
Japan	27.8 percent
Spain	28.5 percent
France	30.5 percent
Germany	30.6 percent

Source: Organization for Economic Cooperation and Development.[1]

This means that the rich in the Netherlands received somewhat less than seven times as much as the poor. In the United States, the rich absorbed fifteen times the income of the poor, nineteen times in Spain, and twenty-two times in France.

In America, this great discrepancy in wealth (which, of course, grows even to more majestic levels when one compares Americans with citizens of developing nations) has numerous implications. As we show in Chapter 5, inequality affects differences in political influence, treatment before the law, educational attainment, health, and, indeed, almost every facet of life.

In the American context, inequalities in wealth are further aggravated by inequalities that derive from racial and sexual status. In Chapter 6, we examine some of the profound effects of these forms of discrimination.

Since the founding of the nation, some American leaders have been deeply disturbed by the various forms of inequality that have scarred the nation. They have launched a number of programs to reduce inequality and, most recently, a "war on poverty." In Chapter 7, we evaluate the consequences of some of these more important strategies to end inequality.

Note

1. Cited in Clyde H. Farnsworth, "France, the Income Disparity Is Great," *The New York Times*, September 10, 1976.

5

THE IMPACT OF
STRATIFICATION
IN AMERICA

Despite prevailing ideals of equality and equality of opportunity, contemporary America is a nation of vast discrepancies in power and privilege. The differences between the various social strata are revealed not only in wealth and the material possessions it buys but also in such aspects of life as:

the possibility of changing occupation

the chance of finishing college

the degree of political involvement and power

the possibility of leading a healthy life

the chance of convincing a legislature to pass a law

the risk of mental disease

the odds of being arrested by the police

the degree of autonomy in work

all the basics of life—from clothes to food

Few Americans are consciously aware of how their position in the social stratification system affects their existence. In this chapter, we will document some of the more crucial effects of social stratification upon Americans.

Objective Differences in Wealth: America and the Third World

With the exception of depressions in 1891, early 1921, 1929, and 1975, the American economy has been steadily growing and producing more and more goods. Because of this expansion, the material lot of Americans has been greatly improved: the dream of equality of opportunity would seem to have been fulfilled—yet there are two major qualifications.

First, the limits of economic expansion in America may have been reached. In their dreams of equality, few Americans have realized the consequences of this fact. Second, although objective differences in income between various social strata have not decreased, most Americans believe that the gap between rich and poor has narrowed. The ramifications of these facts for stratification in America must be examined since these two phenomena may radically alter the traditional ideals that have pervaded American life.

HAVE THE LIMITS OF ECONOMIC GROWTH BEEN REACHED?

Robert Heilbroner, among other sophisticated social scientists, believes that several factors severely limit the hope of future economic expansion.[1] Among several pieces of evidence, Heilbroner bases his gloomy assessment on such facts as these:

1. The growth of world population, if uncontrolled in the next thirty generations, will result in each human being occupying $1/32$ of a square inch of the globe's surface.[2]

2. One H-bomb would release one thousand times the energy of the atomic bomb that destroyed Hiroshima. In 1974 America possessed 11,000 warheads of the H-bomb capacity and Russia had at least 1,200.[3]

3. The sheer increase in energy around the earth could, in the quite near future, result in an increase in the earth's temperature to about 50°C., "a condition totally unsuitable for human habitation."[4]

These startling statistics may spell an end to the American quest for economic advancement.

As a first step to understanding their position in the world's stratification system, Americans must realize that a good part of the world's population is diseased, starving, and near death. Parasitic diseases, where organisms attach themselves to the internal organs of the host-victim, afflict up to 50 percent of South American children, 60 percent of African children, and 92 percent of Asian children.[5]

World population has grown from about one billion in 1650 to approximately four billion in the 1970s, and a conservative estimate is that it will reach five billion by the year 2000.[6] The population expansion began around 1750 with the advent of industrialization. Until that point, population had been relatively constant. In the twentieth century the world population doubles every thirty-seven years. This means that a relatively small country such as Mexico could have two billion people in one hundred years.[7] There is simply not enough food on this planet to feed so many people. As Johnson C. Montgomery has stated: "There have never been more miserable, deprived people in the world than there are right now."[8]

Population increases necessitate greater food production, the consumption of more energy, and the depletion of resources. Americans were shocked by the energy crisis of the 1970s, and some authorities doubt that food supplies and energy reserves can continue to support our own population in the immediate future.[9] To maintain the standard of living of the 1970s in America, this nation must necessarily be involved in a series of confrontations with countries that control some of our energy resources, such as the Middle Eastern countries, and with those that desperately need our extra food supplies, such as India. On a world scale, then, maintenance of "the American standard of living" could require other nations to remain at a poverty level or prompt them to try to seize some of America's abundance through military force.

Further, as population increases, the quest for food becomes more urgent. Food production has increased with the introduction of new seeds, fertilizers, and methods. This has been called the "green revolution." On a per capita basis, however, food production went up briefly during the early 1970s and then returned to approximately the same rate that had prevailed in 1956.[10] This failure of agriculture to outstrip population has serious effects. For instance, in 1975 India lacked an unprecedented seven million tons of grain to feed her population.[11] Obviously, this gap meant starvation of thousands in the less-rich agricultural regions of India such as Assam, West Bengal, Bihar, and Orissa. In the same year Nigeria, an oil-rich African nation, earned enough to spend $2.5 billion to improve its agricultural production. Simultaneously, Ghana, a near neighbor without oil, inaugurated a program to try to feed itself. It was an impossible goal since the cost of Ghana's oil imports, much of them from Nigeria, rose from $53 million in 1973 to $200 million in 1975.[12] Thus in the same geographical region the fortunes of one nation meant disaster for another. Similarly, in 1975 Morocco was able to raise the world price of phosphate, one of the basic ingredients of fertilizers, by 450 percent. Without fertilizers, nations like Bangladesh and Pakistan face famine. Yet, these nations have no way of paying Morocco the price of these commodities. Again, there is a temporary advantage of one nation over others that remain in severe need.[13]

Changes in the world's climate have further endangered the world's already meager food supply. Central Africa, Bangladesh, and parts of China and Russia have experienced droughts and floods. A drought in a huge section of central Africa destroyed arable lands for the foreseeable future.[14] Some experts believe that changes in the climate over the next century will condemn large masses of people to starvation.[15]

Unless relatively well-endowed nations such as the United States voluntarily give food, sell it below world price, or exchange it for such other resources as oil, there is no way that most people of the globe can avoid mass starvation. Unfortunately, at the current rate of consumption, it appears that all the world's known sources of energy will soon be exhausted[16] and there will be nothing left to trade for food.

"Consumption of the earth's stores of fossil fuels has barely started," Harrison Brown observed in 1954, "and yet already we can see the end."[17] In fact, all other forms of energy are rapidly disappearing. Shortages of oil, coal, and electrical power became acute in the 1970s, just as some scientists had predicted in the 1950s.

Scientists hope that nuclear fusion can eventually provide the planet with the energy it requires. The development of new technologies, however, carries with it the danger that the planet may become uninhabitable because of the intense heat which is generated.[18] The Council on Environmental Quality warns that even the slightest increase in the amount of radiation generated on earth could overheat the atmosphere to the point of melting the polar icecap.[19]

Because of the imminent danger that the world's sources of energy will be depleted by the beginning of the next century, some authoritative groups have suggested that the United States should drastically reduce consumption and begin to ration energy.[20] A commission of scientists has suggested that rationed "energy stamps" should be issued, that all cars should conform to minimum energy-use standards, and that the growth in energy use in America should be reduced from a rate of 4.5 percent a year to 2 percent a year.[21] According to one opponent of the report,[22] such a policy could result in "perpetual economic stagnation" for the nation.

The world may also be running out of oxygen, at least for residents of such cities as Los Angeles and New York. News reports in these cities predict whether the air level will be "acceptable" or not the next day. Los Angeles residents who suffer from diseases such as emphysema and older people stay indoors when smog covers the city.[23]

Poisoning of America's waters offers another threat to human survival. Great bodies of water—the Hudson River, Great Kills Bay, Lake Erie, the bays of New York—have become inhospitable to people and deadly for fish. Industries dump chemicals into rivers, lakes, and oceans that kill life and drastically upset the ecological balance. Occasional oil spills off the coast of places like Santa Barbara, the closing of a river near New York, and the obliteration of life in the lake bordering Cleveland underline the hazards of the pollution of water resources.

The potential effects of water poisoning go far beyond these incidents. As David W. Ehrenfeld has pointed out, any hope for desalinating water so that it will be drinkable or of cultivating the sea for new sources of food depends on two conditions.[24] First, the seas of the world must remain unpolluted, but this is unlikely to occur if unmonitored industrial growth occurs in both advanced and underdeveloped nations. Second, huge quantities of existing energy would have to be expended to achieve these goals and, as we have already noted, the energy resources of the globe are close to being exhausted.

One further threat to the American standard of living must be noted. Many of the poorest nations in the world have either developed or have the capacity to manufacture nuclear weapons. Although it may take decades before they can make the necessary delivery systems, the potential for human devastation still exists. Heilbroner has made the grim but not unreasonable forecast that since many nations possess nuclear capabilities the nuclear bomb "may be used as an instrument of blackmail to force the developed world to undertake a massive transfer of wealth to the poverty-stricken world."[25] As Heilbroner has commented: "Two considerations give a new credibility to nuclear terrorism: *nuclear weaponry for the first time makes such action possible; and 'wars of redistribution' may be the only way by which the poor nations can hope to remedy their condition.*"[26] He reasons that this may occur because industrialized nations will never give more than token aid to developing nations, which will increasingly be faced with population pressures that make any increase in their income inconceivable. Other social scientists believe that "the politics of catastrophe" will become a reality in the 1990s and that the twenty-first century may be the "era of Annihilation."[27]

If the limits of economic growth in America have been reached—either because of population pressures, the exhaustion of resources, or the threat of nuclear warfare—Americans must drastically revise their expectations. Instead of an expanding economy, which in the past supported the American stratification system, Americans face a steadily shrinking supply of wealth. Conceivably, for the next few generations, Americans, particularly of the upper class, might be able to maintain their privileges— an island of plenty in the midst of a world of increasing misery and desperation. Somehow, however, consumption will eventually have to be cut—with unpredictable, possibly violent repercussions for America's class system.

The ramifications of a spread in global poverty on the existing American system of social stratification would be immense. Faced with a decrease in consumption or a stagnant economy, the average American will begin to face a fact of social life that he or she has long ignored: the stark discrepancies that separate the upper strata in America from the lower.

EXISTING DIFFERENCES IN WEALTH IN AMERICA

Within American society there are profound gaps between the wealth of different social strata. In 1973, 14.6 percent of all American families lived at the poverty level, earning less than $5,000 per year. In contrast, 1 percent of American families received $50,000 a year or more in income.[28] If income had been distributed with absolute equality, the average family in 1973 would have earned $19,648 a year.[29] Although the total income of Americans approximately doubled between 1947 and 1973, because of an expansion in the economy, the distribution of income among different strata remained highly unequal.[30]

Private corporations control much of the wealth in the United States. General Motors, for example, owned fifty times the wealth of the entire state of Nevada and eight times that of New York State.[31] As A. A. Berle has observed:

> Not only do 500 corporations control two-thirds of the non-farm economy but . . . a still smaller group has the ultimate decision-making power. This is, I think, the highest concentration of economic power in recorded history. Since the United States carries on not quite half of the manufacturing production of the entire world today, these 500 groupings—each with its own little dominating pyramid within it—represent a concentration of power over economics which makes the medieval feudal system look like a Sunday-school party.[32]

Because of their economic power, corporations such as General Motors may easily defy the public interest. As Ralph Nader has pointed out, General Motors did its best to prevent the installation in its cars of anti-pollution catalysts, seat belts, and other safety devices.[33] In consequence, as Nader has remarked, "For decades millions of unrestrained flying objects called Americans were flung inside their vehicles, crushing bones and ending life, because the industry's leaders focused competition towards variations of stylistic pornography instead of toward engineering integrity."[34] Further, this corporation could continue to charge high prices to the public because of its lobbying efforts in the Congress and the expenditure of $200 million a year in advertising.

American corporations are, in turn, controlled by relatively few people. In 1967, for example, the *Fortune* list of the 500 largest companies indicated that particular families dominated 150 of them.[35] In opposition to the image of "people's capitalism," 95 percent of laborers and farmers do not own a single share of stock.[36] In contrast, 56 percent of those in occupations that produce higher incomes, such as professionals who are high in the bureaucratic hierarchy, own shares in American corporations.[37] A partial result of this corporate inequality has been that the top 20 percent of the nation's families received 41 percent of all income in 1970, while the bottom 20 percent received less than 5 percent.[38]

Some theorists have argued that such a disparity in income is a natural part of human society. Vilfredo Pareto, for example, argued that inequality of income followed an exact statistical curve and, short of a revolution, could not be changed. Observing that the distribution of income has been relatively fixed in all places and at all times, some social scientists postulated "Pareto's law," which specified that inequality of income would follow exact dimensions throughout all time.[39] Subsequent studies have demonstrated the partial falsity of Pareto's position. For example, the richest 5 percent of the population in the 1920s received about one-third of all income in this country. But during the depression of the 1930s and World War II, the share of the very rich dropped to about 20 percent.[40] Since that time, as economist Herman Miller has established, there have been no significant changes, and the wealthiest group in America still receives a major share of the national income.[41]

Some scholars would argue that during the twentieth century the rich are getting richer and the poor poorer. Using 1910 as a base year, Gabriel Kolko has shown that the richest 20 percent of Americans received about 56 percent of all income at that time. In 1929 the figure dropped to 52 percent; in 1959 it fell to 45 percent; and in 1970 it leveled off at about 41 percent.[42] The poorest 10 percent of the population has become relatively *more* deprived: in 1910 they received 3 percent of total personal income, but by 1970 they received only 2 percent[43] and by 1976, as we have noted, they got only 1.7 percent.

These figures on personal income do not fully reveal the differential in American wealth. Corporate executives may, for example, utilize unlimited expense accounts, which cost some $10 billion a year and which provide them with free cars, houses, country club memberships, restaurant and hotel services, and other privileges.[44] Loopholes in the tax laws also levy an enormous, if not exactly estimated, price. In 1969 alone, 381 Americans with incomes exceeding $100,000 a year avoided paying any federal income tax at all.[45]

Thus, although most Americans adhere to a belief that they live in a land of freedom where the usual class restraints have been removed—a land of equality where any person may become a Henry Ford, Andrew Carnegie, or John D. Rockefeller; a nation composed entirely of a "middle class"—it is abundantly clear that this country is deeply divided between those who have and those who have not.

Subcultures of Stratification

Variations in wealth in America are reflected in a vast number of subcultural differences. Among the many different styles of life, sociologists have devoted their greatest attention to the characteristics of four groups.*[46]

THE UPPER CLASS

Most observers estimate that no more than 3 percent of the American population (typified by the La Jollans described in the introduction in this book) can be considered as members of the upper class, although this group commands about 20 percent of the nation's wealth and exerts a disproportionate share of political power. According to definitive studies of America's upper class conducted by E. Digby Baltzell, males in the upper class usually operate in the higher reaches of the law or in business and political bureaucracies.[47] They live in exclusive residential neighborhoods; attend universities such as Harvard, Princeton, Yale, Amherst, and Stanford; send their children to prep schools like Andover or Exeter; belong to expensive country clubs and city clubs such as the Union League; and list themselves in *The Social Register*.[48]

THE MIDDLE CLASS

The middle class is normally thought of as consisting of salaried bureaucrats, self-employed professionals, salespeople, clerks, and other

---

*Sociologists have noted many other groups but these seem to be the most enduring national strata.

white-collar workers. They ranged in income from an average of $20,000 a year for professionals to $8,600 a year for clerks in 1970.[49] Because of the diverse nature of this class, few generalizations can be made about it. However, a few can be ventured: they generally have at least some college education; they belong to "service clubs" such as the Rotary and Kiwanis; their children go to public schools; they often subscribe to the Protestant religions; and they raise their children with the goals of "maturity," "self-fulfillment," and ambition in mind.[50]

THE BLUE-COLLAR CLASS

This class makes up about 37 percent of the American population and includes craft and industrial workers, laborers, and mechanized farmers. Their income in 1970 ranged from $9,250 for skilled craftsmen to $6,462 for laborers.[51] Usually, this group has not progressed beyond a high school education; they are disproportionately Catholic in religion; they tend to vote Democratic when they vote at all; they have few protections for their homes, health, or children.

Some sociologists would argue that there is no true working-class subculture since its members imitate a white-collar ethos.[52] But others, such as Albert K. Cohen, Harold Hodges, and Walter Miller, believe that members of the working class exhibit an ethic of bravado, strength, courage, and the seeking of immediate pleasure.[53] As Herbert Gans has noted, the family among the working class assumes unique importance since work is boring and the outside world is viewed with indifference, and thus only one's immediate relatives offer pleasure and gratification.[54]

THE IMPOVERISHED

An additional 20 percent of Americans—the impoverished—can barely scrape together the means to subsist. Their life is unpredictable; jobs are won and lost randomly; men seek immediate gratification and pleasure; women are often left with the routine job of maintaining a minimal standard of living for themselves and their children.[55] Beginning in 1958, in part under the influence of the work of Oscar Lewis, many social scientists began to postulate the existence of a "culture of poverty."[56] This culture supposedly involved social isolation, disorganization, acute economic anxiety, an almost total lack in education, and personal debilitation.

In describing these four strata, we are not implying that they are immutable or that every member of each social stratum subscribes to the same values and customs. Clearly, not all white-collar people are Babbitts nor are all blue-collar workers like Archie Bunker.

Further, we do not propose these categories as absolute. Others, such as Lloyd Warner, would place greater emphasis on distinctions in status and mark off subtle differences between, say, the "upper-upper" class and the "lower-upper" class. Marx, in contrast, would insist that only concrete differences in power should constitute the definition of class. Some, such as Chapin, would avoid the concept of power altogether and measure class by such (in our opinion, superficial) measures as the number of utensils around a family's fireplace or how many books the home exhibits.

Although, inevitably, some critics will assail us for not making hard and fast divisions between America's different subcultures, we believe that broad distinctions based on income, occupation, and, of course, power serve as the most pragmatic way of viewing the various social strata in contemporary America. These indices correlate most highly with other important variables such as political influence, health, and education. Despite ideological differences, most sociologists have used these standards, which, taken together, portray the various American subcultures.

Because researchers use different terminology to describe social strata, in discussing their work we must employ their own terms. These vary from labels such as "the rich" or "the poor," "the middle class" or the "working class," "blue collar" or "white collar." Although this lack of definite, hard, rigid definitions may confuse matters somewhat, it is, inevitable that people will apply different terms to the same phenomenon.

We could quibble, of course, about whether a plumber who earned $30,000 a year was *truly* a "blue-collar" worker or whether a professor who made $15,000 a year *really* belonged to the "middle class" in America—but such debates have the same merit as the ancient issue of how many angels could stand on the head of a pin. And the facts *are* clear: huge gaps in income result in differences in every aspect of life style and access to power. It is the nature of these essential, lasting, and profound cleavages that should be of concern, not the labels that sociologists, journalists, or philosophers attach to them. Even the average person in America is confused by these labels. Although undoubtedly aware of differences in power and income, most Americans still prefer to regard themselves as "typical."

This point is further reinforced by the lack of *class consciousness* in America. Americans of whatever group regard themselves as members of the "middle class."*[57] And most people, with the possible exception of the upper class, do not conceive of politics in dimensions of social stratifi-

*There does, however, seem to have been a tendency during the 1970s for minority-group members to identify with their particular group. Blacks, Chicanos, and Puerto Ricans have engaged in a search for their ethnic heritage just as many of the loyalties of older groups such as Germans and Irish have eroded.

cation.[58] Naturally, Americans recognize the existence of inequalities but —because of economic expansion, increasing specialization, ethnic differences, and the American tendency to view "success" as a reward for individual merit—the consciousness of class differences has been muted.[59]

Although people may not be aware of their actual position in the social structure, they still behave according to uniform patterns characteristic of their class. Most important, they differ objectively in the actual degree of power which they possess. This is as true in contemporary America as ancient India, for power continues as the most enduring and important element of stratification in postindustrial societies.

THE POWER OF VARIOUS SUBCULTURES

Essentially, we follow Max Weber in defining power as "the chance of a man or of a number of men to realize their own will in a communal action even against the resistance of others who are participating in the action."[60] As Robert Bierstedt has pointed out, power is always based on force. The use of force may be latent, overt, or legitimated as a normal exercise of authority.[61]

The degree of concentration of power in America has been ingeniously measured by Thomas Dye, Eugene De Clercq, and John Pickering. They selected twelve important sectors of American society, such as banking, education, foundations, government, and the military, and located those people who were at the top of each institution (defined as the group that controlled at least 50 percent of the resources of that sector). They found an incredible concentration of power at the apex of American society: 4,100 individuals dominated 50 percent of the nation's resources. In turn, these same individuals occupied 5,400 command posts in the various institutional sectors. This is possible through multiple appointments of each individual to a number of different positions.[62]

Power may originate, as we noted in Part I, in sheer physical strength, in control over resources, in command of weapons, in one's social prestige, or in one's dominance of an administrative or bureaucratic hierarchy. It may be reflected in prestige, the ability to influence others, phychological dominance, or overt commands.[63] Power is the essence of any stratification system. In the American context, whether the bulk of power is concentrated in the hands of a single elite or, as David Riesman has argued, is dispersed through a series of equally powerful veto groups remains a continuing debate.[64] Clearly, however, different social strata in America possess vastly different amounts of power— no matter how one defines it. One manifestation of this power lies in the political realm.

The Effects of Stratification
on Politics

Throughout American history, the upper and middle strata have virtually monopolized high political office. Members of the blue-collar class may exert some influence through union officials, but they seldom reach high political office. Members of the impoverished strata almost never attain high political office unless they have been fortunate enough to obtain such middle-class credentials as a law degree.

A variety of studies of different segments of American political life in different epochs have demonstrated the truth of this generalization. Donald R. Mathews noted that for 160 years of American history, only 4 percent of presidents, vice-presidents, or cabinet officers could be portrayed as "blue-collar" or impoverished in background.[65] C. Wright Mills found that twenty-four of the last sixty secretaries of defense (up to 1956) had graduated from Harvard or Yale law school and that 60 percent had attended Ivy League colleges.[66] Between 1932 and 1964 more than 60 percent of the most powerful cabinet officers (secretary of state, defense, or treasury) came from the upper class.[67] Another study of senators noted that only 5 to 7 percent of their fathers could have been considered industrial wage laborers.*[68] Even during eras such as the New Deal when the explicit aim of the government was to end an economic depression, stop unemployment, and expand equality of opportunity, the leaders came overwhelmingly from the upper and upper-middle strata of America.[69] At other levels of political power in America, the upper social stratum is heavily overrepresented in state legislatures,[70] as delegates to political conventions,[71] and even as county political leaders.[72] High civil servants in California[73] and military officers exhibit similar patterns.[74]

Thus, from the highest levels of political power in America down through state legislatures to appointed officials such as civil servants and military officers, the upper class or upper-middle class controls the levers of power. This same pattern prevails throughout the "free world" —that is, in those nations that elect their top officials and maintain a capitalistic postindustrial order. After a thorough examination of the political situation in England, France, Germany, and Japan, Ralph Miliband concluded:

---

*Some elitists would argue that this preponderance of upper-class, well-educated people at the higher levels of the federal government merely reflects their greater intelligence, merit, and competence. The inaccuracy of this position is discussed in the section "Stratification and Education" in this chapter.

What the evidence conclusively suggests is that in terms of social origin, education, and class situation, the men who have manned *all* command positions in the state system have largely, and in many cases overwhelmingly, been drawn from the world of business and property, or from the professional middle classes. . . . it has remained a basic fact of life in advanced capitalist countries that the vast majority of men and women in these countries has been governed, represented, administered, judged, and commanded in war by people drawn from other, economically and socially superior and relatively distant classes.[75]

POLITICAL ATTITUDES AND SOCIAL STRATIFICATION

Stratification affects not only the degree of concentration of political power but also the political interests, attitudes, and voting patterns of the population. On economic and social issues, according to most researchers, the upper strata in America support ideologically conservative positions.[76] However, the opposite conclusion—that "the lower strata tend to be radical"[77]—is not necessarily true. On concrete, "bread-and-butter" issues, the lower strata adopt attitudes that are favorable to their interests. On broader issues of civil liberties, privacy, law and order, and suppression of dissidents, the lower strata tend to prefer a less liberal position. Seymour Martin Lipset has labeled this antidemocratic tendency among the lower strata as "working class authoritarianism." He notes:

The gradual realization that extremist and intolerant movements in modern society are more likely to be based on the lower classes than on the middle classes has posed a tragic dilemma for those intellectuals of the democratic left who once believed the proletariat necessarily to be a force for liberty, racial equality, and social progress.[78]

This dilemma among many American intellectuals arose in part because of their neo-Marxist orientation, a belief that the "proletariat" would be the standard-bearer of progressive political beliefs. Tragically, the sheer fact of economic oppression more often leads the lower classes to seek scapegoats and to succumb to the appeals of the Ku Klux Klan, McCarthyism, or other antiliberty movements. Lipset has concluded:

The poorer strata everywhere are more liberal or leftist on economic issues; they favor more welfare state measures, higher wages, graduated income taxes, support of trade-unions. . . . But when liberalism is defined in noneconomic terms—as support of civil liberties, internationalism, etc.—the correlation is reversed. The more well-to-do are more liberal, the poorer are more intolerant.[79]

Studies of political extremism have usually found that those groups who are most threatened by an economic disaster, displacement by other groups, or a decline in their status are most inclined to use violent, antidemocratic means to redress their situation. Other observers have noticed that the lower-middle class in Germany—a group that was most seriously affected by inflation—was most likely to turn to Nazism.[80] In America, the rapid bureaucratization of the land has led to the "dispossession" of certain social groups: the small-town businessman or farmer, the unskilled black, the unrecognized intellectual, or the Southern white sharecropper. Cut off from their usual means of subsistence and status, such groups seek out demagogues like Populist Huey Long, Eldridge Cleaver, or the New Left's Abbie Hoffman.* [81]

In domestic politics, such extremism has been demonstrated by opposition to racial integration, to reform in police policies, and even to such a mundane measure as fluoridation of public water. The groups that oppose such measures normally come from what Bell calls the "dispossessed classes," or Arnold Rogow has termed the "discontinued classes," those with little education, low income, and little status in their communities.[83]

Political ideology cannot, of course, be equated with actual political participation. In America, the upper strata tend to be the most aware of the political situation, most likely to vote, and most involved at all levels of political life.[84] The lower strata, for a variety of reasons, are relatively isolated from political life and generally do not vote. There are several important explanations for this phenomenon.

First, the lower strata has little interest in political affairs, competence in dealing with them, or knowledge about the intricacies of political life.[85]

Second, as Lee Rainwater has argued, the poor avoid political organizations since they feel they are being patronized, exploited, or denigrated.[86] Often, the lower strata prefer to escape their ghettos through their own individual mobility—that is, by moving their families to a new neighborhood or by getting a better job. Disturbed by prying bill collectors, landlords, police, and public-assistance workers, they do not take easily to the blandishments of political organizers.

Third, as Arthur Lee Burnham and Lucille Duberman argue, the rich and powerful consciously prevent the poor from voting. By various mechanisms, such as registration at appointed places, the upper strata hinder, if not curtail totally, the participation of the poor in the voting process.[87] Thus, according to Duberman:

---

*It would be naive to assume that all forms of discontent that lead to political extremism can be traced to objective differences in social strata. The college radicals of the 1960's, for example, appeared to have emerged from conflict-filled yet middle-class homes.[82]

It is not lack of class consciousness, apathy, disinterest, lack of faith, nor status inconsistency that keep the poor from voting. It is that those in power create sociological barriers that restrain the poor from exercising the franchise.[88]

Although there can be little doubt that white Southerners, for example, have systematically excluded blacks from the political process,[89] there is not as yet convincing evidence that the upper strata in America have engaged in a systematic conspiracy to exclude working-class or impoverished people from the voting process. Nonetheless, it is clear that social stratification in all its various forms has a powerful effect upon political behavior.

In summary, we may offer several conclusions. First, the upper strata in America have virtually reserved all high elective and appointive offices for themselves. Second, the white poor tend to be "liberal" on economic issues and intolerant on civil rights, civil liberties, or racial matters, whereas the rich adopt the opposite stance. Third, political extremism from either the right or left develops most easily among classes who feel threatened or have actually fallen in social status. Fourth, the upper strata are more politically active, better organized, and more regular voters than the lower. This combination of facts allows the development of another form of power: the dominance of the upper strata over the nation's laws.

The Effects of Stratification on Law

The potent effects of upper-class control over politics are that they can assure the passage of legislation that favors them; they can use the law as a legitimate instrument to control the lower strata; and they can elect or appoint judges and other legal officers who share their point of view.

The principles of law in the United States today can be traced to certain elitist points of view that were expressed in the eighteenth century by the Founding Fathers. James Madison,[90] for instance, believed that economic inequality was inevitable and just since it reflected natural differences among people. He did, however, understand that economic inequality could lead to a sense of grievance and subsequent social conflict. Madison thought that the proper role of government and law was not to attempt the impossible task of erasing these inequalities but rather to establish rules that would regulate economic disputes and allow people to live peacefully with one another.

In actual practice, this Madisonian view of government and the law has resulted in a current system that Daniel Rossides has condemned in strong terms:

> Basically, law enforcement agencies deal illegally with, and display
> excessive zeal and force against, all members of the lower classes,
> whether white, black, yellow, red, Anglo, Mexican American, Protes-
> tant, Jewish, or Roman Catholic. In short, the main purpose of law
> enforcement agencies, like all branches of government is to defend the
> existing order of things.[91]

Although lawyers espouse ideals of justice, equality before the court, trial by peers, and even-handed treatment, there is abundant evidence to support the view that the law is merely one more, extremely important device for the upper strata to maintain their control. Examples of this may be drawn from almost every province of the law.

Vagrancy laws, ably analyzed by William Chambliss, provide a histori-cal example of the operation of class bias.[92] The original vagrancy laws, passed in England in 1349, punished those people who gave alms to beg-gers. The basic intention of the law was to discourage begging and thereby increase a supply of cheap labor. Since England had just been decimated by the plague, agricultural laborers were in short supply. Lords of the land passed laws to ensure that desperately needed labor would apply at their doors.

The upper classes have redefined vagrancy laws time and again, but always with the purpose of protecting themselves. In the early twentieth century, corporations such as the Ford Motor Company used the law as a ruthless way of dispossessing sit-in workers at Ford plants. If the work-ers, who sought unionization, refused to move, Henry Ford could invoke the vagrancy law and call in hired thugs who beat the workers into sub-mission. During the 1960s Southern sheriffs used the vagrancy laws to arrest civil rights workers.[93]

Housing and zoning laws have consistently favored the upper strata. Zoning laws, for example, protect the rich from inroads by certain racial or economic groups; planning practices forced public housing into already poor ghetto areas; income tax laws favor those rich groups who can afford to buy a house and pay high rates of interest on it. The result has been to isolate the rich in their own enclaves.[94] A 1977 Supreme Court ruling has required affluent suburbs to allow the building of low-income housing in their areas. The response of the upper strata in many areas has been to protect themselves. For example, one upper-middle-class township out-side of New York City passed a ruling that forbade the acceptance of any federal funds to "protect" itself from any federally supported housing for the poor.

Draft laws as exercised during the Vietnam War consistently favored men from the middle and upper social strata. College "deferments" fa-vored middle- and upper-class college students, and draft laws placed discretionary power in the hands of local boards, which were, in turn, dominated by upper-stratum people.[95] The result was that twice as many lower-class men as upper-class men were killed in Vietnam.[96]

Tax laws cause the burden of taxation to fall heavily upon the poor. Perhaps the greatest benefits flow to those who have inherited their wealth or to those who derive their income from invested monies. Those who already have wealth benefit further from a low capital-gains tax, tax-free bonds, and oil and mineral depletion allowances. All these tax policies are specified in the Internal Revenue Code. Simultaneously, other, less fortunate individuals are taxed at the full rate. Further, of course, the rich are able to hire highly specialized tax lawyers and accountants to find every possible loophole in their base rates. The poorer groups have little extra money to invest or to hire tax experts.

Criminal laws in America exact punishments from the poor sector for its crimes while discriminating in favor of the "white-collar" criminal. By white-collar crime we mean those actions that threaten the life or property of citizens but that are committed by otherwise outwardly respectable individuals or corporations. Although illegal, these crimes are rarely if ever punished with the same severity as are lower-class crimes. Edwin Sutherland's classic study of white-collar crime indicated that every one of the seventy largest corporations in America had, at one time or another, been convicted of fraud, tax evasion, collusion, bribery, infringement of patents, restraint of trade, or the stealing of trade secrets.[97] The particular officials in charge of these operations seldom served time in jail; usually, the corporations were only fined.

Every segment of American industrial life has been affected by this plague of crime: manufacturers of surgical instruments,[98] flag-makers,[99] mine owners,[100] television manufacturers[101]—indeed, every conceivable sector of American commercial and industrial activity. The total cost of these depredations to the American public is unknown, but one commissioner of the Federal Communications Commission was able to estimate in 1969 that "a *single* recent price-fixing case involved a 'robbery' from the American public of more money than was taken in *all* the country's robberies, burglaries and larcenies during the years of that criminal price-fixing."[102]

These white-collar crimes go relatively unnoticed by the public since, among other factors, the mass media are owned and controlled by the upper strata. Members of the upper classes have no desire to "wash their dirty linen" in public. When the courts actually convict white-collar criminals of their actions, the fines or punishments imposed are minimal. In 1976 the Watergate defendants, as one example, were either at liberty or, at most, serving brief sentences in minimum-security prisons. Blatant frauds, such as the sale of franchises in the nonexistent Dale Car in 1974, have gone unpunished.[103] Alleged perpetrators of mass stock manipulations, such as Robert Vesco, live in comfort in the Bahamas or Costa

Rica.[104] Huge corporations such as Gulf Oil and Minnesota Mining and Manufacturing publicly confessed in 1975 to criminal violations of election laws; some top executives resigned their lucrative positions but remained far outside prison walls.[105]

In contrast, petty criminals in New York City may remain "in detention" in the Riker's Island prison for up to two years without *any* admission of their guilt or *any* legal defense of their innocence before coming to trial. Most of these inmates are black or Puerto Rican; all come from the more impoverished sectors of the New York environment.

Why does America allow such a blatant discrepancy in legal equity? The reasons are clear. White-collar criminals, as opposed to those from the lower strata, can afford bail. They can hire experienced lawyers and appear before judges who are from their own social strata. They may have paid for the elections of their own prosecutors, and they can hire the lobbyists who push for the legislation that they favor. And they can ensure that political rhetoric does not result in laws that would truly punish their transgressions. They are the end product of a system where power and money can buy an entire legal system.

As Daniel Bell has observed: "Crime, in many ways, is a Coney Island mirror, caricaturing the morals and manners of a society. The jungle quality of the American business community, particularly at the turn of the century, was reflected in the mode of 'business' practiced by the coarse gangster elements."[106] Corporations in the 1970s use the same methods as organized criminals—except perhaps that the businesspeople are more polite, tactful, sophisticated, and pay out greater sums to establish a legal system which allows special consideration of their needs.

Civil law, as Jerome Carlin, Jan Howard, and Sheldon Messinger have shown, also suffers from a bias in favor of the middle and upper classes.[107] Landlords, as members of the upper stratum, generally have a de jure advantage over renters.[108] Courts that deal with the lower classes, such as small claims courts, generally dispense with such legal niceties as observing the rules of evidence.[109] In divorce or other civil cases, the courts attempt to mass-produce justice, which inevitably works to the advantage of those who can hire clever lawyers.[110] Quite naturally, the lower classes develop an antipathy toward courts and are extremely hesitant to launch any type of lawsuit against big corporations or bureaucracies. Civil justice for the lower classes usually dies "not with a bang, but a whimper."

A total suspension of civil liberties has rarely been resorted to by America's upper classes except in situations which they regarded as extremely grave. Thus, in the Japanese-American illustration cited in the Introduction, America's elite (and, one must admit, its masses) feared that West Coast Japanese-Americans might turn traitor. An executive order issued by President Roosevelt in 1941 stripped Japanese-Americans of their citizenship, of their habeas corpus rights, of property contracts, and indeed of all the legal rights associated with the protection of "life, liberty, and the pursuit of happiness." Earl Warren, later Chief Justice of the Supreme Court, applauded this action. The legal profession did not protest. The fact that the United States government has maintained sites for concentration camps in such areas as Pasa Robles, California, as well as lists of those whom the ruling powers could, if they wished to, detain in 1977 testifies that the same abrogation of the most fundamental liberties can occur once again.

In summary, we should note that the upper strata in America control the operation of the law in a number of significant ways. First, the upper strata have been able to redefine the law to suit their particular interests and needs. Second, the upper groups have been able to maintain discriminatory housing, draft, and tax laws to protect them and their descendants. Third, the criminal law has been bent in such a way as to virtually exclude corporations and white-collar criminals from prosecution. Fourth, the actual administration of the civil law has secured the greatest possible rights for the rich while "mass-producing" supposed equity for the poor. Fifth, in matters of extreme emergency, the upper strata have used the law to take away all rights from those who are presumed to be in opposition to the government. Therefore, in many ways, the law is the handmaiden of those who possess wealth and power in America. The labeling of certain persons as "deviant" also follows patterns of social stratification, although the path is sometimes narrow and untrustworthy.

The Effects of Stratification on Deviance

Every society produces a certain number of "deviants"—that is, those "disvalued people" whose behavior provokes hostile reactions from their particular group.[111] Within this context, we consider the relation of social stratification to the pattern of deviance exhibited in four types of behavior: crime, suicide, alcoholism and drug addiction, and mental disorder.

CRIME AND STRATIFICATION

We have already demonstrated that upper-stratum groups in America may commit white-collar crimes with relative immunity from prosecution. In terms of "ordinary" crime, or "street" offenses, there can be little doubt that the lower classes exhibit the highest rate.[112]

Sophisticated social theorists have explained this phenomenon in several ways. Albert Cohen has argued that lower-class children suffer from a gap between the virtues they are raised to admire and the means available for achieving these goals.[113] Richard Gloward and Lloyd Ohlin have followed a similar line: they maintain that lower-class children, denied availability to the usual channels of "success" in America, have greater access to criminal means for fulfilling their aims.[114] Sheldon and Eleanor Glueck contend that specific types of familial environments in lower-class neighborhoods—homes filled with conflict, argument, bitterness, cruelty and rejection—are responsible for criminal behavior.[115]

Other scholars have maintained that differences in the socialization process between different classes do not really account for gaps in the crime rate. Writers such as Richard Quinney[116] and William Chambliss[117] have focused on the power of various social groups. They have maintained that the uses of power in criminal matters has resulted in members of the lower classes more often being identified and convicted as criminals.[118]

Powerful support for this point of view came from the studies of C. J. Judson and his colleagues.[119] Judson examined 238 first-degree murder cases in California. He found that only 4.8 percent of white-collar defendants received the death penalty. Yet 42.1 percent of blue-collar defendants were sentenced to execution. Judson concluded that "the simplest hypothesis to explain this powerful association is that juries are lenient towards white collar defendants on the basis of occupational status alone."[120]

T. Chiricos and G. Waldo have questioned whether this same socio-economic bias permeates all aspects of the criminal sentencing process. They found that criminals in North Carolina, South Carolina, and Florida received the same sentences for their crimes *after* they had been apprehended, tried, and convicted.[121] After an elaborate statistical treatment of this evidence, Chiricos and Waldo concluded that "the socio-economic status of convicted criminal offenders is unrelated to the severity of the state's official sanction."[122] This would seem to indicate the law's impartiality, except that it omits white-collar criminals, the process of arresting people, the nature of prosecuting and defending attorneys, police attitudes, and many other relevant factors. These findings apparently do not support the studies of Quinney, Turk, Chambliss, and Judson. Yet Chiricos and Waldo studied only those people who had been certified and sentenced as "criminal"—a sample that was highly biased.

If one abandons court sentencing as the most reasonable measure of the equity of criminal justice, it is clear by any other measure that membership in the upper classes tends to protect one from criminal punishment. Many studies have demonstrated the favorable bias of police and lower courts toward members of the upper strata.[123]

Realizing the bias of the criminal procedure against relatively helpless lower-class offenders, it is disturbing to contemplate the nation's mood in the 1970s. A genuine concern for law and order has become an obsession that obscures the fact that the vast majority of *victims* of violent crimes are from the same echelons of society as the perpetrators of these crimes —the lower classes.[124] Except for dramatic jewel robberies and rare "murders of passion," the upper classes seldom experience the climate of violence that pervades lower-class urban slums.

Despite this fact, the pendulum of public opinion in the 1970s, even among those who called themselves liberal, has swung toward more severe repression of crime. Many scholars, for example, have given up hope that any form of rehabilitation will work.*[125] Some, like Harvard's James Q. Wilson, have advocated a "lock 'em up and throw the key away" policy. Most persons of this persuasion believe that the best way to control crime is to imprison criminals.[127] This policy, which has been advocated by scholars who themselves occupy higher positions in the stratification system, would take its heaviest toll among lower-class people. The trend toward more severe repression, symbolized by the Supreme Court's reintroduction of the death penalty in 1976, could well be interpreted as one more symptom of socioeconomic bias.

SUICIDE AND STRATIFICATION

Like "street" crime, suicide is linked to the stratification system but in more complicated ways since its victims do not come exclusively from lower socioeconomic groups.

Suicide is, of course, the last resort of a desperate person. For very different reasons, both the upper strata and the lower strata in America choose this alternative more frequently than those who are in the middle of the social stratification hierarchy. Originally, Emile Durkheim, the first major investigator of suicide rates, contended that the upper classes in Europe were most prone to suicide.[128] Subsequent investigators, such as Ronald W. Maris, argued that self-destruction was highest among lower socioeconomic groups.[129] The most sophisticated investigations strongly suggest that suicide reaches its peak in the upper *and* the lowest strata of society.[130] One study of social stratification and suicide showed the following pattern:

---

*This view overlooks a variety of studies that indicate that certain types of criminals can be rehabilitated.[126]

Suicide Rates per 100,000, by Occupation[131]

Professional and managerial	35.1
Clerical-sales	11.6
Craftsmen	14.3
Operatives	20.5
Service workers	21.9
Laborers	38.7

Elwin Powell has suggested a reasonable explanation for this phenomenon.[132] He argues that the upper classes in America are enveloped in an ethic that demands a striving for success and status. If, however, a member of the upper class stumbles in the search for success symbols, he or she is severely crippled in a psychological sense. Thus, a stockbroker who may objectively have a high income but finds that his or her assets are slipping may commit suicide. And a lower-class person, such as a laborer, who lives constantly in an atmosphere of fear, threat, and meaninglessness may view suicide as a reasonable way to end a chaotic life.

The very highest suicide rates in America occur among those who are "left out" of the occupational system. Unemployed males had a rate of 76.6 per 100,000 people in 1965, almost seven times the national average.[133] Retired American males, who have lost their occupational status, also have an extraordinarily high rate of suicide, 89.0.[134] Since unemployed and retired males vastly exceed females in the rate of suicide, the common experience of illness, disability, and feelings of futility characteristic of old age cannot in itself totally explain the difference. It seems more reasonable to suppose that many American men who do not have jobs have also lost the primary meaning of their lives provided by their occupations and the attendant status.

As one might predict, cycles in prosperity and inflation also affect the rate of suicide. As Andrew Henry and James Short have demonstrated, suicide rises and falls according to the general state of the economy. People of the highest economic stratum commit suicide most often during a depression.[135] At this time, of course, they face the severest problems in terms of economic loss and social status.

Although suicide is the ultimate escape from the problems of life, Americans often choose other routes such as alcohol and drugs. This choice, too, is affected by one's social status.

ADDICTION AND STRATIFICATION

Like suicide, alcoholism in America is most prevalent in two social classes: the upper and the lower.[136] The middle classes, perhaps inspired by a belief in the "work ethic," are relatively free from this addiction. In the upper classes, a customary "cocktail culture" prevails where one sips with social approval. Among lower-class groups, drinking a bottle on the streetcorner of a ghetto or dropping into the local bar is a common form of escape. Certain ethnic groups exhibit their own unique patterns: Jews, largely members of the upper or white-collar classes, have a low rate of alcoholism. Perhaps their intellectual tradition and a respect for rationality and a "clear head" serve as barriers to drinking.[137] Irish-Americans, on the other hand, have a proclivity to excessive drinking. This may be a reflection of Irish culture or it may be due to the fact that the Irish, with few exceptions, belong to the blue-collar or working classes in America.[138]

Heroin addicts are concentrated among lower-class urbanites and number some 350,000.[139] Although it is a popular myth that America is being devastated by a plague of drugs, the rate of heroin addiction has probably dropped since 1885.[140] At that time Civil War veterans who had been given opium in hospitals tended to become addicts. Most observers believe that some 1 to 4 percent of the entire population was addicted.[141] The social background of addicts has also drastically changed. In 1915 most addicts could well be described as little old ladies who sipped opium in the form of cough medicine in the comfort of their middle-class homes.[142] Today, addicts come largely from the slums of New York, Chicago, Los Angeles, and other large cities although doctors make up the highest proportion of addicts.

"Pill poppers"—the millions of Americans who take amphetamines and tranquilizers to produce either an "up" or a "down" mood—cannot be reliably related to the social stratification system. Since over 300 of these tranquilizing or energizing drugs are produced in America, one must assume that there is a great demand for them.[143] Preliminary studies suggest that the use of these costly pills is predominant in the upper and middle classes.[144] Because they do not noticeably interfere with the intellectual functioning, economic calculations, or rationality of the person who takes them, such drugs would have a special appeal to the middle or white-collar classes in America.[145]

It is as yet too early for scientific research to have ascertained the social background of pill poppers. However, two facts about other forms of addictive habits are relatively well established. First, both the upper and the lower classes use alcohol excessively. Indeed, lower-class black males die of illnesses related to alcohol at twice the rate of other social groups.[146] Second, heroin addiction, formerly a middle-class female illness, has emerged as a prominent form of escape for lower-class urban males. This relationship can most easily be explained in terms of the availability of certain drugs "on the street" as well as the subculture of each class, which prescribes the form of escape allowed.

MENTAL DISORDER AND STRATIFICATION

Addicts or not, a high proportion of people in America withdraw into a world of delusions or hallucinations that we have come to call "mental disorder." A variety of studies indicate that the overt symptoms of mental disorder are clearly related to one's position in the social structure.

Mentally disordered people, some 6 percent of the American population, suffer from panic, intense anxiety, disorientation, delusions, or hallucinations. Ordinarily, our society isolates them in mental hospitals or, if they are of upper-class status, provides them with the services of a private psychiatrist. Anything ranging from lobotomies, shock treatments, and drugs to psychotherapies may return these despairing people to society. Despite the claims of R. D. Laing and Thomas Szasz, these individuals are filled with pain and have made one last despairing gesture to find a new reality.[147]

Psychoses in America exact a disproportionate toll from the lower classes. Many studies in different historical periods have demonstrated that psychotics either emerge from the lower classes in large numbers or have drifted downward to a lower-class position. In 1939 E. L. Faris and H. Warren Dunham found that the lower classes in Chicago had an extremely high rate of schizophrenia (one of the "grab bag" categories of psychoses).[148] In 1958 Hollingshead and Redlich noted that the prevalence of psychoses in the lower class of New Haven vastly exceeded that in the upper class.[149] Less than 1 percent of schizophrenics came from the upper class while 45 percent originated in the lowest social class. Hollingshead and Redlich were careful to check the records of private psychiatrists and clinics rather than using the customary standard of admission to mental hospitals. They realized that lower-class people are often "dumped" in public mental hospitals because they cannot meet the expense of private treatment. Nonetheless, after controlling for this social bias, Hollingshead and Redlich still found that the lower classes in New Haven had a higher percentage of severe mental disorders.

Later, Leo Srole and his colleagues examined the mental health of the midtown Manhattan area.[150] After in-depth interviews, they found that over 45 percent of lower-class people in the area were noticeably impaired or incapacitated by mental disorder, yet just 12.5 percent of the highest social class could be diagnosed in that fashion. Only 4.6 percent of the lowest social class could be judged as mentally healthy while 30 percent of the upper class in the same area could be classified as "well." Srole is now engaged in a study of how his mid-Manhattan sample fared in later life.[151]

The extreme psychiatric distress of the disadvantaged groups in America can be attributed to any number of factors. First, in a society that values success above all, the poorer classes may well suffer from severe depression about their failure to achieve. Second, according to some elitist hypotheses, the lower classes may have been born with a greater propensity to mental illness. Third, the lower groups suffer from economic and educational hardships. Fourth, parents have transmitted to their children their feelings about the sufferings and defeats they experienced. Fifth, the lower strata occupy a subordinate economic position where even the least deviation—say, continual lateness at work—may result in their being labeled as "crazy"; the upper-class person, although suffering from a severe mental disorder, may choose his own hours and be known only as eccentric, if not creative.

The hypotheses are innumerable. The facts are not: lower-class groups in America suffer from psychoses vastly more than do other groups.

The Effects of Stratification on Physical Health

The poor in America not only suffer from a higher rate of mental disease, they are also likely to die earlier than the rich. One's position in the socialclass structure affects the possibility of dying in war, falling prey to a serious illness, being hurt in an accident, and in fact, the very chances of life expectancy from birth onward.

An important study of mortality rates has demonstrated that the lower classes die younger and have more diseases than the upper classes in all nations.[152] Up until 1650, there was a relatively small class differential. After the advent of modern medicine, however, the gap between various social groups grew. Obviously, the rich can afford to pay for the best doctors, the most advanced medical technology, and rooms in a well-equipped hospital. These advantages plus a better knowledge of nutrition, preventive care, and hygiene allow the upper classes in America to live more healthy lives.[153] As Aaron Antonovsky has demonstrated, many studies show that upper-class people have a life expectancy that is significantly better than that of the lower class.[154] Antonovsky came "to the inescapable conclusion that class influences one's chance of staying alive." Almost without exception, the evidence shows that classes differ on mortality rates.[155] Evelyn Kitagawa and Philip Hauser examined the rates of mortality in Chicago and reached the same conclusion: specifically, lower-class whites die earlier than upper-class whites.[156] Donald Bogue noted a similar tendency.[157]

This class difference is particularly marked when one compares blacks and whites. Blacks, as a group, occupy a large share of the lower class in America, and they also suffer a higher incidence of physical burdens. Among other illustrations, one should note:

Twice as many black children as whites died during infancy in the 1960s.[158]

More than three times the number of black mothers as whites died while giving birth.[159]

Although the general rate of tuberculosis declined in the 1960s, it rose by 23 percent for blacks in New York City.[160]

Black males in America die about seven years earlier than white males.[161]

These class and racial differences occur for obvious economic reasons. They will not disappear until Americans guarantee medical care for all people regardless of their income.

Beyond the economic facts of life, other social elements may have an effect upon physical health. Lee Rainwater, for example, has argued that "lower class people . . . will be inclined to slight health difficulties in the interest of attending to more pressing ones, such as seeing that there is food in the house."[162] Rainwater believes that poor people cannot afford to care for an ill member of the family and, because of lack of knowledge, they confuse psychological with physical symptoms.[163] They have little acquaintance with nutrition or proper preventive measures. Moreover, says Rainwater, the lower classes "do not hold the sacredness of their persons in the same way that middle class people do. Their tendency to think of themselves as of little account is readily generalized to their bodies."[164] Thus, according to Rainwater, "the lower class person cannot afford the conception of himself as ill; he attends to physical symptoms, if at all, only when they pose a crisis in carrying out those functions he considers necessary."[165]

Regardless of whether Rainwater's opinions are correct, there can be no doubt that lower-class people have a higher rate of mortality than upper groups. This social bias is not limited to health. It extends into an area which Americans have traditionally believed was the door to success: education.

Stratification and Education

As in other areas of life, one's position in the social stratification system markedly affects the quality and level of one's education. Biases in education begin before the child even attends school. The number of books in the house, the paintings which the child sees, the level of conversation in the home—all affect children in their family environment. Clearly, too, families at different levels of the socioeconomic system have different educational aspirations for their children. As Rossides has remarked:

> The high value Americans place on education must be qualified carefully . . . if we are to understand its social meaning. For one thing, Americans do not value education as an end in itself. Always, and often explicitly, it is a means to other ends. . . . Speaking broadly, families in the higher classes prepare and motivate their children for success in school, while families in the lower classes prepare and motivate their children for average academic performance or even failure.[166]

Children enter school, then, with expectations that are conditioned by the class to which they belong.

The school environment is, in turn, affected by the economic conditions in the neighborhood. Schools in poor areas cannot afford to hire the best teachers, buy the best equipment, or properly supply their libraries.[167] These differences in the quality of schools can easily be measured by expenditures per pupil. In Illinois, for example, an upper-class area spent $1,168 a year per pupil while a poorer, yet adjacent school district could afford only $479.[168] The impact of such gaps in expenditure hardly need be underlined. In the Southern United States before the advent of new political attitudes, the discrepancy between lower-class black children and the average white child was even greater than in Illinois. In 1962, for example, J. M. Tubb, the superintendent of education for Mississippi, reported that the state spent an average of $81.86 for each white pupil while each black child received an average of $21.77.[169] The higher the number of blacks in a particular county, the lower the expenditure on black pupils. In Yazoo County the citizens paid 100 times more for the education of white than for the education of black pupils; in Holly Bluff School District, they spent 200 times more on whites than on blacks.[170] Southern political reforms may have reduced this difference.[171] Still, it is clear that rich suburbs throughout the nation can afford much greater sums for the education of their children than can either rural areas or uban ghettos.[172]

Although not directed strictly to matters of social stratification, the Coleman report documented that enormous differences exist in school expenditures between black areas and white suburbs.[173] The prime author, James Coleman, originally suggested that busing of children from one geographical area to another might help to erase this discrepancy. He has since withdrawn this recommendation, despite the fact that busing has been an historic fact of life for most of America's rural children.

Once launched on a school career, children are "tracked" (assigned to different courses) according to their social background and, supposedly, their ability. In fact, ability may have little to do with "tracking." As Paul Lauter and Florence Howe have noted, "tracking is a sure fashion for making sure that 'insecure' unpopular industries like the Army, or less prestigious occupations, like sanitation work, are supplied with manpower."[174]

The educational system, operating on the basis of children's social background, has a lasting effect on their future. It has been shown that adult occupational groups differ substantially in educational attainment. In 1974, 58.6 percent of people classified as "white collar" by the census had completed high school as opposed to 17.1 percent of "blue-collar" people.[175] This occupational and educational difference is, in turn, reflected in income. As measured in 1972 dollars, those who had finished college earned about 25 percent more than those who had completed high school and approximately 250 percent more per year than people who had attended elementary school for less than eight years.[176] Contrary to popular belief, this gap between the college-educated and others had not narrowed in the 1970s.[177]

One could argue, of course, that the college-educated deserve this greater income. It would be equitable, for example, to reward a brain surgeon more highly than a ditchdigger since the surgeon's skills are highly specialized and require many years of training as well as some economic sacrifice. The typical brain surgeon in America must spend not only four years in college but also another two as an intern, three more as a resident, and perhaps two learning to be an expert in this specialty. Therefore, until at least the age of twenty-eight the brain surgeon must labor at relatively meager wages while mastering the craft. In later life, of course, the brain surgeon's income soars far above that of a ditchdigger. Many, particularly those who are members of the American Medical Association, would regard this differential as a fair exchange for the services of the surgeon.

Those who argue in this fashion, however, ignore one salient fact: the entire system of American higher education is biased in favor of those from the upper strata. Thus people of intelligence, skill, and competence from the lower strata may well fall by the wayside before they reach the elevated status of, say, a brain surgeon. The evidence for this assertion comes from many sources.

In the 1860s, most observers who could make reasonable estimates believed that no more than 2.6 percent of college-age people actually graduated from a university.[178] That proportion has gone up significantly because of the demand of business and technocratic organizations for skilled personnel. In 1970, 41 percent of women and 53 percent of men of college age were attending institutions of higher education.[179] Yet definitive studies of the relationship between intelligence, social class, and education continued to indicate that college graduation was highly dependent upon one's social background.

In one major study, William Sewell and Vimal Shah analyzed the careers of all high school seniors in the state of Wisconsin between 1957 and 1965.[180] They were able to gauge both the social-class background and the intelligence score of the students. Social class strongly correlated with the chances of a person's graduating from college.[181]

Percentage Graduating from College, 1964-65

	Males	Females
Lowest social class	7.5%	2.7%
Highest social class	42.1%	35.0%

Many explanations could be offered for this fact. Poverty may have forced some students to quit college even if they desired to stay. Cultural background may have inhibited others. Women may have been forced out more often than men in order to fulfill their marital obligations.

The Wisconsin data also indicated, as one would predict, that people of higher intelligence were more likely to graduate from college than those of low intelligence.[182] In addition, children from the highest social classes also scored better on intelligence tests than those from the lower classes.[183] This result might be due to innate intelligence, however it can be measured, or it might be due to the social biases that are built into intelligence tests.[184] More than twice as many students from the upper class as from the lower class did well on the intelligence tests.[185]

The most important relationship revealed in the Wisconsin tests was that the great majority of intelligent lower-class people failed to graduate from college.[186] In fact, Wisconsin students from the upper social class who were intelligent (as measured by IQ tests) graduated from college about three times as often as intelligent people from the lowest social class.[187]

The pattern of social discrimination is clear. It might be possible to argue that Wisconsin was somehow unique and that such biases do not exist elsewhere. Yet, a very similar pattern exists in France.[188] Optimists might contend that the situation has improved since 1965 and that intelligence rather than socioeconomic standing is more highly rewarded in 1976, but there seems to be no particular reason to believe such an assertion. In fact, the conservative trend of the late twentieth century would tend to indicate that social class may be an increasingly important factor in achieving a college education. The situation of the City University of New York stands as a case in point.

For more than 150 years the City College of New York offered a free college education to all who could meet its academic standards. Generations of new migrants passed through its halls, including such Nobel Prize winners as Jonas Salk and Kenneth Arrow, statesmen like Henry Kissinger and Bernard Baruch, and politicians such as Abe Beame and Herman Badillo. In 1970 the City College, along with other units of the City University of New York (CUNY), engaged in another experiment. CUNY opened its doors to all high school graduates in the city regardless of class standing. The university was flooded with unprepared students, many of whom could not even read at an eighth-grade level. Officials instituted remedial programs in almost every area of instruction. By 1974 the faculty realized that these programs had failed.[189] The disadvantages imposed on lower-class students by their familial backgrounds, by ghetto elementary schools, and by the often chaotic conditions in New York high schools could not be overcome by relatively superficial remedial programs at the college level. In 1976 a fiscal crisis brought about by bad financial management of the city, an erosion of the tax base, and political manipulations by officials at all levels forced the imposition of tuition.

One result of this new policy at CUNY was a change in the composition of the student body. Students from very poor families could receive aid from the state or federal government, and students from wealthier families had the funds to take advantage of CUNY's facilities, but a middle group, those from white-collar and blue-collar backgrounds, was eliminated from the system. Therefore, in one of the nation's more extensive attempts to remove class and ethnic barriers to higher education—an experiment that involved 278,000 students in 1976—American society failed to produce reasonable alternatives to the socioeconomic bias that pervades higher education.

All these differences—in education, income, health, political power—that separate various socioeconomic groups in America naturally produce fundamental contrasts in basic attitudes and beliefs.

Stratification and Attitudes

We have already noted that one's social position affects one's political beliefs, educational aspirations, and attitudes about health, as well as the possibility of falling prey to delusions and hallucinations. Indeed, it would be fair to say that socioeconomic status affects every aspect of human personality. Among the most salient of these effects, one should take note of the child-rearing practices, conformity, and alienation.

Social classes differ drastically in *child-rearing practices*. First, the actual stability of parent-child relationships contrasts in important ways. At one extreme, the upper-class family lays great stress upon knowing one's ancestors, learning the "proper" ways to behave in terms of the family's tradition, and hiding any differences between the father and mother over the best ways to raise a child.[190] Middle-class (or white-collar) families tend to be accepting and egalitarian in relation to their children; the parents discipline them by reasoning and the threat of withholding love.[191] Blue-collar families, on the other hand, tend to use direct physical punishment, have lower aspirations for their children, and wish to maintain the strict obedience and conformity of their children.[192] An atmosphere of lovelessness often affects impoverished families, since they suffer from the highest rates of desertion, divorce, and separation.[193] More than the other social groups, they are likely to be headed by the mother.[194]

The results of these different child-rearing practices are predictable. Children from white-collar families, for example, more often say that they feel secure, loved, and trusted than do children from impoverished families.[195] Children from blue-collar or impoverished families have little access to information, are given meager verbal training, and are offered few educational aspirations.[196] Because of the economic pressures and familial insecurities, children who grow up in such an environment typically lack self-confidence, distrust both themselves and others, try to make up for their problems by presenting a facade of bravado, and generally face a situation where their life chances are severely restricted.[197]

One's occupation affects another crucial dimension of life: the degree of *conformity*. In a cross-national study that included all parts of the United States and Turin, Italy, as well, Melvin L. Kohn found that upper-class people generally believe that they control the nature and pace of their work.[198] They think that they are "self-directed." In turn, they carry over this attitude from their work to other aspects of life and are generally less conformist in all spheres of behavior. Blue-collar workers, on the other hand, are often subject to strict control, are highly organized, and deal with things rather than with people. Kohn argues that the lower-class person tends to be conformist in other matters as well and to view the outside world as controlling and threatening.[199] This relationship between occupation and self-direction cuts across educational, cultural, and religious boundaries. Thus, Kohn concludes: "The job does mold the man—it can either enlarge his horizons or narrow them. The conformity of the lower social classes is only partly a result of their lack of education; it results also from the restrictive conditions of their jobs."[200]

Gavin Mackenzie also argues that one's occupation is a crucial determinant of values and behavior.[201] And Alex Inkeles, in classic international studies of values and industrialization, has shown that classes develop specific values that are independent of their particular culture, and that urbanized, industrialized groups tend to be more tolerant, nonconformist, self-directed, and empathetic than those from rural regions.[202]

One's position in the social structure also vitally affects the degree of *alienation* that one may suffer. For the professional person or other members of the upper class, work is often an end in itself; a source of pleasure, satisfaction, dignity, and self-enhancement.[203] For the white-collar worker, an occupation "does not have an intrinsic value; it is rather a means to an end."[204] And the unskilled laborer is almost totally alienated from his or her occupation:

> The work satisfies no psychic, physical, or mental need, and lacks intrinsic value, being completely and absolutely utilitarian. The unskilled worker brings little or no effort, interest, or motivation to labor, and derives nothing from it beyond the means of subsistence.[205]

Many studies have confirmed this generalization. Duberman noted, for example, that 59 percent of professional workers reported that they were "highly involved" in their work as opposed to 25 percent of blue-collar workers who reported this.[206] Bidnick and Lopreato found that twice as many blue-collar workers as other groups said they "disliked everything" about their jobs.[207] In fact, most lower-status Americans are so alienated from their work that they would never wish their children to take up the same occupation.[208]

Some observers have contended that the advent of bureaucratization in postindustrial societies increases alienation among workers, whereas others have suggested that it decreases it.[209] Nevertheless, the bureaucratization of contemporary society has indeed vitally affected the attitudes and behavior of people.

Stratification and Bureaucracy

There have been bureaucrats throughout history: the courtiers surrounding a pharaoh, a Roman emperor, or a French king. What is new is that, as Joseph Bensman and Bernard Rosenberg have aptly stated, "not bureaucracy, but the bureaucratization of society is unique to modern times."[210] And bureaucracy is of great importance for social stratification.

As we have already noted in Chapter 4, bureaucracy is fast becoming the predominant characteristic of postindustrial societies. Whether one functions in the army, an industry, a religion, or a university, the bureaucratic style of life that Max Weber originally delineated prevails: payment by fixed salary; holding of an office by tenure; written rules and regulations; and rigidly defined rights, privileges, duties, and procedures.[211] This spread of bureaucracy, as Weber noted, has its advantages, for it facilitates efficiency, predictability, and impersonality. Also, as we have previously argued, promotion within a bureaucratic system is the surest route to power and privilege in contemporary society.

The effects of this link between bureaucracy and the socioeconomic system are extremely important. Bensman and Rosenberg have noted some of the more crucial effects. For one thing, a bureaucrat must *identify* with his organization if he is to rise within it. Even his wife and children may become auxiliaries to his desire for power. Yet, "to play his role as a bureaucrat at all adequately is to pay a heavy social and psychological price. The official has to repress certain . . . sentiments . . . instilled in him as a youth,"[212] and he will have to neglect certain social roles that he might otherwise enjoy but that are not compatible with his profession. He must also "begin to view himself as a merchandisable product that he must market and package like any other commodity."[213] He tends to become an "organization man" whose bureaucratic behavior becomes his "real" self.

According to Bensman and Rosenberg, this organization man typically experiences three types of stress: a feeling of impersonality; isolation from others (made up for partially by membership in a clique); and a sense of powerlessness, which may be expressed in any form of behavior from rejecting completely the goals of the bureaucracy to identifying himself totally with the organization. Frustrated by these stresses, the individual may well withdraw into a ritualistic or legalistic observance of the bureaucracy's procedure. Bensman and Rosenberg have discovered a classic example of this phenomenon.

Nazi documents captured after World War II indicate that on the day Adolf Hitler committed suicide and Russian troops were marching through the streets of Berlin, officials of the Reichschancellery were too busy to look out of their windows. They were estimating and ordering paper clips for the next fiscal year.[214]

Authoritarianism also flourishes in a bureaucratic atmosphere. As the Watergate crimes suggest, faceless officials may well feel compelled to carry out crimes in the name of loyalty to a particular organization.

Child-rearing practices of bureaucrats may follow a certain pattern. Parents seek to mold a child who will grow up to be flexible, charming, amiable, tactful, and conforming.[215]

Politically, bureaucrats must conform their outward attitudes to those of the organization. It is the fear of the loss of their jobs that motivates them to do this.

Physical mobility is required by modern bureaucracies—a constant shifting of residence to suit the needs of the company. This may uproot friendships and family traditions, serving to isolate a person even more from other social contacts than those of the bureaucracy in which he or she functions.

In short, bureaucracies have a vast and, as yet, largely uncharted effect upon the social stratification system and every other aspect of life. One of the prime tasks of social scientists in the future will be to map out the specific effects of bureaucratic life on every aspect of human existence from child rearing to politics, from education to feelings of autonomy.

Can one escape the effects of bureaucracy, stratification, and the class system? Generations of Americans dreamed that they could. Migration to America originally represented social (as well as geographic) mobility. The great majority of our ancestors believed that they could gain both freedom and economic advancement in America. Because of the opening of the frontier and the general advance of the economy, many of those dreams were fulfilled. A penniless laborer from Scotland, Ireland, Russia, or Italy could become a millionaire or a president. Recent research, however, suggests that present and future generations of Americans may well be disappointed in their hopes for social mobility.

Stratification and Social Mobility

Because of their belief in equality of opportunity, Americans have been deeply concerned with the possibilities of *social mobility*; that is, the chances of a person moving from one social stratum to another. American sociologists have, in turn, devoted a great deal of energy and debate to this issue.*

In fact, the first book on social mobility appeared as early as 1927, when Pitirim Sorokin pointed out that no society is completely closed or open in social mobility.[218] In 1936 Ralph Linton made a distinction that

---

*The issues that divide sociologists are intricate and complex. They have argued over such arcane issues as whether one should use the word "attained" status instead of "achieved" status, the proper ways for measuring social mobility, the "permeability" of social class, whether people do in fact deserve more power and privileges, and how one should draw proper comparisons between different nations or historical periods. Since these methodological issues have been exhaustively discussed by Duberman[216] and Rossides,[217] we will not attempt to elaborate upon their arguments.

has since been used by many sociologists.[219] He noted that some people receive their power and privileges in life because of their *ascribed status* (that is, their hereditary position) or their *achieved status* (that is, the position that they eventually attained in life because of merit, effort, or luck). If this difference did indeed exist, America could be viewed as a fairly open nation since it did not, for example, automatically accord people privileges because they were born as members of an aristocracy.

In 1972, however, John F. Scott pointed out the fallacies in this position.[220] He noted that all members of an American family generally receive the same social status and that an eventually higher "achieved" status may merely reflect the family's contribution to the child's education and placement in the occupational structure. Joseph Kennedy, for example, may have "achieved" his millionaire status through, among other activities, his bootlegging operations. Because of their "ascribed" status, his children received the money to attend prep schools, matriculate at Harvard, and finance their political campaigns. Without denigrating the actual achievements of a John Kennedy, it is clear that his career was not harmed by his "ascribed" status.

Can people in America rise in social level if they are not members of the upper class? The evidence is somewhat contradictory. In comparison to Great Britain, Japan, and the Netherlands, a somewhat higher proportion of Americans in the working class achieve upward mobility. About 30 percent of manual workers and some 32 percent of nonmanual workers in America are apparently able to achieve a higher occupational status than that of their fathers.[221] It should also be noted, however, that about 18 percent of manual workers and 19 percent of nonmanual workers have *fallen* in social status compared to that of their fathers.[222] Thus individuals may rise or fall in the socioeconomic system in America, but the general proportions of each social class remain rather stable. Naturally, one should recognize that manual occupations throughout the industrialized world have shrunk while white-collar groups have increased.[223]

Peter Blau and Otis Dudley Duncan have generally supported the cross-national findings of other studies.[224] They gathered records on some 20,000 people and found that children generally occupy the same socioeconomic position as their parents; more people in America move upward than downward; and people generally move up or down only by one occupation.[225] (In other words, it is extraordinarily unlikely that the son of a longshoreman would become president of a bank. At best, he might become a foreman on the docks.)

Thus, except for general shifts in the entire economy or in the occupational structure, most Americans must reconcile themselves—happily or not—to occupying a similar place in the occupational structure to the one their parents occupied. This may be due in part to the early socialization process of children as well as to their economic position.[226] It may also be accounted for by the fact that many people do not in fact wish to rise in occupational status. They may realize, as Kenneth Kessin has proved, that upwardly mobile people have more signs of anxiety, psychosomatic illnesses, and neuroses. Perhaps they do not wish to pay the price.[227] They may, if they are women, count on a fortunate marriage to improve their socioeconomic standing.[228] They may be lulled into complacency by the fact that long-term economic trends until the 1970s generally replaced lower-class jobs with white-collar jobs.[229]

Whatever the reasons, it would be extreme to say that social mobility has ended in America. Nonetheless, it is evident that many of the elements that contributed to people's good fortune in the past no longer exist. It is reasonable to expect that one's chances of enormous gains in power and privilege in America are virtually ended unless one is fortunate enough to inherit one's parents' upper socioeconomic position.

Conclusions

Because of her vast resources, America has enjoyed an especially privileged position among the world's nations. Economic growth has fostered a feeling that opportunities are unlimited and that "anyone can grow up to be president." But with the depletion of the world's natural resources and the globe's population explosion, the American dream of ever-increasing affluence has been brought to an end. Further, those Americans who have shared this dream would be shocked to learn the facts of existing inequality. Distinct subcultures have arisen in this country that divide the socioeconomic structure in a variety of ways.

Americans differ, of course, in the actual amount of wealth they possess and in their material consumption. Since 1900 the gaps in American wealth have not changed radically: the richest part of the nation receives slightly less of the economic "pie," but the poorest segment of the population is also getting relatively less than before.

The upper strata occupy the most important political offices, tend to be more active politically, and hold more conservative positions on economic issues than do the lower strata. People who fall in socioeconomic standing are most likely to adopt extremist political positions. People in the lower strata lean toward conservative positions on matters involving civil liberties or civil rights.

Because of their political and economic power, the upper strata have managed to pass laws that favor them in matters as diverse as vagrancy and taxation. White-collar criminals who generally emerge from the upper strata have usually managed to evade the law's penalties.

"Street" crime, mental disorder, alcoholism, addiction, and suicide have reached epidemic level among the lower socioeconomic groups. Yet, despite their affluence, the upper strata also suffer from high rates of alcoholism and suicide.

Physically, the upper strata have a longer life expectancy, are less likely to be killed in war, and are less subject to chronic diseases.

Educationally, people in the lower strata suffer from deprived family backgrounds, impoverished school systems, and systematic biases in higher education. High intelligence alone will not salvage their careers since many who score well on IQ tests but come from the lower strata cannot finish college.

The lower strata experience different forms of socialization than the middle or upper groups and, in consequence, develop a set of attitudes that hamper them in a later life that is dominated by higher social groups. Alienation pervades the lower social strata since they can find little meaning in their work. Their routinized occupations tend to breed conformity rather than a feeling of self-direction.

The bureaucratization of society has had serious repercussions for the stratification system. Most potently, bureaucracy has created an "organization man" whose behavior and attitudes conform to the demands of the system.

Although promotion within a bureaucracy has emerged as the major path of social mobility, there is little chance for an American to break the mold that his or her socioeconomic background established.

These are the major dimensions of social stratification in contemporary America. A person's health, criminal pattern, political influence, feelings of alienation—and a multitude of other facets of life—are established by his or her place in the socioeconomic system, and there is little opportunity for escape.

This molding is particularly rigid for two groups in our society: women and ethnic minorities. They are affected by sexism and racism, which are, in turn, closely linked with the system of stratification.[230] In the case of women, as Joan Acker has argued, "females can be viewed as constituting caste-like groupings within social classes."[231] For blacks, as Alphonso Pinkney concluded after a review of their history, "a caste system developed which continues to relegate the former slaves and their descendents to a subordinate position in society."[232] Because of their unique importance, we will now consider the special position of women and minorities in the stratification system.

Notes

1. Robert Heilbroner, *An Inquiry into the Human Prospect* (New York: Norton, 1974).
2. See Paul R. Ehrlich, *The Population Bomb* (New York: Ballantine, 1968).
3. See Hans S. Bethe, "The Hydrogen Bomb II," in *Scientific American Reader* (New York: Simon & Schuster, 1953), pp. 194–195.
4. See Robert U. Ayers and Allen V. Kneese, "Economic and Ecological Effects of the Stationary State," *Resources for the Future*, Report 99, December 1972, p. 16.
5. Walter Sullivan, "Experts Voice Some Hope Despite the Vast Global Scope of Disease and Malnutrition," *The New York Times*, April 14, 1975, p. 25.
6. *Scientific American,* September 1974.
7. Kingsley Davis, "The World Population Crisis," in Robert K. Merton and Robert Nisbet, eds., *Contemporary Social Problems* (New York: Harcourt Brace Jovanovich, 1971).
8. Johnson C. Montgomery, "The Island of Plenty," *Newsweek,* December 23, 1974.
9. See *Report of the Commission on Population Growth and the American Future,* Washington, D.C., 1972.
10. Agency for International Development, quoted in *The New York Times,* January 26, 1975.
11. Ibid.
12. Ibid.
13. Ibid.
14. "Climate Changes Endanger World Food Output," *The New York Times,* August 13, 1974.
15. Ibid.
16. Lester R. Brown, with Erik P. Eckholm, *By Bread Alone* (New York: Praeger, 1975).
17. Harrison Brown, *The Challenge of Man's Future* (New York: The Viking Press, 1956).
18. See Heilbroner, *Inquiry into the Human Prospect.*
19. See Council on Environmental Quality, *First Annual Report* (Washington, D.C.: Government Printing Office, 1976).
20. See Ford Foundation Report, *A Time to Choose* (New York: Ballantine, 1974).
21. Ibid.
22. William B. Tavoulareas, quoted in *The New York Times,* October 18, 1974.
23. Louis G. Battan, *The Unclean Sky* (Garden City, N.Y.: Doubleday, 1966).
24. David W. Ehrenfeld, *Biological Conservation* (New York: Holt, Rinehart & Winston, 1970).
25. Heilbroner, *Inquiry into the Human Prospect.*
26. Ibid.
27. Ibid.
28. Department of Commerce data cited in Daniel W. Rossides, *The American Class System* (Boston: Houghton Mifflin, 1976), p. 115.
29. Ibid., p. 117.
30. Ibid., p. 114.
31. John Kenneth Galbraith, *The New Industrial State* (Boston: Houghton Mifflin, 1967).
32. A. A. Berle, "Economic Power and the Free Society," in Andrew Hacker, ed., *The Corporation Take-over* (New York: Harper & Row, 1964), pp. 101–102.
33. Ralph Nader, *Unsafe at Any Speed* (New York: Grossman, 1965).
34. Ralph Nader, quoted in Jerome Skolnick and Elliot Currie, *Crisis in American Institutions* (Boston: Little, Brown, 1970), p. 143.

35. Robert Sheehan, "Proprietors in the World of Big Business," *Fortune*, June 15, 1967.

36. New York Stock Exchange, *1970 Census of Share-Owners*.

37. Ibid.

38. Paul Blumberg, *The Impact of Social Class* (New York: Crowell, 1972), p. 84.

39. See Herman P. Miller, *Rich Man, Poor Man* (New York: Crowell, 1964), for a discussion of "Pareto's Law."

40. Ibid.

41. Ibid.

42. Gabriel Kolko, *Wealth and Power in America* (New York: Praeger, 1960).

43. Blumberg, *Impact of Social Class*.

44. Kolko, *Wealth and Power in America*.

45. Philip M. Stein, *The New York Times Magazine*, April, 1969.

46. See August Hollingshead and Frederick C. Redlich, *Social Class and Mental Illness* (New York: Wiley, 1958), for a further definition of "classes."

47. See E. Digby Baltzell, *Philadelphia Gentlemen* (Glencoe, Ill.: Free Press, 1958), and *The Protestant Establishment* (New York: Random House, 1964).

48. Ibid.

49. U.S. Bureau of the Census, *Current Population Reports, 1971*.

50. See C. Wright Mills, *White Collar* (New York: Oxford University Press, 1951); and Eleanor Maccoby and Patricia Gibbs, "Methods of Child Rearing in Two Social Classes," in W. E. Morton and C. Stendler, eds., *Readings in Child Development* (New York: Harcourt, Brace, 1954).

51. *Current Population Trends, 1971*.

52. Rossides, *American Class System*, p. 406.

53. See Albert K. Cohen and Harold M. Hodges, "Characteristics of the Lower Blue Collar Class," *Social Problems* 10 (Spring 1964); Walter Miller, "Lower-Class Culture as a Generating Milieu of Gang Delinquency," *Journal of Social Issues* 14 (1958).

54. Herbert Gans, *The Urban Villagers* (New York: Free Press, 1962); and Mirra Komarovsky, *Blue Collar Marriage* (New York: Random House, 1964).

55. Gans, *Urban Villagers*.

56. See Oscar Lewis, *Village Life in Northern India* (Urbana: University of Illinois Press, 1958).

57. See Harold R. Wilensky, "Class, Class Consciousness and American Workers," in William Haber, ed., *Labor in a Changing Society* (New York: Basic Books, 1966).

58. See Oscar Glantz, "Class Consciousness and Political Solidarity," *American Sociological Review* 23 (1958): 375, 83.

59. See John C. Leggett, *Class, Race and Labor* (New York: Oxford University Press, 1968).

60. Cited in Reinhard Bendix and Seymour Lipset, *Class, Status and Power* (New York: Free Press, 1966), p. 21.

61. See Robert Bierstedt, "An Analysis of Social Power," *American Sociological Review* 15 (1950): 730–738.

62. Thomas Dye, Eugene De Clercq, and John Pickering, "Concentration, Specialization, and Interlocking Among Institutional Elites," *Social Science Quarterly* 54 (June 1973): 8–28.

63. Ibid.

64. See Mills, *White Collar*, for one side of the argument and David Riesman et al., *The Lonely Crowd* (New Haven, Conn.: Yale University Press, 1961), for the other side. William Kornhauser in "Power Elite or Veto Group?" in Bendix and Lipset, *Class, Status and Power*, pp. 210–218, analyzes the differences and similarities between the various schools of thought.

65. Donald R. Mathews, *The Social Background of Political Decision Makers* (New York: Random House, 1954).
66. Mills, *White Collar.*
67. G. William Domhoff, *Who Rules America?''* (Englewood Cliffs, N.J.: Prentice-Hall, 1967).
68. Donald R. Mathews, *The Social Class Background of U.S. Senators* (Chapel Hill: University of North Carolina Press, 1960).
69. Frederic C. Jaher, *The Rich, Well Born, and the Powerful* (Urbana: University of Illinois Press, 1973).
70. Harmon Zeigler and Michael A. Baer, "The Recruitment of Lobbyists and Legislators," *Midwest Journal of Political Science* 12 (November 1968).
71. Lee Webb, "A Welfare State for the Rich," *Ramparts,* October 26, 1968.
72. Dennis S. Ippolito, "Political Perspectives of Suburban Party Leaders," *Social Science Quarterly* 49 (March 1969).
73. Bruce M. Hackett, *Higher Civil Servants in California* (Berkeley: University of California Press, 1967).
74. Morris Janowitz, *The Professional Soldier* (New York: Free Press, 1960).
75. Ralph Miliband, *The State in Capitalist Society* (New York: Basic Books, 1969), p. 181.
76. See, for example, Richard Centers, *The Psychology of Social Classes* (Princeton, N.J.: Princeton University Press, 1949); and Joseph Lopreato and Lawrence Hazelrigg, *Class, Conflict, and Mobility* (San Francisco: Chandler, 1972).
77. Lucille Duberman, *Social Inequality* (Philadelphia: Lippincott, 1976), p. 183.
78. Seymour Martin Lipset, *Political Man* (Garden City, N.Y.: Doubleday, 1960), p. 97.
79. Ibid., pp. 101–102.
80. Ibid.; and Seymour Martin Lipset and Earl Raab, *The Politics of Unreason* (New York: Harper & Row, 1970).
81. Daniel Bell, ed., *The Radical Right* (Garden City, N.Y.: Doubleday, 1964).
82. Richard Flacks, *Youth and Social Change* (Chicago: Markham, 1970).
83. William Kornhauser, "Power and Participation in the Racial Community," Health Education Monographs, No. 6 (Oakland: Society of Public Health Educators, 1959).
84. Sidney Verba and Norman H. Nie, *Participation in America* (New York: Harper & Row, 1972).
85. Ibid.
86. Lee Rainwater, ed., *Social Problems and Public Policy* (Chicago: Aldine, 1974).
87. Walter Dean Burnham, "Equality of Voting," in ibid.
88. Duberman, *Social Inequality,* p. 186.
89. William McCord, *Mississippi: The Long Hot Summer* (New York: Norton, 1965).
90. See James Madison, *Federalist Paper No. 10.*
91. Rossides, *American Class System,* pp. 409–410.
92. William J. Chambliss, "A Sociological Analysis of the Law of Vagrancy," *Social Problems* 12 (Summer); reprinted in William Chambliss, ed., *Crime and the Legal Process* (New York: McGraw-Hill, 1969).
93. McCord, *Mississippi: The Long Hot Summer.*
94. Lawrence M. Friedman, *Government and Slum Housing* (Chicago: Rand McNally, 1968).
95. James W. Davis and Kenneth Dolbeare, *Little Groups of Neighbors* (Chicago: Markham, 1968).
96. M. Zeitlin, R. A. Lutterman, and J. W. Russell, "Death in Vietnam: Class, Poverty, and the Risks of War," *Politics and Society* 3 (Spring 1973): 312–328.
97. Edwin Sutherland, *White Collar Crime* (New York: Dryden, 1949).
98. Edwin Sutherland, "Crime and Business," *Annals of the American Academy of Political and Social Science* 217.

99. Nicholas Johnson, "The Silent Screen," *TV Guide*, July 5, 1969.
100. Ibid.
101. Ibid.
102. Nicholas Johnson, quoted in Jerome Skolnick and Elliot Currie, *Crisis in American Institutions* (Boston: Little, Brown, 1970), p. 141.
103. *Newsweek*, March 3, 1965.
104. Robert A. Hutchinson, *Vesco* (New York: Praeger, 1975).
105. "How 3M Got Tangled Up in Politics," *The New York Times*, March 9, 1975.
106. Daniel Bell, "Crime as an American Way of Life," *Antioch Review* 13 (Summer 1953).
107. See Jerome Carlin, Jan Howard, and Sheldon Messinger, *Civil Justice and the Poor* (New York: Russell Sage Foundation, 1967).
108. Ibid.
109. Ibid.
110. Ibid.
111. See Edward Sagarin, *Deviants and Deviance* (New York: Praeger, 1975), for a brilliant discussion of the complexities in analyzing the problem of deviance.
112. William McCord, Joan McCord, and Irving Kenneth Zola, *Origins of Crime* (New York: Columbia University Press, 1959); and I. Taylor, P. Walton, and J. Young, *The New Criminology* (New York: Harper & Row, 1973).
113. Albert Cohen, *Delinquent Boys* (Glencoe, Ill.: Free Press, 1955).
114. Richard Cloward and Lloyd Ohlin, *Delinquency and Opportunity* (New York: Free Press, 1960).
115. Sheldon and Eleanor Glueck, *Unraveling Juvenile Delinquency* (Cambridge: Harvard University Press, 1950).
116. See Richard Quinney, *Critique of Legal Order* (Boston: Little, Brown, 1973).
117. William Chambliss, "Functional and Conflict Theories of Crime," Module 17, (New York: MSS Modular Publications, 1975), pp. 1–23.
118. Ibid.
119. C. J. Judson, et al., "A Study of the California Penalty Jury in First Degree Murder Cases," *Stanford Law Review* 21 (1970): 1297–1431.
120. Ibid., p. 1379.
121. Theodore Chiricos and Gordon P. Waldo, "Socioeconomic Status and Criminal Sentencing," *American Sociological Review* 40 (December 1975): 753–772.
122. Ibid., p. 766.
123. Jerome Skolnick and Thomas C. Gray, *Police in America* (Boston: Little, Brown, 1975).
124. President's Commission on Law Enforcement, *Crime and Its Impact* (Washington, D.C.: Government Printing Office, 1967), Prologue.
125. See Enid Nemy, "Violent Crime by Young People: No Easy Answer," *The New York Times*, March 17, 1975.
126. See William McCord and Joan McCord, *The Psychopath* (Princeton, N.J.: Van Nostrand, 1965), for a review of studies conducted by Aichhorn, Bettleheim, Redl, and the authors.
127. See James Q. Wilson, "Lock 'em Up," *The New York Times Magazine*, March 9, 1975.
128. Emile Durkheim, *Suicide* (Glencoe, Ill.: Free Press, 1951).
129. Ronald W. Maris, *Social Forces in Urban Suicide* (Homewood, Ill.: Dorsey, 1963).
130. Elwin W. Powell, *The Design of Discord* (New York: Oxford University Press, 1970).
131. Elwin W. Powell, "Occupation, Status, and Suicide," *American Sociological Review* 23 (April 1958): 136.
132. Powell, *Design of Discord*.
133. Powell, "Occupation, Status, and Suicide."

134. Ibid.
135. Andrew Henry and James Short, Jr., *Suicide and Homicide* (Glencoe, Ill.: Free Press, 1954).
136. John Dollard, "Drinking Mores of the Social Classes," in *Alcohol, Science, and Society* (New Haven, Conn.: Journal of Studies of Alcohol, 1945).
137. Robert Bales, "Attitudes Toward Drinking in the Irish Culture," in David Pittman and Charles Snyder, eds., *Society, Culture and Drinking Patterns* (New York: Wiley, 1962); and Charles Snyder, *Alcohol and the Jews* (Glencoe, Ill.: Free Press, 1958).
138. Bales, "Attitudes Toward Drinking in the Irish Culture."
139. Isidor Chain, *The Road to H* (New York: Basic Books, 1964).
140. Charles Terry and Mildred Pellens, *The Opium Problem* (New York: Committee on Drug Addiction, 1930).
141. Ibid.
142. Ibid.
143. William McCord, "Tranquilizers and College Students," mimeo, 1976.
144. Ibid.
145. Ibid.
146. Ibid.
147. See Edward Sagarin, *The Reality of Mental Illness* (New York: Free Press, forthcoming).
148. E. L. Faris and H. Warren Dunham, *Mental Disorders in Urban Areas* (Chicago: University of Chicago Press, 1939).
149. Hollingshead and Redlich, *Social Class and Mental Illness.*
150. Leo Srole et al., *Mental Health in the Metropolis* (New York: McGraw-Hill, 1962).
151. Leo Srole, unpublished manuscript.
152. Aaron Antonovsky, "Social Class, Life Expectancy, and Overall Mortality," in Blumberg, *Impact of Social Class.*
153. Ibid.
154. Ibid.
155. Ibid., pp. 486–487.
156. Evelyn M. Kitagawa and Philip H. Hauser, *Differential Mortality in the United States* (Cambridge: Harvard University Press, 1973).
157. Donald J. Bogue, *Principles of Demography* (New York: Wiley, 1969).
158. Antonovsky, "Social Class, Life Expectancy, and Overall Mortality."
159. Ibid.
160. Robert P. Semple, "Negroes' Health Is Found Lagging," *The New York Times*, March 14, 1967.
161. Antonovsky, "Social Class, Life Expectancy, and Overall Mortality."
162. Lee Rainwater, "The Lower Class: Health, Illness, and Medical Institutions," in Lee Rainwater, ed., *Social Problems and Public Policy* (Chicago: Aldine, 1974), p. 180.
163. Ibid.
164. Ibid., p. 182.
165. Ibid., p. 184.
166. Rossides, *American Class System*, p. 204.
167. Charles A. Daly, ed., *The Quality of Inequality: Urban and Suburban Public Schools* (Chicago: University of Chicago Center for Policy Study, 1968).
168. Arthur E. Wise, *Rich Schools, Poor Schools* (Chicago, University of Chicago Press, 1968), chap. 6.
169. J. M. Tubb, cited in McCord, *Mississippi: The Long Hot Summer*, p. 35.
170. Ibid.
171. Wise, *Rich Schools, Poor Schools.*
172. Daly, *The Quality of Inequality.*

173. *Equality of Educational Opportunity* (Washington, D.C.: Government Printing Office, 1966).

174. Paul Lauter and Florence Howe, "How the School System Is Rigged for Failure," in Robert Lejeune, ed., *Class and Conflict in American Society* (Chicago: Rand McNally, 1972).

175. U.S. Bureau of Labor Statistics, *Special Labor Force Report,* Nos. 1, 125, 161, and 170, 1974.

176. U.S. Bureau of the Census, *Current Population Reports, 1972.*

177. U.S. Bureau of Labor Statistics, *Special Labor Force Report.*

178. Christopher Jencks and David Riesman, "On Class in America," *The Public Interest* 10 (Winter 1968).

179. Robert J. Honigheit and Bernice Neugarten, *Society and Education* (Boston: Allyn & Bacon, 1975), p. 391.

180. William Sewell and Vimal Shah, "Socioeconomic Status, Intelligence, and the Attainment of Higher Education," *The Sociology of Education* 40 (Winter 1967).

181. Ibid.

182. Ibid.

183. Ibid.

184. Ibid.

185. Ibid.

186. Ibid.

187. Ibid.

188. Jean-Jacques Servan-Schreiber, *The Radical Alternative* (New York: Dell, 1971).

189. See Joel Perlman, "Open Admissions at City College," City College of New York, February 8, 1974, p. 94.

190. Ruth Cavan, *The American Family* (New York: Crowell, 1969).

191. U. Bronfenbrenner, "Socialization and Social Class Through Time and Space," in Eleanor Maccoby et al., eds., *Readings in Social Psychology* (New York: Holt, Rinehart & Winston, 1958).

192. M. L. Kohn, "Social Class and Parent-Child Relationships," *American Journal of Sociology* 68 (1963): 471–480.

193. Cavan, *American Family.*

194. Ibid.

195. Eleanor Maccoby and Patricia Gibbs, "Methods of Child-Rearing in Two Social Classes," in W. E. Martin and C. Stendles, eds., *Readings on Child Development* (New York: Harcourt Brace, 1954).

196. See Srole et al., *Mental Health in the Metropolis.*

197. G. Knopfer, "Portrait of an Underdog," *Public Opinion Quarterly* 11 (Spring 1947).

198. Melvin L. Kohn, *Class and Conformity: A Study in Values* (Homewood, Ill.: Dorsey, 1969).

199. Ibid.

200. Ibid., p. 190.

201. Gavin Mackenzie, *The Aristocracy of Labor* (London and New York: Cambridge University Press, 1973).

202. Alex Inkeles, "Industrial Man," *American Journal of Sociology,* 66 (July 1960).

203. Duberman, *Social Inequality.*

204. Ibid., p. 151.

205. Ibid.

206. Ibid.

207. See Joseph Lopreato and Lionel S. Lewis, *Social Stratification* (New York: Harper & Row, 1974).

208. Arline McCord and Willaim McCord, *Urban Social Conflict* (St. Louis: Mosby, 1977).

209. Robert Blauner, *Alienation and Freedom* (Chicago: University of Chicago Press, 1964).
210. Joseph Bensman and Bernard Rosenberg, *Mass, Class, and Bureaucracy: An Introduction to Sociology* (New York: Praeger, 1976), p. 277.
211. Max Weber, in *From Max Weber* (New York: Oxford University Press, 1946).
212. Bensman and Rosenberg, *Mass, Class, and Bureaucracy*, p. 303; also see Joseph Bensman, *Dollars and Sense* (New York: Collier, 1974).
213. Bensman and Rosenberg, *Mass, Class, and Bureaucracy*, p. 305.
214. Ibid., p. 315.
215. Ibid., p. 323.
216. Duberman, *Social Inequality*, chap. 4.
217. Rossides, *American Class System*, chap. 3.
218. Pitirim Sorokin, *Social Mobility* (New York: Harper, 1927).
219. Ralph Linton, *The Study of Man* (New York: Appleton-Century, 1936).
220. John Finley Scott, "Ascription and Mobility," in Gerald W. Thielbar and Saul D. Feldman, eds., *Issues in Social Inequality* (Boston: Little, Brown, 1972), pp. 580–597.
221. T. Fox and S. M. Miller, "Intra-Country Variations: Occupational Stratification and Mobility," *Studies in Comparative International Development* 1 (1965).
222. Ibid.
223. Ibid.
224. Peter M. Blau and Otis Dudley Duncan, *The American Occupational Structure* (New York: Wiley, 1967).
225. Ibid.
226. Alan C. Kerckhoff, *Socialization and Social Class* (Englewood Cliffs, N.J.: Prentice-Hall, 1972).
227. Kenneth Kessin, "Social and Psychological Consequences of Intergenerational Occupational Mobility," *American Journal of Sociology* 77 (1971): 1–18.
228. Andrea Tyree and Judith Trear, "The Occupational and Marital Mobility of Women," *American Sociological Review* 39 (1974): 293–302.
229. Blau and Duncan, *American Occupational Structure*.
230. Ibid.
231. Joan Acker, "Women and Social Stratification," *American Journal of Sociology* 78 (1973): 936–945.
232. Alphonso Pinkney, *Black Americans* (Englewood Cliffs, N.J.: Prentice-Hall, 1975).

6

RACE AND SEX
AS BASES OF
DIFFERENTIATION AND
STRATIFICATION

Introduction

The intricacy of stratification in American society is demonstrated in the variety of descriptions of it found in social science literature.[1] In addition to the transformation of the class structure of specific communities over time,[2] and the variation in descriptions due to methodological differences,[3] there is the complexity of differentiation and stratification by race and sex.[4]

Race and class differences have long been identified as major interrelated features of the American stratification system. As early as 1930, for example, John Dollard described "Southerntown" in terms of the caste line between the white and the black populations. He also associated behavioral and attitudinal characteristics with the various classes that he identified.[5] However, to this time, a sociological theory has not been formulated to explain the relationship between the various bases of differentiating and stratifying racial groups in America.

The concept "ethclass" was introduced by Milton Gordon as a means of discussing certain aspects of the relationship between class and ethnicity.[6] An ethclass, according to Gordon, is created by the intersection of class and ethnic identity. Whereas people of different ethnic groups, but the same class standing, have been found to share similar behavioral and attitudinal characteristics, those who share an ethnicity but are of different social classes were found to share a sense of identity or "peoplehood."[7]

The ethclass concept has many advantages. Beyond allowing consideration of heretofore separate features of the American stratification system, it can aid in delineating similarities and differences in the degree of acculturation (that is, internalization of norms) and type of assimilation (that is, nature and degree of interaction) of subgroups within broader categories. The descriptions of the distribution of the population thus obtained, as well as attendant attitudes and adaptations of the various groups, are surely informative. Moreover, the distinction that Gordon draws between assimilation and acculturation can help to identify selected groups that may be acculturated but maintain social distance and group identification (such as the American Orthodox Jewish population)[8] or those groups that partially assimilate but maintain a distinct subculture (such as the Mohawk Indians).[9]

Gordon's conceptual scheme, moreover, appears to imply that only the dominant group and its culture retains the power and high status to which other groups differentially adapt themselves. For this reason, his concepts do not add to our understanding of the power processes in society; that is, the conditions surrounding the emergence of group solidarity within the categories of identification, or the relationship between the members of different subgroups. In addition, Gordon's framework does not aid in the specification of conditions of social mobility. For example, it does not tell us much about the mobility problems of those who may be acculturated but remain highly visible.

The problems of power and social mobility are, of course, related. In order to maintain their special privilege, a dominant group must place limits on the social mobility of members of a subordinate group. The limitation is made possible through formal and informal restrictions on participation in the nation's economy or polity. These restrictions, in turn, may be effected through social domination legitimated on the basis of presumed cultural, mental, and physical inferiority of the subordinate group: that is, racism.[10]

Most newly arrived immigrant groups in the United States were treated by the superordinate white Anglo-Saxon Protestant population as subordinate immediately after their arrival. There is, however, a difference between the subordination of the Irish in the 1900s and the still pervasive subordination of black Americans, Mexican-Americans, American Indians, and Orientals. White immigrants from Europe, especially if they became economically successful, were able to disappear into the superordinate white population: black immigrants, visible because of physical characteristics, could not.

The differentiation of people on the basis of race has been long debated and discussed by social and physical scientists.[11] In this chapter, we have chosen to categorize by race those who are defined as black, red (American Indians), or Oriental (for instance, Chinese and Japanese). Classification of people along these lines was selected because differences in skin color, hair, and eye form provide visibility and relatively easy differentiation, and in addition are congruent with the definition of race given by many anthropologists and geneticists.* Moreover, the categorization was chosen because it is familiar to most Americans and, despite the variability of specific physical attributes within the individual populations, has been associated with social meanings.† The social meanings that have been attached to these groups serve as the bases of racial-caste stratification.

The arbitrary nature of the classificatory scheme as it is used in American society is indicated by the inclusion of Mexican-Americans and Puerto Ricans in our discussion of American racial-castes. Both groups, of course, have Spanish backgrounds and a wide range of physical attributes. However, the visibility of these groups is increased by physical characteristics probably introduced at an early point in history by Indians, in the case of Mexican-Americans, and by Indians and blacks, in the case of Puerto Ricans and their language.

In contrast to Gordon, who focused on the more inclusive term "ethnicity,"** Robert Blauner[14] has chosen to direct his attention to the relationship between racial groups in the United States. Drawing on a paradigm of colonization, Blauner develops the theme that subordinated racial

---

*The term "race" as it is used in this chapter refers to "a group or population characterized by some concentrations, relative as to frequency and distribution of hereditary particles (genes), or physical characteristics, which appear, fluctuate, and often disappear in the course of time by reason of geographic and/or cultural isolation."[12]

†The arbitrary nature of even such a definition is indicated by the fact that the definition of an American Indian followed by the United States Census Bureau has been: "A person of mixed white and Indian blood should be returned as an Indian, if enrolled on an Indian Agency or Reservation roll; or if not so enrolled, if the proportion of Indian blood is one-fourth or more, or if the person is regarded as an Indian in the community where he lives." Similarly, the question of just who a Negro is had been resolved by the courts of different states. For example, Missouri makes "one-eighth or more Negro blood" the criterion, while Georgia and a number of other states classify as colored all persons with "any ascertainable trace of Negro blood in their veins."[13]

**"Race" is a term that is most commonly associated with physical characteristics. "Ethnicity," on the other hand, generally refers to a self-identification that an individual may make with others on the basis of nationality, religion, cultural or racial similarities, and common values and beliefs. Racial groups or ethnic groups may or may not form interest groups as a mode of protecting their own interests.

groups in American society are internal colonials. These groups, he argues, in contrast to the immigrants of European descent, were not allowed to compete in the capitalist system. Blockage was facilitated by physical attributes that could not be easily altered and was perpetuated by the ideology and stereotypes that developed.

The internal colonial status emphasizes the fatelessness of subordinate racial castes. The black community, contends Blauner, has experienced outside ownership of business and administrative decision-making, just as colonial peoples in Africa and Southeast Asia have. In addition, he notes that despite the numerical superiority of the black population, compared to that of many other groups, black Americans have held little political power. Other racial groups, such as the Chinese, although more successful than blacks in obtaining wealth and political power *within* their own community, have remained powerless and controlled by outside political and economic conditions. The different, yet similar situations of black Americans and other groups, such as the Chinese, writes Blauner, rest on the strength of their own business and community institutions, which in turn appear to be related to their traditional cultural and social organization. Moreover, he notes that it may be the group's small size that has made systematic oppression less central to those in power. Blauner's analysis of race and class in American society focuses on the subtleties and the explicitness of caste in his descriptions of the relationship between racial groups in American society.

The question of the castelike nature of race relations in the United States was investigated by W. Lloyd Warner and his associates as far back as 1936. Whether blacks (and other racial groups) can legitimately be considered "castes" has served as a point of continuing controversy among social scientists.[15] Oliver Cox[16] has been one of the major protagonists of the view that blacks constitute a class, not a true caste. Using as his basis of comparison the Indian caste structure, Cox's major argument centers around the fact that discrimination on the basis of caste was legal in India, whereas similar acts were illegal in the United States. He also argues that higher Indian castes do not exploit members of low castes. American blacks, however, have been exploited by whites.

Both of the arguments against the analysis of American race relations in terms of caste are incorrect. As discussed in Chapter 2, discrimination against a low-caste person in India, *is* illegal. Further, in India, as in the United States (and elsewhere), work defined as "undesirable" is always relegated to those at the bottom of the stratification system. If the majority of people within a given society define specific labors as undesirable (for instance, cleaning the floor, collecting refuse, or handling dead persons), then it can be said that those who are systematically forced to engage in such actvities are being "exploited." It hardly matters whether restriction in occupational choice is based on having been born of low caste or having been born of a particular low-status racial group.

Whether or not the situation in the United States with regard to people of different racial categories is similar to the Indian caste system is an academic question. It is significant, nonetheless, in that it allows social scientists to make cross-cultural comparisons and perhaps to develop some generalizations. Aside from comparisons, the most important issues are the consequences of caste (or castelike) characteristics for the people of a given society and the quality of life experienced by them.

Race (as opposed to nationality—for instance, Irish, Italian), because it allows an inescapable identification, has provided convenient bases of discrimination. Lack of mobility across occupations, relatively low income, little political power, and subjection to arbitrary decisions by those in power have been the lot of those who are not white in the United States. The history of slavery and conditions of life associated with being black in America,[17] the infamous treatment of American Indians,[18] and the discreditable government action against Japanese-Americans in 1942[19] are only a few flagrant examples of the racism that is part of the American heritage.

A Brief Look Backward

Racism, in overt and covert forms, and its companion ideology, white supremacy, disembarked with the earliest arrivals to the New World. The roots of these attitudes and beliefs are based in ethnocentrism and feelings of cultural superiority common in history to all who make distinctions between "us" and "them."[20] Even a brief historical review of the relationships between some of the groups who converged on the North American continent should add depth and perspective to the nature of present and future relationships between them.

THE AMERICAN INDIAN[21]

The European invaders and colonizers viewed the continent of North America as wilderness. With the exception of the Pueblo Indian, most of the Indians subsisted either as hunters or gatherers or as modest horticulturalists in areas such as river bottoms. The Europeans saw the land as unused and unclaimed when they looked at the large forests and the lack of fencing or border demarcations.

The intensive agricultural techniques, the cattle ranches, the home-steads, and the railroad all contributed to the displacement of the Indians from their former territory. Their vulnerability was increased through decimation by illnesses that the Europeans had brought with them, including tuberculosis, measles, smallpox, mumps, scarlet fever and diphtheria. Genocide aided in quieting the Indians' claims to their own land.

Treaties, whereby the Indians surrendered their use of vast areas of land in return for some form of annuity, were the most common mechanisms used by the government. The Indians continued to lose bargaining power in transactions with the government, and as a result they were eventually forced to adapt in ways that made for a different and depressed life style.

The history of Indian-white relationships has included almost the full range of ideologies of race relations. As summarized by Murray Wax, it includes:

> . . . the early pluralistic notion of separate Indian nations, and also the melting pot notion of intermarriage which, while it invariably involved White male and Indian female, nonetheless allowed the couple to establish their home in either society. Simultaneously, there was the operation of the ideology of genocide (extermination). An effective counter to this latter ideology was that of missionization . . . to achieve "cultural (rather than biological) extermination" . . . the emergence of American anthropology, with its focus upon the native peoples of this hemisphere, gave a formidable boost to the ideology of Cultural Pluralism.[22]

THE AMERICAN BLACK

The relationship of white people to black people in American society has provided the most powerful and best-documented form of racism. Prejudice, in this instance, was transplanted from the earliest European experiences with Africa. The first explorers from Portugal, Spain, and England rarely failed to comment on the complexion of the people in the newly discovered areas of Africa. Even sympathetic observers found the color of the people a most salient feature for discussion. As one such observer noted: "although the people were blacke and naked, yet they were civil."[23]

The English, who were the last of the Western powers to explore the sub-Saharan region, defined the Africans as black; the color connoted many negative attributes. The *Oxford English Dictionary* states that one definition of "black" before the sixteenth century was "Deeply stained with dirt; soiled, dirty, foul. . . having dark or deadly purposes, malignant; pertaining to death, deadly, disastrous, sinful. . . . Foul, iniquitous, atrocious, horrible, wicked."[24] The English, confronted with black people, set themselves against what they thought to be the contrasting qualities of people of this color, including their religion, style of life, personality, and morality.[25]

In the light of English actions in North America, it appears that they had learned their lessons well: people of color were different from themselves. By 1790 there were approximately 700,000 black people (both free and slaves) in the United States. This number represented 19 percent of the population. In 1807 Congress enacted legislation that legally ended the importation of slaves. However, by this time, prejudice and discrimination against blacks was strong; this was reflected in the many early efforts to resettle black freedmen outside the boundaries of what was then defined as the United States. Alan Grimes[26] describes attempts at such action by five different states in 1816 and 1817. The proposals by these states ranged from a specific resolution passed by the Virginia House of Delegates requesting the purchase of land on the northern Pacific Coast for "emancipated Negroes" to more general pleas to help colonize the "free people of color" anywhere.

Although the Civil War brought the practice of slavery to a dramatic halt, the general acceptance of white supremacy continued. Discrimination and prejudice against black people was not restricted to the South; indeed, racism was institutionalized in all regions of the United States.[27] It continues today.

THE AMERICAN ORIENTAL

During the latter part of the nineteenth century and early part of the twentieth century, the migration of Asians to the West Coast of the United States resulted in another biracial confrontation. The Chinese came into California shortly after the Gold Rush of 1849.[28] Their migration was facilitated by a system called contract labor, which, according to Grimes, had many parallels to the earlier importation of black slave labor.[29] Under this system, shiploads of Chinese laborers would serve labor contractors for a term of a year or more in return for passage and four or five dollars a month. The contractor would deposit his human cargo, sell his contracts to the highest bidder, then return to China for a new shipload of strong backs and arms. Between 1852 and 1854 more than 33,000 Chinese were admitted into the United States. By 1880 approximately 75,000 Chinese had been brought to California.[30]

The Chinese workers performed many of the menial jobs, first for the miners, then in the fishing, agricultural, and manufacturing industries.[31] Conflict between the whites and the Chinese was found in each of the occupations in which the latter were engaged. In 1852, for example, a special tax was levied upon all aliens engaged in mining. In 1859 and 1867 agitation and rioting against Chinese cigarmakers and the Chinese in the shoe and boot industry took place. The 1870 smallpox epidemic was blamed on the Chinese; "anticoolie" clubs were organized, and mass meetings and riots ensued.

Humanitarians began to direct some attention to the system of contract labor. However, the inhuman treatment of the coolies became entangled with the issue of depressed wages of white labor resulting from the competition. Under the leadership of Samuel Gompers of the American Federation of Labor, the immigration of Chinese (or any other) contract labor was prohibited.[32]

The arrival of most Japanese immigrants on the West Coast coincided with the blockage of Chinese immigration. Although there were little more than 2,000 Japanese in the United States in 1890, approximately 92,000 Japanese came via Hawaii during the first decade of the twentieth century. Almost immediate reaction followed in the form of anti-Japanese meetings, newspaper attacks (1905), and various proposals for discriminatory and repressive measures. President Theodore Roosevelt negotiated the famous "Gentleman's Agreement," limiting implicitly the wave of migration, and executive orders were issued to halt all Japanese immigration. Hostilities of the American population against the immigration of people from Asia culminated in 1924, when the law barring the immigration of all persons ineligible for citizenship was passed by Congress.[33]

Racism, though institutionalized in the fabric of American life, does not always take forms as explicit as mass meetings or pogroms. Confronted with a diversity of race as well as nationality, religion, and creed that espouses the value of all people, American society has evolved a multitude of resolutions as to the position of these people in the social organization of the nation. In addition, sex, as another basis of differentiation, has been used to oppress a large portion of the population. In the sections to follow, the nature of racism and sexism is explored through the use of statistics to examine the relative positions of selected groups. Such statistics perhaps will aid in a refinement of our understanding of the nature of oppression in the United States.

Caste and Class in American Society in the 1970s

Approximately 17 percent of the American population has been subject to disadvantages due to racism. Before beginning our examination of some facets of the life experiences of the groups selected as the subject of this section, let us briefly outline some basic demographic facts about the racial and cultural groups in the United States.

TABLE 6.1   U.S. Population, 1970

Total American population	203,235,000
Blacks	22,581,000
Mexicans	5,023,000
Puerto Ricans	1,450,000
Cubans	626,000
Other Latins	1,851,000
American Indians	792,730
Japanese	591,290
Chinese	435,062
Filipinos	343,060
All others (Koreans, Polynesians, Indonesians, Hawaiians, Aleuts, Eskimos, Asian Indians, and others)	721,000

Source: Statistical Abstracts of the United States, 1973 and 1975 *(Washington, D.C.: Government Printing Office, 1973, 1975), Tables 31, 33, 34, 41, and 63.*

It can be noted from Table 6.1 that in 1970 blacks represented the largest racial caste population. Although nonwhite groups have remained a relatively small proportion of the population, statistics indicate that there has been a substantial increase in these populations just over the past few decades. Blacks, for example, represented 9.7 percent of the American population in 1940 and more than 11 percent in 1970. Within the same period, Japanese increased from .09 to .3 percent of the total population. New York City, which is the center of Puerto Rican migration, reported 45,000 Puerto Rican residents in 1930; by 1970 the number was close to 1 million first- and second-generation Puerto Ricans.[34] The Indian population has more than doubled since 1900, and it is believed that it is now increasing at approximately 1.7 to 2 percent a year, which is slightly higher than the rate for the total population of the United States.[35]

While the increase in the total number of racial-caste members is due to some immigration during this period, it is more largely due to the higher fertility rate of these people compared to that of the white population. The fertility rate of blacks, for example, is 25.2 per 1,000 women and that of whites is 15.5 per 1,000 women.[36] Fertility rates reflect many social factors, the most consistent of which is socioeconomic position. People of the same social class tend to have the same birth rate. More members of racial-caste groups, however, are economically disadvantaged, and the more disadvantaged groups tend to have higher fertility rates.[37] An obvious consequence of population increase through higher fertility rates is the number of young people in the population. Children under thirteen years of age make up 30.3 percent of the black population, but only 23 percent of the white population,[38] portending eventual changes in population growth.

Population increases may also be a result of an altered death rate. Medical advances appear to have benefited all groups. For example, the infant death rate for American Indians between 1955 and 1967 had declined by 48 percent, compared to a 15 percent drop in the rate for all races in the United States during that same period. However, combining all causes of death, the Indian and Alaska native adjusted rate remained 40 percent above the rate for all U.S. races at the end of the 1960s.[39]

While the difference between relative death rates of racial-caste members and white people has narrowed since the turn of this century, economic disadvantage continues to be reflected in the nature of fatal diseases each group is prey to. Alphonso Pinkney reports that three times as many blacks as whites die of diseases that modern medicine has brought under control for most people, that is, tuberculosis, syphilis, diabetes, gastritis, kidney infections, measles, influenza, and pneumonia.[40]

Further, the inadequacy of medical services is reflected in prenatal care and mother-child mortality rates. One Puerto Rican woman in three gets no prenatal care, and the infant mortality rate for Puerto Ricans stands at 37 per 1,000 live births.[41] Black women in 1970 were six times more likely to die in childbirth than whites, and 34.5 black infants per 1,000 died of birth injuries compared to a national average of 19.2 for white infants.[42] The lower class standing of blacks and other racial groups is further supported by data regarding the relative birth weights of newborn infants; birth weight reflects prenatal care and the nutrition available to the population. In 1973 the median birth weight of white infants was 7 pounds, 6 ounces; the median birth weight of other groups was almost a half pound lighter.[43]

Lower caste groups not only begin life with a relative disadvantage, they also die at an earlier age.[44] Whereas the life expectancy for a white man is 71.7 years, it is 64.6 years for blacks and 46 years for an American Indian on a reservation. [45]

The majority of racial-caste members live in cities. More than four times the number of blacks who reside in rural areas live in urban areas. In 1970 this meant that more than 80 percent of blacks compared to 73 percent of whites lived in a metropolitan area. Almost all Puerto Ricans, more than 96 percent of the Chinese, 88 percent of the Japanese, and 80 percent of the Mexicans[46] live in urban areas.

Within the city there exists a segregation along racial-caste lines. Earlier, most European migrants to urban areas had been free to move as they prospered; by force or through choice many racial-caste members have remained in their own residential enclave.[47] Blacks, however, have remained the most highly segregated population in American cities. This condition applies to cities of all sizes and regions in the country.[48]

Stanley Lieberson has argued that segregation of some groups is a result of their competitive position.[49] That is, low-status groups are isolated from high-status groups partly because the latter avoid locating their residence in some areas. Further, low-status groups are not able to compete for more attractive residential sites.

The segregation of populations may also serve the pragmatic interests of the superordinate population.[50] Rose Hum Lee reported some years ago that Chinatowns provide the services that were desired by the larger communities—for instance, Chinese hand laundries, specialty foods, and Oriental crafts.[51]

The statistics that have been presented depict the disadvantage of racial-caste groups in the United States. The overall demographic portrait of almost all racial-caste groups includes the following: high birth and death rates, shortened life expectancy, death from diseases that have been controlled in the dominant population, and a rapid migration into segregated sections of urban areas.[52] That is the lot of many Americans.

Statistics may, of course, be deceiving.[53] The daily life experiences of most racial-caste members cannot be fully portrayed by life-expectancy tables or residential distribution patterns. A discussion of specific social institutions should provide a broader understanding of life as a member of a racial-caste in American society. Let us first turn attention to the encounters of racial-caste members with agents of law enforcement.

CRIME

The increase in violent crimes over the nation has alarmed both urban and suburban[54] dwellers. Statistics presented in Table 6.2, for example, demonstrate the dramatic nature of the increase in crime even during as short a period as the past decade.

Urban dwellers in general experience more crime than do suburban or rural residents. Within the city, dwellers in the black ghetto have the highest number of encounters, both as criminals and as crime victims, with law enforcement agents. In 1972 the black population represented a relatively small proportion of the American population,[55] but adjusting

TABLE 6.2   Increases in National Crime Rate, 1960–70

Crime	Increase
Murder	+56%*
Assault	+92%
Rape	+85%
Robbery	+186%
Larceny	+204%

*Percentage increases based on rates per thousand population.

Source: FBI Uniform Crime Reports, 1970 (Washington, D.C.: Government Printing Office, 1970), p. 6.

the number of arrests by this proportion, the disproportionately high ratio of black to white arrests is indicated (see Table 6.3, Col. 3).

TABLE 6.3   Number of Arrests, 1972

Crime	Whites	Blacks	Disproportionality Rate of Blacks to Whites*
Murder and nonnegligent manslaughter	5,145	8,347	14$\frac{1}{2}$:1
Forcible rape	8,684	8,776	9:1
Robbery	28,236	536,553	19:1
Aggravated assault	72,976	62,890	8:1

*Adjusted for population size.

Source: Ben J. Wattenberg, The Real America (New York: Doubleday, 1974), p. 117.

That the nature of contact between law enforcement agents and members of racial-caste groups varies in frequency and nature is indicated by a comparison of the categories of arrests of American Indians with those of blacks. Whereas a large proportion of black arrests involve serious crimes, a disproportionate number of American Indians are arrested for crimes related to alcohol.[56] Moreover, the statistics indicate a disconcerting proportion of Indians in penal institutions. In South Dakota, for example, where Indians make up approximately 5 percent of the total state population, they constitute over one-third of the prison population.[57] Murray Wax says that these figures may suggest differences in conduct. On the other hand, he notes they may also denote differences in social status and wealth that affect the ways criminal justice deals with deviant behavior.[58] Middle- and upper-class whites commonly drink in the privacy of their home. If they should be so indiscreet as to appear on the street intoxicated, they are likely to be sent home, whereas others are more likely to be arrested.[59] The vulnerability of racial-caste groups to control by law enforcement agents would appear to be increased by their visibility and perhaps by the stereotypes accepted by various agents of social control.[60]

A large number of factors have been used to explain the crime rates of blacks and other racial groups, including physical and psychological conditions. In his classic discussion of the relationship between crime and race, Marvin E. Wolfgang has noted that since "criminal behavior is learned, and what is learned comes from experience with our surrounding environment, it is to the environment we must turn our attention."[61] The environment for most of the oppressed racial-caste members, however, is not conducive to supporting the "good life" as it is defined in American society. Tremendous human resources are lost through illness, death, and lack of training as well as criminal behavior.

FAMILY LIFE AND SOCIALIZATION

In 1965 the Moynihan report attributed much of the apparent disorganization of black communities to the state of the black family.[62] Daniel Moynihan drew attention to the relatively high rates of illegitimacy, divorce, welfare recipients, and female heads of families. While the statistics about the black American family were no doubt valid, critics of the report pointed to the fallacy implicit in his work: that is, that black people were to be blamed for their condition.[63] Lee Rainwater, for example, from his study of lower-class family life styles, pointed out that while the tendency toward matrifocality might appear intensified among lower-class black families, the pattern is also much in evidence in lower-class white families.[64] Anthropologist Oscar Lewis, in his study of Puerto Rican families,[65] and Helen Safa, in her work on the cultures of poverty,[66] also confirmed Rainwater's conclusion.

There is, then, little doubt that class position of subordinated groups does affect the structure and nature of family life. The majority of families of subordinated racial groups, however, are *not* fatherless. Table 6.4 indicates that only slightly less than one-third of all nonwhite families have female heads. The Census Bureau did, however, report that black and Puerto Rican families ranked highest of all nonwhite families in terms of female heads of families.[67]

In 1974, 34.6 percent of black families and 33.2 percent of Puerto Rican families had a female as head of the unit. The majority of nonwhite families, however, consist of both husband and wife. As Charles Willie[68] and Alphonso Pinkney[69] have independently commented: given the conditions of being black in a white society, it is indeed noteworthy that so many black families have remained stable. Emphasizing the strengths rather than the weaknesses of the black family, Reubin Hill, a specialist in the American family, noted that in spite of their problems, the strengths of the black families derives from the strong kinship bonds established between generations, the religious orientation and flexible family roles, and work and achievement orientations.[70]

Many reasons have been cited for the comparatively large number of female-headed families.[71] In the case of the black female-headed family, for example, the most commonly cited reasons include: (1) a history of slavery, when blacks were forced to develop alternative arrangements to the traditional nuclear family;[72] (2) the higher divorce rate of blacks compared to whites;[73] and (3) "abandonment" (real or falsified) of the family by black husbands in order to make the family eligible for welfare.[74]

TABLE 6.4 Comparison of American Families by Race, 1974

	Male Head (married, wife present)	Other Marital Status	Female Head
Black and other nonwhite groups	63.9%	4.3%	31.8%
White	87.7%	2.4%	9.9%

Source: Based on U.S. Bureau of the Census, Current Population Reports, Series P-20, No. 276 (computed), 1974.

More generally, Safa has argued that families in poverty are female-child-centered rather than husband-wife-centered because wives "cannot be sure that men will be adequate providers or will not have to leave to find work elsewhere, or may not abandon them for another woman." Moreover, Nathan Glazer and Daniel Moynihan point out that a common form of migration to the United States mainland from Puerto Rico is for the father to migrate alone, reside here for a while, and, when established, bring his family. Another form of migration is for a mother separated from her husband or an unmarried mother to move with her children to New York City, hoping to find life easier than on the island of Puerto Rico.[75] Class position and concomitant stresses, then, compound the life situation of people who find it difficult, if not impossible, to escape the problems of caste.

Examples that would appear to contradict the generalizations concerning lower-class position and family stress are to be found in the family organization of the Chinese, Japanese, and Mexican communities in the

United States. Traditional family loyalties and the extended-family structure associated with their culture provide part of the explanation for the relative family stability.[76] In each of these instances, however, oppression by the larger society has resulted in the forced retreat of these peoples into their own protective enclaves. Segregation, in turn, has allowed the maintenance of traditional customs. Family loyalties have carried over to the community; they established temples, published newspapers, continued to celebrate festivals, and settled their own disputes among themselves. The erosion of these communities has recently been marked.[77] Ironically, under these conditions, acculturation has meant an increase in divorce, delinquency, crime, and other symptoms of disorganization comparable to that of the society at large.[78]

The overall state of family life in different groups is itself interesting and informative. In modern society, which is frequently described as alienating, impersonal, and achievement-oriented, the family is assumed to provide a source of emotional expression, security, and commitment. The family structure of racial-caste groups, which differs from that of the "normal" (that is, middle-class) family appears, however, to have detrimental consequences for the socialization of children and for the well-being of adults. Lewis concluded on the basis of his work that disadvantaged children he studied took on responsibility for their own care and that of younger children at an early age. They also had fatalistic attitudes, an inability to defer gratification, and a relatively low level of aspiration for educational and occupational achievement, as well as a poor self-image. All these characteristics, however, cannot be attributed to females or single parents. Mexican-Americans, for example, hold many of these same attitudes, which in their case are derived from their traditional culture.[79] Poor self-image, on the other hand, has been found to be related to exposure to the broader white society. Bernard Rosenberg and Roberta Simmons noted in children they studied that it was *not* until a child experienced exposure to white middle-class teachers and peers that a negative self-esteem became most prominent.[80] This conclusion is contrary to commonly reported findings.[81] A child of any racial-caste, if he or she is loved and is an integral part of some kind of family has little reason to experience self-rejection.

The problem of socializing youngsters is, of course, exaggerated for those who have one parent, regardless of class. Middle- or upper-class, one-parent families, however, may ask friends, hire help, or rely on family to aid them in their time and energy allocations.[82] The problem of socializing youngsters is compounded for the one-parent, poverty-level family, commonly resulting in consequences such as that reported by Martin Deutsch and Bert Brown.[83] These researchers reported a relationship between a father's presence in the home and the child's school grades and IQ score.

Tragically, more single-parent families, especially female-headed ones, suffer from economic deprivation than do others of their own general class level. During 1972 approximately 53 percent of the black female-headed families had incomes below the poverty line ($4,275). This figure dropped to 16 percent for families in which the husband was present.[84] The meager income represented by this figure had to be stretched over the 2.84 children whom female heads of black families had to support. In 1972 approximately 70 percent of black children from female-headed families were living below the poverty level.[85]

Questions concerning the effect of family environments different from those of the two-parent middle-class family on academic achievement have been prominent in the literature since the late 1950s. The interest was prompted by the well-known longstanding academic disadvantage of lower-class children,[86] and more specifically of the children of racially subordinated groups such as blacks, Mexicans, Puerto Ricans, and Indians. Many explanations have been proffered. First, based on the work of Deutsch, the concept of cultural deprivation has been used to explain the differences between groups of children who performed below national norms. The basic argument behind this concept is that the characteristic interaction between children and adults inhibits the development of verbal skills and cognitive awareness necessary to success in school. Middle-class children, it is contended, are commonly exposed to a greater variety of colors, shapes and verbal utterances than are lower-class children, thus giving them an advantage as they begin and proceed through school.[87] However, it has been pointed out by many social scientists that lower-class children are *not* exposed to less stimulation than are middle-class children; rather, the stimuli have less variety or range appropriate to the skill development necessary for success in middle-class schools.[88]

Rather than describing lower-class culture and parental deficiencies in socialization practices, a second type of explanation for the lower achievement of racial-caste children has been suggested by anthropologists such as William Stewart[89] and Stephen and Joan Baratz.[90] They suggest that the culture of each group is different from that of white Americans. The cultural-difference hypothesis was demonstrated primarily on the basis of linguistic differences found in the speech of many black youngsters, as well as differences in their folklore and music.[91]

The implication of the cultural-difference hypothesis for socialization is readily apparent. Successful socialization, if it should also include negative attitudes toward education and occupational achievement, or behavior and attitudes different from those of the dominant population, can result in school failures when the children are forced to compete in an environment controlled by middle-class whites. Such would seem to be case of the lower-class Mexican-American youth.[92]

The source of particular cultural differences varies. Lower-class black culture no doubt emerged from the caste status into which blacks were forced and from segregation from the mainstream white society. The process of segregation facilitates the further development and retention of divergent cultural behaviors and attitudes.

In some instances, the cultural differences between groups may be attributed to the traditions that the first migrants brought with them. Colleen and Frank Johnson report that Japanese-Americans, for example, have retained a complex of behaviors (identified as "enryo") that is not only in opposition to the dominant models of behavior (thus laying the basis for misunderstanding, mistrust, and stereotyping) but may also prove disadvantageous in competitive situations. Enryo, as defined by Johnson and Johnson in practical terms is "the communication of humility, deference, reticence and ritualized inferiorization."[93] Japanese-American parents stress respect for elders as well as reticence in verbal and active performance in the socialization of their children; and they do not reward behaviors defined as independent or verbally aggressive.

A third explanation for variation in achievement has been suggested by Charles Valentine,[94] who argues that members of subordinated groups in society are, in fact, bicultural. That is, blacks, Mexicans, Puerto Ricans, Orientals, and Indians, who are familiar with their own unique subcultures, at the same time are taught the mainstream culture, which they do not totally absorb because of discrimination, poverty, and segregation. Moreover, it has been argued that loyalties to racial, ethnic, and religious groups tend to be important to those below the upper middle class.[95] Group ideologies have been formed in all groups subjected to poverty and discrimination for extended periods of time. The advantage of commitment to these ideologies accrues primarily to individuals who cannot overcome social obstacles through personal actions. It may, on the other hand, hinder the progress of those who can lose their visibility.

Beyond such explanations of variation in achievement as cultural deficiency, idiosyncracy, or biculturalism, the advantages of the superordinate population have been also attributed to genetics. Differences in shape of head, hair form, eye shape, consistency of earwax, susceptibility to specific ailments, and so on, have been attributed to genetic differences between the racial groups. Is it not equally plausible, argue men like Arthur Jensen and H. J. Eysenck, and Richard Herrnstein (see Chapter 9), that genetic variation also accounts for differences in verbal and nonverbal abilities?[96] Few accept this position as the full explanation.

Only a few aspects of family life and racial-caste have been discussed in this section. However, it is apparent that much remains to be learned about family life and the consequences of experiences within it. Let us now turn to those experiences that most obviously reflect the racism of American society: education, occupation, and income of selected racial-caste groups.

EDUCATION

For many individuals locked into a subordinate class as well as caste position, formal education has been viewed as a necessary, if not sufficient condition for upward mobility. In many respects the truth of this view is almost self-evident. Technological society demands the "proper" certification of expertise of people for occupations. If disadvantaged people gain increased education, it stands to reason that they would be better equipped to compete. Educational attainment and income are, in fact, positively related.[97] Moreover, if the minorities are successful in education and income, this would enable them to translate their altered status into political power.[98] Concomitantly, education provides a broadened perspective of the world and positive self-concepts as well.[99]

Few Americans doubt the veracity of these generalizations. This line of reasoning has even been accepted by most members of the subordinated group, even though, as for the Cherokee Indian, hopes for an education and aspirations may be altered by the reality of their experience.[100]

Some blacks hailed the *Brown* vs. *Board of Education* decision in the Supreme Court (1954)[101] as a "second Emancipation Proclamation." Educational leaders at a conference in Hot Springs, Arkansas, declared that the decision was "a significant milestone in the nation's quest for a democratic way of life and in the Negro's long struggle to become a first class citizen."[102] Indeed, educational gains have been made by young blacks.

Except for a slight decline in 1973, the Census Bureau has reported a steady growth in the number of black college students. During the 1975–1976 school year nearly a million black students were on college campuses across the country compared to 274,000 only ten years before.[103] Although enrollment by whites in college grew by 60 percent during this decade, the increase in the number of black students during that same period represented a 246 percent gain. There has been a significant narrowing of the black-white college-enrollment gap over the last decade. In 1965 only 10.3 percent of black young people (eighteen to twenty-four years) were enrolled in college compared to 25.5 percent of white young people of the same ages. By 1975, with the increased enrollment of black students, 41 percent of black high school graduates (ages eighteen to twenty-one) were in college compared to 43 percent of white high school graduates of that age group.[104]

By 1970 the majority of black students (55.6 percent) were enrolled in predominantly white colleges. In the northern and western regions of the United States, 80.7 percent of all black undergraduates were in predominantly white colleges. Even in predominantly white colleges, however, the pathologies in the relationship between white and black members of American society have been revealed.[105] Sadly, many black students actually found more prejudice and discrimination and less integration than they had expected to encounter when they began their college experience.[106]

In spite of the gains made by black students, many members of racial-caste groups continue to reflect and reinforce their position in society through their lack of education. About a decade ago, the Carnegie Cross-Cultural Educational project reported a median educational level of 5.3 years for adult male and 5.8 for adult female American Indians over twenty-five years of age.[107] Moreover, even in 1974 more than one-quarter (26.5 percent) of adult Puerto Ricans had completed less than five years of school compared to 4.4 percent of the total American population.[108] And only slightly more than one-quarter of Mexicans and Puerto Ricans (29.6 percent) had completed four years of high school or more compared to 61.2 percent of the total adult American population.[109] Somewhat in contrast to the oppression revealed by the statistics on other racial-castes, Orientals in American society have surpassed the median educational level of the dominant population.[110]

However, for upward mobility to occur, educational advantage must be accompanied by provision of opportunities to obtain appropriate jobs. The mid-1970s have seen unemployment and underemployment among college graduates.[111]

The means of equalizing opportunities within education have been found to be extremely difficult to accomplish, beyond the issuance of court orders or the changing of admission standards.

The Coleman report on academic achievement,[112] for example, indicated the disparity in the test scores of youngsters from the first to the twelfth grades. These scores clearly showed a marked relationship (except in the case of Oriental-Americans) between racial-caste or white status and academic achievement. Whereas the median verbal score for the white youngsters in the first grade was 53.2, the median verbal score for black, Puerto Rican, and Mexican children lagged 5 to 8 points below this. The median verbal score for Oriental youngsters in the first grade was only 1.6 points below that of the white pupils. The median nonverbal score for white children was 54.1; black and Puerto Rican children scored

9 to 11 points below this. Indian, Mexican, and Oriental children had median nonverbal scores of 53.0, 50.1, and 56.6, respectively. After completing twelve years of school, white students maintained their advantage of 5 to 12 points in median score in tests of reading, mathematics, general information, and verbal and nonverbal skills, over Indian, Puerto Rican, Mexican, and black students.

Many compensatory programs[113] were introduced in an attempt to provide opportunities for all children. The complexity and scope of the problems, however, is indicated by the number and experimental nature of these attempts. Sometimes hampering the attempts are the many factors beyond the immediate control of schools that play important roles in educating youngsters, for example, the emotional and physical health of youngsters,[114] regularity of attendance, parental participation, and the values and attitudes of those who enter and complete teacher-training programs.[115] In addition, access to higher education and opportunities for high-prestige careers depend on the availability of scholarships, achievement within college,[116] and the state of the economy, as well as equitable treatment within the work setting.

OCCUPATION AND INCOME

Occupational distribution and income provide two important indicators of the status of various groups in society. Available statistics regarding the occupational distribution of blacks, Puerto Ricans, and Mexicans compared to whites clearly point out their subordinated position. Table 6.5 presents data for 1960 and 1974 for black and white workers and indicates gains made by blacks in the white-collar occupations. A larger proportion of blacks than whites, however, continued to occupy blue-collar and service occupations.[117]

Data regarding the occupations of Mexicans and Puerto Ricans for 1974 indicate a distribution similar to that for blacks with a few differences: Mexicans and Puerto Ricans are represented by only 5.2 and 4.5 percent, respectively, of the workers in the professions and technical occupations; larger proportions of Mexican and Puerto Rican workers are craftsmen (19.2 percent and 10.8 percent, respectively) and operatives (26.8 percent and 31.6 percent, respectively) than of either blacks or whites. Further, a significant proportion of Mexicans (11.4 percent) are farm laborers.[118]

Given their occupational distribution, it is not unexpected that the median incomes of black, Puerto Rican, and Mexican families is lower than that of white families. In 1974 the median income for all white families was $12,541. The median incomes for black, Mexican, and

Puerto Rican families, on the other hand, were $7,807, $8,434, and $6,779, respectively.[119] Perhaps more outstanding than these comparisons is the fact that almost one-quarter (23.5 percent) of Mexican-American families and more than one-third (34.1 percent) of Puerto Rican families, compared to 11.1 percent of all Americans, were described as below the poverty line in 1974.[120] Slightly less than one-third (31 percent) of black families, as opposed to 8 percent of white families, were below the poverty line in 1973.[121]

TABLE 6.5 Occupations of Blacks and Whites, 1960 and 1974

	Blacks		Whites	
Occupation	1960	1974	1960	1974
White-collar workers	16.1%	32.0%	46.6%	50.6%
Professional-technical	4.8	10.4	12.1	14.8
Managers and administrators	2.6	4.1	11.7	11.2
Sales workers	1.5	2.3	6.9	7.3
Clerical	7.3	15.2	15.7	17.8
Blue-collar workers	40.1	40.2	36.2	34.0
Craftsmen	6.0	9.4	13.8	13.8
Operatives	20.4	21.9	17.9	15.5
Nonfarm laborers	13.7	8.9	4.4	4.6
Service workers	31.7	25.1	9.9	11.8
Private housework	14.2	5.1	1.7	1.0
Other	17.5	20.0	8.2	10.8
Total employed (in thousands)	6,927	9,136	58,850	76,620

Source: Statistical Abstracts, 1975.

Further, unemployment figures even more pointedly indicate the position of blacks in the American economy. Unemployment takes a greater toll on black workers than it does on white workers (13.3 percent to 6.8 percent);[122] and the jobless rate for black teenagers had reached an explosive 40.3 percent (compared to 16.1 percent for white teenagers) in July 1975.[123]

The truly depressed nature of those disadvantaged by racial-caste is clearly evidenced by the situation of the American Indian. The median family income for reservation Indians was approximately $1,500 and more than three-quarters (76 percent) of reservation Indians were defined as below poverty level in the late 1960s.[124] In 1969 to 1970 approximately 40 percent of adult Indian males on the reservations were not able to obtain even temporary employment.[125]

Approximately one-half of the Indian work force is hired by the federal government; the government also provides income in the form of food, health care, welfare, and so on. In an attempt to ameliorate the problems of poverty and unemployment of the reservation Indian, the Bureau of Indian Affairs initiated employment or relocation-assistance programs for reservation Indians. These programs, established on the basis of the Indian Vocational Training Act (1956), were instituted because few reservation Indians are employable in occupations above the unskilled category. Through the 1960s more than a million Indians participated in the training or relocation programs. In his report of a sample of participants, Alan Sorkin[126] noted that, like blacks, Indian migrants to urban areas were slightly better educated, and that approximately one-third of the relocatees returned to the reservation within a year after they left. Those Indians participating in the program were reported to have earned twice what they would have made on the reservation for the three years after their training. The more successful relocatees tended to remain in urban areas, whereas the less successful returned to the reservation.[127]

The occupational income status of Oriental-Americans at first glance appears to contradict the examples of racial-caste subordination outlined thus far. In 1966 William Petersen described Japanese-Americans as "better off than any other group in our society, including native born whites. . . . Even in a country whose patron saint is the Horatio Alger hero, there is no parallel to this success story."[128] The success that Petersen describes was based in large part on occupational attainment. In 1960, for example, there were almost as many Japanese-Americans in the professional and technical fields as in agriculture; more managers, proprietors, clericals, and salespeople than craftsmen or foremen.[129]

Like others in upwardly mobile working-class groups, many Japanese-American women prepared for teaching occupations.[130] The civil service provided another area of opportunity. Before 1941 it was estimated that five Japanese-Americans held federal civil service positions; by the end of the 1960s, not only had their number increased (estimated to be at 10,000), they were also reported in a Civil Service Commission study to be in the upper-middle category in the wage scale.[131]

Audrie Girdner and Ann Loftis, in their thorough description of the evacuation of Japanese-Americans in 1942 and its aftermath, provide substantiation of the caste nature of subordinated racial groups. They note that in spite of the advances made by many Japanese-Americans in the civil service and private industry, chief executive positions are usually closed to them. "This may account for the fact that though Japanese Americans have more education than the average American and a larger proportion of them are in professional or white collar occupations, their median income is lower."[132]

The consequences of racism can be seen as pervasive but extremely subtle.

PROTEST: DEMANDED EQUITY

The anger of Rosa Park and her refusal to sit in the section of the bus reserved for black people in the mid-1950s is commonly cited as the first signal of recent outrage from the American blacks.[133] In fact, organizations such as the NAACP had mounted many attacks on Jim Crow laws. They achieved a memorable victory in 1954 when the Supreme Court demanded an end to school desegregation.

Legal triumphs, however, bring few immediate tangible changes. De jure segregation in the South and de facto segregation in the North dragged on. Economic opportunities, housing, and a host of practices bent on keeping black people "in their place" continued. A nonviolent protest movement, led by the Reverend Martin Luther King, Jr., and supported by Southern black students and Northern black and white students and professionals, was launched in the South. The aim of the campaign was to bring an end to segregated public facilities and to obtain the voting franchise. The climax of the movement came in Mississippi in 1964, when civil rights workers forced federal intervention.[134]

The mid-1960s witnessed an eruption of violence in Watts,[135] Detroit, Newark, and other large cities with black ghettos. Toward the end of that decade Americans were introduced to the "black is beautiful" slogan, and some gains, as we have noted, in education and politics were made. With the large urban concentration of blacks, who are now exercising more political power, black mayors, city councilmen, and congressmen have been elected. If the migration of blacks and the outmigration of whites continue in urban areas, certainly this should provide a political advantage. How advantageous this will be in an age when the older cities are going broke remains debatable.

The black protest movement of the last quarter-century has significance for American society beyond the political, legal, and educational gains that black people have made. It has served as a source of inspiration for other oppressed groups in the United States.

Organizing American Indians have encountered many problems, since American Indians have long considered themselves members of a specific tribe or locality. Vine Deloria, an articulate leader of the Indian movement, claimed that at the conclusion of the 1960s these loyalties remained of paramount importance.[136] The first intertribal group of Indians designed to advance their own political interests was the National Congress of American Indians (NCAI), which was created in 1944.[137] The NCAI has assumed as its primary duty serving as a lobby in Washington for the organized Indian tribes. Basically, reports Wax, the NCAI has sought to improve the position of Indians within the present federal government structure.[138] The effectiveness of the organization, however, was limited by a lack of funding and support. Stimulated by the young, college-educated Indian "radicals" who saw the value of organization, a new intertribal association, the National Indian Youth Council (NIYC), emerged in 1961. Organizations such as the NIYC have condemned the entire structure of Indian-white relationships. They would abolish the federal Bureau of Indian Affairs and channel funds directly to Indians rather than through bureaucracies, to be used for community development.[139]

The tactics employed by the more radical of the Indian organizations include picketing and the direct confrontation techniques used by black and Mexican militants. The NIYC sponsored the "fish-in" of the 1960s as a protest against the imposition of state fishing laws, which would have violated rights guaranteed to Indians years ago by treaty. For the most part, the fish-ins, like most of the protests of American Indians, have been symbolic actions. Other examples are provided in the two-year occupation of Alcatraz Island and the battle at Wounded Knee.[140]

"Indian power," despite remaining tribal loyalties, has come to mean the expression of two desires on the part of the Indians: first, retention of the land allotted to them but under new terms; second, retention of their identity as Indians.[141]

In general, the Puerto Ricans address themselves to the same issues as the blacks: schools, housing, and poverty. They have, like blacks, also demanded control over agencies affecting their own communities and endorsed the passage of legislation to deal with poverty. For example, Puerto Ricans have promoted their own interests in the election of Herman Badillo as a congressman from New York City; and in street organizations, such as the Young Lords, which direct their attention to political issues rather than to street crime.[142]

Organized Mexican-American protest has taken place largely among agricultural workers. The history of this protest dates back as early as 1903 when Mexican and Japanese sugar beet workers went on strike in Ventura, California. Protest is not new to the Mexican-American. The new element that was infused into the 1965 grape-pickers' strike action was the movement beyond the bread-and-butter issue: it became a crusade to assert the dignity of Mexican-Americans.[143] Led by Cesar Chavez, former general director of the Community Service Organization (CSO), an urban-based organization, the farm laborers' actions had un-

precedented impact because of three factors: (1) the end to the recruitment of Mexican nationals as farm labor ("braceros") in 1964 stabilized
farm labor; (2) a corps of Mississippi "veterans" of civil rights struggles
was available in 1965 to supply know-how in the organization of poor
people; and (3) the Chavez movement was led by Mexican-Americans.

As mechanization increases even more, the focus of the Mexican-
American struggle will eventually have to move into urban areas. The
development of a political sense among street gangs in areas such as East
Los Angeles leads to the prediction of such a move.[144] The exact nature
and form of the protest, however, like that of other groups, depends on
the circumstances in which people find themselves.

In spite of the actions of white Americans against them, their relative
educational and occupational success has led most Japanese-Americans
to avoid an active role in the civil rights movement. Most react uncom-
fortably to extremism, separatist movements, and extralegal tactics.
Much like blue-collar workers who have achieved middle-class status,
many Japanese-Americans believe that to raise oneself out of poverty one
should "get an education and a decent job" or "pull yourself up, don't
expect handouts."[145]

Although the attitude of Japanese-Americans might be understood in
terms of their own family and community conditioning, as one Japanese-
American noted, "these attitudes are naive and bigoted."[146] That Oriental-Americans, in general, do not support civil rights issues was demonstrated in the 1964 vote in California to block open housing. An opinion
poll prior to the vote indicated that 52 percent of Oriental-Americans in
the Los Angeles area were against open housing.[147]

The Japanese American Citizens League (JACL), however, has apparently moved ahead of its constituent population in its support of civil
rights. Although the organization is not strongly supported by all Japanese-Americans, it has worked for reform within the constitutional-legal
framework. The espousal of a cause outside of their own community is a
recent phenomenon among Japanese-Americans.[148] Perhaps it will be the
task of the JACL to remind its constituents that the racism that they faced
in 1942 is not yet a thing of the past.

Like Japanese-Americans and other racial groups, women in America
have also often been placed in a castelike status. Although the forms of
oppression have sometimes differed, women have often been treated as
subordinate creatures in America. This historically important, pervasive
form of discrimination has cut across class lines and, like other forms of
caste in America, requires close attention.

Sexism

The position of women in American society is only similar in part to that of subordinated racial-castes. For example, although the consequences of inadequate medical care and nutrition, unhealthy working conditions, and other factors operate to shorten the life expectancy of disadvantaged racial groups, women have experienced a longer average life expectancy than men. In 1850 a woman could be predicted to outlive her husband by 2.2 years (40.5 years). By the 1970s, with improved nutrition and advances in obstetrical services, the difference between the average length of a woman's life (74.6 years) and that of her husband's increased to 6.9 years. Thus, American women could not and cannot be pictured as medically deprived.

Another major difference between the position of women and that of racial groups in the United States is in the area of economics. Because of the desire to avoid tax laws as well as their predicted shorter life span, men have transferred much of their wealth into women's hands. Although women serve largely as "absentee" owners of industrial facilities, more stocks in private corporations are owned by women than men. Men, however, have retained control over the administration of the capitalist system. Within this system, as we shall soon see, women are "kept in their (subordinated) place."

The visibility of women is relatively unimportant to an understanding of their position vis-à-vis men in American society. Physical difference,[149] in this instance, places women in a disadvantaged position because American society is geared to direct one's life toward an occupation. The most prestigious occupations, for example, require extended education which in the case of women is often interrupted by childbirths.[150]

Socially, by marriage, and physically, by childbearing, American women have in the past been prevented from following the singleminded pursuit of the more prestigious occupations. Gladys Harbison has summarized the problem faced by many women as that of living three different lives in the course of one. She says:

> There are first the years of formal schooling in which she will usually receive some preparation for occupational competence outside the home. These are followed by a very short period in paid employment. She next experiences the more confining period of child-rearing, and finally the much longer span of years in which she will probably return to paid or voluntary employment outside the home. Each of these three stages has a distinct character, contrasting sharply with the others in

occupational and emotional involvement. The woman's problem is to find coherence.[151]

The difficulty of combining marriage, child-rearing, and a career apparently has not led to the complete devaluation of the importance of marriage and the wife-mother role. Most Americans are married at some time in their lives. In 1972 and 1973, for example, there were 10.9 marriages for every thousand Americans, which was the highest rate since 1950.[152] Most Americans also want to have children,[153] although there has been a small increase in the number of couples who prefer childlessness.

That marriage and the family maintain high valuation for most women is a testament to successful socialization. The proportions of persons delaying marriage and children and of those divorcing[154] or expressing a desire for childless marriage reflect the alternative life options that many women have chosen as well as the strains induced by dual roles.

The position of women is not identical to that of oppressed racial groups in American society. However, the second-class citizenship long experienced by women in terms of opportunity to fulfill the marital and other valued roles or to obtain equity in various institutions does not speak well for a society espousing freedom and opportunity for all people.

A Brief History of the Woman's Position in Society

Throughout history, men have relegated women to debased roles as servants, slaves, pieces of property, or, in some societies, as animals with less status than dogs. Although accidents of birth such as being born a queen or the recipient of the privileges of an upper-class economic position have eased the burdens of a few women, most have generally ranked low on any scale of prestige, power, or wealth. To understand the unique position of women in twentieth-century American society, it is informative to examine the history of women here as well as in other areas of the world.

A BRIEF LOOK BACKWARD

In most simple societies, women were regarded as the literal property of their fathers, eldest brothers, or husbands. Generally, in hunting societies, women did all the basic work, except for the actual capture of game. "Women were created for work," said one chief of the Chippewas. "One of them can draw or carry as much as two men. They also pitch our tents, make our clothes, mend them, and keep us warm at night. . . . They do everything and cost only a little."[155] In many primitive societies, women were bequeathed as property when their husbands died; in some—New Guinea, Fiji, India—a wife was buried with her husband or was expected to commit suicide after his death.[156] In Fiji, women could not be present at religious services in temples, although certain dogs whom the men favored freely attended the rituals.[157]

The men in most simple societies regarded women as impure, evil, and subject to many taboos. The early followers of the Judeo-Christian tradition shared this view. The strictest taboos had to be observed in most simple societies when a woman was menstruating since any contact with her during this time was assumed to deprive a man of his virtue.[158]

Women were probably the pioneers in the invention of agriculture in agrarian societies, but as these societies prospered, men took over ownership and reduced women to an even more servile status than before. For example, in ancient Sumeria, the cradle of agrarian civilization, adultery by a woman was punished by death (although it was regarded as a mere whim for a man); men could sell their wives to pay debts or hand them over into legal slavery; fathers sold their prettiest daughters to serve as concubines in the temples.[159]

In agrarian India around 400 B.C. the institution of *purdah*—the covering and absolute seclusion of women—began. Women were either abducted or sold as brides, and a marriage by mutual consent was considered a disgrace to the woman.[160]

Preindustrial Japan, relatively isolated from the rest of the world until Commodore Perry's invasion, evolved a classic pattern of female submission. The family was the important unit of the society, with the father the tyrant of the family. Women could be divorced without a word, sent into slavery, or killed because of adultery. Filial piety ruled the society, and the "Three Obediences"—a woman's obligation to father, husband, and son—governed her life.[161]

Ancient Egypt proved an exception to the rule of most agrarian societies. Not only did the Egyptian upper class approve and encourage incest, but it produced a number of queens, such as Hatshepsut and Cleopatra, who had as much power and privilege as any man. Moreover, Egypt was characterized by a mild form of matriarchy, which ensured that all inheritances would be handed down along the female line. Women usually assumed the aggressive role in love, committed adultery freely and, according to Greek visitors, henpecked their husbands.[162] No one knows how the women acquired the powers of inheritance, but it clearly increased their freedom and also encouraged incest: a brother married his sister, perhaps not so much for love as for the property she would inherit.[163]

The dawn of Christianity and of Islam in agrarian societies did not produce any major changes in the status of women. The age of chivalry did, of course, promote a romanticized image of upper-class women and a balladry of love. Some leaders of the Christian Church attempted to provide more stability to marital unions. These two developments within Christendom did not, however, prevent the enslavement of women, deprive men of their basic economic and political power, or substantially reduce the promiscuity of men. In the earlier centuries of the Middle Ages, men could divorce their wives at will; women were banned from education; and the love poems of the troubadours were invariably addressed to the mistresses, not the wives of lords. As Saint Boniface warned King Ethelbald in a letter: "We have heard that almost all the nobles of Mercia follow your example, desert their lawful wives, and live in guilty intercourse with adulteresses and nuns."[164]

In those nations that fell under the sway of Islam, Mohammed improved the position of women somewhat, but generally viewed their subordinate status and legal subjugation as "natural." Positively, the coming of Islam meant that women were no longer considered legal property to be handed from father to son. They could (with some trepidation) attend ceremonies in mosques, and they were allowed to inherit one-half as much of an estate as male family heirs. All these measures could be considered advances over the previous status of women in Moslem states, yet they were balanced by other doctrines that sanctified woman's subordinate role.

The Koran, as did the Talmud, allowed men to leave their wives at will, but women found it extremely difficult to leave their husbands. Even if they succeeded, they had to return their dowries to them. It was believed that a woman could enter paradise after death only if her husband was pleased with her. The great majority of women were condemned to hell. A man could have four wives (possibly a measure to compensate for the high death rate of males), but a woman could have only one husband.[165]

As some agrarian societies entered a commercial or preindustrial era, the lot of women was partially eased. The blossoming of a commercial period in Italy around 1400 and the subsequent Renaissance provided women in the upper economic classes with enough income to release themselves from medieval bondage and the general contempt of male-dominated societies. Women of the upper classes received some education in music, Latin, and poetry; they were allowed to dress flamboyantly, wear jewels and cosmetics, and adopt daring fashions. A rare woman, such as Lucrezia Borgia, achieved high political power in the absence of a

husband. The achievements of the educated woman of the Renaissance
led one historian to exclaim:

> The educated women of the Renaissance emancipated themselves
> without any propaganda of emancipation, purely by their intelligence,
> character and tact, and by the heightened sensitivity of men to their
> tangible and intangible charms. . . . The Italian Renaissance like the
> French Enlightenment, was bisexual; women moved into every sphere
> of life; men ceased to be coarse and crude, and were molded to finer
> manners and speech; and civilization, with all its laxity and violence,
> took on a grace and refinement such as it had not known in Europe for
> a thousand years.[166]

This panegyric to the liberated status of women during the Renaissance
must be read with some caution. Clearly, the peasant woman or the
average urban woman devoted herself totally to the service of her husband, home, and children. She participated even less than her husband in
the cultural glories of the Renaissance. Even for the upper-class woman,
the ultimate authority of her husband or father could never be directly
challenged.[167]

Decisive changes in the status of women began to occur only with the
expansion of the industrial revolution. But even in nineteenth-century
America and England, women had virtually no legal rights.[168] They were
still regarded as tainted with sin. Psychologically, they were considered
as weak, humble, soft, submissive, passive, and unable to assume responsible economic functions—even though they worked both in the fields and
in burgeoning factories.[169] Only reluctantly were women allowed to
achieve an education in the nineteenth century, and then largely in secluded convents, schools, or colleges.[170]

But the coming of a postindustrial society in the twentieth century in
Europe, America, Russia, and Japan entailed a variety of changes in
women's traditional position. Legally, politically, economically, educationally, and socially, women entered a new era of "liberation."

Sexism in American Society Today

Just as some scholars have questioned the conclusion that there has
been a decline in racism in the United States over the past few decades,
data regarding the position of women have also yielded contradictory
interpretations concerning the state of sexism.[171] For example, statistics

indicating the increased numbers of women in professional and technical positions during the decade of 1950 to 1960 have been interpreted to mean that women made significant employment gains.[172] This movement of women into presumably more "challenging careers," as defined by the Labor Department, has even led some persons optimistically to suggest that sexism has declined.

The position of women and the state of sexism, however, cannot be determined by an examination of any single gain made by women—in this case, in certain categories of employment. The overall status of women, Dean Knudsen reminds us,[173] must be assessed in terms of multiple indicators and is always relative to the status of men. Structural changes may yield increased opportunities for both men and women in terms of occupation, as in fact they have. But, although women increased their participation as professionals in the labor force by 41 percent from 1950 to 1960, the proportion of males who occupied those positions during the same decade increased by 51 percent.[174] In order for anyone to achieve a more prestigious, higher-income occupation, one must receive preparation through higher education. For this reason, the proportion of women in higher education, and perhaps the early socialization experiences that promote the pursuit of this education, should also be examined in evaluating the current position of women in American society. In addition, to understand the subtleties of institutionalized sexism, one must look not only at the data concerned with women's changes in occupation, income, or education but also at the daily experiences of women.

EDUCATION

Until relatively recently, there was widespread indifference and even opposition to educating females in American society. Women were expected to be wives and mothers. Formal education beyond the elementary level was hardly deemed necessary for this task.[175] In addition, until public education was established, the expense of educating females was thought to be wasteful. Public education and the realization that female school teachers could be paid less than male school teachers served as the incentive to educate females at least through high school.[176]

College was thought to debase and harden a woman's mind as well as strain her physical and mental capacity. Opportunities to pursue higher education were closed to women until the second quarter of the nineteenth century. Oberlin College admitted female undergraduates in 1833, and shortly thereafter Mount Holyoke College (1837) was opened as the first women's college. In 1897 approximately six out of ten college women were in "normal schools," which trained teachers, or private four-year women's colleges.[177] By 1900, however, the majority of colleges and universities became coeducational institutions.[178]

There are few today who would argue that women are too frail to attend college. Although the change in the proportion of women attending college has increased over the past few decades, the total number of women enrolled in colleges in 1974 still did not equal that of men.[179] As Table 6.6 indicates, the proportion of women attending colleges increased between the periods 1950 to 1960, 1960 to 1970, and 1970 to 1974, but the total number of women in college was still only 3.9 million (or 44.3 percent) in 1974, as compared to 4.9 million (55.7 percent) for men.

TABLE 6.6   Female and Male College Enrollment, 1950-74

	Female	Male
1950	31.8% (.7 million)	68.1% (1.5 million)
1960	34.3% (1.2 million)	65.7% (2.3 million)
1970	40.5% (3.0 million)	59.5% (4.4 million)
1974	44.3% (3.9 million)	55.7% (4.9 million)
Percentage change		
1950–1960	76.1%	54.4%
1960–1970	144.8%	88.2%
1970–1974	29.5%	11.9%

Source: U.S. Bureau of the Census, Current Population Reports, Series P-20; reprinted in Statistical Abstracts 1975, p. 114, Table 180 (computed).

The increase in the number of female college students may be interpreted as an indication of women's increased opportunity and motivation to achieve greater equality. Two other types of statistics, however, invite caution in such optimism. Robert Havighurst and Bernice Neugarten report, on the basis of the 1973 report of the Carnegie Commission on Higher Education, that although 50.4 percent of high school graduates are female[180] and that although they earn better grades and score higher on academic achievement tests in high school,[181] the proportion of females in upper levels of universities is relatively small. That is, whereas 43.1 percent of B.A. degrees are awarded to women, only 13.4 percent of Ph.D. degrees and 6 percent of professional degrees (M.D., D.D.S., and others) are awarded to women. This is true despite the fact that women, on the average, have better undergraduate records in college irrespective of their field of study.[182] Moreover, in graduate school a larger number of women than men expect to take terminal M.A. degrees, and the women have a higher attrition rate.

A number of reasons have been cited for the discrepancy in educational attainment of women as compared to men. The structure of higher education, for example, is more restrictive to females than males because of timing.[183] It is assumed that a college education should be pursued as a full-time activity between eighteen and twenty-five years of age. In the 1970s, the average American woman, however, marries at twenty and has her last child at twenty-six. Extended interruptions and the leisurely pursuit of an education are not encouraged. Admission requirements and entrance examinations discourage delays in entering college. Procedures regarding the transfer and evaluation of credits taken at different schools, as well as pressure to specialize early in order to fulfill the requirements for a particular program of study, may discourage many women from resuming an interrupted education.[184] Selective admission, based on the assumption that men are more likely to graduate, and the availability of financial aid in the form of grants or jobs as teaching assistants or research assistants also work to the disadvantage of those women who want to attend graduate school.[185]

Many females have not been motivated to achieve. Rather, stereotyped role expectations of the wife-mother roles have been pushed by parents, friends, and the mass media, as well as reinforced through textbooks in school. A survey of elementary textbooks done by feminists in New York and New Jersey, for example, found that 72 percent of the stories in 144 readers representing 15 major publishers centered around boys; more than 85 percent of biographies of famous people were about men.[186] Further, those that did deal with women held less interest since they were typically restricted to domestic set-ups.[187]

The question of individual motivation is, of course, very complex and cannot be considered solely on the basis of exposure and socialization. Havighurst and Neugarten, for example, suggest that many women must make rational decisions about "the balance they wish to create between family and career responsibilities and related thereto, the financial commitments they wish to make to continued education."[188] Research has also suggested that for some women fear and anxiety about the loss of femininity are created by outstanding academic or other achievement.[189] Expectations to achieve and succeed, on the other hand, are more clearly integrated into the male role.[190]

There are, then, many reasons that can be cited as to why many capable women do not seek the credentials necessary to obtain high-status occupations. Statistics on the occupational and income distribution of women, compared to men, clearly demonstrate the consequences of this lack. The relative position of women in American society can also be seen by income comparisons between men and women of equal education.

WORK

Few areas of activity have received more attention in the study of sexism than that of women's participation in the economy of the nation. Women, of course, have always participated in economic activity as producers of food and clothing, housekeepers, cooks, and baby sitters. It has only been since productive activity moved out of the home that the subject of women at work and the possible consequences of women's work for family life has been raised.[191]

There has been a rapid increase in the proportion of women who have entered the labor force. Whereas in 1940 only 27.4 percent of females were employed outside the home, by 1975, 45.9 percent of all women had joined the labor force.[192]

The growth of female representation in the labor force is due largely to the greatly increased numbers of working married (rather than single, widowed, or divorced) women. In 1940, 48.5 percent of the female labor force was single, and 15.1 percent was divorced or widowed; by 1975 these women represented only 23.2 and 14.6 percent of the female labor force, respectively. Married women, on the other hand, made up 36.4 percent of the female labor force in 1940 and 62.2 percent in 1975. Of married women in the labor force the largest increase has taken place among those with children. In 1950, for example, married women (husband present) with children under six and those with youngsters between six and seventeen years of age made up 11.9 and 28.3 percent, respectively, of married women in the labor force; by 1975 the proportions had grown to 36.6 and 52.4 percent, respectively.[193] One of the recurrent questions concerns the effect on children of mothers working outside the home.[194]

Whatever the motivation or consequences of work, it is clear that increasing numbers of women seek occupations aside from housewifery. This remains true although the majority of women are employed in occupations that require little creativity or initiative and that possess little authority. As noted earlier, the relative increase in the number of female professionals has been smaller than that of male professionals. Table 6.7 indicates that the largest proportion of women are employed in clerical (35.5 percent of the female labor force) or in service work (21.5 percent of the female labor force).

These statistics would appear to support those who contend that in spite of the women's liberation movement of the past decade, there may

TABLE 6.7 Percentages of Females and Males Employed in Various Jobs, 1940-75

	Females						Males					
	1940	1950	1960	1965	1970	1975	1940	1950	1960	1965	1970	1975
Professional, technical	13.4	10.3	12.4	13.2	14.5	16.1	6.1	6.4	10.9	12.1	13.9	14.8
Managers and administrators	3.5	5.7	5.0	4.5	4.5	4.8	9.6	12.9	13.6	13.4	14.2	13.9
Sales	7.3	8.2	7.7	7.5	7.0	6.9	6.7	5.6	5.8	5.7	5.6	6.4
Clerical	21.1	26.3	30.3	31.8	34.5	35.5	6.0	7.2	7.2	7.1	7.1	6.8
Craft and kindred	1.2	1.1	1.0	1.1	1.1	1.6	14.9	17.7	18.9	19.3	20.1	20.0
Operatives	18.1	19.1	15.2	15.2	14.5	11.4	17.9	20.9	19.6	20.7	19.6	17.6
Service workers	11.0	22.0	23.7	23.2	21.7	21.5	5.8	6.4	6.5	6.9	6.7	8.7
Farm workers	2.9	6.9	4.4	3.1	1.8	1.1	8.3	14.7	9.6	7.1	5.3	4.7
Total (in millions)	11,178	17,493	21,874	24,748	29,667	33,142	33,892	42,156	43,904	46,340	48,960	50,407

Source: 1940 percentages from Dean Knudsen, "The Declining Status of Women," Social Forces 48 (December 1969): 185, computed on basis of U.S. Bureau of the Census, U.S. Census of Population: 1960, vol. 1 (Washington, D.C.: Government Printing Office, 1964), Table 89, p. 1. Figures for 1950, 1960, 1965, 1970, and 1975 computed on the basis of data from Statistical Abstracts, 1975.

have been a decline in the status of women.[195] Certainly, many of the experiences of women—even those in relatively high-status positions—support this conclusion. For example, there is a positive relationship between educational attainment, job status, and income.[196] However, women's income in all occupational categories is lower than that of men. Women in the professions (technical and kindred) only earn approximately 65 percent of the income earned by men in that category. Women workers designated as managers, officials, or proprietors, as well as female service workers and operatives, reportedly earned little more than one-half of the income of males in these same categories.[197] In 1964 a federal law was put into effect that provided that every employer must pay equal rates within an establishment to all doing the same work. Equity, in this instance, has as yet proved impossible to legislate.

The differences in income that have been noted result largely from differences in the type and level of jobs that women hold within the broad general occupational categories. Andrea Tyree and Judith Treas[198] report that within the professions, 42 percent of males are in high-status jobs, but only 6.5 percent of females are in comparable positions. Whereas 47 percent of men in sales work occupy superior positions, only 9 percent of the women in this category are in comparable positions. It is only in the lower-prestige occupational categories that women are equally represented in specific jobs of somewhat higher prestige.

Not only do fewer women hold top administrative positions, even when they do attain them, women are subjected to different and disadvantageous organizational experiences. Jon Miller, Sanford Labowitz, and Lincoln Fry concluded on the basis of their research that

> . . . unlike men, women who improve their position by increasing their expertise, by moving up occupationally, or by moving into positions of authority also run the risk of losing friendships and respect, influence and access to information. They can expect the strain created by the work might increase and almost none of this will improve over time.[199]

Such is not the lot of those women who stay in their place. It was postulated by Miller and associates that the problems that upwardly mobile women experienced were a result of the threat to male dominance. This apparently does not occur when women remain in their traditional place—that is, subordinated.

SOCIALIZATION AND SEX ROLE

In general, the socialization of girls in America, as in other societies, is likely to be aimed at achieving passivity, emotional expression, affection, and the development of a concern about interpersonal relationships. Qualities such as nurturance, obedience, and responsibility are rewarded.[200] This pattern of role socialization is in contrast to that of boys, who are more commonly encouraged to be active, aggressive, self-reliant, achievement-oriented, and emotionally controlled.[201]

These different emphases in socialization are related to the roles that females and males are expected to assume upon reaching adulthood. Females, as we have already noted, are expected to be wives and mothers. Males, on the other hand, while they may be fathers and husbands, are expected to succeed in their chosen occupation.

The extent to which socialization practices support rigid gender differentiation varies by social class. In general, parents with more education tend to minimize differences in the way they treat their sons and daughters; the less education the parents have, the greater the likelihood of encouraging sex-typed behavior. The differences in socialization emphases, however, are a bit more complex than this proposition implies.

Both middle- and lower-class parents socialize their sons to be active, aggressive, competitive, independent, physically strong, and courageous. Janet Stazman Chafetz found, however, that lower-class males are taught to deemphasize or even denigrate school success, whereas middle-class parents emphasize active mastery and competition in academic success. In addition to these characteristics, middle-class parents strive to instill a greater tenderness or nurturance in their sons than do lower-class parents in their sons.[202]

Girls, on the other hand, are taught similar things by both middle- and lower-class parents. Middle-class parents, however, encourage their daughters to develop a high degree of independence and assertiveness. These traits are viewed as masculine and therefore undesirable in girls by lower- and working-class parents.[203]

The reasons for sex-role differentiation established by parents of different social classes include tradition;[204] authoritarianism[205] on the part of working- and lower-class parents; differences in values[206] and expectations regarding education and their children's occupational future;[207] anxiety in regard to achieved status, with consequent emphasis on ascribed (sex) status.[208] Such bases of sex-role differentiation provide some understanding of the deep-seated nature of attitudes expressed by women today. These attitudes have been expressed by some women in antisocial behavior and by others in their support or rejection of the women's liberation movement.

CRIME

The number of criminal acts for all categories of people has increased: black and white, male and female. In 1973 a total of 749,374 females were charged with crimes; of this number, over 192,000 of the charges were listed as "serious." Just as the overall numbers of violent crimes committed by women have increased, so too have the number of women who have been arrested. Whereas 406,000 females were arrested in 1960, 1,-057,000 were arrested in 1972.[209] These changes in absolute numbers, however, represent only slight changes in the proportional representation of women arrestees: in 1960, female arrestees represented 11.0 percent of all those arrested; in 1972 females represented approximately 15 percent.[210]

These facts would seem to contradict Freda Adler, who announced the passing of female passivity in her discussion of the increased number of female criminals.[211] Adler's analysis of the relationship of sex and crime implies that the increased rates can be attributed to the women's liberation movement. Before this conclusion is accepted there must be closer scrutiny of the social class of women committing crimes. Upon such examination, one may find that the same social forces associated with crime in oppressed racial-castes in general are operative. It hardly seems likely that the middle- and upper-class women most interested in the female liberation movement would be involved in criminal activity because they are "passing through a stage in which they are imitating men's roles because identification is the most expedient way to learn."[212]

WOMEN ON THE MOVE

One of the many reform movements of the 1960s is known as the women's liberation movement. The women in this social movement have attempted to equalize power and prestige of women relative to that of men in American society. Another of their aims is to alter many of the stereotypic sex-related behaviors and attitudes of women. Multiple goals have directed the leaders of the present movement through its various phases. Women have agitated to obtain specific changes such as equal pay for equal work and day-care centers; they have also organized themselves so as to gain political clout and representation in the more prestigious professions.[213]

This reform movement, like most others, had its origins among women of the upper middle class, just as the feminist movement of the nineteenth century and the suffragette movement of the early twentieth century drew their leadership from those women who were most articulate and who recognized the inequities of the social system.[214]

The success of the women's movement will depend in the future on the abilities of women to prove themselves indispensable to the economy and unified in terms of political power. This, in turn, hinges on the alteration of attitudes and behaviors of both men and women. At this writing there still seems to be some question in the public mind as to the desirability of such changes, at least as reflected in attitudes toward the adoption of the Equal Rights Amendment. It would appear that some women themselves question the necessity, if not the propriety, of the proposed legislation to further the cause of equal status. Such an attitude is a reflection of the castelike position that women have held for so long.

Conclusions

Clearly, oppression in America is subtle, pervasive, and important to all of us. The caste system in America—whether it affects blacks or women, Orientals or Chicanos, Puerto Ricans or Indians—cuts across the usual class divisions (and, in some cases, deepens them). Racism and sexism have an impact on diverse aspects of American life.

Socialization. Males and females, blacks and whites, Japanese and Puerto Ricans are raised with different values, attitudes, and beliefs. These may conflict with the dominant, middle-class, male, white values. Yet, many of the people of subjugated groups also adhere to the goals of the superordinate group. They commonly find themselves ill-equipped to compete in the continuing American search for "success." This, of course, has predictable results in rates of crime and other forms of deviance.

Education. Many racial minorities and women are excluded from the formal educational process with calculable effects on their future occupations, income, and status.

Family life. For castelike groups, the family may serve as a barrier against the injustices of the dominant group. However, families may collapse in the face of the frustrations, continual pressures, and insecurities of caste existence. The reverberations of familial disintegration on every aspect of life are measurably significant.

Work. Some minorities, like Mexicans and American Indians, have been continually thrust into menial occupations outside the mainstream of American life. Others, like blacks, have struggled upward in the economic scale, only to be left behind in the cities' decaying slums. Women have apparently made some progress, yet they remain at the lowest end of the prestige ladder, and women professionals have actually lost ground to males. In every area of life—not the least of which is the crucial variable of income—castelike groups of America suffer from intense and continuing discrimination.

Americans have launched a variety of movements from SNCC to JACL to NIHY attempting to change the system. At times in American history, the government has used its formidable power in head-on challenges to caste, poverty, and class. Have these movements succeeded? Can reasonable people hope that they will succeed? This important, intricate, and perhaps even eternal question is the next issue that must be faced.

Notes

1. See, for example, Milton Gorden, *Social Class in America*(Durham, N.C.: Duke University Press, 1958), especially chaps. 3, 4, 5, 6.
2. See, for example, W. L. Warner and Paul S. Lunt, *The Social Life of a Modern Community.* (New Haven, Conn.: Yale University Press, 1941); and Richard P. Coleman and Bernice L. Newgarten, *Social Status in the City* (San Francisco: Jossey-Bass, 1971).
3. See, for example, John Dollard, *Caste and Class in a Southern Town* (New Haven, Conn.: Yale University Press, 1937); and Hortense Powdermaker, *After Freedom* (New York: Viking, 1939).
4. See Lucille Duberman, *Social Inequality* (Philadelphia: Lippincott, 1976), chap. 9, for a discussion of other bases of caste differentiation: ethnicity, religion, and age.
5. Dollard, *Caste and Class in a Southern Town.*
6. Milton Gordon, *Assimilation in American Life* (New York: Oxford University Press, 1964).
7. Ibid. p. 27.
8. Ibid. pp. 173–193.
9. Murray L. Wax, *Indian Americans.* (Englewood Cliffs, N.J.: Prentice-Hall, 1971), pp. 164–166.
10. See, for example, Ashley Montagu, *Race, Science and Humanity* (New York: Van Nostrand Reinhold, 1963); Peter I. Rose, *The Subject Is Race* (New York: Oxford University Press, 1968); Willem Adriaan Bonger, *Race and Crime* (Montclair, N.J.: Patterson Smith, 1969).
11. See Brewton Berry, *Race and Ethnic Relations* (Boston: Houghton Mifflin, 1951), chap. 3.
12. "Statement on Race, 1950," in *What Is Race* (Paris: United Nations Educational, Scientific and Cultural Organization, 1952), Appendix II, p. 76.
13. Cited in Berry, *Race and Ethnic Relations.*
14. Robert Blauner, *Racial Oppression in America* (New York: Harper & Row, 1972).

15. For a review of this discussion, see W. Lloyd Warner, "American Caste and Class," *American Journal of Sociology* 42 (September 1936): 234–237; Oliver Cox, "Race and Caste: A Distinction," *American Journal of Sociology* 50 (March 1945): 360–368; and Maxwell R. Brooks, "American Class and Caste: An Appraisal," *Social Forces* 25 (December 1946): 207–211.
16. Cox, ibid.
17. Eugene D. Genovese, *Roll Jordon Roll* (New York: Vintage, 1976).
18. See Wax, *Indian Americans*.
19. Audrie Girdner and Anne Loftis, *The Great Betrayal* (London: Collier-Macmillan, 1969).
20. Rose, *The Subject Is Race*, p. 11.
21. Wax, *Indian Americans*, especially Chapter 1.
22. Ibid., pp. 59–60.
23. "The Voyage of M. George Fenner . . . written by Walter Wren" (1566), Hakluyt, *The Principal Navigations*, VI, 270, cited in Winthrop D. Jordan, *White over Black* (Williamsburg: University of Virginia Press, 1968), pp.
24. Jordan, *White over Black*, p. 7.
25. Ibid., p. 43.
26. Alan Grimes, *Equality in America* (New York: Oxford University Press, 1964).
27. Louis L. Knowles and Kenneth Prewitt, *Institutional Racism in America* (Englewood Cliffs, N.J.: Prentice-Hall, 1969).
28. Berry, *Race and Ethnic Relations*, p. 287.
29. Grimes, *Equality in America*, p. 60.
30. Berry, *Race and Ethnic Relations*, p. 287.
31. Grimes, *Equality in America*, p. 55.
32. Berry, *Race and Ethnic Relations*, p. 288.
33. Ibid., p. 299.
34. John R. Howard, *The Cutting Edge* (Philadelphia: Lippincott, 1974).
35. Wax, *Indian Americans*, Appendix C, pp. 215–227.
36. See Duberman, *Social Inequality*, p. 244; and Alphonso Pinkney, *Black Americans*, 2nd ed. (Englewood Cliffs, N.J.: Prentice-Hall, 1975).
37. Letha Scanzoni and John Scanzoni, *Men, Women, and Change* (New York: McGraw-Hill, 1976), pp. 366–367.
38. Department of Commerce, Bureau of the Census, *Statistical Abstracts, 1975* (Washington, D.C.: Government Printing Office, 1975), Table 35.
39. Wax, *Indian Americans*, pp. 220–221.
40. Pinkney, *Black Americans*, pp. 42–43.
41. Howard, *The Cutting Edge*, p. 103.
42. Pinkney, *Black Americans*.
43. U.S. National Center for Health Statistics, *Vital Statistics of the United States, 1975*.
44. Pinkney, *Black Americans*.
45. See Howard, *The Cutting Edge*.
46. Bureau of the Census, *Statistical Abstracts, 1975*.
47. Noel P. Gist and Sylvia Fleis Fava, *Urban Society* (New York: Crowell, 1974), pp. 186–187.
48. Ibid. p. 194.
49. Stanley Lieberson, *Ethnic Patterns in American Cities* (New York: Free Press, 1963).
50. Gist and Fava, *Urban Society*, pp. 190–191.
51. Rose Hum Lee, "The Decline of Chinatowns in the United States," *American Journal of Sociology* 54 (March 1949): 422–432.
52. Pinkney, *Black Americans*, p. 52.

53. The average life expectancy is affected by rates of infant mortality and also illnesses such as tuberculosis that affect certain age groups, thereby reflecting itself in the average age of death for a given population. This is not to detract from the inequalities reflected by the age variation in life expectancy.

54. See Hassim M. Solomon, *Community Corrections* (Boston: Holbrook, 1976).

55. Ben J. Wattenberg, *The Real America* (New York: Doubleday, 1974).

56. Wax, *Indian Americans*, pp. 153–154.

57. Ibid., p. 154.

58. Ibid., p. 155.

59. Ibid., p. 154.

60. See Paul K. Clare and John H. Kramer, *Introduction to American Corrections* (Boston: Holbrook, 1976).

61. Marvin E. Wolfgang, *Crime and Race* (New York: Institute of Human Relations Press, 1964).

62. Daniel P. Moynihan, *The Negro Family: The Case for National Action* (Washington, D.C.: Department of Labor, Office of Policy Planning and Research, 1965).

63. Pinkney, *Black Americans*, p. 248.

64. Lee Rainwater, "Crucible of Identity: The Negro Lower Class Family," *Daedalus* 95 (Winter 1970): 172–216.

65. Oscar Lewis, *A Study of Slum Culture* (New York: Random House, 1968).

66. Helen Safa, "The Matrifocal Family in the Black Ghetto: Sign of Pathology or Pattern of Survival?" in Charles O. Crawford, ed., *Health and the Family: A Medical Sociological Analysis* (New York: Macmillan, 1971).

67. Cited in Gist and Fava, *Urban Society*, p. 393.

68. Charles V. Willie, ed., *The Family Life of Black People* (Columbus, Ohio: Merrill, 1970).

69. Pinkney, *Black Americans*.

70. Robert B. Hill, *The Strengths of Black Families* (New York: Emerson Hall, 1972), p. 4.

71. Duberman, *Social Inequality*, p. 247.

72. Ibid.

73. Eric C. Lincoln, "The Absent Father Haunts the Negro Family," *The New York Times Magazine*, November 28, 1966.

74. Safa, "The Matrifocal Family."

75. Cited in Gist and Fava, *Urban Society*, p. 394.

76. See, for example, Lee, "Decline of Chinatowns."

77. Ibid. See also Girdner and Loftis, *The Great Betrayal*, pp. 456–457, for a discussion of the ecological distribution of Japanese-Americans.

78. Dr. Harry Kitano, cited in *Pacific Citizen*, February 17, 1967. For a discussion of delinquency and family life in the Mexican-American population, see Celia S. Heller, *Mexican American Youths: Forgotten Youth at the Crossroads* (New York: Random House, 1966); and Joan W. Moore, *Mexican Americans* (Englewood Cliffs, N.J.: Prentice-Hall, 1970).

79. Nathan Murillo, "The Mexican American Family," in Nathaniel N. Wagner and Marsha J. Haug, eds., *Chicanos* (St. Louis: Mosby, 1971), p. 97.

80. Morris Rosenberg and Roberta G. Simmons, *Black and White Self-Esteem: The Urban School Child* (Washington, D.C.: American Sociological Association, 1971).

81. See, for example, Chad Gordon, *Looking Ahead: Self-Conceptions, Race and Family Factors as Determinants of Adolescent Achievement Orientations* (Washington, D.C.: American Sociological Association, 1972); Kenneth Clark and Mamie P. Clark, "Racial Identification and Preference in Negro Children," in T. M. Newcomb and E. L. Hartley, eds., *Readings in Social Psychology* (New York: Holt, 1947).

82. See Paul Glasser and Elizabeth Navarre, "Structural Problems of the One Parent Family," *Journal of Social Issues* 21 (January 1964): 98–109.
83. Martin P. Deutsch and Burt Brown, "Social Influences in Negro-White Intelligence Differences," *Journal of Social Issues* Vol. 12 (1964): 24–35.
84. *Current Population Reports, 1973*, no. 46, pp. 28–29.
85. Ibid.
86. See Calvin W. Burnett, "Urban Education in Low-Income Areas: An Overview," in Allan C. Ornstein et al., eds., *Educating the Disadvantaged 1969–70* (New York: AMS, 1971), p. 279.
87. Martin P. Deutsch, "The Disadvantaged Child and the Learning Process," in A. Harry Passow, ed., *Education in Depressed Areas* (New York: Bureau of Publications, Teachers College, Columbia University, 1963).
88. Harry L. Miller and Roger R. Woock, *Social Foundations of Urban Education*, 2nd ed. (Hinsdale, Ill.: Dryden, 1973).
89. Ibid., p. 175.
90. Stephen S. Baratz and J. C. Baratz, "Early Childhood Intervention: The Social Science Bases of Institutional Racism," *Harvard Educational Review* 40 (Fall 1970): 29–50. Also see *ibid.*, p. 176.
91. Baratz and Baratz, ibid.
92. Murillo, "Mexican American Family."
93. Colleen Leahy Johnson and Frank Arvid Johnson, "Interaction Rules and Ethnicity: The Japanese and Caucasians in Honolulu," *Social Forces* 54 (December 1975).
94. Charles A. Valentine, "Deficit, Difference and Bicultural Models of Afro-American Behavior," *Harvard Educational Review* 41 (May 1971): 137–157.
95. Marcia Guttentag, "Group Cohesiveness, Ethnic Organization, and Poverty," *Journal of Social Issues* 26 (1970): 105–132.
96. See Arthur Jensen, "How Much Can We Boost IQ and Scholastic Achievement?" *Harvard Educational Review* 39 (Winter 1969): 1–123, and "The Differences Are Real," *Psychology Today*, December 1973, pp. 80–86; and Richard Herrnstein, "IQ," *The Atlantic*, September 1971, pp. 43–64.
97. *Statistical Abstracts, 1975*, Table 240, p. 126.
98. Tamotstu Shibutani and Kian M. Kwan, *Ethnic Stratification: Comparative Approach* (New York: Macmillan, 1965).
99. Alex Inkeles, "Becoming Modern: Individual Change in Six Developing Countries," *Ethos* 3 (Summer 1975).
100. Wax, *Indian Americans*, pp. 111–112.
101. "*Brown* vs. *Board of Education*," 347 U.S. 483 (1954).
102. Official statement adopted at the Conference of Southern Negro Educators in Hot Springs, Arkansas, October 1954.
103. Diane Ravitch, "Blacks' College Gains," *The New York Times*, July 8, 1976.
104. Ibid.
105. Charles V. Willie and Arline S. McCord, *Black Students on White College Campuses* (New York: Praeger, 1972).
106. Ibid., especially chap. 3.
107. Cited in Wax, *Indian Americans*, pp. 106–107.
108. Daniel W. Rossides, *The American Class System* (Boston: Houghton Mifflin, 1976).
109. Ibid.
110. Girdner and Loftis, *The Great Betrayal*.
111. See "Who Needs College?" *Newsweek*, April 26, 1976, pp. 60–69.
112. James S. Coleman et al., *Equality of Educational Opportunity* (Washington, D.C.: Government Printing Office, 1966), p. 20.

113. See, for example, Edmund W. Gordon and Doxey A. Wilkerson, *Compensatory Education for the Disadvantaged* (New York: College Examination Board, 1966).
114. See Herbert G. Birch and Joan Dye Gussow, *Disadvantaged Children: Health, Nutrition and School Failure* (New York: Harcourt Brace Jovanovich, 1970).
115. See Robert E. Doherty, "Attitudes Toward Labor: When Blue Collar Children Become Teachers," *School Review* 71 (Spring 1963); and Howard S. Becker, "Social Class Variations in the Teacher–Pupil Relationship," *Journal of Educational Sociology* 25 (April 1952).
116. Merrill Sheils et al, "Minority Report Card," *Newsweek*, July 12, 1976, pp. 74–75.
117. Bureau of the Census, *Current Population Reports*, "The Social and Economic Status of the Black Population in the United States, 1973" (Washington, D.C.: Government Printing Office, 1974), Table 34.
118. Bureau of the Census, *Current Population Reports*, "Persons of Spanish Origin in the United States: March 1974," Table 10.
119. *Statistical Abstracts, 1975*, p. 163.
120. Ibid.
121. Rossides, *American Class System*, p. 163.
122. Michael Ruby and Rich Thompson, "The Great Job Debate," *Newsweek*, July 26, 1976, pp. 62–63.
123. Ibid.
124. Wax, *Indian Americans*, p. 70 and Howard, *The Cutting Edge*, p. 108.
125. Wax, ibid.
126. Alan L. Sorkin, "Some Aspects of American Indian Migration," *Social Forces* 48 (December 1969): 243.
127. Ibid.
128. William Peterson, "Success Story, Japanese American Style," *The New York Times Magazine*, January 9, 1966.
129. Bureau of the Census, "Nonwhite Population by Race, 1960," p. 108.
130. As in the instance of many others with working-class backgrounds, college-educated Japanese-Americans have specialized in highly pragmatic areas such as education (during the 1960s) and engineering.
131. Girdner and Loftis, *The Great Betrayal*, p. 461.
132. Ibid.
133. See Melvin Steinfeld, *Cracks in the Melting Pot* (Beverly Hills, Calif.: Glencoe, 1970).
134. See William McCord, *Mississippi: The Long Hot Summer* (New York: Norton, 1965).
135. See William McCord et al., *Life Styles in the Black Ghetto* (New York: Norton, 1969).
136. Vine Deloria, *Custer Died for Your Sins* (London: Macmillan, 1969).
137. Howard, *The Cutting Edge*.
138. Wax, *Indian Americans*, p. 144.
139. Ibid.
140. Deloria, *Custer Died for Your Sins*.
141. Howard, *The Cutting Edge*, p. 108.
142. Ibid., p. 101.
143. Ibid., p. 91.
144. Ibid., p. 100.
145. Girdner and Loftis, *The Great Betrayal*, p. 470.
146. Ibid.
147. Ibid., p. 467; see also *Pacific Citizen*, editorial, July 29, 1966.
148. Ibid., p. 471.
149. For a different perspective, see Steven Goldberg, *The Inevitability of Patriarchy* (New York: Morrow, 1973).
150. See, for example, Cynthia Epstein, *Woman's Place* (Berkeley: University of California Press, 1971), pp. 20–24.

151. Gladys E. Harbeson, *Choice and Challenge for the American Woman* (Cambridge, Mass.: Shenkman, 1967), pp. 13–14.
152. Scanzoni and Scanzoni, *Men Women and Change*, p. 141.
153. Ibid.
154. Lois Wladis Hoffman and Martin L. Hoffman, "The Value of Children to Parents," in James T. Fawcett, ed., *Psychological Perspectives on Population* (New York: Basic Books, 1973); and Veevers, *Current Population Reports, 1972*, P-20, no. 269, p. 5.
155. F. Muller-Lyner, *Evaluation of Modern Marriage* (New York: Macmillan, 1903), p. 112.
156. Havelock Ellis, *Studies in the Psychology of Sex* (New York: Random House, 1936).
157. E. Crawley, *The Mystic Rose* (New York: Macmillan, 1927).
158. Robert Buffault, *The Mothers*, 3 vols. (New York: Macmillan, 1927).
159. C. Leonard Wooley, *The Sumerians* (Oxford: Oxford University Press, 1929).
160. *Mahabharata*, III, xxxiii, 82.
161. Captain F. Bunkley, *Japan: Its History, Arts, Literature*, 8 vols. (Boston: Little Brown, 1894).
162. Adolf Erman, *Life in Ancient Egypt* (London: Canterbury, 1894).
163. Ibid.
164. Saint Boniface's letter to King Ethelbald, A.D. 756.
165. See the *Koran*, xi, 3.
166. Will Durant, *The Renaissance* (New York: Simon and Schuster, 1953), pp. 585–586.
167. See Jacob Burkhardt, *The Civilization of the Renaissance in Italy* (Berne: Bruengner, 1914).
168. See Eleanor Flexner, *Century of Struggle* (Cambridge, Mass.: Harvard University Press, 1959).
169. See, for example, Eleanor Maccoby and Carol Jackin, *Psychology of Sex Differentiation* (Stanford, Calif.: Stanford University Press, 1975).
170. See Thomas Woody, *History of Women's Education in the United States* (New York: Macmillan, 1904).
171. An assumed near equality of men and women is contained in *Victory, How Women Won It* (Anonymous, New York: Wilson, 1940), which in its Foreword states: "The Century from 1840 to 1940 may appropriately be called the Woman's Century." Cited in Dean D. Knudsen, "The Declining Status of Women: Popular Myths and the Failure of Functionalist Thought," *Social Forces* 48 (December 1969).
172. Interdepartmental Committee on the Status of Women, *Report on Progress in 1966 on the Status of Women* (Washington, D.C.: U.S. Women's Bureau Publication, 1966).
173. Knudsen, "Declining Status of Women."
174. U.S. Department of Labor, Women's Bureau, *Job Horizons for College Women in the 1960's* (Washington, D.C.: Government Printing Office, 1964), Table 2, p. 67.
175. Harbeson, *Choice and Challenge*, pp. 4–5.
176. Edwin G. Dexter, *A History of Education in the United States* (New York: Macmillan, 1904).
177. David W. Swift, *American Education: A Sociological View* (Boston: Houghton Mifflin, 1976), pp. 370–386.
178. Mabel Newcomer, "Women's Education: Facts, Findings, and Apparent Trends," *Journal of the National Association of Women Deans and Counselors* (October 1960): 35–56.
179. See Knudsen, "Declining Status of Women," which reports that there has been a decline since 1940.
180. Carnegie Commission on Higher Education (1973), cited in Robert J. Havighurst and Bernice L. Neugarten, *Society and Education* (Boston: Allyn & Bacon, 1975), p. 392.
181. *Report of the Commission On Tests: I. Righting the Balance* (Princeton, N.J.: College Entrance Examination Board, 1970).

182. John K. Folger, Helen S. Astin, and Alan E. Bayer, *Human Resources and Advanced Education,* Staff Report of the Commission on Human Resources and Advanced Education (New York: Russell Sage Foundation, 1970).
183. Elizabeth Cless, "A Modest Proposal for the Educating of Women," *American Scholar* 38 (Autumn 1969): 622.
184. Swift, *American Education,* pp. 386–387.
185. U.S. Office of Education, *Digest of Educational Statistics: 1972,* September 1972, Table 98, p. 83.
186. Judith Hole and Ellen Levine, *Rebirth of Feminism* (New York: Quadrangle, 1971), p. 334.
187. Marjorie B. U'Ren, "The Image of Women in Textbooks," *Women in Sexist Society* (New York: Basic Books, 1971), p. 218.
188. Havighurst and Neugarten, *Society and Education,* p. 393.
189. Matina S. Horner, "Fail: Bright Women," *Psychology Today,* November 1969, p. 393.
190. William H. Sewell, "Inequality of Opportunity for Higher Education," *American Sociological Review* 36 (1971): 793–809.
191. Alice Rossi, "Equality Between the Sexes: An Immodest Proposal," *Daedalus* 93 (Spring 1964): 607–652.
192. *Statistical Abstracts, 1975,* Table 563, p. 346.
193. Ibid.
194. Ivan F. Nye and Lois W. Hoffman, *The Employed Mother in America* (Chicago: Rand McNally, 1963).
195. Knudsen, "Declining Status of Women."
196. Harbeson, *Choice and Challenge,* p. 49.
197. U.S. Department of Commerce, *Current Population Reports: Consumer Income,* Series P60, no. 53 (Washington, D.C.: Government Printing Office, 1967), cited in Knudsen, "Declining Status of Women."
198. Andrea Tyree and Judith Treas, "The Occupational and Marital Mobility of Women," *American Sociological Review* 39 (June 1974): 293–302.
199. John Miller, Sanford Labovitz, and Lincoln Fry, "Inequalities in the Organizational Experiences of Women and Men," *Social Forces* 54 (December 1975): 365.
200. Jean Humphrey Block, "Conceptions of Sex Role—Some Cross Cultural and Longitudinal Perspectives," *American Psychologist* (June 1973): 512–526.
201. Ibid.
202. Scanzoni and Scanzoni, *Men, Women, and Change,* p. 33.
203. Ibid., p. 34.
204. Harriet Holter, *Sex Roles and Social Structure* (Oslo: Universitetsforiaget, 1970).
205. Donald G. McKinley, *Social Class and Family Life* (New York: Free Press, 1964).
206. Scanzoni and Scanzoni, *Men, Women, and Change,* p. 34.
207. Ibid., pp. 38–39; see also Pauline B. Bart, "Why Women See the Future Differently from Men," in Alvin Toffler, ed., *Learning for Tomorrow: The Role of the Future in Education* (New York: Random House, 1974).
208. McKinley, *Social Class and Family Life.*
209. *Statistical Abstracts, 1975,* Table 266, p. 158.
210. Ibid., Table 264, p. 157.
211. Freda Adler, *Sisters in Crime: The Rise of the New Female Criminal* (New York: McGraw-Hill, 1975).
212. Ibid., p. 253.
213. See Hole and Levin, *Rebirth of Feminism,* especially Chapter 10.
214. See Arline McCord and William McCord, *Urban Social Conflict* (St. Louis: Mosby, 1977).

7

STRATEGIES TO END INEQUALITY

Europeans did not "discover" America in a search for equality. Spaniards sought gold, the supremacy of their king, and the rule of their religion; the French wanted beaver skins and any other form of wealth; the vaunted Pilgrims wished the right to persecute and exclude those of other religious faiths. And, contrary to Rousseau's myth, the native American Indian had created complex forms of social hierarchy that would have been far beyond the comprehension of a "noble savage." The founders of America were, in no sense, egalitarians.

Whatever their origins, however, Americans of the last two hundred years have entered into debates about equality and equity. The reasons are clear: many, such as the convicts who were Georgia's original residents, migrated to the huge continent from humble sources that were innately antagonistic to the privileges of wealth and nobility in their home countries; others, like Alexander Hamilton, found the new taste of wealth and privilege in the colonies an inspiration for their own elitist conceptions; still others, like Thomas Jefferson, savored the vast bounties of the new nation and hoped to create a mutually equal group of agricultural producers. In the early nineteenth century, the Jeffersonian ideology prevailed: America was, ideally, a land of equal opportunity that rewarded hard-working individuals regardless of their origin.[1] Alexis de Tocqueville, the eminent European visitor to America, echoed the prevailing concepts of the time:

> The more I advanced in the study of American society, the more I perceived that . . . equality of condition is the fundamental fact from which all others seem to be derived and the central point at which all my observations terminated. . . . [It is] an irresistible revolution which has advanced for centuries in spite of every obstacle.[2]

Yet, even at the time of Jefferson's sweeping electoral victories, or later during de Tocqueville's journey, the reality of American life hardly reflected the ideal. Early in the nineteenth century, the Northeast had developed a class of rich entrepreneurs and merchants; Virginia's landholders played at being aristocrats; and even Jefferson himself did not free his slaves until after his death.

Slavery in America prevailed until the Civil War, a bloody event that some historians mark as the triumph of an industrialized North over an agrarian South. The war did not, as we have noted, end the pervasive effects of racism in America; it succeeded at best in ending de jure slavery of blacks, who then often became part of the industrialized lower classes in the rest of the nation. The myth of equality still dominated American minds, however, and nowhere as strongly as among Northern industrial classes, freed slaves, and new migrants to the nation.

During the last part of the nineteenth century, the vast expanse of the frontier kept open for many the hope of equality of opportunity and the belief in true social equality. Although specific social groups—the backers of Shay's Rebellion, or Irish migrants to New York, or blacks in the Deep South—tasted the dregs of American inequality, most Americans believed that the frontier's vast resources beckoned them to lives of prosperity and true equality.

As industrialization, the exhaustion of land, and the growth of monopolies destroyed this myth, Americans by 1900 turned to social or political measures in order to build a nation of equal opportunity. Trade unions, a conscious expression of class conflict, burgeoned during this period. Socialist parties, muckrakers, and trustbusters came to prominence. Legislators, warned anew of the dangers of gross and increasing inequality, passed several measures to ensure an end to child labor, the enslavement of women, and cruel factory conditions.

As the twentieth century began, many Americans no longer believed that even these relatively radical (for their time) measures could ensure, or "re-establish," equality of opportunity. Some put their faith in private philanthropy; and Jane Addams, for instance, established settlement houses in Northern slums to educate the poor. Others hoped that the spread of public education would give poor Americans the tools to "raise themselves" out of their misery. Still others thought that legislation could radically change opportunities for the poor. As a strategy which, as a side effect, aimed at reducing inequality, the introduction of the progressive income tax has been by far the most important piece of legislative action in the twentieth century.

Taxes and Social Security

The income tax and its supplements, creations of twentieth-century legislators, served ostensibly to shift the burden of supporting the government to those who had "the ability to pay." Supposedly, too, inheritance taxes discouraged idleness and the influence of inherited, unearned wealth. Proponents of the income tax conceived of it as a massive redistribution of wealth, and opponents of it saw it as a major step toward socialism and total equality. Whatever these views, the income tax was merely a pragmatic measure to meet the exigencies of government costs. Daniel Rossides has pointed out that despite numerous reforms, over the years, the income tax is not very "progressive" at all and has failed to affect measurably the inequality of incomes in America.[3]

Moreover, the federal tax structure—through tax-free bonds, oil and capital depletion allowances, and a low rate of taxation on the sale of property—gives an enormous benefit to the property-owning, coupon-clipping classes.[4] By favoring those who gain money through stocks and bonds, the tax system rewards the idler who does not need to work for a salary.

The tax system also favors inequality by its generous provisions for inheritance. In 1976, for example, a couple could leave $120,000 in inheritances, in addition to $60,000 in gifts, and $3,000 each year to their children. If fully utilized, these benefits hardly encouraged the children to work and did little to reduce income gaps between generations.

Thus, the imposition of the income and inheritance tax has not radically changed the pattern of inequality in America. As one expert on the subject observed, "The American tax code not only reflects the power and privilege of the class-prestige structure, but also facilitates and legitimates their accumulation over time."[5]

In 1935, reacting to the economic pressures of the Great Depression, America's government instituted Social Security, a measure of social insurance that was denounced at the time as leading to sloth and economic leveling. Although the Social Security system provides pensions and other forms of security for the aged, in its financing it presents a highly regressive tax burden to the poor. Using a flat rate on a portion of income, Social Security does not take into account the number of dependents. Payments eventually come at an extremely low rate in relation to payments. For many ethnic groups, such as lower-class blacks, the mandatory age of retirement at sixty-five is a mythic goal since many will die before attaining it. Thus they will never benefit from all the monies they have paid into the system. Because the Social Security Act has been indiscriminately amended since 1935, administrators in the 1970s doubted that its originally well-financed trust funds would last until the end of the century.

Since neither the charity of the nineteenth century, the introduction of a new tax system in the early 1900s, nor the launching of Social Security in 1935 significantly changed the pattern of inequality, many Americans in the 1960s—spurred on by the civil rights movement—tried to wage a "war on poverty."

The Ideology of Poverty: The 1960s

"The ideal of our economic system," President Herbert Hoover declared prior to the depression of the 1930s, "is that the door of opportunity and equality of opportunity may be held open to all."[6] In 1964 Sargent Shriver followed in a hallowed American tradition by commenting that the goal of the newly funded Office of Economic Opportunity was to ensure that opportunity is equal to all.[7] As President Hoover said in 1928, "Today we are engaged in a war against depression," so President Johnson reiterated in his State of the Union speech in 1964, "This administration, here and now, declares unconditional war on poverty in America."[8] The words were the same, the melody lingered on.

Undeniably, some changes in emphasis had occurred in the American ideology of poverty by the 1960s. Hoover's stress on individual initiative gave way to Roosevelt's attempt to provide minimum security for all, which, in turn, was superseded by Johnson's drive to eliminate even the social-psychological roots of poverty. Yet the same basic themes—opportunity, militancy, and optimism—recurred.

Over the last decades, an establishment ideology concerning the causes and cures of poverty crystallized, and even its critics from both the right and the left tended to accept similar propositions. This establishment ideology can be summarized in five propositions:[9]

1. Poverty is a massive problem in our affluent society. As Michael Harrington argued in his influential book *The Other America,* some 25 percent of Americans (in 1963)

> . . . are, at this very moment, maimed in body and spirit, existing at levels beneath those necessary for human decency. If these people are not starving, they are hungry, and sometimes fat with hunger for that is what cheap foods do. They are without adequate housing and educa-tion and medical care.[10]

For reasons of both humanitarianism and economy, poverty had to be eliminated once and for all. At the time, tabulations of the poor varied from eight million to as many as fifty million Americans. Using the arbi-trary definition that families earning less than $3,000 a year constituted the poor, President Johnson adopted an official position that one-fifth of Americans lived at a bare subsistence level.

2. While poverty afflicted the aged and disabled, the core of the prob-lem, as the president stated in his 1964 message to Congress, is "the young man or woman who grows up without a decent education, in a broken home, or in a hostile and squalid environment, in ill health or in the face of racial injustice."[11] Since automation demands an upgrading in education, the youth—particularly school drop-outs—should be the cen-tral concern of those launching an assault on poverty.

3. Measures that expand opportunity by alowing people to develop and use their capacities had to be the primary instruments in the war against poverty. By investing in the skills of people, prosperity would incrase, without altering the fundamental distribution of power in Ameri-can society.

4 Traditional education, while important, would not suffice since "the culture of poverty," the basic cause of the problem, must also undergo change. Apathy, fatalism, and low aspirations must be replaced by a new hope and dynamism. This goal, while garbed in the newest sociological fashion, differed little from President Hoover's desire in 1929 to "restore confidence" or President Roosevelt's reassurance in 1933 that "the only thing we have to fear is fear itself."

5. Properly conducted, the war on poverty would result in a society where people fulfill their potentialities to the utmost. With the expendi-ture of some $1 billion a year, President Johnson expected "total victory" to result from his program.

In its optimism, emphasis on "motivating" the poor, faith in educa-tion, focus on youth, and glorification of opportunity, the establishment ideology reflected a broad American consensus about the nature of ine-quality in the 1960s. De Tocqueville would have found it remarkably similar to the nineteenth-century American temper.

Conservative critics in the 1960s carped with details in the antipoverty program, criticized its waste, and described the administration's efforts as a political slush fund. Yet the rightist attacks, a somewhat subdued version of anti-New Deal slogans, were seldom directed against the essential assumptions of the war on poverty. The failure of rightist critics to develop an alternative doctrine that would appeal to conservative members of Congress underlined their basic agreement with the administration.

Similarly, critics on the left differed from the prevailing ideology only on issues of *methods* rather than *strategy* in the war on poverty. Indeed, it was difficult to decide whether the more influential spokesmen for the left —Saul Alinsky, Michael Harrington, Bayard Rustin, S. M. Miller, LeRoi Jones—were "in" or "out" of the establishment. Before the ink had dried on their manifestoes, their suggestions were often appropriated and their projects financed by the administration.

Leftist critics believed that the administration had underestimated the scope of the problem of poverty and should have spent more to eradicate economic blight from America. Some writers advocated a continuous redefinition of the "poverty line" since there could be no *objective* definition of a poor person. Some leftist critics believed that as society grew in abundance, people would demand more. The left believed even more strongly than the administration that automation caused poverty and that America had created a class of able people forced into leisure. Administration spokesmen did not necessarily disagree with these views. Rather, they countered with the argument that President Johnson was doing all that he could within the realm of that which was politically feasible.

The New Left relied on three arguments to define its unique ideology of poverty. Its first criticism was that the war on poverty was simply a token measure designed to mollify the civil rights conflict. It was, in their view, a transmutation of the civil rights movement designed to protect the power position of whites. Since this conspiratorial interpretation lacked evidence, it was accepted only by those on the farthest fringe of the left or by those such as disillusioned slum blacks who anticipated an immediate increase in income from the antipoverty program.

Its second criticism was that the war on poverty did nothing to eradicate economic inequality. The poverty programs, they argued, made no effort to reduce inequalities produced since World War II. Since economists disagree about whether the gap between rich and poor was greater in the 1960s than, say, before World War II, the basic premise of this view remained in doubt. It was, in any case, irrelevant. The administration's announced goal was equality of opportunity, not equality of income. Whatever one's ethical beliefs, it was unrealistic to expect that a politically astute president, at that juncture of history, would seek unabashed equalitarianism.

Its third contention was more to the point. The poor, so the argument went, had to undergo a political mobilization to achieve all the goals that, however inarticulately, they desired to fulfill. Thus the poor had to evolve into a political constituency, aware and powerful enough to enforce their demands. Otherwise, the antipoverty money would land in the hands of corrupt administrators or of social workers who knew little of the real needs of the poor. This position suffered from the basic fault that urban blacks, poor Southern whites, old people in Los Angeles, deserted women, and migratory workers had few interests in common, except for their poverty. How could one forge a powerful national coalition out of such a diverse—and sometimes antagonistic—conglomeration of groups? Further, as we have noted, the most deprived groups in American society are least susceptible to political mobilization.

Despite the utopian element in leftist thinking, the establishment was sufficiently flexible so that even these opinions were more or less absorbed into the antipoverty program. The Office of Economic Opportunity financed LeRoi Jones's "Black Arts Theater," supposedly a center of black ideology in Harlem, an action that could hardly be regarded as a way of diverting attention from civil rights issues. The Council of Economic Advisers proposed that all people receive a minimum income in order to further economic quality, surely a step toward the classless society envisioned by the left. And VISTA as well as Community Action Program workers devoted much of their attention to organizing indigenous, politically oriented protest movements.

In its implementation of the war against poverty, America was leftist, but with a mixture of ideologies. Even in this most debatable area of domestic politics, a consensus emerged. There was only one difficulty: the basic doctrines about poverty were often mistaken.

THE EXTENT OF POVERTY

Critics first questioned the massiveness of the problem of poverty. The number of Americans who truly suffered from economic privation was, at times, grossly exaggerated. Michael Harrington's original estimates, for example, ludicrously lumped Appalachian farmers and Harlem dwellers together with the "self-chosen" poor, for instance, Bohemians and skid-row alcoholics.[12] If one omits these latter groups, a more realistic estimate of the number of poor ranges from 8 to 34.6 million. The lower figure referred only to those receiving some form of public assistance, while the higher came from a Social Security Administration report. By the Social Security Administration's definition of the poverty line—an income insufficient to provide a minimum diet and other living essentials—14 percent of Americans would have been considered poor in 1964.

This yardstick of poverty of course obscured the fact that America's poor lived at a level that would seem incredibly opulent to most of the world's peoples. If, for example, one defined as poor simply those who did not live in an adequate house and did not own a television set, the census revealed that only 10 percent of blacks and 5 percent of whites would fall into such a category. Even among the low-income groups of Tunica, Mississippi—the poorest segment of the poorest county of the poorest state in America—52 percent owned televisions, 46 percent had automobiles, and 37 percent possessed sewing machines.[13] And, despite justified concern about the state of American youth, it should be remembered that more children attended school in the 1960s—and fewer dropped out—than at any other time in history.

Poverty in America, then, was not quite the massive problem depicted by certain social critics. Compared to the destitution of two-thirds of the world, it was—to use sociological jargon—a matter of "relative deprivation." Nonetheless, to view American poverty in its proper perspective—to recognize that it seldom involved starvation, homelessness, and total ignorance—was not a conservative glorification of the status quo. The poorest one-seventh in America suffered. As we have noted, they fell ill more often, died earlier, and left their progeny with little hope.

THE NATURE OF POVERTY

To achieve a final "total victory" over poverty obviously requires a sound knowledge of its sources. Establishment ideology, however, too often has led the public to portray the poor as gaunt farmers, migrant agricultural workers, unemployed Appalachian miners, or hordes of youth unable to find jobs because of a lack of education. This picture of the poor, while quite accurate during the depression, had little relevance in the 1960s. Such groups existed, of course, but they were only a small number of the poor. In contrast, as various studies have demonstrated, four overlapping segments of the American population were peculiarly vulnerable to poverty.

The helpless poor: the disabled and mentally disadvantaged people. No educational program designed to equalize opportunity could accomplish much in helping, say, those 3 percent of Americans who were mentally deficient. Rather, the solution to such poverty lay in medicine, custodial care, or other types of therapy.

The aged: people over sixty-five, particularly women, accounted for approximately five million of the poor. Equality of opportunity had little meaning to this group. Many of the poor aged led comfortable lives before retirement; they were not bred by the "culture of poverty"; they could not have benefited from vocational training.

Fatherless families: about two million poor families were headed by a mother whose husband had died or had deserted or divorced her. These single parents, in turn, raised about 50 percent of the fifteen million children who were normally included in poverty tabulations during the 1960s. In such matriarchal families, the basic problem (aside, often, from an inadequate knowledge of birth control) was not a lack of jobs, but simply an income insufficient to allow the mother to raise her children, without resorting to work outside the home.

Blacks: nearly half of American blacks had incomes of less than $3,000 in the 1960s. This group had more unemployment, the greatest incidence of illness, and the highest number of premature deaths.

The preponderant importance of these "pockets" of poverty was well illustrated in the studies concerning how much money the government would have had to allocate to raise the poor above a subsistence level. Forty-three percent of such a subsidy would go to the fatherless families alone; another 27 percent to the aged. In contrast, however, only about 6 percent would be needed to care for all the groups associated with the *Grapes of Wrath* image of poverty: West Virginia farmers, migratory workers, and all other poor rural families.

With the significant exception of blacks, the average impoverished person of the 1960s was not a victim of automation and unemployment. The previously cited studies showed that the poor could not be helped by extensive job-training programs. Even the provision of more and better jobs would have done little to aid most of the poor. Two-thirds of families headed by unemployed or partially employed males cited bad health, retirement, or other reasons for their situation, not an inability to find jobs. And a review of the case load of New York's welfare department indicated that only 3 percent could be considered as underemployed. Even this definition included people who had severe physical or mental problems.

Given the nature of poverty in contemporary America, a retreaded New Deal program did not go far in alleviating the situation. Agencies reminiscent of the CCC, the WPA, or the settlement houses affected, at best, only a minority of the poor. And such programs often ignored the plight of the poor who were disabled, mentally deficient, aged, or members of fatherless families. The establishment assertion that the best way out is through education seems most doubtful when one examines the actual condition of the poor.

The prevailing belief that the culture of poverty was at the heart of the problem also raised several issues. Many observers noted that attempts to change the culture of poverty actually entailed not a war on poverty but a war on the poor. Critics argued that the goal was to infuse the poor with middle-class values. Whether, in fact, those supposed virtues should or could be inculcated remained in substantial doubt. Clearly, the sick aged woman or the unemployed black or the crippled worker was often apathetic, despairing, and fatalistic. But was this the cause of their predicament? In attempting to better the conditions of these people, it seemed more pertinent to concentrate upon changing the structure of society—an America where the old could not live on Social Security payments, where the skilled black could not find an appropriate job, and where the disabled had to struggle on an inadequate workmen's compensation. Would not the psychological climate of poverty change if these aspects of society were altered?

In some cases, of course, psychological attitudes passed from generation to generation may "cause" poverty. It may well be that the disintegration of the black family permanently crippled children who were raised in this environment. Yet, many social scientists believe that efforts to uproot the culture of poverty are, however laudable, motivated by romanticism and guided by naiveté. Past experiments in changing people's attitudes and emotions—without altering either their total environment or their basic personality—have been notorious failures. It seemed unlikely that relatively superficial measures such as Head Start or the Job Corps could make notable inroads into the culture of poverty.

In several of its premises, therefore, the establishment ideology was questioned. Sheer expansion of opportunity had little relevance to most poverty-stricken groups. The provision of more or better jobs did not accomplish much for the majority of the poor. Education hardly proved a panacea since, in itself, it could not change the causes of poverty among many significant groups. Head-on attempts to alter the entire culture of poverty met with failure. Attempts to change the political direction of America without altering its socioeconomic structure were greeted with contempt by local city halls or by outright opposition. Because of the massive attempts to change the status of the poor and the unprecedented expenditures of national monies, the actual results of the war on poverty deserve more detailed consideration.

The Antipoverty Program: A Balance Sheet

Although often based on false premises, the antipoverty program of the 1960s should not be rejected as a total failure. Two of its greatest achievements, for example, were the extension of legal and medical aid to the poor.

The original Economic Opportunity Act of 1964 and subsequent innovations by the Nixon administration in 1974 have had moderate success in providing free legal services to the poor. The new forms of legal aid not only covered criminal defenses of the poor but provided mechanisms whereby the poor could initiate cases to protect their interests and empowered lawyers to launch class actions on behalf of entire groups of people.[14] These changes worked to the advantage of the poor by barring certain discriminatory trade practices, deceptive contracts, and garnishee actions.[15] In a nation where law has evolved as an instrument for serving the propertied classes in their eternal conflict with the poor,[16] these advances should not be underestimated. Yet, as Daniel Rossides has commented, "It should not go unnoticed that such legislation helps to legitimate the class system by incorporating into our legal understanding and sense of justice that the law protects only the equal right of poor and rich to consume according to class standing."[17]

In the field of medicine, the establishment of programs of health insurance for the elderly and health care for the poor relieved many but not all of the financial burdens of the aged and poor. Despite this advance and the provision of federally financed legal aid, the war on poverty, in the judgment of most experts, did not fundamentally affect the poor. In the opinion of one knowledgeable observer, "The rest of the War on Poverty has become indistinguishable from the dependency-creating, dirt-under-the-carpet welfare system. Its programs have gradually been incorporated into local government, dismantled or starved for funds."[18]

The failures of the war on poverty occurred on many fronts. The Community Action Program (CAP) was, for example, originally designed as an agency to be led by the poor themselves to change the conditions of their own lives. Supposedly, CAP was to mobilize the poor into effective political pressure groups. It utterly failed for two essential reasons.[19] First, efforts to mobilize the poor in most cities met with apathy, suspicion, and even antagonism in the ghettos. The organizers of CAP should have recognized that the lowest socioeconomic groups are politically passive. Perhaps discouraged by past experience, perhaps overburdened by their daily lives, perhaps ignorant of political complexities, lower socioeconomic groups seldom participate in political activity—even to the extent of casting a vote.[20]

As Sidney Verba and Norman Nie demonstrated in a nationwide study, most people in the lower classes are totally uninvolved in politics, lack political interests, are devoid of requisite political skills, and do not possess a sense of political competence.[21] Those few among the poor who do participate in American politics generally come from the ranks of big-city Catholics who contact officials on particular, parochial issues.[22] Confronted with such passivity, CAP officials generally failed to rally the poor to political goals.

Second, in those relatively rare cases where CAP succeeded in generating a mass movement among the poor, local city and state officials—normally drawn from other class groups—moved quickly to either stifle or co-opt the lower classes. In Houston, for example, white politicians paid black ministers to collect votes, black politicians were gerrymandered into new districts, and leaders of community programs were put into jail on trumped-up charges.[23] On a national level, Congress voted in 1967 to restrict the membership of the poor on CAP boards to one-third and directed local governments to form the goals of CAP. Thus, even in those areas where CAP had made some headway, the movement was quashed or integrated into the existing structure of class power.

In a variety of other fields, the war on poverty proved to be less than a spectacular success. Some programs—the Neighborhood Youth Corps, the Job Corps, and Work Experience and Training for adults—were launched during the 1960s in the belief that, through training, people could escape the vicious circle of the culture of poverty. Although the results of these attempts have not been fully evaluated, in the 1970s President Nixon declared them bankrupt and withdrew most federal monies. More radical critics had long attacked these programs for spending more money on their staffs than on their clients.

Head Start, designed to give deprived children preschool education, seemed promising at first. Studies indicated that ghetto children who had participated in Head Start did indeed do better in school. Later research, however, indicated that this initial advantage soon wore off. The oppressive atmosphere of ghetto schools lowered the achievement scores of both Head Start students and those who had not been in the program.[24]

For a short time, the Housing Act of 1968 rapidly expanded the construction of housing for the poor. The immediate result, however, "was a massive expenditure of funds that often lined the pockets of corrupt builders and officials and produced shoddy housing."[25] In 1972 the Nixon administration ended even this abortive program.

Specific attempts to aid those who existed in pockets of poverty either failed or were terminated by government officials. After centuries of being ignored, for example, Mexican-Americans received direct federal aid in the 1960s. For the first time, Mexican-American organizations in the Southwest and West received funds to aid their own ethnic group. As in other areas, however, the Nixon administration feared the political consequences of this initiative. Between 1968 and 1973, government officials ended direct grants to Mexican-American organizations and funneled the money to local politicians.

In most of its important endeavors, therefore, the antipoverty program failed to change the lot of the American poor. Hampered by an unrealistic ideology and a "service strategy" designed to remake the character of the poor,[26] the war on poverty had little chance, even as it began, to change the nature of the American class system. Subsequent onslaughts by conservative political administrations eroded its financial foundations. And the recession of the 1970s with its accompanying apathy doomed the movement to failure.

What to Do with the Poor

As the failure of the antipoverty program became clear, new strategies were suggested. If it is true that most of the poor could not be helped by more jobs, more opportunity, more education, or more middle-class virtues, then it seemed to many social critics in the 1970s that the nation should provide, out of public money, a minimum guaranteed annual income. This type of subsidy had after all long been used to support police departments, the post office, and public schools. Would it not also be equitable and, in the long run, quite efficient to provide federal subsidies that would raise incomes above the poverty level so that every person could afford a decent life?

Providing a minimum level of security in America can be done in many ways: broadening the base of Social Security and increasing its allotments; extending medical care to neglected groups (particularly fatherless families); reducing taxes for the poor (who, proportionately, actually pay more than the rich); giving direct grants that would ensure a minimum diet and would guarantee the other essentials of a decent life. Such a program would, at its inception, require some $11.5 billion annually. Most of this sum, $8.1 billion, would go to fatherless families and to elderly people. And most of the money would flow back into the economy since the subsidy would be spent immediately for consumer needs. In the 1970s, while presidential advisors suggested providing such a minimum income and Congress appropriated miserly rent subsidies, much of the public—still believing in education as a bootstrap way to equality of opportunity—regarded the provision of a minimum income as contributing to laziness and a lack of desire to seek a job.

The suffering of the white aged, the white fatherless family, or the white farmer could, theoretically, be reduced, if not eliminated, by one stroke of the presidential pen. Without invoking the specter of social Darwinism, it seems reasonable to agree with Kenneth Galbraith that white poverty is either of the "insular" variety (a relatively minor problem) or it is "case poverty," which is due to afflictions such as age, mental deficiency, bad health, inability to adapt to the discipline of modern economic life, or excessive procreation.[27] In a humane society, as Galbraith has eloquently argued, the government has a duty to care for people crippled by these disabilities rather than condemning them to a life of poverty. A subsidy ensuring a minimum income, in addition to various other corrective measures, could indeed reduce the problems of poverty among American *whites.*

The situation of the black in America, however, presents a more complex and intransigent problem. In one of the most incisive of writings during the 1960s, economist Alan Batchelder revealed the true extent of black poverty.[28] Batchelder has shown that the black dollar is second-class money. Operating in a market of "restricted supply," the ghetto or the plantation, the black pays relatively more than the white for housing, durable goods, and even food. Thus, $3,000 in "black money" buys only the equivalent of $2,500 in "white money."

Further, measures such as urban renewal, which benefit whites who are on the margin of poverty, have at times damaged the black. When a city, for example, erects a housing project, 60 percent of the families who are dispossessed are black. This means even more dense settlement of the ghetto, since, on the average, urban renewal projects that displace 190,-500 families result in a net loss of 75,000 housing units.

In the job market, changes that have benefited the general public have either left blacks untouched or have hurt them. Between 1950 and 1960, for example, the number of Southern factory jobs rose by 944,000. None of these went to black men, Batchelder asserts, and only 12,000 went to black women. Clearly, as automation eliminates unskilled jobs, blacks suffer the most.

These facts suggested that antipoverty programs could best accomplish their purposes by investing in blacks, for it is primarily in the black community where unemployed adults or potentially able youths could benefit from the programs offered by VISTA, Head Start, and the Neighborhood Youth Corps. Nonetheless, the heritage of racial discrimination and inadequate education can hardly be overcome by any antipoverty program based on the assumptions of the 1960s. An even more sweeping strategy has to be invented.

The Strategies of the 1970s

Social critics of the 1970s agree that the prime task of any new war on poverty is to get money into the hands of the poor. This apparently very simple assertion actually has wide-ranging implications, for all the efforts of the 1960s failed to increase the actual cash income of the poor between 1970 and 1974.[29] Although expenditures for various forms of public aid jumped from $77.2 million in 1965 to $286.5 million in 1975, a large portion of these sums went to education, staff salaries, and other activities that did not directly put cash in the hands of the poor.[30] Other approaches, including expenditures for Social Security, which the poor might or might not eventually enjoy, also skyrocketed as a reflection of fad and inflation.[31]

The fact that the poor did not directly increase their incomes as a result of these expenditures prompted responses from three areas. First, conservative critics sought the end of the welfare state itself and put their faith in the operation of a free-enterprise economy as the best device for putting income into the pockets of the poor. Second, liberal critics argued for various monetary innovations such as a guaranteed annual income (or a "credit income tax") to accomplish the same goal. Third, radicals believed that mere economic changes in the existing system would not help the poor and that direct confrontation between the poor and the "establishment" was the only method for producing the social revolution they desired. Thus strategists of the 1970s, although seeking the same goal, envisaged very different means for achieving it. Since the premises underlying each strategy would lead to contrasting national policies, they must be closely examined.

THE CONSERVATIVE STRATEGY

As enunciated by economist John A. Davenport, the basic strategy of conservative economists "is not to redistribute wealth but to *create* it."[32] To this end, Davenport would end minimum-wage laws, curtail the power of labor unions, and drastically cut payments for both welfare and Social Security. Davenport believes that the economy would then be freed from restrictive controls, high productivity would result, and only the "truly deserving" poor would remain on welfare rolls.

Davenport believes that the great leap forward in welfare costs "creates little or no welfare in terms of the actual production of goods."[33] He contends that "the American assumption . . . has been that the true source of welfare in its broadest meaning is private economic activity. . . . The general welfare has been promoted most effectively by the freedom, and the desire, of individuals to scamper across class lines."[34] Increases in welfare spending have not reduced indices of social pathology such as crime, divorce, or illegitimate births. In fact, Davenport believes increases in welfare spending have not measurably narrowed the gap between rich and poor. He allows one major exception: grants-in-kind such as the food stamp program, which has allowed the poor to buy essential groceries at their basic cost. Thus Davenport and other conservative thinkers would drastically cut any attempts at income redistribution:

> In the end, therefore, the curbing of so-called public welfare spending is only part of a much larger task. It is to turn our thinking around in a way that puts overwhelming priority on the growth of the private economy which is not only the source of employment for most people but also the key to higher living standards for all.[35]

As one substitute for welfare payments, some conservatives such as Milton Friedman have suggested a negative income tax. It is a plan to assure people below a given income level that they would receive a direct grant upon submission of their tax returns. In a modified form, President Nixon adopted a family assistance plan that proposed a minimum income of $2,400 for a family of four. Nixon's scheme did not involve actual redistribution of wealth. Some sociologists such as Daniel Patrick Moynihan applauded this plan when it first appeared in 1972, even though it would still have left the best-paid of poor families below the poverty line.[36] However inadequate, the family assistance plan provided a viable conservative version of a guaranteed annual income.

THE LIBERAL STRATEGY

Liberal social critics from John Kenneth Galbraith to Michael Harrington basically disagree with the conservative point of view. Instead, they urge much greater attention than before to the public sector of the economy. The position of such liberals has been most fully enunciated by sociologist Herbert Gans.[37] Along with many other liberals, Gans views increasing discontent among such varied minority groups as blacks, women, and workers as presaging an inevitable movement toward greater equality in income and in other spheres of life.[38] He envisages an "equality revolution" and believes that "how much liberty must be redistributed for this to happen will be the burning issue of the coming generation."[39] Gans rejects equality of opportunity as a laudable goal: "People who start their lives at a disadvantage rarely benefit significantly from equality of opportunity because . . . they can never catch up with the more fortunate."[40] Thus Gans and others seek greater equality of results.

Gans recognizes that there are many "positive functions" of poverty for other members of American society. The existence of poor people ensures that the dirty work of a society is done; the poor "subsidize" the rich by freeing the rich for leisure activities; and the poor "create" a number of jobs for such groups as social workers and policemen.[41]

To close the gap between the rich and the poor, various liberal plans have been proposed. Perhaps the most publicized one was that put forward by Senator George McGovern during his 1972 presidential campaign. McGovern suggested the adoption of a credit income tax, which would tap the "unearned" income of the rich, which is now exempted by various tax shelters for bonds, real estate, and oil. The concept of the credit income tax was developed by Earl Ralph and James Tobin,[42] it would have eliminated all exemptions and given a cash grant to any family that fell below a certain level. In effect, a family that earned $6,000 at 1972 levels would have received a one-third increase in income. Half of all Americans would not have had to pay any income tax; welfare would have been virtually eliminated; and unemployment rates would have been reduced to a minimal level.[43] Perhaps because it would have meant that the very rich in America would have surrendered part of their income—particularly that derived from gains in the stock market, real estate tax shelters, and oil-depletion allowances—the McGovern plan did not meet with universal approbation.

THE RADICAL STRATEGY

Discouraged by the political prospects for plans such as McGovern's, radical critics have demanded more severe measures to end poverty. Richard A. Cloward and Frances Fox Piven contend that most efforts to help the poor in America have failed. They call for a new theory of political action based on the recognition that the existing political system is closed to those at the bottom. They believe that the poor, particularly urban blacks, can achieve nothing through the usual political channels. They, therefore, advocate that the poor disrupt the entire system as a way of mobilizing political support. Essentially, they argue that the poor "should defy the rules governing their behavior on which major institutions depend"[45]—by withholding rent from slum housing, by encouraging many more thousands of people to go on relief, or by creating "confrontations" with caste norms in the South. Cloward and Piven argue:

> Such institutional disruptions would, in turn, have widespread political repercussions, activating significant electoral groups—some hostile, some sympathetic, but all aroused. . . . This capacity to create political crises through disrupting institutions is . . . the chief resource for political influence possessed by the poor.[46]

Cloward and Piven's appeal to disrupt, bankrupt, and polarize the American system is based on their disillusionment with the events of the

1960s. They believe that the marches, protests, rent strikes, and other efforts of the poor during the 1960s were often self-defeating. They also view the prospect of black masses for achieving political power in urban centers as extremely dim. They dismiss war on poverty programs, including manpower training and mental health programs, as useless. In fact, they argue, such approaches benefited the middle class rather than the black urban poor. For them, disruption of the system remains the most important tactic the poor can employ. Their theory stimulated the creation of the National Welfare Rights Organization, which organized welfare recipients to flood state and federal offices with demands.

Cloward and Piven's theory of disruption has produced no more tangible results than other theories since, as they recognize, those who control the system always have a choice: they may institute reforms or they may turn to even more repressive measures than have been used in the past. In the 1970s the choice has usually been greater repression. Attempts at school desegregation in Boston met with the rage of white mobs; the City University of New York—with its open admissions, free tuition policy to aid the poor—had to close its doors temporarily and end free tuition when its funds ran out; faced with increasing demands for services from the urban poor, mayors of America's cities quit their jobs at an unprecedented rate, declaring the cities "ungovernable."

The strategy of disruption had little effect on the poor of the 1970s, since city leaders claimed they had no money left to meet the demands of the poor who increasingly dominated the urban centers of America. The urban crises rendered the strategy of disruption ineffective. A typical comment of urban mayors came from Mayor Kevin White of Boston, who said in 1971:

> Boston is a tinderbox. . . . The fact is, it's an armed camp. One out of every five people in Boston is on welfare. Look, we raise 70 per cent of our money with the property tax, but half our property is untaxable and 20 per cent of our people are bankrupt. Could you run a business that way?[47]

In the face of such a massive fiscal crisis, the nation's mood of conservatism, and the increasing concentration of the poor in America's cities, the radical strategy of the 1970s had little to offer.

Conclusions

By the 1970s America was in the midst of a crisis. The incompetency of basic policies for helping the poor had been demonstrated and the increasing concentration of the poor in urban centers lent a forceful dimension to their protests. Public services throughout the nation—welfare, education, housing, criminal justice—were collapsing. And yet the nation's leaders, particularly in the cities, claimed that the erosion of their tax base made it impossible to deal with the multiple, complex problems of the poor. Strategies proposed by thoughtful conservatives, such as the negative income tax, had not really been tried; liberal strategies, such as the credit income tax, had not been given a fair chance either; radical strategies, emphasizing class polarization and disruption, seem doomed to plunge the nation into a worse economic crisis.

Faced with this paralysis of policy, some Americans looked abroad for other strategies to end poverty. They recognized that some industrialized nations faced with essentially similar problems had long ago erased the plague of poverty. Scandinavian nations—Denmark, Norway, and Sweden—stand out as possible examples for America's emulation.

SCANDINAVIA: AN END TO POVERTY?

Following a middle way between the extremes of unbridled capitalism and communism, Sweden, Norway, and Denmark have virtually abolished all the outward vestiges of poverty.[48] A class system continues to exist in these nations, and they are pervaded with bureaucracy. Yet they have successfully eliminated the basic deprivations suffered by their lower classes. Health insurance covers virtually all people and provides entirely free hospitalization and free medical attention as well as the costs of most medicines and special treatments.[49] Families receive payments for each child, free preschool care, and, of course, free education for all. Ninety percent of the population receives the same basic income, and there is virtually no unemployment.[50] Older people, if leading a solitary and lonely existence, live in "old people's towns" where they enjoy their own apartments, communal kitchens, and gardens. While a housing shortage has persisted in most Scandinavian nations since World War II, there are abundant public-housing facilities, and no one is condemned to live in the rural or urban slums that characterize America.

All these benefits, of course, come at a high economic cost. Sweden expends 22 percent of its gross national product on welfare (not including education), whereas in comparison America spends about 10 percent of its GNP on this.[51] The high level of taxation in Scandinavian countries is a perennial subject of debate, and yet no successful political party actually advocates dismantling the welfare apparatus.

Sweden's economic policies since the 1930s have allowed the nation to escape the worst effects of worldwide depression, to provide cradle-to-grave security, and to maintain one of the world's highest rates of growth.

In 1976 Swedish leaders considered extending their social experiment one step further.[52] Since Sweden has already entered the postindustrial stage (only 25 percent of workers are involved directly in industrial production), some leaders have proposed plans to eliminate the more formalized, stifling aspects of bureaucracy. Trade union economists have proposed the Meidner Plan, which calls for the transfer of 20 percent of annual profits to workers' groups. If carried out, the plan would give workers control over Swedish businesses in some twenty years and would, theoretically, enhance their autonomy.[53]

To assert that Scandinavian nations have abolished poverty and are now experimenting with ways to mitigate the effects of bureaucracy does not mean that they have ushered in a paradise. Economic growth rates are high, but some conservatives in Scandinavian countries maintain that they could be even higher without government "interference." One Swedish industrialist, Anders Pers, who is particularly opposed to government interference, has two signs prominently displayed in his office: "Smile—you may be on radar" and "Do it now—tomorrow there may be a law against it."[54]

Certainly, too, particular kinds of social pathology, such as suicide and alcoholism, are extraordinarily high in the Scandinavian countries. Since World War I, for example, Denmark has consistently been in the top rank of industrialized nations with a suicide rate of over 200 per million inhabitants.[55] And some Scandinavians, most notably the director Ingmar Bergman, have taken affront at the uniformity and bureaucratic rule that they believe pervade their home countries; Bergman expressed his indignation by self-exile from Sweden in 1976. Many Danish authors carp at the materialism of their nation, bemoaning its lack of spiritual vitality and the absence of a spiritual conscience.

Such criticisms, of course, overlook the fact that the vast majority of Scandinavians are relatively well off, comfortably housed, magnificently fed, and healthy (the average Scandinavian's life span exceeds the American's by some three years). Moreover, the Scandinavian nations' prosperity has not blunted their concern for less fortunate peoples; Sweden, for example, contributes a higher portion of its income than any other nation for aid to developing countries.

Can Scandinavia's abolition of the worst effects of the class system be emulated by America? It could be argued that the racial homogeneity of these nations, their small size, and their fortunate escape from the ravages of the last century of warfare make them unique. Yet, in common with America, they are highly urbanized, industrialized, capitalistic nations. There seems no inevitable reason why America could not benefit from the Scandinavian experiments. As Marquis Childs has commented about Sweden's relevance to America, "If we could only learn the value of compromise, of making haste slowly, that would in itself be a valuable lesson."[56]

In that spirit, a number of Americans have increasingly addressed themselves to the basic philosophical issues of power, equality, and equity. Conceptually, they have tried to develop just societies that more closely approximate an ideal of equity than does contemporary America. Humbled by the failure of our own war on poverty and heartened by the success of Scandinavian endeavors, we should pay close attention to these new attempts to envisage a truly just society.

Notes

1. See Albert Jay Nock, *Jefferson* (New York: Hill and Wang, 1960).
2. Alexis de Tocqueville, *Democracy in America*, 1843.
3. See Daniel Rossides, *The American Class System* (Boston: Houghton Mifflin, 1973), p. 373.
4. See Robin Barlow, Harvey E. Brazer, and James N. Morgan, *Economic Behavior of the Affluent* (Washington, D.C.: Brookings Institution, 1966).
5. Rossides, *American Class System*, p. 375.
6. Herbert Hoover, "Inaugural Speech," 1928.
7. Sargent Shriver, "Speech to Boston OEO," 1964.
8. Lyndon Johnson, "State of the Union Speech," 1964.
9. A spate of books in the 1960s stated positions about poverty and, sometimes unknowingly, illustrated the historical continuity of these views: Ben Seligman, ed., *Poverty as a Public Issue* (New York: Free Press, 1965); R. M. MacIver, ed., *The Assault on Poverty* (New York: Harper & Row, 1965); Philip M. Stern, *The Shame of a Nation* (New York: Obolensky, 1965); Louis Ferman, Joyce Kornbluh, and Alan Haber, eds., *Poverty in America* (Ann Arbor: University of Michigan Press, 1965); Robert E. Will and Harold G. Vatter, eds., *Poverty in Affluence* (New York: Harcourt, Brace and World, 1965); Samuel E. Wallace, *Skid Row as a Way of Life* (Totowa, N. J.: Bedminster, 1965); Arthur Pearl and Frank Riessman, eds., *New Careers for the Poor* (New York: Free Press, 1965); Albert Tomansco, *The Poverty of Abundance* (New York: Oxford University Press, 1965); Caroline Bird, *The Invisible Scar* (New York: McKay, 1965); and Charles A. Valentine, *Culture and Power* (Chicago: University of Chicago Press, 1968).
10. Michael Harrington, *The Other America* (New York: Macmillan, 1963), p. 2.
11. Johnson, "State of the Union Speech."
12. See Harrington, *The Other America*.
13. See William McCord, *Mississippi: The Long Hot Summer* (New York: Norton, 1965). 1965).
14. See Jacques Ten Broek, ed., *The Law of the Poor* (San Francisco: Chandler, 1966).
15. See Jerome E. Carlin, Jan Howard, and Sheldon Messinger, *Civil Justice and the Poor* (New York: Russell Sage Foundation, 1967).
16. See Jacques Ten Broek, *Family Law and the Poor* (Westport, Conn.: Greenwood, 1971), for one example.

17. Rossides, *American Class System*, p. 414.
18. Ibid., p. 461.
19. See Ralph M. Karmen, *Participation of the Poor* (Englewood Cliffs, N.J.: Prentice-Hall, 1969); and Dale Rogers Marshal, *The Politics of Participation in Poverty* (Berkeley: University of California Press, 1971).
20. See Sidney Verba and Norman H. Nie, *Participation in America* (New York: Harper & Row, 1972).
21. Ibid.
22. Ibid.
23. See William McCord et al., *Life Styles in the Black Ghetto* (New York: Norton, 1969).
24. See Ronald Corwin, *Education in Crisis* (New York: Wiley, 1974).
25. Arthur Shostack, Jon Van Til, and Sally Bould Van Til, *Privilege in America* (Englewood Cliffs, N.J.: Prentice-Hall, 1973), p. 20.
26. See Lee Rainwater, "The Service Strategy vs. the Income Strategy," *Transaction*, October 1967.
27. John Kenneth Galbraith, *The New Industrial State* (New York: Signet, 1968).
28. Alan Batchelder, "Poverty: The Special Case of the Negro," *American Economic Review*, May 1965.
29. See John A. Davenport, "The Welfare State vs. the Public Welfare," *Fortune*, June 1976, p. 134.
30. Ibid.
31. Ibid., p. 135.
32. Ibid., p. 206.
33. Ibid., p. 132.
34. Ibid., p. 133.
35. Ibid., p. 205.
36. Daniel Patrick Moynihan, *The Politics of a Guaranteed Income* (New York: Random House, 1973).
37. Herbert Gans, *More Equality* (New York: Vintage, 1974).
38. See also Harold Sheppard and Neal Herrick, *Where Have All the Robots Gone?* (New York: Free Press, 1972).
39. Gans, *More Equality*, p. 33.
40. Ibid., p. 64.
41. See Herbert Gans, "The Positive Functions of Poverty," *American Journal of Sociology*, 78 (September 1972): 275–289; and Lee Rainwater, *Beyond Ghetto Walls* (Chicago: Aldine, 1970).
42. See Earl Ralph, "A Credit Income Tax," in Theodore Marmon, ed., *Poverty Policy* (Chicago: Aldine, 1972); and James Toben, "Raising the Incomes of the Poor," in Kermit Gordon, ed., *Agenda for the Nation* (Washington, D.C.: Brookings Institution, 1968).
43. Marmon, ibid.
44. Richard A. Cloward and Frances Fox Piven, *The Politics of Turmoil* (New York: Pantheon, 1974).
45. Ibid., pp. 70–71.
46. Ibid., p. 71.
47. Cited in James Reston, "The President and the Mayors," *The New York Times*, March 24, 1971.
48. Marquis Childs, *Sweden: The Middle Way* (New Haven, Conn.: Yale University Press, 1936; reprint, New York: Penguin, 1948).
49. See Jean Bailhache, *Denmark* (New York: Vista, 1961).
50. Ibid.

51. Davenport, "Welfare State vs. Public Welfare."
52. Leonard Silk, "Post-Industrial Capitalism," *The New York Times*, June 13, 1976.
53. Ibid.
54. Ibid.
55. Bailhache, *Denmark*, p. 155.
56. Childs, *Sweden*, Introduction.

PART III

Liberty, Equality, and Fraternity: Philosophical Aspects of Social Stratification

Should humankind strive to achieve greater equality of material goods, power, and privilege? If so, how can this be accomplished? If not, how can the current drift toward greater equality in many nations of the world be stopped? Ideally, what would be an equitable distribution of rewards in the best possible society?

These essential problems are at the core of the political and social conflicts of the twentieth century. A knowledge of the facts of social stratification provides an empirical framework for assessing answers to these questions. The facts themselves cannot, however, provide answers, for these basic questions involve issues of morality and justice that must be faced on the philosophical level. Ultimately, an image of the good society informs any policy concerning social stratification. Too often, out of ignorance or malice, statesmen and politicians do not examine the philosophical roots of their positions. Yet, the cogency of these philosophic issues can hardly be exaggerated.

On the international level, for example, the Chinese and the Russians fought their revolutions with the explicit ethical goal of helping the masses to greater equality and self-fulfillment. Hitler and Mussolini launched World War II in an effort to establish the supremacy of their favorite elites. In the postwar world, we have witnessed the blossoming of "welfare" states aimed at decreasing inequalities that doom the lower classes to poverty, ill health, and ignorance. Most recently, newly independent Third World nations in Asia, Africa, and South America have asked for a redistribution of the world's resources to alleviate their suffering. If these requests for greater international equality are not met, as Robert Heilbroner has warned, global "wars of redistribution" may well result.[1]

In America, similar battles have seared the domestic landscape. Adherents of the civil rights movement of the 1960s contended that American blacks had been treated both unequally and inequitably.[2] The war on poverty sprang from a deep-held American belief that inequality of opportunity should and could be abolished.[3] And the feminist movement of the 1970s is but another expression of the opinion that no single group should be held in a state of unfair or unjust subjugation. Opponents of these social movements also gained their impetus from philosophical beliefs that many specific changes would be disastrous for an equitable or just society. Opponents of busing, for example, believed that it would be unfair to mix their children with poor blacks; enemies of open admissions to American colleges claimed that such a policy undermined standards of merit; attackers of quota systems in business or education claimed that this was reverse discrimination, which destroyed equality of opportunity.

American proponents and opponents of greater equality have both used arguments derived from the same ethical premise: that equality of opportunity is an admirable goal that should be realized in a good society. Although they disagree on the means and consequences of a particular approach, few Americans in the 1970s openly question this ideal. Fewer still realize that theirs would be a totally foreign, exotic belief in those societies that flourished under an estate, caste, or slavery system. To even question this ideal, which may be traced to the French Revolution's slogan of *Liberté, Egalité, Fraternité,* one must have some acquaintance with its philosophical origins.

Origins of the Debate on Inequality

Throughout most of recorded history, as we have seen, inequality in wealth, power, and privilege has been accepted as an unquestioned fact. Today, even in China, once suffused with Confucianism, or India, where caste distinctions still retain their meaning, concepts of equity, equality of opportunity, and human progress reign supreme, even if they are not always fulfilled. These vast changes in sociopolitical ideology occurred partially because of changes in technology. More fundamentally, however, these changes are regarded as offspring of Western civilization—a Judeo-Christian ethic that flourished in the West and was, for good or evil, disseminated throughout the world by such forces as colonialism and the mass media.

The roots of this heritage may be traced to Judaism. Clearly, such prophets as Amos, Hillel, and Isaiah questioned the justice of social stratification in ancient Israel. These Hebrew prophets denounced the rich and the powerful of their times. With the possible exception of the Essenes, a minor sect that may have inspired Jesus, such prophets did not condemn stratification or private property in itself. They did, however, denounce the "wickedness," the misuse of power, and the violence of the powerful who seized the homes and lands of the weak.[4] In Micah's eyes, such actions "pervert all equity."[5] Although the God of the Hebrews mysteriously reserved all justice to himself (witness His persecution of His faithful adherent Job), some prophets derived their own concept of equity and used it to condemn the wealthy of Israel. Thus one may contend that the debate over social stratification originated some eight hundred years before Christ and revolved around a concept of "equity" and "equality of opportunity."

Elements in the teaching of Jesus have also been construed as a plea for equality or, at the minimum, as an attack upon the rich. St. Luke portrayed Jesus as admonishing a rich man: "Sell all that thou hast, and distribute unto the poor and thou shalt have treasure in heaven; and come, follow me. . . . For it is easier for a camel to go through a needle's eye, than for a rich man to enter into the kingdom of God."[6] Similarly, St. Paul declared in Galatians: "there is neither bond nor free . . . for you are all one in Jesus Christ."[7] And St. Augustine believed that man in the Garden of Eden was equal and free; only man's fall from God's grace led to differences in power and privilege: "The prime cause of servitude is sin."[8]

It would be ridiculous, of course, to picture Christians as pure egalitarians. The same tradition produced Jesus' admonition "to render unto Caesar," St. Paul's justification of slavery, and the important role of the Church as a serf-holder in medieval times. Yet, when interwoven with other skeins that make up the fabric of Western civilization, the Judeo-Christian ethic can be considered as one important source of contemporary egalitarianism.

Another significant influence on contemporary egalitarian thought is ancient Athens, despite its own practice of slavery. It was in Athens, after all, that thinkers first elaborated three aspects of the concept of equality: *isonomia* (all equal before the law), *isotimia* (equal respect), and *isagoria* (political freedom).[9] These ideas were, in turn, taken up by enlightened Romans. Particularly in the Stoic and Epicurean philosophies, men were portrayed as essentially equal, brothers who should rightfully treat each other with compassion in the face of the eternal threat of death. Although the Stoics obviously did not abolish slavery in the Roman Empire, their thought led logically in that direction.[10]

Later Western philosophers drew upon this tradition in quite different ways. Rousseau, for example, pictured men in an innocent state of nature as free and equal. Social stratification, for Rousseau, began only when men introduced the concept of private property. John Locke believed that men had entered into a "social contract" with a sovereign, exchanging some control over their fate in return for other privileges. Voltaire disagreed with both of these thinkers and viewed humankind as essentially brutish and selfish; only the imposition of civilization forced people to tolerate others. Despite their differences, however, all these philosophers sought political and legal freedoms for all men and, to that degree, viewed men as essentially equal.

With the French Revolution, the ideas of freedom, equality and fraternity, as expressed in the *Déclaration des droits de l'homme*, became enshrined in the social and political thought of Western nations. This is hardly to say that Western nations universally created institutions that advanced the goals of liberty and equality. It required the industrial revolution and great convulsions like the American Civil War to end such enduring social forms as serfdom and slavery. And the debate over the ideas expressed by the slogans of the French Revolution continues today. It is an argument that has been formed in a unique climate of ideas, drawing its inspiration from Judaism and Christianity, Athens and Rome. Today, philosophical schools of thought concerning social stratification may be roughly, but not unreasonably, divided into four groups: elitism, liberalism, libertarianism, and egalitarianism.

Philosophical Schools of Thought

It is always hazardous to categorize forms of political and social thought. The more brilliant the individual thinker, the more easily he or she escapes pigeonholing. In a matter as difficult and complex as equality, equity, and justice, however, some degree of simplification is necessary if one is to understand the bewildering array of opinions on the subject. With apologies, then, to thinkers who object to labeling or to the particular school to which we attach them, let us proceed to analyze the philosophies of social stratification that have been offered in the contemporary era.

As a first step, we should largely avoid the conventional labels of "conservatism," "liberalism," and "socialism" that have been used in the past and, for the sake of simplicity, in this book. In the area of social stratification, these categories no longer apply. Contemporary "liberals," for example, are willing or even eager to see an expansion of state power if it can be used to extend equality of opportunity, an idea which would have been anathema to their nineteenth-century precursors. Similarly, contemporary "socialists" are intrigued by the idea of decentralizing economic power through profit sharing rather than seeking the total nationalization of property under central control that their ancestors desired. Contemporary "conservatives," for their part, would just as soon be known as "eighteenth-century liberals." And so the argument goes. Let us, then, attempt to understand what contemporary thinkers actually believe rather than decipher the flags they fly under.

ELITISTS

It seems reasonable to identify one large group of social philosophers as elitists; that is, as people who believe that a natural elite of merit rules (or should rule) society, and that attempts at equalization of power and privilege are inequitable, dangerous, or at best, misguided. Elitists generally agree on three propositions.

1. They believe that liberty and creativity are the prime goals of a good society. Nineteenth-century philosophers such as Nietzsche argued, in fact, that the only goal for most of us is to provide favorable conditions for the "overman," the great creative figure in history.[11] Allowing the masses greater participation in society, according to writers such as Ortega y Gasset, serves only to debase the "high culture" of Western civilization.[12] And other elitists, like Ayn Rand, believe that a small economic and cultural elite must be zealously guarded if our civilization is to survive.[13]

2. Elitists therefore are suspicious of most attempts to erase differences in wealth, power, and social esteem. Such efforts can never

succeed in making people truly equal, but they may, intentionally or not, erode the base for individual liberty and threaten the existence of a natural elite. As Irving Kristol has argued:

> The equality proclaimed by the Declaration of Independence is an equality of natural rights—including the right to become unequal (within limits) in wealth, or public esteem, or influence. Without *that* right, equality becomes the enemy of liberty . . . it is a dangerous sophistry to insist that there is no true equality of opportunity unless and until everyone ends up with equal shares of everything.[14]

3. In addition, elitists entertain a pessimistic view concerning the nature of man. They are impressed by the evidence produced by Freud and others that people are, at base, irrational, brutal, and lusting after power. Therefore, they are suspicious of movements that seek to "liberate" people from the constraints of their society, tradition, and such conventional institutions as the family, religion, and the class system. Some elitists, such as B. F. Skinner, believe that proper conditioning, guided by wise men, might erase the "baser" tendencies of humankind.[15] Others, such as Kristol, do not embrace notions of establishing new, elite-controlled utopias. Rather, they tend to "be respectful of traditional values and institutions" and seek to maintain them. They contend that "the individual who is abruptly 'liberated' from the sovereignty of traditional values will soon find himself experiencing the vertigo and despair of nihilism."[16]

In sum, elitists seek to maintain natural inequalities between men as the best way of preserving liberty and creativity in modern society. Chastised for their beliefs concerning the nature of man, they hesitate to abandon traditional, civilized constraints upon the masses in the name of such elusive goals as equality and fraternity.

LIBERALS

Like the elitists, contemporary liberals put an extraordinarily high value upon the defense of liberty as a superior goal of man. Yet, since the time of John Stuart Mill, liberals have argued that the defense of liberty is inseparable from issues of social equity. They maintain that freedom of speech, for example, is meaningless to a starving child in Africa, an unemployed man in Harlem, or a caste-ridden untouchable in India. For the liberal, the goal of ensuring maximum liberty for all can be achieved only if everyone can be assured of genuine equality of opportunity.

In a world riven by class and caste inequalities and vast discrepancies in power, liberals believe that only a strong measure of economic equality can truly free humankind. How to achieve such equality has often divided the liberals. Some, such as John Rawls, contend that any step toward greater economic equality, unless an unequal distribution of wealth benefits everyone, would be advisable. Others, like Daniel Patrick Moynihan, retain some faith in the market mechanism and "benign neglect" by government of racial inequalities to ensure an eventual state of equality of opportunity.

Economist Arthur M. Okun takes a middle ground by advocating a moderate transfer of wealth from the rich to the poor. In *Equality and Efficiency,* Okun, former chairman of the president's Council of Economic Advisers, argues that the goal of equally distributing the goods of our society must be balanced against the demands of economic efficiency.[17] Because the output lost from poverty, illness, and ignorance exceeds the cost of eliminating these human burdens, Okun advocates transferring income from the very rich to the very poor through taxation.

In general, therefore, liberals wish to create a welfare state. By this, they mean a society that would assure a minimum level of economic security, health, and education to all. Translated into concrete policies, most contemporary liberals advocate national health insurance, wage-assistance plans, school "voucher" plans, and tuition aid for students attending college. These policies, they believe, should be implemented with a minimum of bureaucratic intrusion, for bureaucratic control and paternalism can more easily circumscribe the individual's liberty than extend it.

Liberals buttress their views on social policy by a cautious assessment of human nature. Like the elitists, liberals such as Arthur Schlesinger, Jr. believe that people have an inevitable tendency to use power corruptly for selfish, brutal ends. People are often governed by unconscious passions that are not always overcome by their better qualities. Informed by the experience of Nazism and Communism, contemporary liberals put their faith in a system of checks and balances to control the baser human tendencies. Following Michels and Pareto, most contemporary liberals also acknowledge that societies, whatever their ideals, inherently tend to become oligarchies—a social situation where the leadership defends its own interests, often at the expense of its constituency.

Elitists normally stop at this point, convinced of human sinfulness. Liberals, however, do not succumb totally to such a denigration of human potentialities. Rather, they believe that people, although plagued by passion, are capable of reason; although consumed by a power lust, can also be cooperative, generous, and gentle. They also believe that even oligarchies may be controlled in such a way as to provide opportunities for all people.

Thus liberals believe that the state has a duty to provide opportunities for goodness, beauty, and individual development, but it must avoid forcing people to conform to a particular goal. "It is not the business of parliament to make men good," Joseph Grimmond, the English Liberal, has commented, "but to create conditions in which they make themselves good."[18]

According to Charles Frankel, most liberals believe that

> . . . the existence of a variety of social interests and values was legitimate; more than legitimate, we thought it desirable. Fixed distinctions of class or status were looked upon as gratuitous. When there were conflicts of social interest, or disagreements between social classes, something like a rational compromise was considered possible.[19]

In their hardened view of the scope of liberty, their vision of a society open to talent and merit, and their cautiously optimistic assessment of human nature, liberals drastically differ from elitists. A third school, "libertarians," occupies an ambiguous position in between these two camps.

LIBERTARIANS

Writers such as Robert Nozick, Frederick Hyack, and Milton Friedman share the liberal passion for freedom but they believe that conscious attempts to promote equality are economically misdirected and may lead to totalitarianism. Most importantly, they contend that the drift toward state-induced equality violates basic canons of equity. Robert Nozick argues that the state must protect people from fraud, force, theft, and arbitrary abridgment of contracts. Beyond this, the state has no justified role whatsoever.[20] The state may not aid people or protect people for their own good.

It follows, therefore, that the state should not attempt to redress previously unequal distribution of privilege and wealth. It has no positive role in ensuring equality of opportunity and surely not in promoting conditions of absolute equality. The only equitable society, Nozick believes, is one based on the slogan, "From each as they choose, to each as they are chosen."[21]

Nozick thinks that an equitable society affords the greatest possible liberty to the individual. This goal, he believes, is incompatible with achieving the greatest possible degree of equality. According to Nozick, any social philosophy that endorses a "patterned" distribution of goods—each according to merit, need, or contribution—is inherently unjust since it takes away goods to which people are "entitled." Nozick postulates that all people are rational, calculating, and, above all, oriented to their own self-interest. He qualifies his principles with only one exception: a person is not entitled to his property if the system of holdings prior to his birth was itself unjust. An originally just situation happens if the person's predecessors acquired their holdings from unclaimed land.

On a more pragmatic level, economists such as Milton Friedman also seek to limit the government's role in the economy. They oppose any sacrifice of economic efficiency that occurs because of the actions of those who give priority to equality.[22] In general, libertarians like Friedman stand in opposition to those who wish to extend the benefits of the welfare state.

As a group, libertarians apparently subscribe to an optimistic and flattering doctrine concerning the nature of man. Nozick appears to assume that man is inherently rational, cooperative, and capable of voluntary choice. Such a premise lies at the very heart of his theory, a position that we will later describe in some detail.

Erich Fromm, a very different breed of libertarian, projects a portrait of man as potentially generous, rational, and self-regulating.[23] Following in the tradition of Proudhon, Fromm believes that men should seek to create small, politically independent, and economically self-sufficient communes. In units such as these, modeled after French "communities of work" or Israeli kibbutzim, differences in power, wealth, status, and privilege would supposedly wither away. As they disappeared, Fromm argues, so would man's greed, lust, and aggression. In the absence of social stratification and political oligarchies, the "true" nature of man would blossom.

EGALITARIANS

Although they deride Fromm's vision of decentralized communes as hopelessly utopian in this postindustrial, urbanized world, egalitarians share his vision of ending inequality. Above all, they wish to stop exploitation of one man by another. To accomplish this goal, they believe that we must strive to eliminate artificial systems that allow one person to inherit a vast fortune at birth while many starve; we must abolish inequalities that allow the rich to purchase the best of medical care while others suffer miserably from diseases that might be cured; we must ensure that all people, however lowly their position in existing society may be, have a right to education, to political participation, and to the full development of their potentialities. Only the destruction of existing forms of social stratification, they say, will accomplish these goals.

In one way or another, most contemporary egalitarians derive their vision from the writings of Karl Marx, who believed that poverty was not only an unjust feature of modern society but an unnecessary one as well. In Marx's view, the progress of world history, unfolding in a series of class conflicts, doomed contemporary bourgeois society. Capitalism's inner contradictions derived essentially from the urge to secure increasing "surplus value" from perenially exploited workers. Despite such last-ditch efforts as neocolonialism (basically an attempt to turn the entire Third World into a ghetto supporting the rich of industrialized nations), capitalists face ultimate destruction. Marxists believe that capitalism would be replaced by socialism and eventually by communism. Under a true communist system, all social stratification would disappear and "each would contribute according to his ability and receive according to his needs."

Some orthodox Marxists believe that this vision can be fulfilled only through revolution, since capitalists will not willingly or peacefully abandon their privileges. Those in the camp of democratic socialism, such as R. H. Tawney and Michael Harrington, believe that great strides can be made toward the establishment of equality within the framework of democracy.[24]

Although they differ on most other matters, egalitarians and libertarians agree that people are potentially rational, generous, and creative. Egalitarians believe that people will exhibit these qualities in complete freedom once they are released from the alienation caused by the class system.

Conclusions

Clearly, contemporary social philosophers offer drastically different answers to the basic issues concerning social stratification. They fundamentally disagree, for example, on such questions as these: Is greater equality of rank a desirable goal? Would the creativity and liberty of individuals be harmed by greater equality? Should we attempt to provide the conditions for equality of opportunity or go further and attempt to ensure true equality? Does the nature of man require the imposition of authority, assured by the power of an elite?

Or, rather, do present institutions debase man by introducing coercion and alienation? What would be an ideally just or equitable society?

One's responses to the practical issues in the contemporary world rest ultimately on one's answers to these philosophic questions. If you follow the path of elitism, you find yourself in company with those who oppose aid to developing nations, who condemn the welfare state, and who view our contemporary culture as debased by the masses. If liberalism is your choice, you are interested in ending school segregation, in expanding national health insurance, and in curbing discrimination against women. A commitment to libertarianism usually involves an attack upon progressive taxation, an opposition to big government and bureaucratic "meddling," and a desire for the decentralization of political power. Egalitarianism may well involve support for open admissions to colleges, caution concerning the power of big corporations, and a willingness to promote a redistribution of wealth among the rich and the poor nations of the world.

Because of the pervasive importance of these practical and philosophical issues concerning social stratification, the arguments of each of the four basic schools of social philosophy should be closely examined. The adherents of each of the positions have a long and honorable heritage; they can muster well-supported, reasonable arguments for their views; and they have convinced large segments of the world's population throughout recorded history. As the oldest articulate school of thought, elitism deserves our attention first.

Notes

1. Robert Heilbroner, *An Inquiry into the Human Prospect* (New York: Norton, 1974).
2. See William McCord, *Mississippi: The Long Hot Summer* (New York: Norton, 1965).
3. Michael Harrington, *Socialism* (New York: Bantam, 1972).
4. Micah, *Revised Standard Version of the Bible* (New York: Nelson, 1953).
5. Ibid.
6. Luke, 18:18–25.
7. Galatians, 3:28.
8. Augustine, *De Civitate Dei*, XIX, Chapter XV.
9. See J. P. Mayer, "Reflections on Equality," in L. Kolakowski and S. Hampshire, eds., *The Socialist Idea* (New York: Basic Books, 1974), for an interesting discussion of the evolution of these ideas.
10. See Whitney J. Oates, *The Collected Writings of the Stoic and Epicurean Philosophers* (New York: Modern Library, 1940).
11. F. Nietzsche, *Thus Spake Zarathustra* (London: Bozman, 1946).
12. Jose Ortega y Gasset, *The Revolt of the Masses* (New York: Norton, 1932).

13. Ayn Rand, *Atlas Shrugged* (New York: Macmillan, 1960).
14. Irving Kristol, "What Is a 'Neo-Conservative'?" *Newsweek*, January 19, 1976, p. 17.
15. B. F. Skinner, *Beyond Freedom and Dignity* (New York: Knopf, 1971).
16. Kristol, "What Is a "Neo-Conservative?"
17. Arthur Okun, *Equality and Efficiency: The Big Trade-Off* (Washington, D.C.: Brookings Institution, 1975).
18. Joseph Grimmond, *The Liberal Future* (London: Faber & Faber, 1959).
19. Charles Frankel, *The Case for Modern Man* (New York: Harper & Row, 1955).
20. Robert Nozick, *Anarchy, State, and Utopia* (New York: Basic Books, 1974).
21. Ibid., p. 160.
22. Milton Friedman, *Capitalism and Freedom* (Chicago: University of Chicago Press, 1962).
23. Erich Fromm, *The Sane Society* (New York: Rinehart, 1955).
24. Harrington, *Socialism.*

8

ELITISM

William F. Buckley, the popular columnist, has succinctly posed the generic question that separates elitists from all other schools of social philosophy. In his *Up from Liberalism,* he rhetorically asked "whether the minority in a democratically organized community is ever entitled to take such measures as are necessary to prevail, politically and culturally, over the majority?"[1] The inheritor of an oil fortune, a Yale graduate, and a presumed member of America's elite, Buckley answered his own question: "Surely yes, there are circumstances when the minority can lay claim to preeminent political authority, without bringing down upon its head the moral opprobrium of just men."[2] Such a circumstance, according to Buckley, was the response of white Southerners to the civil rights conflict in America, since "the leaders of American civilization are white."[3] Similarly, the British had the right in 1952 to suppress the "eruption" in Kenya for "there the choice was dramatically one between civilization and barbarism."[4] Although Buckley never defined his meaning of "civilization," he clearly believed that he and other members of the Western, economically privileged elite represented its finest blossoms. Buckley's arguments typify the various ones used by elitists.

This defense of elitism has ancient roots. As we have seen, the lords of medieval Europe, the slaveholders of Rome, the priests of India, the oil barons of contemporary America, were all assured by at least some of the philosophers and publicists of their age that their power was just and right. Despite America's familiar designation as the land of equality, elitism has had a strong tradition in this nation, too.

Some Origins of Elitism

Alexander Hamilton and John Quincy Adams, John Randolph and Henry Adams, all held to the conviction

> . . . that civilized society requires orders and classes. The only true equality is moral equality; all other attempts at levelling lead to despair, if enforced by positive legislation. Society longs for leadership, and if a people destroy natural distinctions among men, presently Buonaparte fills the vacuum.[5]

This same credo of elitism has been eloquently echoed throughout American history. John Randolph, the Virginian who so dearly defended slavery, proclaimed in 1829: "I am an aristocrat: I love liberty, I hate equality."[6] He entertained many reasons for his beliefs, but the most basic was his (and Calhoun's) belief in slavery. The South, in its revolt against the Union, proclaimed many ideas under the slogan of states' rights. Its true reasons, however, were revealed by General Nathan Bedford Forrest, an inheritor of Randolph's teaching. At a convention of Confederate veterans, who defended the "glory" of their lost cause, the ex-cavalryman scoffed at high-sounding ideals and announced that he had gone to war for only one reason, "to keep my niggers, and other folks' niggers."[7]

Many Southern "aristocrats" drew their inspiration from the English statesman Edmund Burke. A commoner by birth, Burke became the greatest defender of piety, prejudice, prescription, and the "established order" of classes in eighteenth-century England. His eloquent defense of aristocracy inspired England to resist the French Revolution, gave intellectual substance to the claims of white Americans, and established him, in Russell Kirk's phrase, as "the first truly modern conservative thinker."

A complicated man much devoted to individual liberty, Burke was not merely a mindless defender of those classes who monopolized power and privilege. He felt, for example, that the king was foolish in his handling of the American Revolution. Indeed, he once proclaimed, "I am no friend of aristocracy. . . . If it should come to the last extremity, and to a contest of blood, God forbid! God forbid!—my part is taken; I would take my fate with the poor, the low, and feeble."[8]

And yet the author of these words provided the most articulate defense of elitism in the recent history of the Western world. Above all, Burke was convinced that a Divine Order ruled our world. Consequently, God had ordained the particular system of classes, the distribution of property, and the inequalities of power that prevailed in any social order, but particularly in eighteenth-century England.

Social philosophers who ignored tradition, who lacked reverence for the customary ordering of inequalities, and who attempted to "reform" inequalities in society undertook a vain task. In Burke's view, the French Revolution was a particularly catastrophic example of man's foolish attempts to establish a kingdom of God on earth.

From his point of view, men were equal only in the sight of God and in no other sense. Arbitrary attempts to achieve political or economic leveling ended either in anarchy or despotism. Therefore, Burke set himself resolutely against the reform movements and revolutions that proclaimed greater equality as their paramount political goal. Burke noted terrible signs of disunity within the England of his time—the dispossessed condition of agricultural laborers, the vast unrest of new industrial workers, a series of riots in London—all of which suggested to him that the egalitarian slogans of the French Revolution might well inspire a conflagration in England. Invoking the principle of the "grand design of piety," Burke fought to maintain the established class order.

Burke strongly defended the conception of man as a sinful, "fallen" animal. He rejected all notions of human perfectibility and attributed poverty and misfortune to human sinfulness. From this point of view, of course, it was the height of arrogance to try to change man's natural inequality by legislation, by social reform, or by revolution.

Burke particularly opposed Rousseau's belief that man had once existed in a free, equal, propertyless, and happy condition. In Burke's opinion, man, as a depraved being who had fallen away from God's law, had forever lived in a state of inequality, and this condition would prevail eternally.

Burke's only hope for human kind lay in the defense of a natural aristocracy, an elite whose reasonable and benevolent rule would keep man's brutish nature under control. Thus, from Burke's position:

> Equal justice is indeed a natural right; but equal dividend is no right at all. The laws of nature, ordained by Divine wisdom, make no provision for sharing goods without regard for individual energies or merits, nor is political power naturally equalitarian.[9]

In his opposition to equality, his glorification of a natural aristocracy, and his contempt—bordering on fear—for the masses, Burke established the classic theme of modern elitism. In quite different forms, and yet in ways that clearly reflect an elitist orientation, some modern social philosophers have adopted the Burkean position.

The most influential branches of this contemporary elitism fall generally into four groups. First, *cultural elitists* believe that various forces, most notably the rise of industrialism, have created rancorous masses who threaten to destroy liberty and high culture. Second, *psychological elitists* argue that conditioning carried out by properly chosen supervisors could create a humane, creative society. Third, *economic elitists* contend that the economic health and efficiency of a society require a stern opposition to egalitarian measures. Fourth, *biological elitists* maintain that certain human groups have a genetic monopoly on such abilities as abstract thinking. Because of their immense importance in contemporary American life and the profound impact of the policies that they endorse, each of these types of elitists deserves attention.

Cultural Elitists: The Defenders of "High" Civilization

Taking their inspiration from such diverse sources as Europe's aristocratic traditions, the Germanic idealism of Hegel, Oswald Spengler's gloomy prognostications about the decline of the West, and Pitirim Sorokin's dismay about the onslaught of a secularized culture, many Western intellectuals have abandoned hope that a "high" culture can survive an age of democratic egalitarianism.[10] Above all, they fear that the mediocre taste of the masses—encouraged by the spread of mass media, nourished by a desire to cater to the lowest common denominator, and facilitated by majority political rule—will destroy the last existing bastions of human learning and arts.

In the twentieth century many voices have cried out against the "degradation" of high culture, the threat of "massification," and the decline of aristocratic standards. The poet T. S. Eliot, originally from St. Louis, chose to live in England because of his admiration for its monarchy, aristocracy, and culture. Other exiles—from Ernest Hemingway to Richard Wright—have found solace in the civilized atmosphere of an urbane Parisian culture. American movie and television critics have lambasted the nation for its supposedly low-brow tastes in the arts. Whether exiled or indigenous, many prominent Americans have decried an "erosion" of culture by the masses.

In the first half of the twentieth century, many of these cultural elitists discovered a responsive chord in José Ortega y Gasset's *Revolt of the Masses*.[11] This immensely popular work by the Spanish philosopher inspired some intellectuals of the 1930s and 1940s with a belief that the rise of the masses entailed the death of Western culture.

Ortega y Gasset served briefly in the Spanish parliament in 1931. With the advent of Franco's fascist revolution, this wealthy defender of culture fled to France. After Franco's victory, Ortega y Gasset returned to Madrid, where he lived until 1955 as the more or less official philosopher of Franco's authoritarian regime.

In *The Revolt of the Masses* Ortega y Gasset stated his basic philosophy, which has served to bolster the position of contemporary elitists: the "common" people of the world have rebelled against the usual standards of culture and traditional order. They are nihilistic and have become a law unto themselves. Lacking the standards of a superior culture, they find their lives empty and boring. According to Ortega y Gasset, they can easily be swayed to join any movement that provides them with a sense of meaning. Despising the masses, who he believed had gained inordinate power without possessing the wisdom to utilize it, Ortega y Gasset predicted in 1930: "There will be heard throughout the planet a formidable cry, rising like the howl of innumerable dogs to the stars, asking for someone or something to tke command, to impose an occupation, a duty."[12] In one sense, this elitist was absolutely correct since soon after his forecast Mussolini and Hitler, Stalin and Mao, issued their commands to the "doglike" masses.

Ortega y Gasset believed that the natural aristocracy, those distinguished by their merit and by the fact that they made demands upon themselves, had been replaced by the "masses," who had no sense of duty, no knowledge of culture, and no feelings of social responsibility. His implied solution to the current "crisis" was to return control of politics and culture to people of talent and nobility. Religion, he believed, might be the most appropriate source of this new system since, "without a spiritual power, without someone to command . . . chaos reigns over mankind."[13]

Ortega y Gasset's opinion temporarily bolstered fascist regimes but foundered in its own ambiguities. Most important, he failed to specify the nature of this natural elite who should dictate the basic culture of others. Nor did he actually identify the masses. They could not be located, in his opinion, within any specific group. Lacking a firm definition of the division between the cultural elite and the masses, Ortega y Gasset left the creation of his new society to those who could wield the most force and define themselves as the elite. Since his terms were totally unclear, it became impossible to measure his empirical generalizations (for example, that the masses had debased high culture) or to gauge the actual implications of his political prescriptions (for example, which particular elite would use its power in the most beneficial way).

Despite the ambiguity of Ortega y Gasset's beliefs, some contemporary sociologists have echoed his disdain for the masses and his feelings about the deleterious effects of democracy upon high culture. Perhaps the most eloquent of these cultural elitists is Edgar Z. Friedenberg, a professor of education. Friedenberg has frequently defended his belief that cultural privileges and distinctions should be maintained. Writing in journals such as *Harper's, The Nation,* and *The New York Review of Books,* Friedenberg has contended that the belief in equality has bred profound discontent among the world's peoples. In *The Disposal of Liberty and Other Industrial Wastes* Friedenberg argues that jealousy and rancor have become rampant among the "masses" in democratic societies.[14] He contends that liberty is best preserved in a society such as pre–World War II England that is not hostile to privilege and social distinctions.

Friedenberg develops the concept of "conscript clienteles": people who are treated in "mass society" as members of an unrepresented minority. From his point of view, men sacrifice liberty in exchange for a "mess of packaged breakfast cereals."[15]

As one might predict, Friedenberg dislikes a society supposedly dominated by "horselike" people: "Life in an industrial democracy possesses some of the characteristics one might expect of an equestrian society in which horses could vote."[16]

Friedenberg readily admits:

> I have been radically critical and indeed contemptuous of the institutions of industrial society. Yet, I have been, on the whole, considerably more hostile to the values, folkways, and political roles of the mass of that society's members than I have toward its elites who are held to be much more powerful and presumably bear much more responsibility for the abuses and barbarities I condemn.[17]

Friedenberg opines that "the people" are not aware of their own best interests and are not capable of defending individual liberty. On the whole, he prefers rule by elites:

> The elites, at their worst, have at least the virtue of acting in their own interests. They are usually ruthless and often vicious, but rarely punitive and spiteful—certainly, not to the point of ruining their own chances in order to keep somebody else down. . . . The powerful can afford civility.[18]

Friedenberg is convinced that the growth of equality in industrial societies has led to a diminution of liberty. He also condemns equality of opportunity since it "makes it harder to identify the talented among so many strangers."[19] In consequence, he glorifies societies that institution-alize unequal power and privilege:

> I would suggest that a society which affords some of its members extraordinary privilege and celebrates this fact, instead of apologizing for it and validating its less privileged members in their sense of griev-ance, will enjoy an unparalleled sense of human possibility.[20]

Friedenberg apparently believes that business corporations in North America provide the best and last hope for the preservation of an elitist culture:

> With all its constraints and often stifling conformity, the corporate world is the only one left that legitimates privilege and hierarchy. From the very beginning it lets the flesh off the egalitarian hook and openly admits, without apology, not only that some people who are obviously not superior in character or intellect have more power, prestige, and affluence than others, but that they want these, prize them, feel entitled to them, do not propose to relinquish them to more worthy claimants, *and will be supported by the organization in their pretensions to them.*[21]

Few would deny Friedenberg's condemnation of *ressentiment*, that feeling of rancor that supposedly pervades many people in the American lower classes. It is a sentiment, surpassing jealousy, that leads its victims to deny any satisfaction to other people, particularly to their "superiors" in the class system. Friedenberg fails, however, to present any evidence that this profoundly angry attitude is more prevalent in industrialized, egalitarian societies than in other types of societies. Nor does he give proof that *ressentiment* is more often noted today in the American lower classes than in any other group.

Like Ortega y Gasset, Friedenberg never clearly articulates his con-cept of the "masses" or of "elites." Thus, his condemnations of modern society remain debatable and essentially immeasurable.

As a group, the cultural elitists themslves often come from modest backgrounds. Friedenberg, for example, openly describes his own mid-dle-class origins. Conceivably, thinkers such as Friedenberg may be suf-fering from an even deeper *ressentiment* than the vague "masses" whom they despise. In America, bitterness flows most strongly in the blood of those "elitists" who never quite "made it."

Psychological Elitists:
Conditioning the Masses

Like the cultural elitists, some people throughout history have thought that they were wiser than the "masses" and could establish a perfect society. Plato is, of course, the epitome of this school of thought. He wished to create an elite of philosopher-kings. This dream has reappeared in many forms.

Since the Enlightenment, some intellectuals—for instance, Saint-Simon, Fourier, Bellamy—have believed that they could utilize scientific methods to build utopias fashioned in their own image. Often, as Marx noted, such thinkers failed to analyze exactly how society would move from "now" to "then."

In the twentieth century, however, some psychological elitists have discovered a mechanism that they contend will lead to a better society. Specifically, they envision a community, presumably led by them, that will condition people by subtle rewards to act "correctly," hold the "best" values, and behave in an equitable manner toward each other.

The psychological elitists maintain that people in the modern world are constantly subjected to unplanned conditioning. This may be manipulated by advertising agencies or political candidates, or it may be a natural process whereby parents and peers instruct others in "proper" behavior. According to psychological elitists, the conditioning power is currently in the hands of irresponsible people and is used in a rather haphazard fashion. Yet, should this be the case?

Why should not the wiser members of the elite condition people to accept such goals as peace, equity, altruism, and creativity? Would it not be better, the psychological elitists ask, to consciously control the conditioning process rather than to leave it to parental whims or to commercial exploitation?

Perhaps the most famous exponent of this school of thought is Harvard psychologist B. F. Skinner, whose novel *Walden Two* describes the creation of a scientifically molded utopia.[22] Written in 1948, the book has been reprinted many times and has won praise from those who believe that a science of human behavior can eliminate human problems. Others have condemned the book as sinister and corrupting. In the novel Skinner depicts a commune where a benevolent "supervisor" eliminates human aggression and assures peace of mind by means of thorough psychological conditioning. Although Skinner wishes to create people who will treat each other with equal dignity, his vision in the novel necessarily implies the existence of an elite who would bring about this best of all possible worlds.

In 1971 Skinner extended this argument in *Beyond Freedom and Dignity*, an equally controversial analysis of how people might stunningly redesign their culture and shape a new society in which many of the nation's social problems would be solved. Skinner begins with the contention that man lacks free will in any traditional sense of the term: "Personal exemption from a complete determinism is revoked as a scientific analysis progresses, particularly in accounting for the behavior of the individual."[23] Since man is controlled by rewards and punishments, Skinner raises (but never answers) the question: "Who is to construct the controlling environment and to what end?"[2]

From Skinner's point of view:

> It should be possible to design a world in which behavior likely to be punished seldom or never occurs. We try to design such a world for those who cannot solve the problem of punishment for themselves, such as babies, retardates, or psychotics, and if it could be done for everyone, much time and energy would be saved.[25]

The saving of time and energy is one of Skinner's prime concerns. Skinner believes that we behave "correctly" only after the behavior demanded by our supervisor (parent, boss, and so on) has been inculcated. Even if our supervisor disappears from our environment, we listen to the "still, small voice of conscience" that he or she has implanted in us:

> The absence of a supervisor is easily misunderstood. It is commonly said that the control becomes internalized, which is simply another way of saying that it passes from the environment to autonomous man, but what happens is that it becomes less visible.[26]

Skinner wishes to establish less visible, but still very real supervisors for us all. Although he recognizes that the choice of supervisors poses a problem, he believes that psychological conditioning could be adopted by any group of rulers: "Such a technology is ethically neutral. It can be used by villain or saint."[27] Skinner consistently refuses to specify the terms for choosing the supervisors, but he approximates a definition of his own particular elite by designating it as made up of those who further the survival of their culture:

> Those who have been induced by their culture to act to further its survival through design must accept the fact that they are altering the conditions under which men live and, hence, engaging in the control of human behavior. Good government is as much a matter of the control of human behavior as bad. . . . Nothing is to be gained by using a softer word.[28]

Skinner's arguments have raised questions on a number of different levels. Philosophically, one should contemplate his basic premise. Is there, in some sense, free will? Are we merely the products of our immediate environment and of our history? Many social scientists admit that we do not yet have sufficient evidence to make sweeping claims for determinism. Others, noting the Heisenberg principle in physics, believe that the causes of human behavior can never be totally established.

On a practical level, many social scientists question the total efficacy of the conditioning that Skinner advocates. They believe that we do not now, and perhaps never will, possess the means for controlling human behavior in the way Skinner suggests.

Even if Skinner were correct philosophically and practically, fundamental problems remain. Who is to choose the supervisors to do the psychological conditioning, who would, by definition, be members of the elite? Skinner seems to believe that this crucial selection process would occur through automatic Darwinian means. On the other hand, he does not imply that those who currently possess the brute strength—physically, economically, politically, or socially—should automatically become members of the governing elite. His ambiguity in this critical matter renders his entire position suspect.

Further, if this new elite of psychological supervisors could be elected by some method that would satisfy the members of democratic societies, who would then control *them*? If the conditioning were successful, no one would have the motivation to oppose the elite. As Skinner explicitly acknowledges, the methods of conditioning may well be exploited by villains. Who would call the supervisors to responsibility? How could people appeal their decisions since, by definition, everyone would be conditioned successfully to accept their decisions automatically? How would conflicts *within* the elite be resolved? Skinner never faces these issues in a forthright manner.

Perhaps we should not expect it of him since, by his own reasoning, Skinner has no free will. His destiny forced him to express certain opinions. Yet, if this is the case, then Skinner's question of "who is to control the environment and to what end" is meaningless. In his framework, there is no choice and therefore no reason to debate the question. Who governs a society and for what ends is, from a Skinnerian point of view, already determined. Whether or not one writes tracts about the issue is *also* determined and ultimately pointless since the readers' beliefs have been predetermined. Thus if Skinner's society is to emerge, it will do so because of forces far beyond his control and regardless of his personal wishes.

Why bother, then, to fulminate against modern society and issue impassioned pleas for a new elitist order? Clearly, by Skinner's logic, the only reason is that external conditioning has compelled him to write brilliant books such as *Walden Two* and *Beyond Freedom and Dignity*. But we doubt that he actually wrote his detailed plans for the creation of more equitable societies because of a belief that fate had guided his pen into stirring a nationwide debate.

Economic Elitists: Inequality as the Handmaiden of Productivity

A third school of elitists, those who entertain the belief that economic efficiency requires inequality, differs drastically from those who subscribe to the ideas of B. F. Skinner, and yet both groups are convinced that society will not survive without its own particular brand of "aristocrats."

Led by economists such as Joseph Schumpeter and Milton Friedman, this variety of elitist believes that we must preserve a free-enterprise system whatever the cost may be to social equality.[29] Economic efficiency and complete equality are inherently incompatible from their point of view.

In 1976 the British government came to the same conclusion on a pragmatic level. Although inspired by a socialist vision of equality, the leaders of the Labour government attempted to drastically slash Great Britain's welfare budget. The British have traditionally been extremely generous in expenditures for health and welfare. Yet the Labour government felt that the "welfare state" had become too expensive, that the balance of trade was radically out of line, and that individual initiative would be undermined by further expenditures aimed at ensuring equality.

On a theoretical level, the argument that egalitarian policies may conflict with economic efficiency has been persuasively advanced by Clair Wilcox.[30] Wilcox, a political liberal, recognizes many of the usual arguments against inequality. He argues that many great fortunes were made because the owners had a monopoly of scarce natural resources or because they engaged in financial misappropriations. He does not regard this use of private resources as socially beneficial. In Wilcox's opinion, a timberman, a miner, or an oilman deserves some profits for his efforts. "But the person who first took possession of these resources, paying little or nothing for them, and then sold them, did not earn the money that he made. . . . He simply converted nature's gifts to all mankind into a fortune for himself."[31] Wilcox also recognizes that contemporary inheritance laws make it possible to perpetuate these great fortunes. Why should these unearned fortunes be inherited by the lucky children?

Wilcox found that it would be extremely hard to defend social inequality on grounds that huge private fortunes give other people employment or that they promote culture by providing museums and art galleries to the public. He writes:

> Extreme inequality is unnecessary. It is also socially undesirable. It perverts social values. . . . It denies those with lower incomes an equal opportunity to participate in the life of the community, robbing them of their self-respect. . . . It checks the flow of sympathy and hinders action for the common good.[32]

Nonetheless, Wilcox argues, certain forms of social inequality have merit and we should preserve them. First, economic inequality is a strong incentive for people to work: "Unequal wages persuade men to work harder. . . . Pecuniary motivation is both effective and convenient."[33] In other words, high production depends upon unequal incomes—a conclusion that has been endorsed by even the strongly socialist nations.

Second, Wilcox argues, without the unequal incomes entailed by the operation of a free market, society would have to resort to even more brutal forms of compulsion; laborers, for example, would be forced to produce goods that the rest of the people wished. Thus, Wilcox says, "Of the possible methods of accomplishing the allocation of resources among competing uses, variation in income appears to be the most desirable."

On balance, Wilcox and others of his persuasion believe that differences in profit, interest, and wages are useful as the least imperfect way of inducing people to work. He rejects such measures as the total confiscation of inheritances since "exact equality is not to be obtained in a market economy. It would require the public ownership and operation of all industry and the concentration of economic authority in the hands of the state."[34]

Economic elitists believe that egalitarianism will not only lead to lower productivity but also to the demise of political liberty. Although this is an ancient contention, many modern writers repeat it. Walter B. Wriston, for example, president of Citicorp, a major American banking firm, fears that any social planning aimed at ensuring social equality will lead to political tyranny:

> Like most attacks on individual freedom, the current proposals for economic planning—even though they are wrapped up in a package labelled 'progress'—attract people who should know better. . . . The collision course between centralized economic planning and personal liberty is inevitable because, in the end, government allocation of economic resources requires force.[35]

In Wriston's view and that of many economic elitists:

> Centralized planning would come to the inevitable conclusion that it would be more efficient to allocate scarce resources on a national level by mandating university curriculums in a standardized fashion.[36]

Thus, according to Wriston, economic and social planning would necessarily lead to a standardization of thought: "The loss of economic liberty is always accompanied by the loss of individual liberty."[37]

Economic elitists envision two profound problems in the expansion of equality. First, current attempts at equalizing opportunity will lessen productivity. If this occurs, the "economic pie" that we must all share would shrink in size. Second, attempts at economic planning guided toward a decrease in gross economic inequalities will necessarily entail a loss of individual liberty.

However, critics of the economic elitists point out that the equalization of a particular society has not, in fact, necessarily led to a decline in productivity. Indeed, an ideological movement toward egalitarianism may at least temporarily increase a nation's productive power. China is a clear example. Egalitarianism in China has spread since the advent of Mao, while simultaneously her production of economic goods has grown steadily. And although there have been misadventures in several enterprises (for instance, production of steel in backyard furnaces),[38] China's total production has grown vastly. Further, as we have noted, Germany, Japan, Scandinavia, and the Netherlands are more equal in income distribution than the United States—and yet they have achieved vigorous economic growth.

To assert that social and economic planning aimed at equalization inevitably results in a loss of political liberty ignores the Scandinavian nations that enjoy as much political liberty as America, if not more, and yet they are more egalitarian than we are and have highly planned economies.

Further, one must question the identification of a free-enterprise economy and its attendant inequalities with the preservation of liberty. The economic elitists' picture of capitalism as a free market, in which consumers "vote" their wants through the use of money, ignores the manipulation by advertising of "wants," the disguising of inarticulated or unfulfillable wants, and the existence of monopolistic bureaucracies that can often dictate which desires will be satisfied.

Therefore, the economic elitists have hardly presented a solid case that egalitarianism *must* bring about a loss in productivity. They have also failed to prove their point that a socially planned, egalitarian society *must* lead to political tyranny or that capitalism is *always* a bastion of political freedom. Perhaps the most reasonable position is that although economic inequality in most societies stimulates the economy, in others, it retards it. Similarly, social planning can lead to the demise of individual liberty, in many instances; in other societies, political freedom may flourish with relative social equality.

The Biological Elitists: The Controversy over Genetics

Clearly, humans differ in intelligence and speed, in height and beauty, in strength and longevity. Do these differences represent inherited traits? Should these differences, regardless of origin, serve as the basis of social inequalities in contemporary society? These two issues have produced serious divisions among contemporary social thinkers.

The sources of these problems may be traced to the controversy that began over Darwin's position that man originally derived from apes. His interpreters believed that if man was a mere animal, and if the imperative of "destiny" was for each species to favor those who survive, then social inequalities should be based upon the principle of the "survival of the fittest." Many social theorists adopted this theme.

Herbert Spencer, for one, embraced this idea and consequently deplored the introduction of social welfare, feeling that it artificially preserved the "unfit." Friedrich Nietzsche, also influenced by Darwinism, attacked the Christian ethic of ennobling the meek and poor. William Graham Sumner, one of the first American sociologists, warned that giving benefits to the lower classes would enfeeble the more intelligent groups in society.[39] Although such contentions are not so blatantly expressed today, many influential thinkers have voiced similar arguments. In contemporary times, they have focused on supposed genetic differences between American blacks (largely lower class) and whites.

People such as H. J. Eysenck,[40] Richard Herrnstein,[41] and Arthur R. Jensen[42] argue that complete equality is impossible because of the supposed limits that biology imposes upon all of us. "Biology," says Eysenck, "sets an absolute barrier to egalitarianism."[43] Such thinkers believe that genetic factors largely determine intelligence and, therefore, one's social position. For them, intelligence, ambition, talent, merit, and ability are largely innate factors that no social system can alter.[44] Herrnstein argues that the mating of people of similar IQ's will inevitably result in a castelike hereditary meritocracy.[45] For his part, Jensen contends that American blacks have consistently scored some 10 to 15 IQ points below American whites.[46] He believes that this difference should be attributed largely to heredity rather than to environmental differences. Therefore, the schooling of blacks should not be oriented to abstract thinking. Clearly, if these assertions were true, a hierarchical, racist society based on intelligence would be inevitable. Genetic inequality would dictate a class-stratified society.

Many observers have seriously questioned the evidence produced by the "biological elitists." Some critics have shown, for example, that performance on standard intelligence tests is strongly affected by one's parents' social class, by nutrition, and even by the type of person who administers the test.[47] Other investigators, most notably Howard Taylor, have demonstrated that the work of the biological elitists suffers from grave statistical errors.[48] As Taylor has shown, the most common problems in the work of Jensen, Eysenck, and Herrnstein include:

> . . . reification, incorrect calculations of "heritability," invalid syllogisms, equating SES [Socio Economic Status] with environment, misreading of tables and figures, problems of culture-bias, unnecessary statistical manipulations, incorrect causal inferences and inconsistent interpretations of regression toward the mean.[49]

Regrettably, the biased evidence of the biological elitists has often had "the dubious honor of offering social science observations that sustain or encourage those who would reverse the national momentum of social reform."[50] Such research has encouraged those who believe that "if IQ determines success in society, then success in society will become virtually genetically determined" because of the interbreeding of "higher" strains of humanity.[51]

In America, the arguments of biological elitists have been used particularly by those who believe that opening educational opportunity will have no effect in lessening the social and economic inequalities that separate American blacks and whites. The work of Taylor and his colleagues has eroded, if not totally discredited, such assumptions.

Conclusions

In all their various manifestations, the elitists offer eloquent, persuasive arguments. Too often, however, these are arguments without evidence.

Admittedly, nature has created "elites"—whether of brains, brawn, or beauty. Defenders of this natural aristocracy have mistakenly, if understandably, identified it with the existing social elites of their society and, indeed, with their own particular group, usually themselves.

The cultural elitists, such as Ortega y Gasset and Friedenberg, rail against the low tastes and rancorous behavior of the masses. Yet they fail to define their basic terms or to present empirical evidence for their beliefs. Has "high culture" actually been undermined in industrialized, relatively equalitarian societies? No one really knows. But the sheer growth in numbers of libraries, the spread of education, and the increase in public museums would lead a reasonable person to question this proposition.

Psychological elitists such as B. F. Skinner condemn our present culture with equal vigor. They believe that advertising agencies and other groups condition our behavior, often in malicious ways. Their solution, however, raises as many questions as it solves. In a true Skinnerian society, we can never assure who will be the supervisors, what their goals are, or who would resolve disagreements among them. A superb manipulator such as Hitler might well lead a "Walden Two." Even assuming the truth of the behaviorist's point of view, would it not be wiser to surrender ourselves to the whims of fate rather than to a Hitler?

Similarly, grave considerations undermine the position of economic elitists, who believe that most attempts at social reform result in economic decay or political tyranny. Rational evaluations of their arguments suggest that economic efficiency and political liberty may well flourish in some societies under conditions of great social equality.

Biological elitists have contended that intelligence is inherited, that it correlates with "success" in life, and that it is found more often in some ethnic groups (whites) than others. If this were so, biology would doom egalitarian measures to failure or, if these reforms were successful, would eventually condemn human society to extinction. Many critics have effectively questioned all the basic assumptions of this school of thought.

Thus contemporary elitists—bedeviled by illogic, unable to define their crucial terms, and impoverished by a dearth of evidence—are on the intellectual and political retreat throughout the modern world. Their traditional antagonists, the liberals, suffer, however, from their own problems —internal contradictions and intellectual malaise. In this age of sweeping egalitarianism, often accompanied by dictatorship, it is doubtful that either a classic elitist such as Burke or a liberal such as John Stuart Mill would feel comfortable. Nonetheless, liberals are putting up a battle and their fight demands recognition.

Notes

1. William F. Buckley, *Up from Liberalism* (New York: Hellman, 1961), p. 146.
2. Ibid.
3. Ibid.
4. Ibid., p. 147.
5. Russell Kirk, *The Conservative Mind* (Chicago: Regnery, 1953), p. 130.
6. Quoted in ibid.
7. Quoted in ibid., p. 131.
8. Edmund Burke, "Thoughts on the Present Discontents," *Collected Works* (London: Hillyard), vol. 1, p. 323.
9. Quoted in Kirk, *Conservative Mind*, p. 48.
10. See Pitirim Sorokin, *Social Philosophies of an Age of Crisis* (Boston: Beacon, 1950), for a summary of some of these views.
11. José Ortega y Gasset, *The Revolt of the Masses* (New York: Norton, 1932).
12. Ibid.
13. Ibid.
14. Edgar Z. Friedenberg, *The Disposal of Liberty and Other Industrial Wastes* (Garden City, N.Y.: Doubleday, 1975).
15. Ibid., p. 3.
16. Ibid., p. 79.
17. Ibid., p. 84.
18. Ibid., p. 87.
19. Ibid., p. 153.
20. Ibid., p. 155.
21. Ibid., p. 177.
22. B. F. Skinner, *Walden Two* (New York: Macmillan, 1948).
23. B. F. Skinner, *Beyond Freedom and Dignity* (New York: Knopf, 1971), p. 18.
24. Ibid., p. 19.
25. Ibid., p. 62.
26. Ibid., p. 63.
27. Ibid., p. 143.
28. Ibid., p. 172.
29. See, for example, Milton Friedman, *Capitalism and Freedom* (Chicago: University of Chicago Press, 1962).
30. See Clair Wilcox, *Toward Social Welfare*, (Homewood, Ill.: Irwin, 1969). For an interesting comment on Wilcox, see Jon Van Til, "Traditional Views: Liberalism and Conservatism," in Arthur B. Shostak, Jon Van Til, and Sally Bould Van Til, *Privilege in America* (Englewood Cliffs, N.J.: Prentice-Hall, 1973).
31. Wilcox, ibid., p. 18.
32. Ibid., p. 21.
33. Ibid., pp. 22–23.
34. Ibid., p. 23.
35. Walter B. Wriston, "An Economic Police State," *Newsweek*, October 15, 1975, p. 15.
36. Ibid.
37. Ibid.
38. See William McCord, *The Springtime of Freedom* (New York: Oxford University Press, 1965).

39. William Graham Sumner, *Folkways* (Boston: Ginn, 1906).
40. H. J. Eysenck, *The Inequality of Man* (London: Temple/Smith, 1973).
41. Richard Herrnstein, *I.Q. in the Meritocracy* (London: Penguin, 1973).
42. Arthur R. Jensen, *Educability and Group Differences* (London: Methuen, 1973).
43. Ibid., p. 224.
44. Ibid., pp. 159, 224.
45. Jensen, *Educability and Group Differences*.
46. Ibid.
47. See William McCord and Nicholas Demarath, "Negro vs. White Intelligence: A Continuing Controversy," *Harvard Educational Review* (Spring 1958).
48. See, for example, Howard F. Taylor, "Quantitative Racism: A Partial Documentation," *Journal of Afro-American Issues* 1 (Summer 1972): 1–20; Howard F. Taylor, review of Herrnstein, *I. Q. in the Meritocracy, Journal of the American Statistical Association* 69 (December 1974): 1041–1044.
49. Taylor, "Quantitative Racism," p. 1.
50. Ronald Edmons et al., "A Black Response to Christopher Jencks' *Inequality* and Certain Other Issues," *Harvard Educational Review* 43 (February 1973).
51. Howard F. Taylor, "A Causal Analysis of Meritocracy Arguments," *Social Science Research* (in press, 1977).

9

LIBERALISM

Origins of Liberalism

Two issues, the nature of equity and the proper extent of equality, have fundamentally divided liberals since the end of the eighteenth-century. Traditionally, by liberalism we mean a form of political thought that portrays the advancement of human liberty as the prime goal of a good society. Liberals, retaining some faith in human nature, have fought to free the individual's potentialities from the constraints of a particular society. Practitioners of the earliest political forms of liberalism merely wished to expand the realm of political and intellectual liberty. In the nineteenth century they fought for "economic freedom," usually defined in terms of the "rights" of the capitalist. In the twentieth century most liberals defined an equitable society as one that would provide minimum standards for economic survival as well as the fullest possibilities for equality of opportunity to every citizen.

Liberalism in the Western world can be traced to four historical bases. First, from the seventeenth to the nineteenth century, a variety of social philosophers—from Milton to Locke to Voltaire—argued for religious and intellectual liberty. Their followers during the Enlightenment period sought to replace authoritarianism with individualism, belief in original sin with hope for progress, and a conviction of predestination with the opinion that man can shape his own future.

Second, the advance of natural science laid the material foundations for liberalism. The development of advanced technology turned people's minds increasingly to thoughts of this world and to the belief that if their natural environment could be altered, their social environment could be as well.

Third, the commercial revolution, which dated from roughly the thirteenth through the nineteenth centuries, created a new, independently powerful "middle class." This group demanded its rights from the landed gentry.

Fourth, the industrial revolution, which culminated in the twentieth century, produced "proletarian" classes who were based largely in urban areas, who worked in factories, and who began to enjoy the benefits of mass literacy. These classes, in their turn, advocated such egalitarian measures as free public education and a universal franchise.

Two quite different figures, John Stuart Mill and Alexis de Tocqueville, may properly be regarded as the prophets of nineteenth-century liberalism. Although at one in their defense of liberty, the two disagreed radically on the role of equality in a good society.

John Stuart Mill was a child prodigy educated by a distinguished father. By 1814, at the age of eight, he had read all of Herodotus in the original Greek, and by age ten, he had read all of Plato. Mill ran into trouble at age twenty, when, suffering a "nervous breakdown," he began to regard himself as a mere intellectual machine, an unloved person with no appreciation for the beauty of life. He joined the East India Company, the colonizing agent of India, and rose eventually to its head. In 1865 he was elected to Parliament, where he supported such egalitarian measures as the extension of the franchise and the granting of women's rights. A lonely man, he carried on a platonic love affair for twenty years and only married his great love, Mrs. Taylor, in 1851. She died soon after. He retired to Avignon, where he lived in seclusion until his death in 1873.

His consuming passion, an interest in "political economy," truly occupied his thoughts and life. Perhaps his two greatest books were *Principles of Political Economy* (1848) and *On Liberty* (1859).[1] In these books he developed a form of liberalism that continues to influence contemporary readers.

His political thought represented a classic statement of nineteenth-century liberalism. First, he believed that the only legitimate goal of the state was the protection of individual liberty: "The only purpose for which power can be rightfully exercised over any member of a civilized community, against his will, is to prevent harm to others. His own good, either physical or moral, is not a sufficient warrant."[2] Mill constantly revised his opinion of the areas of action that could harm others. Beginning as a laissez-faire capitalist, for example, he emerged as a strong champion of workers' rights.

Second, throughout his life Mill demonstrated a fear of the possible tyranny of the state, and of uniformity. Yet this did not stop him from advocating laws that limited child labor and forbade certain of the more brutal practices that English entrepreneurs of the time used upon the "lower classes."

Third, in his later life Mill increasingly condemned inequalities of economic opportunity and recognized that they could undermine such treasures as freedom of speech. He observed the destructive effects that industrialism had brought to the life of the English community and strongly advocated state intervention as a way of securing greater equality between the classes or the sexes.

Alexis de Tocqueville, the great French social thinker, underwent a similar transformation but reached contrasting conclusions. In a life span that roughly paralleled that of Mill, de Tocqueville served as a jurist and statesman. In his capacity as a legalist, de Tocqueville visited America to observe its new prison system. In the course of his wanderings he was struck by the extraordinary degree of equality that prevailed in America in the early part of the nineteenth century. In *Democratie en Amerique* he praised many aspects of it:

> The more I advanced in the study of American society, the more I perceived that equality of condition is the fundamental fact from which all others seem to be derived and the central point at which all my observations terminated . . . the gradual development of the principle of equality is, therefore, a providential fact . . . an inestimable revolution which has advanced for centuries in spite of every obstacle.[3]

Yet, as a man dedicated to liberty, de Tocqueville foresaw dangers in the advance of egalitarianism. In reviewing the history of the French Revolution, for example, he noted that the people "wanted to be free, to be able to make themselves equal, and in the same measure that equality is consolidated with the help of freedom, freedom itself is brought into question."[4] Although he was contemptuous of existing aristocracies, de Tocqueville feared that a movement toward egalitarianism might result in centralization and the death of individuality. He believed that in a nation without castes or classes, people increasingly resemble one another, and it is possible, although not inevitable, that the spirit of individuality will be destroyed. He hoped that the advance of egalitarianism might result in free, decentralized communities but he knew that "in matters of social constitution the field of possibilities is much wider than people living within each society imagine."[5]

The trends that Mill and de Tocqueville had foreseen blossomed by the end of the century. Between roughly 1890 and 1914 the demands of the new industrial classes for social equality reached a peak. In England,

America, and Scandinavia, new trade unions demanded social reform. They denied the old liberal, middle-class equation of liberty with laissez-faire economics. Instead, they argued that liberty without equality was a squalid, meaningless concept: there must be an equitable distribution of the goods of life and true equality of opportunity. In nations such as Sweden, Denmark, England, and even Germany, the ruling classes acceded to this plea. In England, for example, the Liberal party in 1906 introduced limits on workers' hours, protection for the existence of trade unions, provision for the health and safety of the working classes, pensions, and income taxes. With more or less alacrity, other Western nations followed suit (France waited until the 1930s; Italy, until the 1950s) in introducing provisions for workers' security.

Even in its early manifestations, however, liberalism found difficulty in dealing with the general ideal of equality. In the nineteenth century this problem arose in three profound issues.

First, liberals could not agree on the proper role of the state in assuring equality of opportunity. As we have noted, Mill, toward the end of his life, advocated state intervention in economic life, but subsequent leaders of the English Liberal party feared this innovation.

Second, liberals could not agree on the proper role of nationalism in social life. Some, like the great Italian leader Mazzini, identified nation-states with "individuals" and believed that the spread of nationalism would lead to greater equality among all people. Others, like Mill, were convinced that only a cosmopolitan ethic linking all people in a common fate would lead to the greatest liberty and opportunity for all.

Third, liberals could not decide on their stance on colonialism. Logically, the spread of European rule over Asia and Africa entailed an implicit if not explicit elitism. As we have noted, Mill himself served as a steward of colonial advance in India. Most liberal leaders, such as the English Prime Minister Gladstone, sanctioned colonialism as simply the assumption of power by a civilized people over other forms of tyranny. Most contemporary people who call themselves liberal would shudder at the implications of this position.

By 1914, partially because of its internal contradictions, liberalism as a political movement had reached its height. With the onslaught of World War I, it virtually changed its nature. The war brought an end to unbridled optimism concerning humanity's future and the rationality of human nature. Under different political labels, however, liberals have continued to flourish in Western nations—and now, to some degree, even in generally authoritarian regimes such as Russia. In America they may be known as the left wing of the Democrats; in Scandinavia, as Social Democrats; in Russia, as merely "dissidents." But whatever the label, liberal thinkers continue to have a pervasive influence on contemporary life.

Twentieth-Century Liberalism

The tensions within liberalism over the issue of equality have continued in contemporary times. The debate can be reduced to four basic issues.

1. Can an extension of equality or of equality of opportunity basically change people's nature? The nineteenth-century liberal hoped that the removal of artificial economic and social constraints would lead to a blossoming of human creative, cooperative tendencies. Such twentieth-century liberals as Arthur Schlesinger, Jr., Reinhold Niebuhr, Walter Lippmann, Joseph Grimmond, and Charles Frankel offer a more cautious assessment of the effects of equality.[6]

2. Can the economy be reformed to produce equality both of opportunity and of resulting conditions? Most liberals, led by Herbert Gans, believe that it can and should.[7]

3. Can changes in the educational system result in real alterations in equality of opportunity? Here, the liberals are seriously divided. Most prominently, Christopher Jencks believes this is a hopeless task.[8]

4. Does the concept of justice itself demand a high degree of egalitarianism, far beyond that extended in our society? Philosophers such as John Rawls argue that it does.[9]

On such fundamental issues, there is no consensus among those labeled as "liberals." Without assuming that liberals present a unified front, some aspects of these questions must be examined if one is to achieve a balanced view of the liberal positions on equality and equity.

Liberalism and the Nature of Man

Arthur Schlesinger, Jr. has pointed out:

> The 18th century had exaggerated man's capacity to live by logic alone; the nineteenth century sanctified what remained of his non-logical impulses; and the result was the pervading belief in human perfectability which has disarmed progressivism in too many of its encounters with actuality.[10]

The typical liberal, Schlesinger argues, was totally unprepared for the emergence of elitist or totalitarian movements in the twentieth century:

> More than anything else, the rise of Hitler and Stalin has revealed in terms no one can deny the awful reality of the human impulse toward

aggrandizement and distinction—impulses for which the liberal intellectual had left no room in his philosophy.[11]

Some writers, such as Reinhold Niebuhr, the late theologian and political liberal, have abandoned hope that the wickedness entailed in social inequalities could be eradicated by human effort.[12] Evil in the world comes not simply from the malfunctioning of social institutions but rather from the deeper taint of original sin in man's soul. In different, secularized form this same conviction about the ultimate imperfectibility of man was expressed by such influential thinkers as Freud. From this point of view, attempts to alter the social structure in an egalitarian fashion are ultimately useless since man is basically an evil, aggressive, selfish creature who seeks to elevate himself above his fellows.

Other liberals, while recognizing the flawed nature of man, believe that this does not undermine all hope of social progress. In fact, writes Charles Frankel, "the belief in the undying egoism of human beings, and the persistence in any society of the struggle for power, has in fact been the distinguishing feature of the liberal approach to politics."[13] Like most contemporary liberals, Frankel does not embrace the belief that man's institutions are infinitely perfectible or that a change in social structure—say, greater equality of opportunity—will usher in a utopia. For him, perfectibility is merely a belief in the improvability of the human condition:

> In the end, to believe in "the goodness of man" is not to . . . say that men's good deeds outnumber their evil deeds, or that benevolence is a stronger disposition in men than malice. It is, quite simply, to adopt a policy—the policy of looking for cures for human ailments, and of refusing to take No for an answer.[14]

Armed with this faith in the possibilities of human nature, most liberals regard a move toward greater economic equality as a reasonable step toward improving the human condition.

Liberalism and "Equality of Results"

Many liberals have recently advocated a shift in national goals. They believe that mere equality of opportunity, assuming that this traditional liberal goal could be achieved, is not enough. Instead, they feel, we should seek "equality of results"—a redistribution of income that would ensure the abolition of slums, a decent level of health for everyone, and an eradication of infant mortality among the poor. John Kenneth Galbraith has been in the forefront of those who argue that our affluent society should focus more of its attention and vastly more of its monies on enterprises that are in the general public interest.[15] Arthur Okun, while admitting that the inequalities of capitalism provide strong work incentives, believes that our society could well afford and greatly benefit from a transfer of income from the top 5 percent of the nation's families to the bottom 20 percent.[16]

Herbert Gans, a sociologist and urban planner, takes these arguments further.[17] Gans seeks greater equality of results, by which he means an equalization of both income *and* political power among different class, ethnic, and sexual groups. Gans believes that equality of opportunity is hardly an adequate ethical goal since the more fortunate people in society begin the "race" for success with economic, social, and cultural advantages that can never be matched by the disadvantaged. Similarly, he rejects the aim of complete equality because it could produce a uniform "sameness" in society. Further, he believes a completely egalitarian society is hopelessly utopian since most Americans would not accept an ideal that conflicts so deeply with their belief that people should be rewarded according to their effort. It is a utopian ideal, too, in that it might prove difficult to get people to do the "dirty jobs" that society requires. Thus, in Gans's opinion, "the real issue, at least from the point of view of pragmatic social policy, is more equality, that is, how much present levels of inequality of income and power should be reduced."[18]

Gans argues that no one should receive less than 60 or 70 percent of the society's median income. This redistribution of wealth could occur through steeper income taxes, higher inheritance taxes, or other mechanisms. Gans aims at a greater sharing of the nation's resources rather than an actual similarity in consumption patterns:

> As I interpret the egalitarian ideal, equality of income and power does not mean that every person would wind up with the same consumer goods and services and the same political roles; rather, that everyone would have equal shares of these resources but not be required to use them in the same way.[19]

Gans believes that a number of forces in contemporary America push the society irreversibly toward greater equality. In the 1960s and 1970s, he points out, a number of submerged groups—blacks, women, blue-collar workers—voiced their demands for greater equality and liberty. He argues that the realm of the independent entrepreneur has shrunk while the power of bureaucracies and the expectations of the average person have grown. "These changes in the economy," Gans writes, "may therefore spur people to realize that they can achieve affluence instead through a greater sharing of the available wealth and income."[20]

Gans recognizes a number of powerful arguments against his plea for more equality. First, the American tradition of individualism allows little tolerance for those who receive money without the expenditure of effort. Second, a guaranteed income might not pose enough incentives to keep people working. Third, the desire to invest money in capital expenditures might decline and the entire economy with it. Fourth, scarce resources such as Picasso paintings or high-quality education offered by Ivy League colleges cannot be allocated in an egalitarian manner.

Gans believes that these difficulties could be overcome by a variety of means. Most important, he contends that if the operation of a free market persisted, people would allocate their relatively equal incomes in terms of their own particular choices. Thus the price of an Ivy League education could be raised to such a high level that only those parents who deeply valued this commodity would sacrifice other goods to pay for it; others would spend their money on beer, cigarettes, and movies.

Gans, like other liberals such as politicians Fred Harris and George McGovern, would like to bring about a redistribution of political as well as economic power. They point to the "outvoted" minorities, such as blacks, who cannot exert real political clout within a democratic system. "Under the present structure of American politics and government," Gans argues, "there cannot be and will not be a real solution to the problems of the minorities."[21] As the cities become increasingly dominated by minority groups—blacks, Puerto Ricans, Chicanos—they will receive less attention from the majority whites. Thus Gans questions the continued equity of majority rule: "I believe that the time has come to modernize American democracy and adapt it to the needs of a pluralistic society; in short, to create an *egalitarian* democracy."[22] Specifically, Gans advocates a new political system that would do away with majority government. Further, he would abolish the seniority rule in all legislative bodies, fund all elections through the existing government, require all citizens to vote, and allocate important posts such as cabinet positions on a quota basis to various minorities.

Gans recognizes that his proposals to increase the power of the poor and of blacks in contemporary society are remarkably similar to earlier Southern defenses of slavery—which were, of course, advanced in the name of white supremacy. John C. Calhoun, for example, also fought against national majority rule since a straight vote would have doomed the institution of slavery. Calhoun argued for "concurring majorities," a situation in which each class or community in a nation would reach a majority decision and the sum of the whole would be considered as the nation's "majority" opinion.[23] Both Calhoun and Gans, for quite different reasons, wish to avoid the tyranny of the majority. Gans rejects the comparison with Calhoun, however, on grounds that the basic motives of that defender of slavery were "ignoble" and that an idea should be judged on grounds of "whether the goal being sought is itself desirable, rather than in terms of its origin."[24]

Yet, one must still ask: If Gans's suggestion for abandoning majority rule is good in the contemporary era, why was it not valid in Calhoun's times? Why should minority opinions, either those of Harlem blacks or of nineteenth-century slaveholders, be given special preference in a political system? One must espouse an absolute ethical system, which Gans explicitly disavows, to maintain that minority government should prevail if one ethical goal rather than another is sought.

Will "equality of results" be achieved if one deems it desirable to redistribute income and power in the way Gans suggests? Laying aside questions of incentive and investment—serious issues but ones more within the realm of the economist than the sociologist—one is still left with lingering doubts concerning the practicality of certain of Gans's suggestions. On the political level, is it not utopian to envision a society where the existing political machines will voluntarily relinquish their influence to powerless, voteless minorities? On the economic level, is it not also doubtful that privileged groups in American society will altruistically give up their benefits to the less privileged? As Gans himself observes: "More equality is not likely to come about easily and peaceably in an individualistic, heterogeneous, and non-cohesive society where there is little trust between groups—or, among these groups, in the government."[25]

Gans proceeds to offer a realistic, if condemning comment concerning the scope and limits of egalitarianism:

> That conception suggests, first, the sociological impossibility of a completely egalitarian society, for as long as people have egos, they will strive for differentiation and some inequality. Second, it requires the assumption that people's aspirations will continue to combine self-interest about private matters and the public good, with some limited altruism.[26]

Thus, in the economic realm as in others, liberals strike a note of very cautious optimism—a hope in our potential altruism and our willingness to share the goods of this world blended with a pragmatic recognition that self-interest, if not egoism, motivates all mankind.

Without postulating a major redistribution of wealth and power, some liberals have put their faith in education as a way of bringing about a more equitable, if not equal society.

Liberalism and "Equality of Education"

Since the time of Horace Mann and the introduction of free public schooling in America, many liberals have fought for the equalization of educational opportunity. They believed that education could open the doors for all people to economic, political, and social success. The traditional argument has been that intellectual merit alone—not wealth, not athletic prowess, not social connections, not skin color—should be the criterion for access to any form of education. The waves of migrants who attended and were successful in free public schools, land-grant colleges, and such free universities as the City University of New York reinforced the hope of less-privileged groups in America that education could provide a magic key to advancement in social status.

By the 1960s however, many liberals argued against sheer equality of opportunity in education or other fields. They pointed specifically to the lot of the black person in America. They contended that the nation owed a peculiar debt to blacks who had been enslaved and denied equal access to all the opportunities of American life, including education. Some liberals hoped that "compensatory education" might remedy this evil by narrowing the gap between black and white educational opportunities.

In June 1965, President Lyndon B. Johnson stated at Howard University:

> You do not take a person who, for years, has been hobbled in chains and liberate him, bring him up to the starting line of a race and then say, "You are free to compete with all the others" and still justly believe that you have been completely fair.
>
> Thus, it is not enough just to open the gates of opportunity. All our citizens must have the ability to walk through those gates.
>
> This is the next and most profound stage of the battle for civil rights. We seek not just freedom but opportunity. We seek not just equality but human ability, not just equality as a right and a theory *but equality as a fact and equality as a result.*[27]

Nonetheless, by the 1970s some liberals had rejected the belief in the utility of truly equal education. Johnson's arguments came under serious criticism not just by elitists but by liberals themselves. Nathan Glazer, for example, argues that "affirmative action" in education and in other areas of life has benefited only middle-class blacks who would have "made it" in any case. He maintains that the mass of working-class or unemployed blacks have been unaffected by attempts to equalize educational opportunity, whether in the form of integration, busing, or open admissions policies.[28]

Similarly, Arnold Rogow, a generously open-hearted liberal, has given up hope for equality of education. In *The Dying of the Light* Rogow calls for a social revolution, which his own analysis predicts is impossible.[29] He is particularly gloomy in his assessment of the fate of the American black minority. In the belief that equality of education will not help the ghettos of America, he instead calls for a basic change in the entire structure of America that would redistribute wealth, end poverty, and allocate capital to public needs. Alas, he does not specify the practical implementation of this social change.

Among the most influential works by modern liberals who have given up hope of using the educational system to equalize either opportunities or results are those by James Coleman and Christopher Jencks.[30] The Coleman report, as we have mentioned, found little to support the belief that educational reform could bring about social change in America. In substance, the report "disparaged a decade of educational intervention on behalf of black children."[31] In 1976 Coleman rejected even his own suggestion that school busing might alleviate inequalities in education.

Christopher Jencks published his own condemnation of America's school system in 1972. Apparently armed with invincible statistics, Jencks and his colleagues concluded that equal educational opportunities had no effect upon later achievement in life. National publicity heralded his work—a modest, realistic effort to assess the relation of education to such other factors as adult income—as proof that a widening of educational opportunity cannot change the basic class and caste system of America.

Jencks believes that only fundamental economic policies can alter the school system, not the other way around. His review of compensatory education programs led him to the opinion that they were a majestic failure. Personality, family background, and sheer "luck," Jencks believes, are the primary factors affecting economic success in America.

Children born of rich parents, Jencks argues, "want more education than children with poor parents. . . . Those who want a lot should get a lot and those who want very little should get very little."[32] If Jencks had altered his sentence to read "those who want a lot get a lot," it would be an empirical question. By adding the single word "should" to the sentence, however, he raises a variety of ethical questions.

Jencks believes that schools fail to educate children because of differences in motivation, not the school environment: "Variations in what children learn in school depend largely on variations in what they bring to school, not on variations in what the school offers them."[33] Jencks also dismisses racial and economic segregation as major factors in affecting children's scores on achievement tests.[34] He concludes that "even if we reorganized the schools so that their primary concern was for the student who most needed help, there is no reason to suppose that adults would end up appreciably more equal as a result."[35]

It would seem that for many liberals—quite different from their recent ancestors—changes in educational opportunity are irrelevant to expanding either equality of opportunity or equality of results. Yet, many liberal social scientists have argued persuasively and forcibly on the other side. Ronald Edmonds and his colleagues, for example, have charged that Jencks ignores the fact that the leaders of American schools have failed to make a real attempt to reduce inequality:

> He [Jencks] implies that we have made sincere efforts to reduce inequality via the schools, that our efforts have come to grief, and we ought to stop trying. We assert that the differences in the quality of education in this country are not due to lack of knowledge of how to make schools better but to willful decisions to perpetuate inequality. . . . If decision makers dedicated themselves to the task of improving schools . . . they could succeed.[36]

Other social scientists, most notably Howard Taylor, have severely criticized the methods and therefore the conclusions of Jencks's work. The statistical technique used by Jencks, path analysis, ignores any possible nonlinear relationships and any "interactive" or "conditional" relationships between education, family background, and eventual "success." As Taylor observes:

> In discussing the various determinants of success among blacks, for some unfathomable reason, Jencks utterly omits the painfully obvious one of racism. . . . Jencks' omission of any analysis or discussion whatever of racism, in a book presumably analyzing "inequality" in society, is an omission almost beyond conception.[37]

Obviously, profound disagreements split liberal ranks concerning the effect of education upon inequality. Men like Glazer, Rogow, and Jencks explicitly or implicitly deny the value of education as a cure for inequality. Among other alternative measures, they argue for "income insurance," a salary that would redistribute money by taxation. At the same time, their policy recommendations lead to a decrease in federal or local funding of education.

Edmonds and Taylor, in contrast, believe that equal opportunity in schooling has never been given a fair chance. As ideological liberals and as social scientists, they reject the opinion that our schools have failed to equalize opportunity. On statistical grounds alone, they seem to have won the match in the liberal camp. Further, their own recommendations for an improvement in education are pragmatic, whereas those of Jencks and others, which call for a total social revolution, smack of utopianism. Why should the rich, as Jencks recommends, voluntarily give up their wealth to the poor? Even if it were desirable, could the upper classes be persuaded or forced to adopt this option? The viability of this solution seems doubtful.

Some contemporary liberals have put aside questions about pragmatic issues and instead have addressed themselves solely to the creation of an ideally just, equitable society. Their supposedly theoretical work may survive all the proposals of those who have tried to confront the immediate problems of the twentieth century.

Liberalism and Justice

John Rawls, a philosopher, has produced the most eminent defense of egalitarianism in the 1970s. He considers the issues on a purely philosophical plane, disdaining immediate practical concerns. Although he qualifies his defense of egalitarianism as an ideal society, Rawls believes that it approximates a just or equitable situation.

Rawls argues that every human being possesses an inviolable right to justice. Theoretically, neither the interests of the whole society nor the "calculus of social interests" should overcome the principles that free and rational persons would accept under a "veil of ignorance."[38] This veil of ignorance, Rawls postulates, is a hypothetical situation where no person knows his class position, his intelligence, his social power, or his strength. Indeed, he has no conception of good or evil.

If men were forced to decide their rights and duties—assuming a situation of total ignorance—what might they decide? Remember: at the beginning of the exercise, no one knows his own position and all are theoretically equal. Would they continue to maintain their equality? Or would they decide upon a society that accords men different privileges according to their contributions? Should the creation and provision of food, or honor, or shelter, count most? Should a person's effort, or his years of training, or his total expenditure of strength, be considered? These are the issues that people, under Rawls's veil of ignorance, must consider.

Indeed, we who are actually aware of the vast inequalities of contemporary societies must acknowledge similar issues. We are not covered by the veil of ignorance: we know that a son of an Oxford graduate has a much better chance of graduating from Oxford than the son of a laborer; we know that an upper-class adolescent arrested for drug crimes in Westchester is more likely to be released than a lower-class adolescent in

Harlem; we know that a child who inherits the majority of stock in a company is more likely to become president of that corporation than an outsider. Is this because of merit, or ability, or even nepotism? Usually, it is not. Rather, those who control the universities, the courts, and the corporations advance spurious arguments based on their judgment of intelligence, or innocence, or merit.

Rawls questions these present inequalities:

> The institutions of society favor certain starting places over others. These are especially deep inequalities. Not only are they pervasive, but these affect men's initial chances in life; yet they cannot possibly be justified by an appeal to the notion of merit or desert.[39]

In his opposition to the inequalities of present society, Rawls brings up arguments against the utilitarianism represented by Mill and formulates a theory of justice (or equity) based on two fundamental principles: First, "each person is to have an equal liberty compatible with the liberty of others."[40] Second, "social and economic inequalities are to be arranged so that they are both (a) reasonably expected to be to everyone's advantage, and (b) attached to positions and offices open to all."[41]

These principles, he believes, would be chosen by men under a veil of ignorance. Rawls attaches many qualifications to these assertions. Clearly, however, his principles bear a strong resemblance to traditional liberal goals of assuring liberty as well as equality of opportunity. In reaching his particular conclusions, Rawls developed his theory of justice both as an attack on the usual varieties of utilitarian liberalism and as a defense of his own theory as to how men would react if they were blinded by the veil of ignorance.

This interesting device of philosophical argument deserves further discussion. The veil-of-ignorance argument assumes a high degree of naiveté on the part of all parties involved except that "the only particular fact which the parties know is that their society is subject to the circumstances of justice and whatever this implies."[42] Rawls later adds, however, that they know the general facts about human society, political affairs, economic theory, and psychology.[43] Their task is to suggest a system of justice that can be embodied in the basic structure of society. Each person in the system is assumed to be rational in the sense that he "is thought to have a coherent set of preferences between the options open to him. He ranks these options according to how well they further his purpose."[44]

On this basis Rawls concludes that rational men under a veil of ignorance would decide that the principles of liberty and equality should be observed by all. His defense of equality is not limited even by biological differences. At one point, for example, he poses a rhetorical question: "It seems that even when fair opportunity (as it has been defined) is satisfied, the family will lead to unequal chances between individuals. Is the family to be abolished then?"[45] No, Rawls seems to say, because once his theory of justice is accepted, people will be less inclined to envy and rancor. They will acknowledge differences between family backgrounds and reconcile themselves to them:

> The conception of justice, should it be truly effective and publicly recognized as such, seems more likely than its rivals to transform our perspective on the social world and to reconcile it to the dispositions of the natural order and the conditions of human life.[46]

Clearly, Rawls is a humane person who wishes to establish some theoretical grounds for abolishing current inequalities. His veil-of-ignorance argument is ingenious and highly influential among the general public. Yet, as with all social philosophers, we must examine his basic assumptions. Are men truly free and rational to make such decisions? Would he include psychopaths, paranoids, and schizophrenics in his group of "original parties"? Why not, since they are surely human beings by the usual definition? Clearly, a group made up predominantly of such types would not reach the same firm decisions about liberty and equality as he would. Rawls, therefore, excludes these people from those he calls "moral persons": people who are rational and who are "capable of having (and are assumed to acquire) a sense of justice."[47]

This is arbitrary since it would, of course, eliminate a rather major portion of our population.[48] Such a decision points up the hypothetical nature of Rawls's theory. In fact, there is no innocent state of nature where people debate their ultimate destinies and the nature of a just society. Speculations about these nonexistent "ignorant" people (who, after all, are postulated to know a great deal) are interesting games, but do they illuminate the real world? Do they even tell us much about that best of all possible worlds that we could create out of human clay?

Conclusions

Clearly, contemporary liberalism is in some disarray. But liberals do agree on two broad, general goals. First, they believe that society must protect or enlarge the freedom of the individual: his ability to make choices, to conduct his private life in the way he wishes, and to protect himself from the inroads of political tyranny. Second, in consonance with this goal, liberals seek to enlarge equality of opportunity for the individual by removing artificially imposed barriers to his development.

In their attempt to fulfill this second aim, however, liberals have diverged widely from the "conventional wisdom" and economic policies of their nineteenth-century ancestors, who believed that the public good emerged naturally from unrestrained individualism and competition.

There are many areas of disagreement in the liberal ranks. Some liberals, like Charles Frankel, continue to believe in the improvability of mankind and look to a widening of economic equality as a step in this direction. Others, like Arthur Schlesinger, Jr. take a rather grim view of man's nature and future.

For many liberals, equality of opportunity is no longer a suitable goal. Instead, like Herbert Gans, they seek equality of results. Few liberals have, however, been able to develop specific, workable plans for redistributing either income or political power.

Some liberals, particularly Christopher Jencks, have abandoned hope that education can prove a useful agent in bringing about greater equality. Others, like Howard Taylor, argue convincingly that equality of educational opportunity remains an important goal.

Philosophical liberals such as John Rawls have largely abandoned attempts to solve pragmatic issues and devote themselves instead to abstract questions concerning the nature of a truly just society. While admirable in intent, these efforts often strike the reader as utopian.

Contemporary liberals are probably most divided over the issue of what role the state should play in ensuring equality of opportunity and equality of results. They believe that at the minimum the state should provide basic standards of health and welfare below which no person should fall. They are convinced that certain public needs—education, health care, the advancement of knowledge, the elimination of basic inequalities—require state intervention. Yet most liberals believe that some degree of private enterprise and inequality should be maintained since independent economic "pockets of resistance" will ensure that the life of any individual cannot be totally absorbed into any monolithic social unit —whether it be the state or an encompassing bureaucracy such as General Motors.

Liberals view with alarm situations that, by depriving the individual of private income and by centralizing all economic decisions, would strip a person of economic independence and of the means for resisting possible incursions of the state into his or her political liberty.[49] Thus, although they seek more equality, most liberals believe that private property has a useful, beneficial role in the life of the economy, the polity, and the society.

It is precisely at this delicate point in their conception of the limits on state power where liberals diverge from libertarians. Although libertarians would agree with liberals on basic goals and although they value equally the political liberty and privacy of the individual, they believe that the state cannot and should not bring about fundamental changes in the economic and social order.

Notes

1. John Stuart Mill, *Principles of Political Economy* (London: 1848), and *On Liberty* (London: 1859).
2. Mill, *Principles*, p. 69.
3. Alexis de Tocqueville, *Democratie en Amerique*, in J. P. Mayer, ed., *Oeuvres Complétes,* (Paris: Gallemard, 1953), p. 310.
4. *L'Ancien Régime et la Révolution*, in ibid., pp. 334–335.
5. Alexis de Tocqueville, J. P. Mayer and A. P. Kerr, *Recollections,* (New York: Anchor, 1971), p. xx.
6. See, for example, Charles Frankel, *The Case for Modern Man* (New York: Harper, 1956).
7. See Herbert Gans, *More Equality* (New York: Vintage, 1973).
8. See Christopher Jencks et al., *Inequality* (New York: Basic Books, 1972).
9. See John Rawls, *A Theory of Justice* (Cambridge, Mass.: Harvard University Press, 1974).
10. Arthur Schlesinger, Jr., *The Vital Center* (Boston: Houghton Mifflin, 1949), pp. 39–40.
11. Ibid.
12. Reinhold Niebuhr, *Faith and History* (New York: Scribner's, 1951).
13. Frankel, *Case for Modern Man*, p. 101.
14. Ibid., p. 115.
15. See John Kenneth Galbraith, *The New Industrial State* (New York: Signet, 1967).
16. Arthur M. Okun, *Equality and Efficiency* (Washington, D.C.: Brookings Institution, 1975).
17. Gans, *More Equality.*
18. Ibid., p. 67.
19. Ibid., p. 66.
20. Ibid., p. 5.
21. Ibid., p. 136.
22. Ibid., p. 139.
23. John C. Calhoun, "Letter to General Hamilton," in Richard K. Cralle, ed., *The Works of John C. Calhoun*, vol. 6, (New York: Russell & Russell, 1968).
24. Gans, *More Equality*, p. 148.
25. Ibid., p. 79.
26. Ibid., pp. 81–82.
27. Lyndon B. Johnson, Commencement Address, Howard University, Washington, D.C., June 12, 1965.
28. Nathan Glazer, *Affirmative Discrimination* (New York: Basic Books, 1976).

29. Arnold Rogow, *The Dying of the Light* (New York: Putnam's, 1976).
30. James S. Coleman et al., *Equality of Educational Opportunity* (Washington, D.C.: Government Printing Office, 1966); and Christopher Jencks et al., *Inequality*.
31. Ronald Edmonds et al., "Perspectives on *Inequality:* A Reassessment of the Effect of Family and Schooling in America," *Harvard Educational Review* 43 (February 1973).
32. Jencks et al., *Inequality*, p. 11.
33. Ibid., p. 53.
34. Ibid., p. 186.
35. Ibid., p. 255.
36. Edmonds, "Perspectives on *Inequality*," p. 89.
37. Howard F. Taylor, "Playing the Dozens with Path Analyses," *Sociology of Education* 46 (Fall 1973).
38. Rawls, *Theory of Justice*.
39. Ibid., p. 7.
40. Ibid., p. 60.
41. Ibid., pp. 60–61.
42. Ibid., p. 137.
43. Ibid.
44. Ibid., p. 143.
45. Ibid., p. 511.
46. Ibid., p. 512.
47. Ibid., p. 505.
48. See William McCord and Arline McCord, *American Social Problems* (St. Louis: Mosby, 1977).
49. See Joseph Grimmond, *The Liberal Future* (London: Faber and Faber, 1959).

10

LIBERTARIANISM

Origins of Libertarianism

The libertarian movement in contemporary social philosophy is followed by an odd assortment of social thinkers. Many contemporary adherents of this position, such as philosopher Robert Nozick, believe that liberty and justice are the true goals of a civilized society and that inequality is just.[1] To some degree, libertarians of this vein have derived their philosophy from the works of John Locke and Thomas Hobbes, the eighteenth-century philosophers who glorified the individual, his independence from the state, and his highly limited participation in a "social contract" with his fellow man. One may reasonably argue that these early social philosophers reflected the advance of capitalism in their era.

Other libertarians, such as Erich Fromm, condemn inequality and believe that liberty and justice can be achieved only in small, decentralized communities. Fromm's thought can be traced to Marx and Freud, but most importantly to the anarchist philosopher Pierre Joseph Proudhon. In spite of their contrasting conclusions, both Fromm and a Nozick put their faith in a total decentralization of the state and of the economy. They believe that individuals or small groups of people who work together can build an equitable society.

Locke and Hobbes (together with Adam Smith, the first economist to advocate laissez-faire policies) reflected an ideology that grew hand in hand with the advance of capitalism. By their emphasis upon individual liberties, Locke and Hobbes deviated from the ancient Greek and Roman conception of equity. For Aristotle, for example, justice lay in a person benefiting the fellow members of his society. And, as Sheldon Wolin has pointed out, citizenship in ancient times meant sharing with others: "The very word 'republic' derives from the Latin which translates into "public thing."[2]

Nonetheless, with the onset of capitalism, as Wolin has observed:

> Sharing became suspect, an affront to the sensibilities of a newly emerging type of person. The individual, rather than the community, was the basic unit. . . . Rational calculations of private advantage, rather than public deliberation upon common matters, became the preferred mode of action.[3]

While some contemporary libertarians owe an intellectual debt to this position, others might equally well be regarded as inheritors of the nineteenth-century anarchist position. Proudhon (1809–1865) can, for example, be viewed as a legitimate progenitor of contemporary libertarianism. Proudhon sought the abolition of authority in all areas of human life. He loathed the tyranny of the state and of the church. He esteemed individual freedom and yearned for small, all-powerful communities where everyone could work freely and cooperatively.[4] He hated the capitalist system, asserting that "property is theft." He believed that "God is evil" and yet revered Christianity in its purest form.[5] Equality for him was a "mutuality" of exchange of services.[6] Participation in his ideal communities would leave the individual free to withdraw at any time. Proudhon valued independence, autonomy, and privacy as highly as he did the principle of mutual exchange.[7]

Although Proudhon suffered through various prison terms, intellectual attacks by Marx, and a painful death from cerebral anemia, his ideas survived to spawn a generation of revolutionaries who have come to be known as "anarchists." Above all, they wished liberty and equality for human beings; they attacked elitism wherever it existed in nineteenth- and twentieth-century Europe; and they sought the fulfillment of human potentialities. Many of the early labor leaders in America, some of the founders of Israeli kibbutzim, nihilist assassins in tsarist Russia, and a number of Loyalist troops during the Spanish Civil War absorbed Proudhon's anarchism.

Few contemporary libertarians vow allegiance to Proudhon. And yet, in quite different ways, psychologist Erich Fromm, economist Friederick Hyack (who fears that egalitarianism results in tyranny) and philosopher Robert Nozick have explicitly or implicitly allied themselves with Proudhon. Fromm is perhaps the most influential exponent of anarchism in modern times.

"Communitarian Socialism": Erich Fromm

Erich Fromm, a distinguished psychoanalyst, represents one distinct variety of contemporary libertarians. He might well be called the leader of the movement's "left wing" since, like Proudhon, he accepts equality and liberty as equally desirable goals.

Fromm believes that twentieth-century man is "escaping from freedom" and is totally alienated from his work.[8] He argues that "the countries in Europe which are among the most democratic, peaceful and prosperous ones, and the United States, the most prosperous country in the world, show the most severe symptoms of mental disturbance."[9] Fromm veiws all modern industrialized societies as "sick." Rather than attributing high rates of crime, alcoholism, or suicide to the idiosyncrasies of individuals in these lands, Fromm argues that the infirm, unequal nature of such societies contributes to mental disorders. Fromm assumes that "freedom and spontaneity are the objective goals to be attained by every human being. If such a goal is not attained by the majority of members of any given society, we deal with the phenomenon of socially patterned defect."[10]

For Fromm, all capitalistic societies have socially patterned defects and are "abnormal" in that the social structure itself frustrates man's basic needs. For him, "mental health is characterized by the ability to love and to create."[11] Thus any society that inhibits these capacities is inherently pathological. He agrees with C. Wright Mills that in modern, postindustrial societies, "few individuals manipulate things; more handle people and symbols."[12]

In considering various solutions to the problem of alienation, Fromm arrives at basic criticisms of capitalist society. He contends that these opinions have been shared by a variety of people:

> Whether we think of Burckhardt or Proudhon, of Tolstoy or Baudelaire, of Marx or Kropotkin, they had a concept of man which was essentially a religious and moral one. Man is the end, and must never be used as a means; material production is for man, not man for material production; the aim of life is the unfolding of man's creative powers; the aim of history is a transformation of society into one governed by justice and truth.[13]

In an attempt to create a new society divested of alienation, Fromm suggests several "roads to sanity." Specifically, as an adherent of the old Frankfurt school of sociology, he advocates "communitarian socialism." He would like to establish small social organizations where "every working person would be an active and responsible participant, where work would be attractive and meaningful, where capital would not employ labor, but labor would employ capital."[14] As concrete examples, he cites various "communities of work" in France, Switzerland, and Italy. In such small communes, people employ advanced technological instruments to produce items like watches; they are totally democratic; they allow a diversity of different beliefs (for instance, subgroups of Catholics and atheists in the same commune); and they enjoy complete equality. According to Fromm, "the situation of alienation is overcome, work has become a meaningful expression of human energy, human solidarity is established without restriction of freedom—or the danger of conformity."[15]

In Italy, advocates of "paternal capitalism" such as A. Olivetti have established similar communes which allow workers a major voice in governing the operation of their lives, factories, and homes.[16]

The efforts of an Olivetti, a Fromm, or the founders of French communities of work are essentially aimed at creating egalitarian—and at the same time, totally free—communities. Yet, one may reasonably question the success of such experiments on several grounds.

First, most of these libertarian establishments, except for the Israeli kibbutzim, have in fact collapsed. The usual human needs from lust to greed undermined feelings of cooperation.[17]

Second, such libertarian ideologies tend to denigrate modern life and glorify rural existence. Erich Fromm says, for example, that "undoubtedly a relatively primitive village in which there are still real feasts, common artistic shared expressions, and no literacy at all is more advanced culturally and more healthy mentally than our educated, newspaper-reading, radio-listening culture."[18] However correct he may or may not be in his idealization of rural life Fromm completely ignores the fact that the vast majority of people in both industrialized and developing nations refuse to sacrifice their education, their newspapers, or their television sets.[19] In fact, whether it is conducive to mental health or not, people in the developing world increasingly choose to live in cities. In the industrialized world, citizens move toward suburbs, which are further extensions of metropolitan areas.[20] Therefore, it is completely unrealistic to expect that the people of the world will suddenly give themselves over to the anarchistic ideal of communal living.

Although communitarian socialism has a dim future, other varieties of libertarianism are thriving. One of the most popular is the position of

Robert Nozick. His *Anarchy, State, and Utopia* has been acclaimed by both philosophers and businesspeople as a fundamental challenge to the pervasive egalitarian beliefs of our time.[21]

Libertarianism and "Entitlement": Robert Nozick

Drawing upon John Locke and yet explicitly rejecting anarchism, Robert Nozick speaks eloquently for the "right wing" of libertarianism. Those in his camp, such as writer Ayn Rand and economist Milton Friedman, believe that the state should serve no other function than as a watchdog over individual rights. Nozick opposes any laws that try to force people to do something "for their own good," such as those regulating sexual behavior or drug use.

He is also against laws that regulate business or measures aimed at the redistribution of wealth. People who are better off in ability, talent, and wealth are entitled to their good fortune. Any state intervention to bring about greater equality is both inefficient and unjust in his opinion.

If people have gained their privileges fairly and squarely, Nozick believes, they may dispose of them in any fashion they wish. Thus inheritance or income taxes are inherently unjust for they deprive people of their rights.

A person achieves a right to dispose of his "holdings" in any way he sees fit if he acquired his privileged situation from a prior distribution of holdings that was also just. Nozick postulates an original Lockean state of nature where, for example, each person seized unclaimed portions of land and left enough for others. Totally ahistorical in his writings, Nozick makes no attempt to prove that such a state of nature actually existed. Although a socialist as a young man, Nozick ignores the historical record of castes, serfdom, and slavery, leaving the impression that these were "just" systems and that their remnants in contemporary society are equally just.

For Nozick, the only function of the state is to be a protector against force or fraud and primarily to be the ultimate enforcer of justice. In his view, the state grew as people "bought" increasingly larger "packages" of services from various agencies in the market:

> Presumably, what drives people to use the state's system of justice is the issue of ultimate enforcement. Only the state can enforce a judgment against the will of one of the parties. For the state does not *allow* anyone else to enforce another system's justment.[22]

Nozick objects to the state's interference with a person's liberty to do anything to himself: "My nonpaternalistic position holds that someone may choose (or permit another) to do to himself anything, unless he has acquired an obligation to some third party not to do or allow it."[23]

Nozick rejects Rawls and philosopher Herbert Hart in their "principle of fairness." Both Hart and Rawls believe that people who engage in a cooperative venture mutually restrict their liberties in ways that are beneficial to both parties. Once one has entered such a "contract," one has a right to expect reciprocal obligations.[24]

Nozick believes that "one cannot, whatever one's purpose, just act so as to give people benefits and then demand (or seize) payment."[25] For Nozick,

1. A person who acquires a holding in accordance with the principle of justice in acquisition is entitled to that holding.

2. A person who acquires a holding in accordance with the principle of justice in transfer, from someone else entitled to the holding, is entitled to the holding.[26]

How does one establish such principles of justice? Here, Nozick turns to Rawls's veil-of-ignorance argument but profoundly alters it. Nozick believes that there *are* differential "entitlements" to wealth, power, and privilege. Since people supposedly receive these rewards in an ideally just situation, it would be inequitable to deprive them of their advantages.

Nozick assumes that all people make their choices "voluntarily," and that the only difference among people is that some have more options than others. It may be unfortunate for those who remain at the bottom of the scale, Nozick says, but it is not unjust. Thus Nozick cites the case of the basketball player Wilt Chamberlain and poses the question of whether it would be wrong for people to pay extra money to see this man in action.[27] Under conditions of full freedom, Chamberlain might receive vastly more income than nonathletic types. This would be inegalitarian, according to Nozick, but not unjust.

Thus, for Nozick, an ideal society would be governed by the motto, "From each as they choose, to each as they are chosen."[28] It would be a "minimal" state that people could join or leave at will. Armies might be raised for defense but only by voluntary choice, and "a Rockefeller may —without moral scruple—bequeath a fortune to charity, endow a socialist commune or dump all his money into the Hudson River.'[29] Inequalities would remain but might be cured by the generosity of private philanthropists. Government attempts to establish unrealistic systems of egalitarian, "distributive" justice would disappear as the scope of individual liberty widened.

It is small wonder that Nozick's book has been welcomed not only by philosophers but by capitalists who share his libertarian ethic. Yet, critics of this newest form of libertarianism have not been entirely dazzled by his combination of economic theory and utopian visions. Critics of this type of libertarianism advance four central arguments.

First, do human beings have any "natural rights" at all? Nozick flatly asserts in his first sentence: "Individuals have rights, and there are things no person or group may do to them (without violating these rights)."[30] Who or what has endowed these rights? How would Nozick answer a thorough nihilist who attacked his very first premise, declared that philosophy was bosh, and asserted that human "rights" are a vacuous concoction created by rationalizers who are willing to serve the powerful. Nozick does not answer this. Yet, if such nihilists were right, would there be any purpose at all to libertarian philosophy or to a discussion of "rights"

Second, Nozick provides no way for rectifying past injustices, even defined in his own terms. As he admits: "If past injustice has shaped present holdings in various ways. . . what now, if anything, ought to be done to rectify these injustices? . . . I do not know of a thorough or theoretically sophisticated treatment of such issues."[31] Clearly, however, if the money one spent on seeing a Wilt Chamberlain had been received through the ill-gotten gains of one's "robber baron" father, Nozick would, by his logic, have to regard this as an unjust transaction.

Third, Sheldon Wolin argues that when Nozick ignores the role of real human actions in creating inequality, Nozick turns his account of liberty and inequality into "merely an abstract formulation . . . there is no reference to any historical circumstance, much less any suggestion that patterns of holdings were in fact the result of the political power exerted by powerful individuals and classes."[32]

Fourth, Nozick's naiveté about history and power almost equals his lack of sophistication concerning the "voluntary" nature of human activity. By assuming that all men act on the rational calculus of economic man, Nozick ignores shelves of literature ranging from Freud's conclusions concerning the unconscious motivation of man to contemporary evidence concerning the effects of slavery and racism upon the supposedly "voluntary" nature of human choice.

From their unsupported assertions concerning human rights, to their neglect of history as a force in inequality, to their naive assumptions concerning human nature, the "right wing" libertarians such as Nozick have reaped immense popularity but little tangible action from the world's population. Neither a Fromm nor a Nozick has brought about a genuine advance in human thought concerning liberty, equality, and fraternity. Their very different forms of utopianism have reaped only indifference from the majority of the world's population, which is, for good or evil, enthralled by that most influential of contemporary social philosophies: egalitarianism.

Notes

1. Robert Nozick, *Anarchy, State, and Utopia* (New York: Basic Books, 1974).
2. Sheldon Wolin, review of *Anarchy, State, and Utopia, The New York Times Book Review*, May 11, 1975, p. 1.
3. Ibid.
4. See, for example, Pierre Joseph Proudhon, *De la Creation de l'Ordre dans l'Humanité* (Paris: 1843).
5. See Henri de Lubac, *The Un-Marxian Socialist* (New York: Sheed and Ward, 1948).
6. Yves Simon, "Notes sur le Fédéralisme Proudhonian," *Esprit*, April 1937, p. 58.
7. See, for example, Pierre Joseph Proudhon, *Lettres sur la Philosophie du Progrés* (Brussels: 1853).
8. Erich Fromm, *The Sane Society* (New York: Rinehart, 1955).
9. Ibid., p. 10.
10. Ibid., p. 15.
11. Ibid., p. 69.
12. C. Wright Mills, *White Collar* (New York: Oxford University Press 1956, p. 3).
13. Fromm, *Sane Society*, p. 233.
14. Ibid., pp. 283–284.
15. Ibid., p. 20.
16. A. Olivetti, *L'Ordine Politico della Communitá* (Rome: 1946).
17. See, for example, Daniel Bell, *The End of Ideology* (New York: Free Press, 1962).
18. Fromm, *Sane Society*, p. 348.
19. William McCord and Abdullah Lutfiyya, "Urbanization and World View in the Middle East," in A. R. Desai, ed., *Essays on Modernization of Underdeveloped Countries* (Bombay: Thacker, 1972).
20. See Arline McCord and William McCord, *Urban Social Conflict* (St. Louis: Mosby, 1977).
21. Ibid.
22. Ibid., p. 14.
23. Ibid., p. 58.
24. Herbert Hart, "Are There Any Natural Rights?" *Philosophical Review*, 1955.
25. Nozick, *Anarchy, State, and Utopia*, p. 95.
26. Ibid., p. 151.
27. Ibid., p. 161.
28. Ibid., p. 160.
29. "You're Entitled," *Newsweek*, March 31, 1975, p. 81.
30. Nozick, *Anarchy, State, and Utopia*, p. ix.
31. Ibid., p. 152.
32. Wolin, review of *Anarchy, State, and Utopia*, p. 32.

11

EGALITARIANISM

Origins of Egalitarianism

The desire for equality in privileges, power, and wealth is an ancient human urge. Indeed, some social scientists, such as Jon Van Til, believe that many of the simple societies are characterized by "mutual equality." If this were the case at the beginning of the technological revolution, Van Til believes that the essential question thus posed to social philosophers is: "Why is it that a very natural way of organizing society has given way in our own time to a much more inegalitarian social form—with all the attendant costs that tax us so?"[1]

It is difficult to take this assertion at its face value. As we noted in our discussion of simple societies (Chapter 1), very few people at any time of history have actually lived under conditions of mutual equality. Nonetheless, many in most eras of history have yearned for an egalitarian society. Clearly, the Bible's reminder that all men move from "dust unto dust" is a clear admonition that men are fundamentally equal, as in St. Paul's injunction to the Galatians: "There is neither Jew nor Greek, there is neither bond nor free, there is neither male nor female, for you are all one in Christ Jesus."[2]

Later, the Epicureans and Stoics of ancient Rome embraced a similar, if unsupernatural, view of men as reasoning beings, as identical, equal brothers. As Marcus Aurelius (A.D. 121–180), a great Roman emperor and an opponent of slavery, observed: "Reasoning beings wère created for one another's sake. . . . All is emphemeral—fame and the famous as well. . . . Mark how fleeting and paltry is the estate of man,—yesterday in embryo, tomorrow, a mummy or ashes."[3] Stoics such as Marcus Aurelius had little esteem for the social gradations of their time. Equality of reasoning men was, for the Stoics, an ideal society.

The growth of both slavery and serfdom in the Middle Ages temporarily eclipsed these egalitarian views. The advance of industrialism, buttressed by the individualistic doctrines of Hobbes, Locke, and Smith, militated against egalitarian beliefs. But by the nineteenth century various forms of egalitarian thought began to reappear. Marx, of course, emerged as the giant of egalitarians—both in his own time and into the twentieth century, and he is now revered by some as a kind of secular saint.

As a young man in 1844, Marx regarded the end of man's alienation as the goal of history. A first step would be the abolition of private property and classes. A state of true individual autonomy brought about by equality would ensue. He had an implicit faith "that History will come to it."[4] As we have pointed out, subsequent communist doctrine has been based on the "scientific" theory that the internal contradictions of capitalism would eventually culminate in a classless society.

As Marx later stated in his *Critique of the Gotha Programme* (1875): "In a higher phase of communist society, after the enslaving subordination of individuals under division of labor . . . has vanished . . . only then . . . can society inscribe on its banners: from each according to his ability, to each according to his needs."[5] He believed that only full egalitarianism would produce true freedom. As Marx announced in the *Communist Manifesto:* "In place of the old bourgeois society, with its classes and class antagonism, we shall have an association in which the free development of each is the condition of the free development of all."[6]

Unlike liberals and libertarians, Marx did not seek mere equality of opportunity nor did he believe that people were naturally entitled to their privileges. Rather, in the words of Stephen Lukes, Marx and other egalitarian socialists focused "on equalizing the rewards and privileges attached to different positions, not on widening the competition for them."[7]

The concrete manifestations of Marx's dream led neither to complete equality nor to complete freedom. Although the excesses of Stalinist Russia have been justified on grounds that the nation was not "ripe" for revolution,[8] few sophisticated Marxists still hold to the belief that either Russia or China represents the fulfillment of the Marxist hopes.[9] In the words of Leszek Kolawkowski, a devoted egalitarian who was expelled from the University of Warsaw in 1968:

> We were happy a hundred years ago. We knew that there were ex-
> ploiters and exploited, wealthy and poor, and we had a perfect idea of
> how to get rid of injustice: we would expropriate the owners and turn
> the wealth over to the common good. We expropriated the owners and
> we created one of the most monstrous and oppressive social systems in
> world history.[10]

Some contemporary Marxists cling to the belief that egalitarian principles were essentially correct and that only specific historical and international conditions made the principle unworkable.[11] Others, such as Stuart
Hampshire, reject explicit Marxist theory: "No . . . final liberation of man
is any longer to be expected from any likely socialist transformation of
the social order."[12]

Although vastly influential, Marxism was not the only pregenitor of
contemporary egalitarian thought. Proudhon in France, Sidney and Bea-
trice Webb in England, Prince Eugene Kropotkin in Russia, all developed
different versions of egalitarian social philosophy. Perhaps the most influential of all was R. H. Tawney, whose books *The Acquisitive Society*
(1920) and *Equality* (1931) earned him an international reputation as a
defender of egalitarianism.[13]

The son of an upper-class British official in India, Tawney attended
Rugby and Oxford. Later, he taught at Glasgow, Oxford, and London
universities. Despite his membership in the English "establishment,"
Tawney became one of the most influential defenders of "Fabian," or
democratic, socialism.

Tawney attacked the shibboleth of his day: that poverty and inequality
were merely the result of a lack of production. He responded:

> "But increased production is important." Of course it is! That plenty
> is good and scarcity evil—it needs no ghost from the graves of the past
> five years to tell us that. But plenty depends upon co-operative effort,
> and co-operation upon moral principles.[14]

He assaulted the inequalities of Britain and the recurrent economic crises
from which she suffered:

> An industry, when all is said, is, in its essence, nothing more mysteri-
> ous than a body of men associated, in various degrees of competition
> and co-operation, to win their living by providing the community with
> some service it requires. . . .
> The conditions of a right organization of industry are, therefore,
> permanent, unchanging, and capable of being apprehended by the
> most elementary intelligence.[15]

Tawney proposed two basic principles. First, each industry should provide the best service possible, and those who render no service at all should not be paid. Second, the government of the industry should be in the hands of persons "who are responsible to those who are directed and governed."[16] In effect, Tawney proposed that industry should be rewarded according to the functions it served for the community, and that it should be democratically governed.

These principles ran against conceptions of property rights in his own time—and, indeed, against many of the arguments proposed by some contemporary libertarians who believe that they are "entitled" to dispose of their property in any way they see fit. Tawney well remembered the fights in the nineteenth century between his egalitarian ideals and libertarian theories of property:

> No one has forgotten the opposition offered in the name of the rights of property to factory legislation, to housing reform, to interference with the adulteration of goods, even to the compulsory sanitation of private houses. "May I not do what I like with my own?" was the answer to the proposal to require a minimum standard of safety and sanitation from the owners of mills and houses.[17]

Tawney fought against this position not only because of his own humanitarianism but because it inevitably blocked the creation of what he called a "functional" society.

> A society which aimed at making the acquisition of wealth contingent upon the discharge of social obligations, which sought to proportion remuneration to service and denied it to those by whom no service was performed, which inquired first not what men possess but what they can make or create or achieve.[18]

Although Tawney, unlike Marx, did not yearn for a totally egalitarian society in which all the causes of egotism, greed, and aggression could be eliminated from man's nature, he did foresee a functional society guided by three rules. First, property rights would be abolished if their owners served no function for the society. Second, "the producers shall stand in a direct relation to the community for whom production is carried on, so that their responsibility to it may be obvious and unmistakable, not lost, as at present, through their immediate subordination to shareholders whose interest is not service but gain."[19] Third, the economy should be guided by professional organizations whose ultimate supervision would lie in the hands of consumers.

Tawney, then, did not totally embrace the ideal of complete equality. He advocated instead a moderate advance of humanity toward a situation of greater equality, responsibility, and democracy—a "functional" society where great differences in wealth would be abolished. Has this occurred?

Is Contemporary Society More Nearly Equal?

In the opinion of many social scientists, the egalitarian agitation of the past century (combined, of course, with other factors) has indeed resulted in greater equality. Gerhard Lenski, for example, has flatly stated: "The appearance of mature industrial societies marks the first significant reversal in the age-old evolutionary trend toward ever increasing inequality."[20] Lenski argues that only 1 or 2 percent of the population in agrarian societies absorbed at least half of the total income. By contrast, in industrial societies the upper classes consume a much smaller proportion, around 8 to 12 percent, of national income.[21]

Lenski suggests several reasons for the postulated decline in inequality. Industrial leaders may not command obedience with the same ease as their agrarian counterparts. Rising productivity allows the elite to sacrifice a larger proportion of their income without threatening their absolute profits. The spread of knowledge and literacy makes the masses more aware of their unequal position. Most important, the rise of egalitarian, democratic ideologies has been the spur to greater equality. As this ideology spread, "those who governed had to make substantial concessions in order to avoid massive challenges to their power—challenges which would have been costly to resist, and might even have led to their overthrow."[22]

Lenski adopted a long-range view of inequality, particularly concentrating on the transition between agrarian and industrial societies. Other social scientists, such as Raymond Aron in *La Lutte des Classes* and Seymour Martin Lipset in *Political Man,* have argued that class distinctions even during the brief history of industrialism have considerably declined.[23] Both believe that economic development has reduced the polarization of classes, eroded the bases of class identification, and resulted in an end to ideological conflicts based on class differences. According to such writers, the general increase in economic affluence, combined with the advent of democratic politics, has made debates over equality pointless.

Other social critics have, however, questioned this conclusion. T. R. Bottomore, for one, has argued that working-class levels of income have increased in the industrialized world but that this has made relatively little difference in the gap between upper and lower classes.[24] Bottomore points out that 75 percent of all personal wealth in Britain remained under the control of 5 percent of the population between 1911 and 1960.[25] He recognizes, of course, that the material wealth of all groups in an industrialized society has increased, but "pockets" of absolute poverty continue to exist. As Bottomore comments, "although the *relative* positions of the various classes have changed little, if at all, since before the war . . . the economic bases of class differentiation—the ownership or nonownership of property—remain much as they were."[26]

Have other modern societies that have equality as one of their highest ideals succeeded in fulfilling this goal more than the Western capitalist nations? The evidence indicates a measure of qualified success. The leaders of the Soviet Union, for example, have strongly advocated the ideal of egalitarianism and, as we have noted previously, the wage differentials between the highest members of the Communist bureaucracy and the lowest-paid workers are less than comparable differences in capitalist societies.[27] Yet, the gap is still enormous. Leaders in Communist nations receive a hundred times the income of lowly workers; 73 percent of the delegates to the official party congress in 1959 were at least secondary school graduates.[28] From such evidence, Lenski has concluded that despite the egalitarian ideology of a nation, "there is no alternative to at least partial coordination of the political class system with the occupational and educational class systems in totalitarian states."[29]

Leaders of the Israeli kibbutzim, like the founders of the Soviet Union, envisioned a totally egalitarian society. As Leslie Y. Rabkin has put it, "Before Israel became a state, the kibbutz represented the dramatic fulfillment of Zionist dreams: return to the soil, social democracy at its purest, and the encouragement of strength, purpose and self-fulfillment."[30]

One friendly observer of the kibbutz life found in 1976 that the radical experiment in egalitarianism that had been founded in 1920 had fundamentally changed. In 1920 the leaders had hoped for an austere and simple life involving completely equal ownership of property and the means of production. The kibbutz prospered but "with the rise of affluence, and the march of generations, there have been large departures from the ideology of the founders."[31]

Rabkin found that by 1976 "individualism, private ownership, and personal needs and values are affecting communal life as never before."[32] Specifically, Rabkin noted that concern with family life and individual possessions threatened to submerge the originally egalitarian ideology of the kibbutz.

Changes in "ideal" communities—such as the Israeli kibbutz or the

Soviet society, which seem increasingly dominated by the profit motive—
have not dulled the thrust of contemporary egalitarians. In capitalist,
communist, or communitarian societies, they have still fought for the
same basic ideal: equality.

Some Contemporary Philosophies of Egalitarianism

Many observers have been deeply disturbed by the vast discrepancies
in wealth that continue to afflict affluent contemporary America. They
have been appalled by the misguided pattern of priorities that Americans
follow. In 1974, for example, the nation spent $3 billion for one aircraft
carrier—the same amount required to rebuild all blighted slum areas in the
nation.[33] The cost of the B-1 bomber program ($11.4 billion), a defense
endeavor that many military experts believe is useless, would have been
enough to have brought all Americans above the poverty line in 1971.[34]
Twenty full-time college scholarships at $2,050 per year could have been
paid at the cost of *one* mission by *one* plane during the Vietnam War.[35]
This odd "agenda for the future" obviously allocates huge amounts of the
national income for military needs while neglecting health, welfare, and
education at home.

Moreover, as economist Lester Thurow has demonstrated, the domestic distribution of wealth in 1976 is drastically skewed toward supporting a
small minority of the American population.[36] The Internal Revenue Service indicates that the top .008 percent of the population has as much
wealth as the bottom 50 percent.[37] Viewed somewhat differently, the
same pattern of inequality in wealth obtains: the top 20 percent of the
population owns 76 percent of all wealth (homes, cars, stocks, factories),
while the bottom 20 percent owns 2 percent.[38]

This pattern of inequality dominates America, according to Thurow,
because of lax inheritance laws, generous depreciation deductions for
corporations, and loopholes in capital gains taxes. Thurow points out that
such vast inequality in wealth could easily be reduced if America adopted
the Swedish model and taxed net worth rather than merely income. In
response to the argument that Swedish policies in America would reduce
savings and thus hinder economic growth, Thurow points out that
Sweden has already surpassed the United States in producing the highest
national per capita product of any industrialized nation.

Thurow contends that we have the economic techniques to assure that
the concentration of wealth in America could be broken up. Yet, he
argues, the "real issues" are:

What is a "fair" distribution of economic power? What is a fair distribution of economic resources? At what point should our society stop its wealth from becoming concentrated in the hands of a minority? We are quick to pose these questions for others, particularly underdeveloped societies but slow to pose them for ourselves.[39]

Egalitarians in both Europe and America have not hesitated to face such issues. Whether calling themselves "populists," "socialists," or "communists," egalitarians have consistently maintained that concentrations of private wealth should be broken up for the benefit of the public welfare.

In America, a few politicians—most notably George McGovern, Fred Harris, and, more ambiguously, Jimmy Carter—have been labeled as "new populists." They hope to unite the poor and those of moderate income, whites and blacks, labor union members and students, into a coalition aimed at abolishing America's inequalities.

The doctrine of the new populists draws on two hundred years of American history and bears some resemblance to the beliefs of such diverse figures as Andrew Jackson, Thorstein Veblen, and Robert La Follette. The new populists have, however, shed the anti-Semitic, anti-black, and anti-Catholic sentiments of some of their ancestors such as members of the "know-nothing" movement.

In common with all of their American predecessors, the new populists suggest that the structure of American society is inequitable and that policies aimed at "taming the trusts" or "soaking the rich" should be adopted. In specific terms, the new populists advocate such policies as these:

Tax capital gains at death

Increase inheritance taxes

Abolish oil depletion allowances

End tax shelters and tax loopholes

Tax churches and foundations

Greatly increase the taxes of the "superrich" and decrease those of moderate- and low-income people

Break up all corporate trusts and democratize decision making in all companies

Provide free medical care for all.[40]

In other words, they aim at ending large fortunes, ensuring some public control over giant corporations, setting a minimum standard of living for all, and decreasing the sense of alienation characteristic of many Ameri-

cans. Jack Newfield and Jeff Greenfield contend that "while a new popul-
ism will not mean nirvana or the Final Triumph of Virtue, it can make life
a little more humane for a majority of our countrymen. Nothing more.
But nothing less either."[41]

Other American egalitarians have rallied under the banner of "democratic socialism." Although espousing a form of neo-Marxism, most
American socialists have abandoned the hope that history moves inevitably toward a just society or that contemporary capitalism will disappear in
one gigantic cataclysm. Rather, they believe that basic reforms in American life may be achieved peacefully and gradually with the assent of most
Americans.

The concrete goals of American socialism have been succinctly summarized by Michael Harrington, a leader of American socialism and once
head of the American delegation to the Socialist International.[42] Among
various egalitarian measures, Harrington urges that Americans should
adopt certain policies.

1. Major appropriations for welfare, housing, and health programs
must be undertaken by the federal government. Private enterprise cannot
be counted on for such undertakings since there is no immediate profitable return. Earlier programs, such as the war on poverty, generally
failed, but, in Harrington's opinion, this was because they failed to attack
the political, real estate, "agro-business," and corporate interests, which
had much to gain from maintaining the status quo. As Harrington observes, "In education, housing, agriculture, welfare and every other area
of social life it is necessary to attack the systematic concentration of
economic power in order to achieve serious reform."[43]

2. Socialists advocate comprehensive planning of the economy. Such
planning has already been undertaken by giant corporations such as General Motors. Harrington suggests, however, that federal agencies that are
democratically responsive to elected bodies should assume this role:
"The principle of socialist planning is clear: the people rather than corporations with Government subsidies should decide priorities."[44]

3. The government, as the representative of the people, should gradually nationalize industries and use their profits for the public welfare.
This might be accomplished by abolishing the rights of short-term stockholders (essentially gamblers in Harrington's opinion), prohibiting large
inheritances, and establishing an investment bank to receive and invest
taxes at the death of a millionaire.

4. As part of his approach, Harrington advocates strict enforcement of
existing tax laws, as well as the imposition of new taxes on capital gains
and inheritances. He condemns "parasitic gamblers" on the stock market
because they do not contribute to the economy. Therefore, he suggests,
no one should be allowed to profit from mere stock speculation. He notes

that the actual rate of taxation of the wealthiest Americans declined in the years 1952 to 1967 because they availed themselves of various tax shelters. In instituting tax reforms, Harrington argues, "the point would not be to penalize hard work or actual risk taking but to severely limit, and eventually eliminate, the tribute society pays to passive wealth or to stock gamblers."[45]

5. Democratic socialists not only yearn for political democracy but what might be called "economic" democracy; that is, allowing workers full participation in the decisions of management. Workers should be allowed to decide work assignments, veto the decisions of managers, and elect supervisors. In essence, they should be given a good measure of control over their working lives.

European egalitarians have long emphasized participatory democracy. Yugoslavia, for example, has created "workers' councils," which have ultimate responsibility for production, conditions of work, and even the hiring and firing of managers. A capitalist society, West Germany, has instituted similar proceedings in about 50 percent of its large industries. Maria Hirszowicz, a former professor at the University of Warsaw who was expelled for political reasons and one of the more ardent adherents of industrial democracy, has argued that "participative democracy, incorporated in the system of workers' self-management . . . could be regarded as a safeguard against the organized power of the state by making the workers . . . independent of organization elites and able to resist them if necessary."[46]

The likelihood that such reforms can actually occur in America depends upon creating a coalition of the aggrieved—of such disparate groups as the Boston Irish who oppose the "invasion" of blacks into their schools, Chicano lettuce pickers, residents of Harlem's "Climber's Row," and unemployed Detroit autoworkers. In 1976 it seemed highly unlikely that these groups would, as Harrington hopes, perceive that they had a common interest in advancing the cause of egalitarianism.

In Europe many egalitarians have given up hope that the amorphous proletariat can serve as the "vanguard of the future" or even that such doctrinaire measures as the nationalization of industry will significantly advance the cause of equality.[47] Indeed, the European socialists and even many communists have generally acknowledged their lack of faith in Marx's predictions and prescriptions. At a 1974 conference of such egalitarians, Stuart Hampshire declared:

> Throughout the discussions at the conference, and in reading most of the papers submitted, I thought that the perspective that adaptions of Marxism provided was a false perspective. I had the idea that we were being superstitious, like men still talking about alchemy when chemistry was already proving to be a different science with uncertain prospects.[48]

Hampshire has adopted a moderate credo of egalitarianism. He has proposed a set of moral injunctions that seem to him "clearly right and rationally justifiable." The vast majority of egalitarians would agree with these tenets:

> First, that the elimination of poverty ought to be the first priority of government after defense: secondly, that as great inequalities in wealth between different social groups lead to inequalities in power and in freedom of action, they are generally unjust and need to be redressed by governmental action; thirdly, that democratically elected governments ought to ensure that primary and basic human needs are given priority within the economic system.[49]

Conclusions

It would be rare indeed for any humane person to object to Hampshire's goals. Some conservatives and libertarians, as well as all liberals, would argue that poverty, enormous inequalities in wealth, and undemocratic practices should be eliminated in modern society. Yet they raise serious questions as to the actual effects of the proposals of today's populists, socialists, and communists.

First, antiegalitarians fear that the erosion of private property might entail the eclipse of political liberty. If, at one extreme, the state owned all the means of production, could there be a free press, a judiciary untrammeled by fears for next month's salary, or universities that could pursue independent lines of inquiry wherever they might go? The recent experience of communist nations suggests that state ownership of property militates against free institutions and dissent. Thus, most antiegalitarians fear total confiscation of wealth by the state. This does not prevent some of them, however, from advocating a "co-ownership" plan; that is, a system where property is widely distributed and the workers themselves become owners within the framework of a free-enterprise system.[50] Clearly, too, a condition of mutual equality may exist on a small scale as in French communities of work or Israeli kibbutzim without destroying the privacy or political liberty of the individual. This brings up another criticism by antiegalitarians.

Second, the critics contend, egalitarianism may well lead to uniformity and cultural stagnation, even if it does not destroy political liberty. The relatively egalitarian kibbutzim have not, for example, been noted for their creativity in art, literature, or science. Advances in these areas have instead come either from members of a traditional elite (such as Oxford, Harvard, or Cambridge graduates); or from individuals whose talents eventually gave them a high degree of economic privilege and independence (a Hemingway, Faulkner, or Sartre); or from people who have been economically sponsored by rich elites (a Plato, a Michelangelo, or a Leonardo da Vinci). Antiegalitarians argue that this is no mere accident. Inequalities of privilege and wealth are a necessary protection, in their view, for people of sublime talent, eccentric tastes, and superior vision. Many of those who oppose egalitarianism would open the doors of privilege to all who had the intellect or the esthetic ability to create; they would not, however, abolish differences in rank and privilege as such.

Third, critics of egalitarianism fear that economic efficiency would be undermined if incentives were totally equalized. They contend that it is not merely a matter of inducing people to accept grueling jobs at the top of a society; there will probably always be ambitious people who, regardless of salary, are willing to assume the presidency of General Motors or of the Politburo for reasons of honor, prestige, and self-fulfillment. Rather, the critics say, the question is: Who will be the drudges and drones of society—the bookkeepers, the clerks, the assembly-line workers? These people require monetary incentives to keep them at their essentially boring work. Perhaps ultimately they will be replaced by robots, but for now they must somehow be rewarded for their labor—indeed, it is not inconceivable that the usual correlation between pay and prestige will be reversed as there are increasingly fewer people who will voluntarily do the "dirty work." Unless the state introduces compulsory labor—and thus deprives people of one of their liberties—it may well be that garbage men will be paid more than doctors by the year 2000. Economic inequality will, however, still remain part of society's fabric.

Fourth, critics of egalitarianism raise a final question: Who is to be the agent of change toward a more egalitarian regime? Few egalitarians, as we have noted, still believe that history is on their side and that humankind will inevitably, spontaneously create a more egalitarian society. If the "proletariat" refuses, who will lead?

Some egalitarians offer answers that smack of a hidden elitism and potential dictatorship. Herbert Marcuse, for example, was a hero to rioting French students in 1968 who chanted "Marx, Mao, and Marcuse" as they agitated for a more equitable society. Few realized that Marcuse, a reclusive philosopher who lives in the exclusive California resort of La Jolla, wished for a dictatorship, not of the proletariat but of the intellectual elite.

Marcuse believes that the radical intellectual must lead the masses into a more egalitarian society, even if they do not wish it. Marcuse postulates that capitalist society blinds people to their "true" needs and interests. Thus one may condone repression and intolerance of capitalists as a way of leading people to true freedom.[51] As Andrew Hacker has cogently observed, this theory "confirms his belief that he [Marcuse] alone knows the true needs of the underclasses, that to him has been given the task of defining political goals for those who are unable to perceive their own historic interests."[52] Thus Marcuse emerges in his true garb: as a defender of equality and "freedom" who is quite prepared to force his utopia down our gorge.

These criticisms of egalitarianism—of its potential threat of tyranny, stagnation, and stale uniformity—force the reasonable person to question the entire approach. The egalitarian ideal has been a truly splendid, humane force in history, yet its actual practice and current theories leave one unconvinced that a new egalitarian society would be as marvelous as its advocates promise.

Now, having in hand empirical evidence and philosophical views about contemporary inequality, we are in a strategic position to assay the most basic question: What would be an equitable society and how can we achieve it?

Notes

1. Arthur Shostack, Jon Van Til, and Sally Bould Van Til, *Privilege in America* (Englewood Cliffs, N.J.: Prentice-Hall, 1973), p. 1.
2. Galatians 3:28.
3. Marcus Aurelius, *Meditations*, IV, 3, 35, 48.
4. Karl Marx, *Economic and Philosophic Manuscripts of 1844* (Moscow: Foreign Languages Publishing House, 1961), pp. 123 ff.
5. Karl Marx, *Selected Works*, vol. 2 (London: Lawrence & Wishart, 1942), p. 566.
6. Karl Marx and Friedrich Engels, *The Communist Manifesto* (London: Allen Unwin, 1948), p. 35.
7. Stephen Lukes, "Socialism and Equality," in Leszek Kolawkowski and Stuart Hampshire, eds., *Socialist Idea* (New York: Basic Books, 1975), p. 83.
8. Ibid.
9. Ibid.
10. Ibid., p. 16.
11. Ibid.
12. Stuart Hampshire, "Unity of Civil and Political Society," in *Socialist Idea*, p. 36.
13. R. H. Tawney, *The Acquisitive Society* (New York: Harcourt, Brace, 1948; orig. 1920).
14. Ibid., p. 6
15. Ibid.
16. Ibid., p. 7.
17. Ibid., p. 21.
18. Ibid., p. 29.
19. Ibid., p. 180.
20. Gerhard Lenski, *Power and Privilege* (New York: McGraw-Hill, 1966), p. 308.
21. Ibid., p. 309.
22. Ibid., p. 318.

23. Seymour M. Lipset, *Political Man* (Garden City, N.Y.: Doubleday, 1960).
24. T. R. Bottomore, *Sociology as Social Criticism* (New York: Pantheon, 1974), p. 118.
25. Ibid., p. 119.
26. Ibid., p. 118.
27. Merle Fainsod, *How Russia Is Ruled* (Cambridge, Mass.: Harvard University Press, 1963).
28. See Nicholas DeWitt, *Education and Professional Employment in the USSR* (Washington, D.C.: National Science Foundation, 1961).
29. Lenski, *Power and Privilege*, p. 330.
30. Leslie Y. Rabkin, "The Institution of the Family Is Alive and Well," *Psychology Today*, February 1976, p. 69.
31. Ibid., p. 68.
32. Ibid.
33. See Seymour Melman, "Getting the Biggest Bang for the Buck," *The New York Times*, September 4, 1974.
34. Ibid.
35. Ibid.
36. Lester C. Thurow, "Tax Wealth, Not Income," *The New York Times Magazine*, April 11, 1976, p. 31.
37. Cited in ibid.
38. Cited in ibid.
39. Ibid., p. 107.
40. See Jack Newfield and Jeff Greenfield, *A Populist Manifesto* (New York: Paperback Library, 1972).
41. Ibid., p. 222.
42. Michael Harrington, *Socialism* (New York: Bantam Books, 1973).
43. Ibid., p. 342.
44. Ibid., p. 347.
45. Ibid., p. 375.
46. Maria Hirszowicz, "Industrial Democracy, Self-Management and Social Control of Production," in Kolawkowski and Hampshire, *Socialist Idea*.
47. Ibid.
48. Stuart Hampshire, "Epilogue," in Kolawkowski and Hampshire, *Socialist Idea*, p. 248.
49. Ibid., p. 249.
50. Joseph Grimmond, *The Liberal Future* (London: Faber and Faber, 1959).
51. See Herbert Marcuse, *One-Dimensional Man* (Boston: Beacon, 1964).
52. Andrew Hacker, "Philosopher of the New Left," *The New York Times Book Review*, March 10, 1968, p. 34.

12

A PREFACE
TO EQUITY

"Where, at what final rampart, must a man stand when he fights for human freedom?"[1] In 1936, as he witnessed the onslaught of totalitarianism in Russia and in Europe, Walter Lippmann demanded to know the answer. He had seen the advances of Hitler and Mussolini, who, in the name of elitism, sought to save humankind from the "follies" of its masses. He had watched, too, as Stalin enslaved his peoples for the great goal of egalitarianism. He had been present when liberals quavered in the face of these newly garbed ideologues. He saw the "old" libertarians, such as Barcelona's anarchists, collapse under Franco's armed might.

In a series of articles and books, Lippmann, perhaps America's most renowned social critic, valiantly attempted to define the basic principles of equity for a war-ravaged world. "The problem, as I see it," he wrote in 1943, "is how to reconcile with the comparatively new economy of the division of labor the great and ancient and progressive traditions of liberty."[2] The same problem affects us today: how to preserve liberty and yet expand the realm of social justice. New factors—the emergence of "developing" nations, the spread of technology, the realization that the earth's resources could be exhausted—have increased the urgency of finding solutions.

All too many social scientists, however, have abandoned Lippmann's search—which was indeed the quest of Plato and Aristotle, of Mill and Marx, and of Proudhon and de Tocqueville. Like ostriches hiding their heads in beds of sand, some social scientists pretend that personal values can be excluded from research: they seek pure objectivity.

We believe that it is not possible or—if it were practical—not desirable to obscure ethical goals. In matters as grand, pervasive, and encompassing as differences in power, privilege, and equity, we believe that it is incumbent on reasonable people to take a stand. Too many human beings accept their lot in life—whether it is that of an untouchable or that of a mansion owner—without question, debate, or combat. Such mute, perhaps unconscious, usually inarticulate acquiescence does nothing to enhance human dignity. For social scientists, there is only one choice: remain silent on questions of equity—whether for reasons of "objectivity," self-interest, or deliberate malice—or state their position explicitly. We believe that our own biases concerning liberty and equity cannot, in any case, be disguised.

What Is Equity?

Equity in human affairs involves interrelated, difficult, and perhaps ultimately unattainable principles. Equity means treating each person as if he or she were yourself. Why? Since people are one in birth, suffering, and death. Since we emerge from the same human family. Since we experience the same ultimate fate. Even the most egocentric person should follow this principle once he or she realizes that the highest-placed and most arrogant must fall prey to the whims of nature and fellow human beings. Self-interest, if nothing else, dictates prudence in our concern for others.

This basic principle of equity, the so-called Golden Rule, has been enunciated by philosophers and prophets since the beginning of written time. Confucius holds first rank. As he suggested, "when one cultivates to the utmost the capabilities of his nature and exercises them on the principle of reciprocity, he is not far from the path. What you do not want done to yourself, do not do unto others."[3]

Widely separated from contact with the Chinese, the Indian writers of the Upanishads admonished: "Let no man do to another that which would be repugnant to himself. . . . In refusing, in bestowing, in regard to pleasure and pain, to what is agreeable and disagreeable, a man obtains the proper rule by regarding the case as like his own."[4]

Thousands of miles and hundreds of years away, Hillel and some of the other ancient Hebrews produced the same principle of equity. Later, of course, Jesus told his disciples to follow the Golden Rule. Justin the Martyr, perhaps more than other Christians, adhered to this rule. He said just before he was beheaded: "We must do no one an injury."[5] And Lucian, a cynical Roman who observed Christian life, had one of his rogues, Peregrinus, speak well of Christians in this fashion: "They are all brothers. . . with the result that they despise all worldly goods and hold them in common ownership."[6] Most Romans did not, of course, know the basic Christian rule of "Love thy neighbor as thyself,"[7] as St. Matthew expressed it. Independently, however, many Romans developed their own version of the fundamental principle of equity.

Ironically, reasonable men of every social rank in Rome from emperor to slave came to the same philosophical decision. Epictetus (ca. A.D. 60), a slave who taught aristocrats, developed a belief in the eternal brotherhood of man under a rule of benevolent reason. He, in turn, instructed the Emperor Marcus Aurelius (A.D. 121–180) to observe the same principles in his very elevated station in life. These two men, drawn from such different positions of dominion, wealth, and eminence, stated the same themes in their writings on equity. Epictetus considered that the first duty of one who studies philosophy is "to part with self-conceit."[8] Similarly, Marcus Aurelius, imbued with the Stoic conviction that all is ephemeral, still wished that it might be said of him, "Never has he wronged a man in deed or word."[9]

These Stoics, who believed that a person is but a microcosm of the universe (each fulfilling its particular function and none deserving of either fame or reward), lived far from the times of Gautama Buddha. Yet, Buddha, too, developed his own version of the Golden Rule. "My doctrine," he said, "makes no distinction between high and low, rich and poor. . . . To him in whom love dwells, the whole world is but one family."[10]

Each of these wise men from different epochs and cultures, from slave to emperor, from prince to carpenter, arrived at the same belief concerning equity: that each man should treat others as himself. Should we believe this definition of equity?

Mere antiquity of a belief is not a sufficient guide, for then we should still mistakenly hold the conviction that the world is flat. Yet in human affairs we should pay attention. One should consider that these were often men of experience in worldly matters. They spoke from wisdom in human life. They were men of vastly different cultures, educations, and centuries. Still, they reached the same conclusion: that a Golden Rule should guide human relationships. This experience and unanimity should lead us to accept this eternal principle.

Whether it was Jesus or Confucius, Buddha or Marcus Aurelius, they provided us with a basic principle. But they left many issues unanswered. These are problems that we, the subsequent generations, face. Most prominently, we must confront three problems.

1. What is a person? Should a retarded child or a fetus or even a corpse be accorded the same status of brotherhood as other people? This was an issue, for example, for the Uruguayan "cannibals" whom we described earlier. Our own answer is that the first principle of equity applies to all human beings *if* they possess the prime attributes that separate man from animals: rationality and the ability to endow existence with meaning."[11]

2. May one take a person's life legitimately? Would not killing be the ultimate violation of the principle of equity? Yes, it would. Yet extreme circumstances may demand it. The murder of Hitler in 1938 would have been justified by the saving of millions of others. The basic principle is that the sacrifice of one may be justified by the salvation of others, if it is patently clear that this would be the result. Again, many will disagree.[12]

3. Under what conditions, if any, should preference be given to one human being over another? Tragically, times arise, as in the case of the Uruguayans cited above, where scarce resources *must* be allocated differentially from one human being to another. We believe that such dire circumstances require that a person who obviously and directly contributes to the welfare of others be given preference. The Uruguayans, for instance, decided when they faced starvation that those men who had a chance of saving the lives of the entire group should receive more food.[13]

In principle, this argument does not differ substantially from that of an elitist such as Ayn Rand, except that Rand would reward, say, businessmen on the assumption that they would at some distant, unspecified, and ultimately unprovable point contribute to the welfare of others.[14] We, in contrast, would insist on a principle of "immediacy." There must be unmistakable proof, ascertainable in the near future, that those who are awarded greater rewards directly increase the public welfare.

From these principles, the general outline of an equitable society is one that allocates its resources equally to all its members without prejudice, privilege, or consideration of class, status, power, strength, race, or sex. Greater rewards should be granted only to those who clearly and immediately contribute to the public good in ways that cannot be matched by others. All positions in the society should be open to unhampered, equal opportunity. In this portrait of a good society, we follow in the progressive path of Western liberals. Yet, as we have contended, it is also the way of Confucius and Buddha, the *Upanishads* and the *Meditations* of Marcus Aurelius. It is, in our opinion, the only way to the good society.

Man's Inhumanity to Man

Nonetheless, as our discussion has indicated, most human societies must be considered inequitable. You will recall some of the examples we have cited. Some simple societies, like the Ik, disown their children because they eat too much. The rulers of slave societies legally defined some people as the property of others. They could be disposed of at the will of their masters. Serfs in Russia questioned the will of their lords only if they dared to be whipped by soldiers. Indian untouchables eat cow dung because the higher castes offer them no other food. Industrial societies have forced children into factories, women into servitude, and Japanese-Americans into concentration camps. Postindustrial societies have created new organization types whose dress, religion, politics, speech and attitudes, and perhaps even spouses may be dictated by faceless bureaucrats.[15] America, as one contemporary example, reserves political power for the rich; condemns the intelligent—if they happen to be indigent—to ignorance; and shortens the lives of black males. Despite ambitious efforts to achieve equality of opportunity, these have not been sustained or uniformly successful. America in the 1970s is still the land of the privileged and powerful. A summary of the evidence that has been presented could well be:

> The masters of the government of the United States are the combined capitalists and manufacturers of the United States. It is written over every intimate page of the record of Congress. . . . The government of the United States at present is a foster child of the special interests.[16]

A critic of America did not utter these words. They were written in 1913 by Woodrow Wilson, president of Princeton University and later President of the United States.

History Moves toward Equity

"If by 'progress,' we mean a fundamental elevation in the human estate," pessimist Robert Heilbroner has concluded, "it is plain that we must put away our ideas of progress over the foreseeable vista of the historic future."[17] We believe that this statement is incorrect, misleading, and even, without intention, perverse.

The history of humankind records a movement toward equity. Both in material goods and spiritual freedoms, human societies have inched ever closer to the idea of equity. Consider the evidence.

Materially, as even Heilbroner admits, "something like a huge escalation process, a massive migration upward through the social strata, has taken place"[18] in America since 1929. People live longer, live in better housing, and eat more plentifully today than ever before. Even accounting for inflation, the income of the average American has more than doubled since 1940.

The differences in styles of life of the rich and the poor, while still very large, have lessened in measurable ways in the past quarter-century. In 1976, for example, Americans could afford some nine million new cars. This was an impossible goal for the automobile industry twenty years ago.[19]

For rich and poor alike, leisure time has been increased. In the time of Thorstein Veblen, men worked an average of fifty to sixty hours a week;[20] now the average person labors less than thirty-five hours a week.[21]

Clearly, as we have argued, Americans have not achieved a material paradise. And yet they have moved far ahead in the last centuries.

Humankind has advanced beyond the time of Cardinal Richelieu, for example, that eminent advisor to Louis XIII who held that "it would be impossible to keep the people down if they were suffered to be well off."[22] For his times, he had good intellectual comradeship. Descartes wished kings to kill off all who resisted them; Hobbes never questioned the right of authority; Pascal thought that social reforms were laughable; and Spinoza was convinced that the state should control everything, including religious beliefs.[23]

Material advances since that time, however, have continued without slowing the measured pace. America has been uniquely lucky. Women, if they chose, entered the occupational realm in the 1970s as they never did before.[24] Black families who were counted among the poverty-stricken dropped by almost half between 1959 and 1972.[25] The average income for all blue-collar workers rose in dramatic leaps.[26]

Clearly, as we have demonstrated, economic advances since the time of Richelieu have not been spread equally among all social groups or all nations. Yet no reasonable person can deny that the last century has been an era of increasing, if uneven prosperity for most humans.

Of equal if not surpassing importance, we have advanced spiritually. In those nations influenced by Western ideas, there has been a true progression of liberty, one among the many manifestations of equity.

In the last four hundred years, Western society has been freed from religious bonds; people can express themselves with liberty in print or speech; and they can, for the first time in history, depose their rulers without violence. These are no small gains. They have, in turn, ushered in an era of science, knowledge, and personal security. Contrary to the doctrines of neo-Marxists and liberals, these intellectual changes *caused* an era of technological progress. This economic beneficence emancipated many from the bondage of absolute dominion, unequal opportunity, and special privilege.

The gradual liberation of humankind has come about because of an increasing respect for individuals as inviolable beings. The patriarch in a simple society could treat his subjects as mere objects for his pleasure. The slaveowner had, in one fashion or another, to establish that he had legal dominion over his property. The landowning lord was forced into contractual obligations with his serfs. These were steps to a rule of equity. If one considers this carefully, it is clear that there was definite progress: "the general dominion of men over men has been reduced to definite laws fixing their reciprocal rights and duties."[27]

This progress continued throughout the nineteenth century as people formed trade unions to defend their rights as workers; as they engaged in revolutions to end their subservience as serfs; or as they fought a Civil War to abolish slavery. Admittedly, the path was never easy but the end was always in view: to treat each person as an inviolable being instead of rubbish. In their fight to establish the Golden Rule, people have not been universally successful, yet they have gained ground.

This, we believe, is the development of civilization—and of equity:

> For where men are degraded to the status of chattels, pawns in a game, cannon fodder, robots, they are used as means to the ends of others and the injunction has been suspended. Therefore in all things whatsoever, you would that men should do to you, do ye even so to them.[28]

As history progresses, we each become more of a person and less of a mere object. Can this be true of America—this land of bureaucrats, the monied, and the privileged? Yes, if we Americans have the will, the knowledge, and the foresight to achieve it.

How to Achieve Equity in America

Americans, *if* they were willing, could eliminate the grossest aspects of inequity.

Health insurance plans could be established (as they have been in every other advanced nation) that would reduce infant mortality and ensure that rich and poor alike receive decent medical care. Perhaps then we would climb upwards from our place as the thirteenth of the world in life expectancy.

We could divert money from activities such as building aircraft carriers to those such as rebuilding the burned-out slums of our older cities. We could provide decent housing for all.

Maximum care for the aged, poor, and infants could be provided, as it is in Scandinavia.

As has been noted before, universities that would be free to all with talent could be built. Indeed, the cost of a single atomic submarine equals a twenty-year budget of a free college.

We could provide equality of opportunity for all by legally abolishing preferential hiring in corporations, discriminatory apprenticeships in unions, unequal justice in the courts.

We *could* do all of this and more. Americans are not lacking in specific pragmatic policies—or money. The question is whether Americans have the vision, the nerve, and the good will to establish an equitable society. Some knowledgeable observers doubt it. They consider the obstacles to attaining an equitable society—such as the world crisis in energy, mineral resources, and food—as insurmountable. They conclude that equity, either in America or on earth, is impossible. We disagree. However, because of the cogency, power, and relevance of their arguments, we should consider the pessimists' points of view now.

Are the Obstacles Insurmountable?

We have considered the arguments that any movement toward greater equity would interfere with economic efficiency, erode liberty, hamper creativity, and stifle diversity. We have found them without merit. Nations more equitable than America, such as the Netherlands and Sweden, grow at a faster economic rate, maintain their political freedom, exhibit creativity in a number of fields, and allow diversity to grow at a more luxuriant rate than America dares. In no sense could the Scandinavian nations be debited as tyrannical, monolithic, or decadent. The success of these small nations, however, may not be considered as proof that the principle of equity that has been proposed is right. Their historical experience merely suggests that a just society is possible and workable in the contemporary world. Although acknowledging these qualifications, rational people must recognize the demanding reasons that, ultimately, will establish a rule of equity upon this earth.

Yet time may be running out. The people of the world are gathering at the gates of privilege throughout the world.

Some theorists have advocated a policy of "triage" with the goal of keeping America an "island of plenty." During World War I French army physicians practiced triage in dealing with the wounded who emerged from the trenches. They sorted the wounded soldiers into three categories: those who would die regardless of medical care, those who could possibly live if they were not treated, and those who might live if they received immediate attention. Because of a shortage of doctors and medical supplies, only the third group received medical care. Out of tragic necessity, the rest were left either to die or to recover on their own.

Many believe that this stark choice faces the world's abundant nations: either the poor, mortally sick nations must be abandoned or the world's population will expend its precious resources of food in a hopeless effort to feed the growing population. Are there to be not only societal but worldwide inequities? Most Americans are well fed; they may even be fat; and they dislike facing such grim issues and are perhaps repulsed by the question. Nonetheless, the unceasing expansion of the globe's population condemns all of us to face the basic question posed by the triage policy: "Who shall starve?" The internal policies of each nation-state must be fashioned in the context of the condition of the world's people. No one remains isolated.

Some prominent social and natural scientists believe that the nations of the world are like lifeboats floating in a stormy sea. Because of the onslaught of the population problem, the rich must abandon the poor in fear that we shall all be swamped. If the postindustrialized nations help the poorer nations, some contend, everyone will drown because the lifeboat will be overcrowded. Some people must be allowed to drown.

Scholars of this persuasion argue that a true, equal sharing of food would deplete our resources and that we will all be doomed. From the point of view of these pessimists the postindustrialized nations have little choice but to remain an island of plenty. Robert Heilbroner has articulated this sentiment: "For the next several generations . . . the main restraint on population growth in the underdeveloped areas is apt to be the Malthusian check of famine and disease."[29]

If, through scientific discovery, humankind should escape the disasters of famine, our quest for survival is threatened by other equally difficult challenges. Consider some facts. In 1972 Maurice Strong observed, "a citizen of an advanced industrialized nation consumed in six months the energy and raw materials that last the citizen of a developing country his entire lifetime."[30] In 1973 Americans, who constituted only 6 percent of the world's population, consumed 30 percent of the world's meat.[31] The present use of energy will allow the world's industry to function for about

150 years. At that point, increased heat in the atmosphere might burn us up.[32] At the present rate of consumption, all of this planet's reserves of petroleum energy will be depleted no later than the year 2200.[33] The Club of Rome, an influential group of social and natural scientists, has calculated that the present rate of both industrialization and population increase must be immediately curtailed or *any* type of economic growth on this planet will have to stop by the year 2072.[34] If one accepts these arguments, domestic expenditures on houses, schools, or mass transit would be a dangerous waste of national resources.

As discussed earlier, the postindustrialized nations are using up vastly more energy than are the developing countries. By the year 2000, if present trends continue, America, Europe, Russia, and Japan will produce 90 percent of the world's gross national product.[35] Simultaneously, these industrialized nations will consume three-quarters of the world's income and resources.[36] The United States alone will use half of the remaining energy of the world by the year 2000.[37]

Assuming this enormous difference—which is an entirely reasonable forecast—the gap between rich and poor nations is bound to widen. Put another way, the gap between the 23 percent of the world's people who live in the wealthy regions and the 77 percent who live in poor regions will inevitably widen.[38] As G. R. Urban has aptly stated, "It is not a question *whether,* but *how soon,* the impoverished and ever-growing majority will challenge the rich and ever-diminishing minority for a more equitable distribution of food, space, and resources."[39]

How will the poor nations of the world make their challenge? They have one resource that frightens the poor and rich alike: nuclear weapons.

Although these obstacles are intimately intertwined, three particular threats to the creation of an equitable society must be recognized before it is too late. First, on the ecological level, we face the possibility that basic fuel and energy sources may disappear before the end of the century and that the food supply will not be adequate to feed a burgeoning population. Our befoulment of the air and water around us also threatens our survival. Optimists place their faith in the discovery of new sources of energy, food, and other basic resources that will save society from extinction. Pessimists foresee a Malthusian solution of famine, war, and dictatorial rule.

Second, all forecasts agree that developing nations will bear the burden of the ecological and population crises. A grim likelihood is that they will turn to military or civilian dictatorships in a vain hope to secure a greater proportion of the world's resources. Yet even the most ruthless governments attempting to force further industrialization must face the fact that the earth's resources are being rapidly exhausted. Stabilization of the world economy and cooperation between all the powers of the world could conserve and redistribute the world's resources. However, the more gloomy of social scientists doubt that humankind has the vision or the altruism to undertake the task.

Third, the invention of nuclear weapons and the supremacy of military-industrial complexes in the United States, Russia, China, and many of the underdeveloped nations make a war of extinction (or a "war of redistribution") a ghastly possibility in the coming decades. Some theorists have even hypothesized that the starving regions of the world might resort to "nuclear blackmail" as a way of coercing the richer nations into world cooperation.

No one has a neat, simple, and logical solution to these interlocking problems. Neo-Malthusians believe that nature will apply its traditional methods of checks and balances: famine, pestilence, and disease. Epidemics, small wars, and starvation could indeed wipe out many of the world's people and "solve" part of the population and ecological problem. The Malthusian solution, however, requires that the developing nations do not use their nuclear power against the industrialized nations. For instance, if a nation such as India were to drop bombs, some theorists believe that the industrialized nations could immediately smash her. Such an opinion, of course, overlooks the fact that a series of large nuclear explosions would destroy the ozone layer of the earth, thus extinguishing all forms of life everywhere.

These gloomy scenarios of the future have been drawn because these are the often-ignored facts of human existence in the twentieth century. However, we have a capacity for rationality, kindness, and foresight, even though it may not always be evidenced, and this gives us a chance for survival. Can our base instincts of aggression, greed, and immersion in self-interest be overcome in order to stop the drift toward human annihilation?

A Reaffirmation of Equity

We have drawn a sad portrait of social stratification in America and, indeed, in the world. No one can predict the future with any precision.

Within the postindustrialized nations, the example of Scandinavia offers reasonable hope that with vision, will, and patience people can create an equitable society. For the entire globe, one may hope or expect that science can produce new realms of abundance as yet undreamed of by humankind.

The age-old dream of equity—that we are inviolable beings—must yet be realized. The message of the Stoics and the Christians, that "men are *not* brute things . . . weak, outcast, downtrodden, enslaved,"[40] must echo throughout the world.

From the morass of inequity people have fought their way to the ideal of the Golden Rule. Upon this stately principle, Greeks and Romans, Union soldiers and Russian revolutionaries, anarchists and liberals, have built the foundation of an equitable society. The fulfillment of the ideal remains the task of present and future generations.

Notes

1. Walter Lippmann, *The Good Society* (New York: Grosset, 1943; orig. 1936), p. 574.
2. Ibid., p. xi.
3. Confucius, *The Doctrine of the Mean*, XIII, 3.
4. Mahabharata, XIII.
5. Justin, *First Apology*, 27.
6. Irwin Edman, *Justin Martyr, Christian* (Roslyn, N.Y.: Black, 1945), Introduction.
7. Matthew, *The Bible*, King James Version, XIX, 19.
8. Epictetus, *How to Apply General Principles to Particular Cases*, 17.
9. Quoted in Marcus Aurelius, *Meditations*, 31, from Homer, *Odyssey*.
10. *Dhammapada*, V.
11. For one who disagrees, see R. R. Diwaker, *Satyagraha* (Hinsdale, Ill.: Regnery, 1948). For our argument, see William McCord and Arline McCord, *American Social Problems* (St. Louis: Mosby, 1977).
12. For one who disagrees, see William Westar Comfort, *The Quaker Way of Life* (Philadelphia: American Friends Service Committee, 1952).
13. Piers Paul Read, *Alive* (New York: Avon, 1974).
14. Ayn Rand, *The Virtue of Selfishness* (New York: New American Library, 1964).
15. See Vance Packard, *The Status Seekers* (New York: McKay, 1961), for an interesting if dated commentary on this phenomenon in such varied garbs as housing, job prestige, friendship, sex, clubs, education, and religion.
16. Woodrow Wilson, *The New Freedom* (New York: Doubleday, 1913), pp. 57–58. Also see Ferdinand Lundberg, *The Rich and the Super-Rich*, (New York: Bantam, 1969), for a vivid, contemporary indictment of the power of the wealthy.
17. Robert Heilbroner, *The Future as History* (New York: Harper, 1960), p. 204.
18. Ibid., p. 122.
19. Packard, *Status Seekers*, p. 17. Also see Irving Krauss, *Stratification, Class, and Conflict* (New York: Free Press, 1976).
20. Packard, *Status Seekers*, p. 21.
21. Ben Wattenberg, *The Real America* (Garden City, N.Y.: Doubleday, 1974).
22. Quoted in Lord Acton, "Address on 'Freedom in Christianity,'" in *History of Freedom and Other Essays* (London: Macmillan, 1945).
23. See Lippmann, *The Good Society*, p. 370.
24. Wattenberg, *The Real America*, p. 30.

25. Ibid., p. 140.
26. Ibid.
27. Lippmann, *The Good Society*, p. 374.
28. Ibid., p. 371.
29. Heilbroner, *The Future as History*.
30. Maurice Strong, quoted in "Marx vs. Malthus," *The New York Times*, August 25, 1974.
31. Paul R. Erlich and Anne Erlich, *The End of Affluence* (New York: Ballantine, 1974).
32. See Heilbroner, *The Future as History*, p. 52.
33. Harrison Brown, *The Challenge of Man's Future* (New York: Viking, 1954).
34. See Donella Mathews et al., *The Limits of Growth* (New York: Signet, 1972).
35. Urban, op. cit., p. 24.
36. Ibid.
37. Ibid.
38. Ibid.
39. Ibid., p. 24.
40. Lippmann, *The Good Society*, p. 378.

INDEX